UITGAVEN VAN HET
NEDERLANDS HISTORISCH-ARCHAEOLOGISCH INSTITUUT TE ISTANBUL

Publications de l'Institut historique-archéologique néerlandais de Stamboul
sous la direction de
Machteld J. MELLINK, J. de ROOS,
J.J. ROODENBERG et K.R. VEENHOF

LXXVI

TELL SABI ABYAD
THE LATE NEOLITHIC SETTLEMENT

Report on the Excavations of the University of Amsterdam (1988) and the
National Museum of Antiquities Leiden (1991-1993) in Syria

I

TELL SABI ABYAD
THE LATE NEOLITHIC SETTLEMENT

Report on the Excavations of the University of Amsterdam (1988) and the
National Museum of Antiquities Leiden (1991-1993) in Syria

I

edited by

PETER M.M.G. AKKERMANS

NEDERLANDS HISTORISCH-ARCHAEOLOGISCH INSTITUUT
TE ISTANBUL
1996

Copyright 1996 by
Nederlands Instituut voor het Nabije Oosten
Witte Singel 25
Postbus 9515
2300 RA LEIDEN, NEDERLAND

CIP-GEGEVENS KONINKLIJKE BIBLIOTHEEK, DEN HAAG

Sabi

Tell Sabi Abyad — The Late Neolithic Settlement: Report on the Excavations of the University of Amsterdam (1988) and the National Museum of Antiquities Leiden (1991-1993) in Syria / ed. Peter M.M.G. Akkermans, 2 vols.
Istanbul: Nederlands Historisch-Archaeologisch Instituut;
Leiden: Nederlands Instituut voor het Nabije Oosten [distr.]. — (Uitgaven van het Nederlands Historisch Archaeologisch Instituut te Istanbul; 76)
Met Engelse teksten.
ISBN 90-6258-078-5
SISO 905.1 UDC 902 + 930.85 + 72/73 NUGI 644
Trefw.: opgravingen; Late Neolithicum; Syrië

Printed in Belgium

TABLE OF CONTENTS

VOLUME I

VOLUME II

FOREWORD

PETER M.M.G. AKKERMANS

Since the spring of 1986 the site of Tell Sabi Abyad ('Mound of the White Boy') has been the focal point of a regional research project of survey and excavation, which aims to explore the social and economic structure of late Neolithic society in the Balikh basin of northern Syria (see Akkermans 1993 for a detailed account on the research objectives). The site is situated within a hitherto archaeologically poorly understood region of Syria, close to the Syro-Turkish border.

So far, six campaigns of archaeological investigation have been undertaken on Sabi Abyad, which revealed a series of superimposed and generally well-preserved prehistoric settlements dated between ca. 5700 and 5000 B.C. (uncalibrated). In addition impressive remains were found of a Late Bronze Age or Middle Assyrian fortified settlement, dating from the later 13th and early 12th century B.C. (see e.g. Akkermans and Rossmeisl 1990; Akkermans et al. 1993).

The discoveries at Sabi Abyad have made an important contribution to our knowledge of the late Neolithic in the Near East. The site has yielded wholly new and, sometimes, spectacular data on the history of cultural development in the 6th millennium B.C., which actually belongs among the poorest known in the region so far. Campbell (1992a) already pointed to the fact that prehistoric research in the Near East mainly seems to be concerned with the two great 'revolutions', i.e. the introduction of agriculture on the one hand and the emergence of cities and early states on the other, with only little attention given to the intermediate late Neolithic. The interest in Halaf culture (i.e. the final stage of the Neolithic) has increased in recent decades but active research in the preceding cultures is still of a most intermittent nature.

So far, the results of the excavations at Sabi Abyad have been selectively published season by season in a series of articles in archaeological journals (e.g. Akkermans 1987a, 1987b, 1988c, 1993/94a, 1993/94b; Akkermans and Le Mière 1992; Akkermans and Verhoeven 1995; Akkermans in Weiss 1991; Van Loon et al. 1986/87) and monographs (Akkermans 1993; Akkermans, ed., 1989). The aim of the present report is to present a factual review of the 1988 to 1993 seasons of excavation by the University of Amsterdam (1988) and the Netherlands National Museum of Antiquities (1991-1993), in collaboration with the Maison de l'Orient (Lyon) and the Oriental Institute of the University of Chicago. The emphasis of analysis is upon the excavations in the southeastern part of Sabi Abyad (see chapter 2); the test trenches in the northeastern area await further study and, consequently, will only be referred to whenever there is a specific need. It is stressed that this study is not the final publication, aiming at fullness, of our research at Tell Sabi Abyad, but an extensive

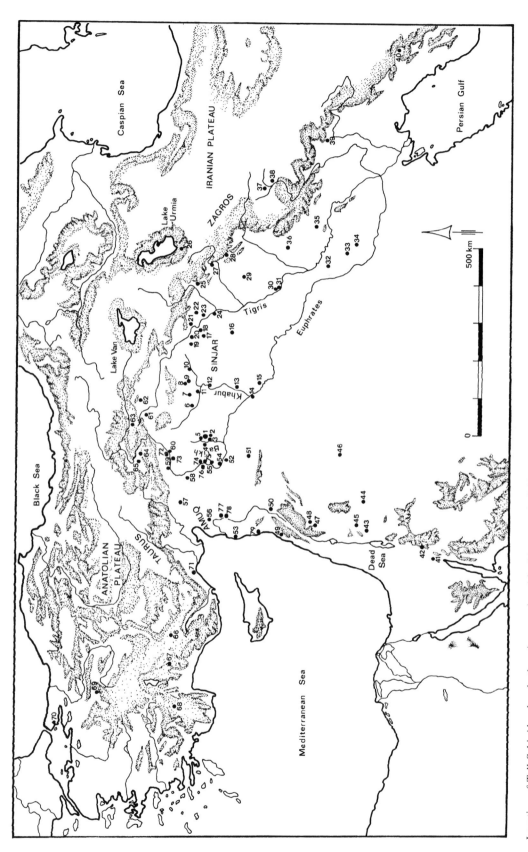

Location of Tell Sabi Abyad and other sites mentioned in this report. 1. Sabi Abyad; 2. Shenef; 3. Hammam et-Turkman; 4. Damishliyya; 5. Assouad; 6. Halaf; 7. Habesh; 8. Aqab; 9. Chagar Bazar; 10. Brak; 11. Kashkashok; 12. Umm Qseir; 13. Sheikh Hamad; 14. Bouqras; 15. Baghouz; 16. Umm Dabaghiyah; 17. Yarim Tepe; 18. Thalathat; 19. NJP 72; 20. Khirbet Garsour; 21. Khirbet Derak; 22. Gawra; 23. Arpachiyah; 24. Hassuna; 25. Banahilk; 26. Hajji Firuz; 27. Shimshara; 28. Jarmo; 29. Mattarah; 30. Samarra; 31. Sawwan; 32. Abu Salabikh; 33. Nippur; 34. Fara; 35. Tell ed-Der; 36. Chogha Mami; 37. Sarab; 38. Ganj Dareh; 39. Sarafabad; 40. Bakun; 41. Nahal Issaron; 42. Beidha; 43. Hesban; 44. Azraq; 45. ʾAin Ghazal; 46. Dhuweila; 47. Ramad; 48. Aswad; 49. Byblos; 50. Arjoune; 51. El-Kowm; 52. Abu Hureyra; 53. Ras Shamra; 54. Mureybit; 55. Shams ed-Din; 56. Judaidah; 57. Sakçe Gözü; 58. Turlu; 59. Hayaz Hüyük; 60. Çayönü; 61. Çavi Tarlasi; 62. Girikihaciyan; 63. Korucu Tepe; 64. Degirmentepe; 65. Arslantepe; 66. Çatal Hüyük; 67. Erbaba; 68. Hacilar; 69. Demircihüyük; 70. Fikirtepe; 71. Mersin; 72. Sürük Mevkii; 73. Kumartepe; 74. Dja'de; 75. Qosak Shamali; 76. Haloula; 77. Tell Aray; 78. Tell Kerkh; 79. Tabbat el-Hammam.

interim report on the past years of fieldwork. Indeed, some chapters are exhaustive in their description of the features investigated. Others, however, will undoubtedly be revised or reworked, as more of the material is analysed. It seems evident that future seasons of excavation will add to the picture and partially shift the emphasis. At present, it has been a deliberate choice to engage only to a limited extent in the discussion of the site in its wider cultural context; instead, the emphasis is on the description and illustration of the local material culture. The research aims and a detailed *evaluation* and *interpretation* of the (first) campaigns of fieldwork have been given elsewhere (Akkermans 1993).

Some remarks on the chronological framework

The chronological framework used in this volume has already been discussed in detail elsewhere (Akkermans 1991, 1993). Basically, the earlier presented views are still valid, although the stratigraphic sequence has been extended considerably and yielded new insights. The original chronological scheme was based upon the 1986 and 1988 seasons of excavation, which revealed eight major building phases or levels. However, subsequent work at the site yielded three more levels until virgin soil was finally reached at a depth of four metres below the level of the surrounding fields (cf. chapter 2). A series of radiocarbon dates firmly supports the present sequence (cf. Akkermans 1991, 1993:113-16 and table 4.1; Akkermans and Le Mière 1992, table 1; see also Akkermans and Verhoeven 1995). All dates mentioned in this report are used in a 'traditional' manner, i.e. uncalibrated.

The earliest levels (11-7) are part of the initial stage of the Pottery Neolithic, referred to as Balikh II in local terms and generally dated around 6000/5900-5200 B.C. Three subphases are suggested, viz. Balikh IIA to C. The fieldwork up to 1988 showed a hiatus of several centuries in our chronological scheme between the Balikh IIA phase and the later phase IIC; however, it was expected that intermediate levels bridging this apparent gap could be found somewhere at Sabi Abyad (Akkermans 1993:119). However, the strata providing this transition have not appeared so far. On the contrary, the excavations in the deep sounding P15 pointed towards a real break in settlement at Sabi Abyad between levels 11 and 10 (see chapter 2), lasting for perhaps 200 or 300 years. Our lowest level 11 at Sabi Abyad is provisionally ascribed to the final Balikh IIA phase on the basis of ceramic parallels with sites like Tell Assouad and Tell Damishliyya (cf. chapter 3) and may date from around 5700 B.C. It is, however, stressed that the flint and obsidian industries of level 11 resemble those of the other Balikh IIA sites to a limited extent only; these industries suggest a somewhat later date for level 11, perhaps better fitting the Balikh IIB phase (see chapter 4).

Levels 10-7 at Sabi Abyad are ascribed to the Balikh IIC phase, more or less contemporary to Amuq B in western Syria. Levels 8-7 were earlier dated at ca. 5300-5200

lab. no.	material	level	conventional date B.P.	conventional date B.C.	calibrated date B.P. 1 sigma*	calibrated date B.P. 2 sigma*
GrN-16804	burnt grain	1	6975±30	5025±30	5842-5762	5934-5916 5866-5730
GrN-16800	charcoal	2	7005±30	5055±30	5936-5916 5870-5802	5944-5910 5884-5764
GrN-16801	burnt seeds	3	7465±35	5515±35	6362-6318 6306-6276 6256-6224	6370-6210 6206-6192
GrN-16802	burnt seeds	3	7065±30	5115±30	5954-5936 5916-5870	5964-5844
GrN-16803	burnt seeds	4	7075±25	5125±25	5956-5942 5912-5880	5966-5932 5918-5858
UtC-1008	charcoal	4	6930±80	4980±80	5926-5924 5848-5684	5950-5906 5890-5620
GrN-19367	burnt grain	6	7075±25	5125±25	5956-5942 5912-5880	5966-5932 5918-5858
GrN-19368	burnt seeds	6	7100±60	5150±60	5986-5934 5916-5860	6024-5780
UtC-1009	burnt seeds	8	7080±80	5130±80	5984-5828	6044-5730
GrN-16805	burnt wood	8	7145±30	5195±30	5990-5958	6008-5950 5906-5888
UtC-1010	burnt wood	(Halaf n.e. mound)	6670±100	4720±100	5595-5480	5700-5430 5400-5390
UtC-1011	burnt wood	(pre-Halaf n.e. mound)	7150±90	5200±90	6110-6096 6052-5936 5914-5872	6168-6134 6130-6080 6072-5786
UtC-1012	charcoal	(pre-Halaf n.e. mound)	7170±90	5220±90	6116-6092 6056-5942 5910-5882	6174-5820
GrN-16806	charcoal	(pre-Halaf n.e. mound	7225±30	5275±30	6105-6098 6048-6000	6116-6090 6056-5984

* According to Stuiver et al. 1993

List of radiocarbon dates from Tell Sabi Abyad

B.C.; the preceding levels 10-9 then may fit around 5500/5400-5300 B.C. These levels have been reached to a limited extent in the deep trenches, and are characterised, among other things, by imported Dark-Faced Burnished Ware and locally manufactured Standard-Ware ceramics (cf. chapter 3). Levels 10-7 antedate the appearance of fine painted ceramics at the site.

The subsequent levels 6-1 represent the more developed stage of the Pottery Neolithic and are dated around 5200/5150-5000 B.C. This phase starts with the appearance of carefully made painted pottery of Samarran and, perhaps, Hassunan style, ultimately resulting in true Early Halaf pottery. Two subphases are recognised at Sabi Abyad, viz. Balikh IIIA and IIIB.

The Balikh IIIA phase comprises levels 6 to 4 and represents the transitional stage between the earlier ceramic Neolithic and the upper Early Halaf. This phase is dated at ca. 5200/5150-5100 B.C. The most spectacular finds came from the level 6 settlement, which appears to have been reduced to ashes due to a violent fire around 5200 B.C. and which contained thousands of small finds in situ. The richness of the inventory recovered from this so-called 'Burnt Village' (cf. Akkermans and Verhoeven 1995) resembles the finds in the famous Burnt House at later Halafian Arpachiyah (Mallowan and Rose 1935). The latter has often been cited as an example of a chiefly residence, whose occupants possessed a considerable control over the surrounding people and settlements. The main reason for this is the outstanding richness of its inventory, including a considerable number of sealings seen as items current in elite circles and used by them to control society in a bureaucratic manner (e.g. Campbell 1992a, 1992b). However, when comparing the finds of the Arpachiyah Burnt House with those of the Burnt Village at Sabi Abyad[1] it seems that, with some exceptions (e.g. the finely made obsidian items present at Arpachiyah but not at our site), both are fairly well comparable. One then wonders whether the extraordinary status ascribed to the Arpachiyah Burnt House so far is not merely due to the absence of any comparisons until the finds at Sabi Abyad, so that the Burnt House was *a priori* presented as unique and exceptional. In other words: may it not be the case that structures similar to the Burnt House were originally a common characteristic of later Neolithic society, present at many sites but simply not preserved to the same ideal level or simply not found yet?

Finally, the Balikh IIIB phase consists of the topmost Early Halaf levels 3-1, dated at ca. 5100-5000 B.C. These levels are characterised by an open agglomeration of both rectangular and circular structures. At present, there can be little doubt that Halaf at Sabi Abyad was the result of a gradual and continuous local process of cultural change; the Halaf was directly derived from earlier Neolithic cultural traditions in the Balikh valley. The transition is characterised by profound changes in artefact assemblages and settlement structure, and must have had a considerable impact upon

---

[1] However, one should bear in mind that the Burnt Village at Sabi Abyad fits in the very beginning of the Halaf era, whereas the Burnt House at Arpachiyah belongs to its final stage.

the organisation of society as well (cf. Akkermans 1993). So far, no other excavated site has provided a similar transitional sequence, as all other investigated sites were newly founded during the Halaf period.

Acknowledgements

It is evident that this report contains the work of many, and I am greatly indebted to those who have contributed to the success of the Sabi Abyad project. I wish to express my sincere gratitude to the Directorate General of Antiquities and Museums of the Syrian Arab Republic for their continued assistance and encouragement, in particular to Dr. Ali Abu Assaf and later Dr. Sultan Muhesen as Directors General, and to Dr. Adnan Bounni as Director of Excavations. Mr Murhaf al-Khalaf, Director of Antiquities of the Raqqa province and head of the Raqqa National Museum, is warmly thanked for his help and hospitality. Sincere thanks are also due to the General Direction's representatives to the Sabi Abyad project, Mr Mohammed Muslim (1988) and Mr Nauras al-Mohammed (1991-1993). Thanks also go to the villagers of Hammam et-Turkman for their friendship, hospitality and often hard labour. Special thanks in this respect are due to the guard of the Sabi Abyad excavations, Mr Salim al-Mughlif.

Numerous people contributed their archaeological skills and unceasing enthusiasm to the Sabi Abyad project in a team-work approach. Foremost I wish to thank the authors of the various contributions in this report for their hard work and warm friendship: Tony Wilkinson, Marc Verhoeven, Peter Kranendonk, Nico Aten, Olivier Nieuwenhuyse, Marie Le Mière, Lorraine Copeland, Kim Duistermaat, Pieter Collet, Richard Spoor, Chiara Cavallo, Willemina Waterbolk-van Rooijen and Willem van Zeist. Maurits van Loon deserves special thanks for his guidance and support throughout the years of research at Sabi Abyad. Many thanks go to the field supervisors at Sabi Abyad, especially to Karin Bartl, Lauren Brüning, Ayla Çevik, Laura van Deelen, Kim Duistermaat, Monica Dütting, David Fontijn, Fokke Gerritsen, Ruurd Kok, Peter Kranendonk, Marie Le Mière, José Limpens, Antoine Mientjes, Miquel Molist, Mohammed Muslim, Olivier Nieuwenhuyse, Hans Piena, Serge Polman, Inge Rossmeisl, Marie Claire Schallig, Richard Spoor, Judith Stoker, Miriam Teeuwisse, Marc Verhoeven, Maarten Wispelwey and Beatrice Wittmann. The drawings were made in the field by Pieter Collet, who also partly took care of the find recording. Photographs were made with the help of Michiel Bootsman, Peter-Jan Bomhof, Anneke de Kemp and Elisabeth van Dorp. Much valuable information concerning the faunal and floral remains was provided by Sytze Bottema, Chiara Cavallo, Gert-Jan de Roller, Loes van Wijngaarden-Bakker and Willem van Zeist. Ingolf Thuesen and Lea Rehhoff took care of the analyses of wall plasters. My gratitude also goes to Tony Wilkinson and his team from the Oriental Institute of the University of Chicago, who with great precision and a lot of humour took care of the landscape archaeology and detailed surveying of the region around Sabi Abyad. The staff of Her Majesty's Royal Embassy in Damascus, in particular Mr Ferdinand Smit, is thanked for their assistance whenever the need arose. Thanks are also due to Ans Bulles who corrected the English texts with great patience.

The 1988 excavations at Tell Sabi Abyad were supported by the Foundation for Archaeological Research, which is subsidised by the Netherlands Organisation for Scientific Research (NWO). The 1991-1993 seasons of excavations were funded by the National Museum of Antiquities in Leiden. Further support was provided by the Foundation for Anthropology and Prehistory in the Netherlands, the University of Amsterdam (Instituut voor Prae- en Protohistorie), the Hamburger Museum für Archäologie, the Centre National de la Recherche Scientifique, the Association des Amis de la Maison de l'Orient (Lyon), the Oriental Institute of the University of Chicago, and some private sponsors. Minibuses were freely put at the project's disposal by HNG Bedrijfswagens (Sassenheim) and Mengelers Automobielbedrijven (Oirsbeek). Some graduate students participating in the excavations were supported in the form of grants by the Stichting Dr. Hendrik Muller's Vaderlandsch Fonds and the Netherlands Organisation for Scientific Reasearch. Prof. Dr. J. de Roos and Dr. J. Roodenberg of the Netherlands Institute of the Near East are thanked for their willingness to publish the present work.

Finally, neither the fieldwork nor the present analysis could have been carried out without the encouragement and support of the staff of the National Museum of Antiquities in Leiden.

Leiden, November 1994

CHAPTER 1

SABI ABYAD: THE GEOARCHAEOLOGY OF A COMPLEX LANDSCAPE

Tony J. Wilkinson

Introduction

In this preliminary interpretation of the landscape around Tell Sabi Abyad in Syria, archaeological, pedological and geomorphological data have been combined to provide an integrated assessment of landscape development. Too often soil and geomorphological studies lack an archaeological component, which is unfortunate because archaeology can provide dating evidence as well as insights into the process of landscape utilisation through time. Conversely, archaeological studies frequently stop at the edge of the site and do not include off-site features or treat the soil landscape. Even if soil studies are included they are frequently simply viewed as part of the 'environmental background'.

Although at this stage no attempt will be made to provide a demographic history of the region, ultimately it is hoped to relate population history to land use and environmental change. The area of study within the Balikh valley (fig. 1.1) is particularly appropriate to this problem owing to its position astride the limit of rain-fed cultivation (ca. 250 mm annual rainfall at Sabi Abyad). Thus during dry years agricultural production on the rain-fed lands would be threatened, perhaps resulting in a population crisis or ultimately a shift towards irrigation. A primary objective of the fieldwork in 1992 and 1993 was to subdivide the landscapes into zones of older, well-developed soils where landscape features would be preserved, and land characterised by recent sedimentation and immature soils where burial of sites and landscape features will have taken place. In addition, by relating soil types to water resources, areas of long term rain-fed farming and irrigation potential could be identified. The fieldwork forms part of a long-term project of archaeological landscape investigations conducted by the Oriental Institute, University of Chicago, in cooperation with the excavations at Sabi Abyad[1].

[1]   Fieldwork was funded by the National Geographic Society (grant nos. 4900-92 and 5095-93) and the Oriental Institute, University of Chicago, as part of a continuing Oriental Institute project investigating the ancient landscape of the Jezirah. I am particularly grateful to Peter M.M.G. Akkermans and his team for logistical support and advice in the field, to Clemens Reichel and Fokke Gerritsen (Oriental Institute) for assistance in the field, to Eleanor Barbanes (University of California, Berkely) for cartographic drafting, to Dr. M.A. Mulders (Agricultural University, Wageningen) for advice on soils, and to Mr Murhaf al-Khalaf (Director Dept. of Antiquities Raqqa) for his assistance during the field season.

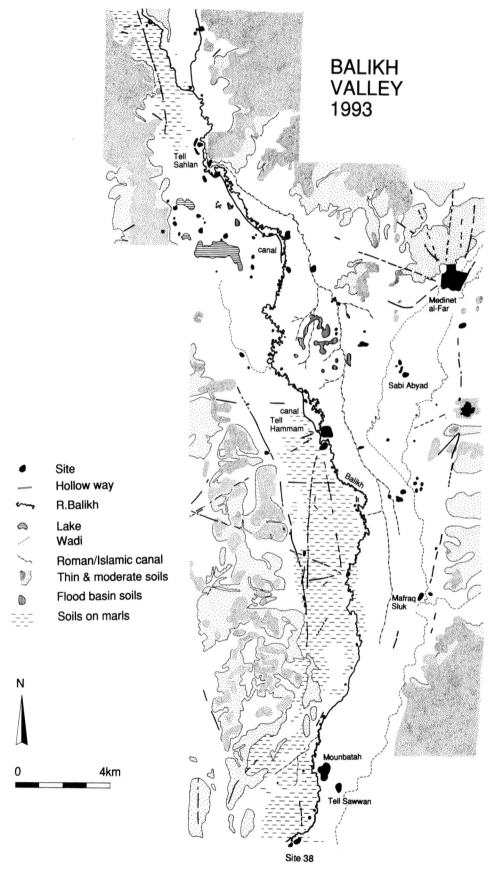

Figure 1.1. The archaeological landscape around Sabi Abyad as surveyed in 1992 and 1993.

Soil Landscape Units (fig. 1.1)

The following summary is based upon air-photo interpretation and field studies conducted in the autumn of 1992, supplemented by additional field information recovered during the 1993 season. No attempt has been made to provide a comprehensive range of soil profiles but key soil/sedimentary sequences have been included when appropriate. A summary of environmental conditions and a review of the relevant soil and geomorphological literature is provided by Boerma (1988) for the area around Tell Hammam et-Turkman, and by Mulders (1969) for the southern part of the Balikh valley.

Valley-side terraces and plateaus

The two or three kilometres wide Balikh valley is fringed along its eastern side by low, rolling hills of Tertiary limestone and gypsum, locally capped by gravel of the Balikh terrace. The hills either have thin soils less than 30 cm deep (dotted on figs. 1.1 and 1.2), or, where capped by gravel and loam terraces, mature soil profiles with well-developed calcium carbonate (calcic) horizons. The gentle slopes which merge imperceptibly into the plain have moderately developed loam soils with well-developed calcium-carbonate horizons. Although absolute dates cannot be provided, by comparison with the carbonate build-up stages of Gile et al. (1966), even the lower, younger soils show evidence for having evolved during much of the Holocene with accumulations of calcium carbonate being in the range of 1-2% by volume.

The soils on the higher terraces exhibit well-developed calcium carbonate horizons of an estimated age of more than 10,000 years (see e.g. fig. 1.2, profile at 89 near Site 10). The soil profiles suggest that, archaeologically speaking, the fringing plateaus and terraces are old landscapes, and with the exception of localised sedimentation in minor valleys and on lower slopes, the archaeological record appears to be highly visible. It is possible to distinguish not only habitation sites of all sizes but also off-site features such as hollow ways and 'field scatters' (see below). Where the mature soil profiles merge with those of the valley bottom there is localised aggradation. For example, at the small Halaf site of Khirbet esh-Shenef (BS 170) the buried soil below the site is ca. 0.4 m below plain level (Akkermans 1993:86), whereas at site BS 305, a little over one kilometre to the east, a mature soil profile is coincident with the modern ground surface. Although relict wadi channels are evident around Khirbet esh-Shenef, it seems that subtle features and very low sites might be buried around the edges of the fringing plateaus and terraces.

Although similar in appearance, the low terraces to the west of the Balikh are developed upon Pliocene marls and associated sediments with shallow, very pale-coloured soils. These soils are highly calcareous with frequent strong accumulations of calcium carbonate (Boerma 1988:5) and like the east bank terraces they possess mature soil profiles. Again hollow ways, small sites and 'field scatters' can be distinguished.

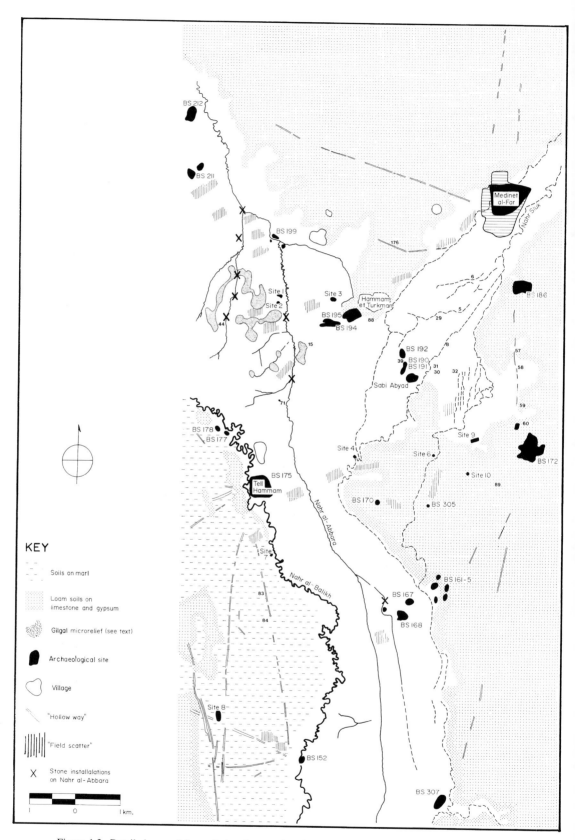

Figure 1.2. Detailed map of figure 1 showing numbered soil pits and other sites examined during 1992.

Valley bottom lands

The two to three kilometres wide Balikh valley contains a deep sequence of some 70 m or more of silt/clay sedimentary fill, which although undated, is probably mainly of Quaternary date. This deposit forms part of a deceptively complex zone comprising the actual channel of the Balikh and its immediate flood plain together with a broad, flat clay plain occupying the remainder of the valley to the east. The latter, although apparently part of the flood plain, being some four to five metres above the present flood plain, is really a low clay terrace (the 'lowest Balikh terrace' of Boerma 1988:7). Towards the east of Sabi Abyad, and oriented north-east-southwest, the Nahr Slouq and Wadi al-Khedr contribute flood water to the Balikh valley.

Recent soils of the Balikh flood plain. Although dry today as a result of over-pumping for irrigation, the Balikh was formerly a river of modest charge (mean annual discharge of 6-12 m^3 per second at its confluence with the Euphrates; Mulders 1969:54) which received most of its water from 'Ain al-Arous near Tell Abyad, some 25 km to the north of Tell Sabi Abyad. During the Pleistocene the Balikh must have occupied various positions to the east, but today it follows a shallow valley situated along the western fringes of the plain, or in places actually cuts through the marl terrace. The present course west of Tell Hammam et-Turkman may result from the diversion of a river channel, originally to the east of the site, which was subsequently diverted by the construction of a canal which chanelled water along the present western course. This channel shift can be inferred from a borehole dug to the west of Tell Hammam et-Turkman which exposed circa one metre of fluvial sands with common pot sherds and bone, including Early Bronze Age diagnostics, at a depth of ten to eleven metres. The overlying ten metres of low-energy sediments include a thin deposit of low-energy water-laid silts ultimately overlain by 3-4 m of wash from the adjacent tell (fig. 1.5e).

The flood-plain soils developed on grey clay alluvium show evidence of water-logging and localised oxidation, but few other signs of soil development. At Tell Hammam et-Turkman, in addition to the above-mentioned channel diversion, archaeological excavations indicate that the flood-plain level has aggraded some two metres since the 5th millennium B.C. (Akkermans 1988:144) raising the possibility that small sites may be buried near the river's edge. The presence of a moderately dense veneer of pottery over the surface of the higher flood-plain soils in the vicinity and downstream of Tell Zkero, and points downstream, suggests that the flood plain was formerly irrigated and intensively cultivated.

The clay soils of the 'lowest Balikh terrace'. These soils form the bulk of the valley-bottom lands and may correspond to the geological Q4a terrace (Boerma 1988:7). Roughly through the centre of this plain is another 'river' the Nahr al-Abbara, which despite its meandering channel is not a natural river but rather a modified ancient canal.

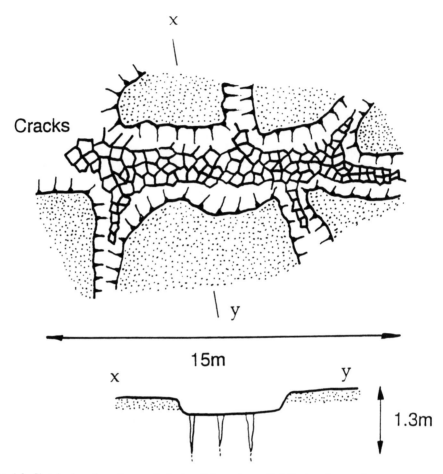

Figure 1.3. Sketch plan of small area of gilgai or Tabra micro-relief (for location see figure 1.2, point 15).

The flat plain is formed of deep but well-drained, calcareous soils locally enriched with calcium carbonate suggestive of a moderate degree of maturity. A conspicuous, but localised, feature of the soils are numerous deep cracks merging into areas of well-developed micro-relief. At one extreme the micro-relief forms large basins of some 300-500 m long axis, 100-200 m across and about 1.5 m deep. Other examples (fig. 1.2:15 and fig. 1.3) comprise alternating risers and basins with heavily cracked intervening depressions. One of the larger basins (south of Site 2 on fig. 1.2) is floored with humic greyish-brown (dry 10YR 5/2; wet 10YR 4/2) silty clays containing occasional broken fragments of shells of freshwater gastropods suggestive of prolonged inundation. Many basins were connected by curving hollows, usually uncracked, which in time of flood may have conducted flood water from basin to basin. The large basins can be classed as 'depression gilgai' (type A of Harris 1958:171 and pl. 1) and were the most common such features, but the heavily cracked lattice type (fig. 1.3) also occurred. The general explanation for gilgai features is that they are caused by heaving of the soil as a result of its expansion upon wetting and subsequent cracking during drying stages. Soil then falls down the cracks, and when re-wetting occurs lateral pressures build up resulting in the soil being heaved up (Young 1976:189). Although this may explain the lattice type, a related mechanism of 'downpacking' and soil compaction can result in the elimination of voids and re-orientation of clay particles which produces an increase in density of the soils associated with the formation of depression gilgai (Harris 1958:182). Alternatively Edelman and Brinkman (1962) have suggested that gilgai micro relief can develop in former lake or swamp areas as a result of swelling, shrinking and 'ripening' of the originally supersaturated mud. Yet another interpretation, which disputes the gilgai label and prefers the term Tabra soils, considers that long-standing water in depressions together with localised channel erosion can produce such basins (White and Law 1969).

Although the Balikh-valley gilgai cannot be satisfactorily explained simply by the above mechanisms, it is clear according to all authorities that the features tended to be related to flood basins which usually occurred between ancient irrigation canals. Harris (1958), White and Law (1969) as well as Edelman and Brinkman (1962) all suggest that standing water or flood basins once existed in such areas. The existence of such an environment is supported by the presence of the humic soil with freshwater molluscs, as noted above, and given the location of the gilgai or Tabra features between distributary channels of the Nahr al-Abbara, it can be suggested that these were originally flood basins associated with irrigation. This, however, requires confirmation by further fieldwork.

It is probable that the lowest Balikh terrace partly aggraded as a result of the deposition of sediments from the irrigation-canal system, but the depth of accumulation cannot yet be stated. However, the presence of a flat Halaf site (Site 1) immediately west of the Nahr al-Abbara gives an opportunity to determine the depth of sedimentary aggradation. On first impression this site, with its abundant Early-Halaf pottery and a minor occupation of the first millennium B.C., appears to be buried to such a point that it now appears to be flat. Similarly the absence of hollow ways on the lowest Balikh terrace suggests that landscape features are buried, but the presence of field scatters, probably of 4th-10th century A.D. date, implies that there has been little significant aggradation over the past millennium.

Valley-bottom lands of the Nahr Slouq. A key problem to be investigated was that of sedimentation around the Neolithic site of Sabi Abyad. On the one hand, some soil scientists maintained that the present land surface has been essentially unchanged since the late Pleistocene or early Holocene (cf. Akkermans 1993:144), thus implying that burial of archaeological sites has been minimal. On the other

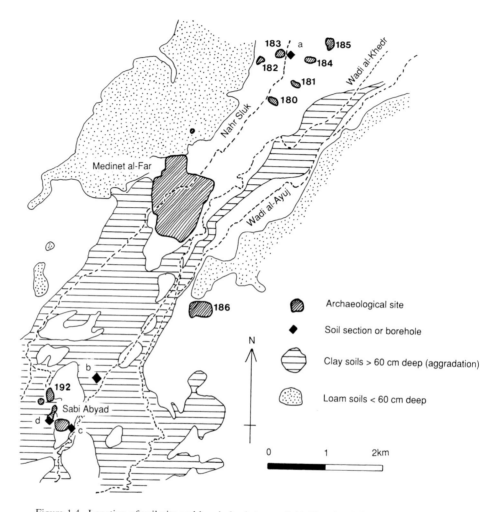

Figure 1.4. Location of soil pits and boreholes between Sabi Abyad and Tell Hajiran (BS 183).

hand, archaeological excavation traced the lowest occupation levels to almost four metres below plain level (see chapter 2). The following account of sedimentation is based upon exposures in pits near Tell Hajiran (BS 183), several deep rectangular pits dug as housings for diesel-pumped wells, a section in a trench exposed below the aceramic Neolithic occupation at Sabi Abyad II (BS 190) and a 22 m well boring made adjacent to the site itself. These are described from the northeast to the southwest (figs. 1.4 and 1.5):

(a) Soil profile in a pit ca. 100 m southeast of Tell Hajiran (BS 183; fig. 1.4).

0-30 cm	Brown loam, weak subangular blocky structure. Recent IA horizon.
30-80 cm	Strong brown (dry 7.5YR 6/6; wet 7.5YR 5/6) clay loam, weak subangular blocky structure, occasional small (5 mm) moderately well-developed white calcium carbonate soft concretions. Soil IBca horizon.
[80-100 cm	Estimated level of old land surface]
80-120 cm	Brown clay loam, tendency to horizontally oriented structure; occasional horizontal cracks and planar voids. Very weak calcium carbonate in form of faint filaments. Occasional sherds were collected from this horizon at various points around trench wall. Buried A (i.e. IIA) horizon.
120-175 cm	Strong brown (dry 5YR 5/6; wet 5YR 5/6) clay loam. Medium to coarse subangular blocky structure with well-developed extensive white calcium carbonate soft concretions with tendency to vertical orientation. Towards base tendency to redder hues and more well-developed structure. IIBca horizon.

The above sequence comprises a buried soil (IIA and IIBca) horizon with a well-developed calcium carbonate horizon (IIBca) and an upper soil horizon (IIA) containing occasional small sherds. One of the six sherds recovered, one with a combed exterior, may be diagnostically of Uruk date and contemporaneous with nearby Tell Hajiran; the others are indeterminate. This IIA horizon may either comprise an old ground surface strewn with sherds from the nearby Uruk site or it may be a buried soil treated with settlement debris used as manure (see below). Then followed deposition of 80 cm of overlying loams, which are without sherds. Following the cessation of loam accumulation, a weak soil horizon (IBca) developed within this upper loam, which presumably accumulated over the past 5000 years.

(b) Sections exposed in pump-housing pits of wells. The most deeply accessible of these, at 8, about one kilometre east of Sabi Abyad (figs. 1.2 and 1.4), is located on flat, ploughed and usually irrigated land a little north of an old irrigation canal and yielded the following sequence (fig. 1.5b):

0-10 cm	Reddish-yellow (dry 7.5YR 6/6; wet 7.5YR 4/4, dark brown); silty clay loam; coarse structure with slightly platy tendency. Common fine root hairs; occasional woody roots. Top soil.
10-80 cm	Reddish yellow (dry 7.5YR 7/6; wet 7.5YR 4.4, dark brown); silty clay loam; medium subangular blocky with platy tendency; occasional filled-in voids of micro-fauna. Occasional woody roots.

T.J. WILKINSON

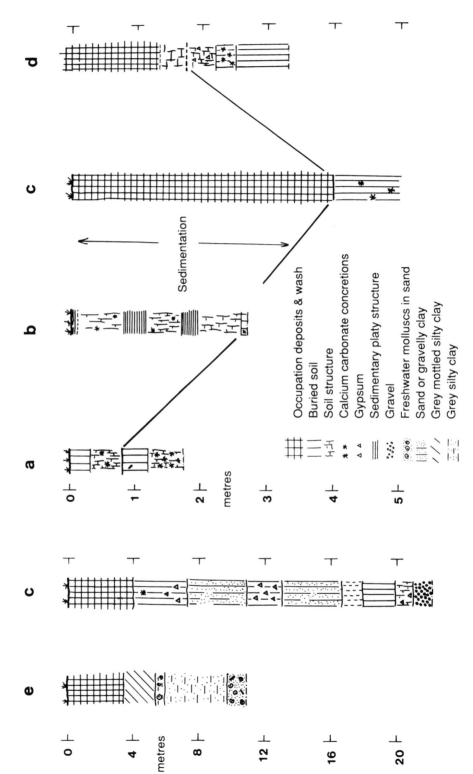

Figure 1.5. Selected soil and sediment sections from around Sabi Abyad. For locations of a-d, see figure 1.4. Note that the full sequence at c (22 m) is given to the left; e refers to the borehole sunk immediately to the east of Tell Hammam et-Turkman.

80-115 cm   Reddish yellow (dry 7.5YR 7/6; wet 7.5YR 5/6, strong brown); fine sandy silt loam. Well-developed platy structure with fine sand on plate faces. Occasional woody roots.

115-170 cm   Reddish yellow (dry 7.5YR 7/6; wet 7.5YR 5/6, strong brown); firm silty clay; weak medium to coarse subangular blocky structure; weak $CaCo_3$ filaments along fine root channels and in voids. Occasional roots to 8 mm.

170-195 cm   Reddish yellow (dry 7.5YR 7/6; wet 5YR 5/6, strong brown); silt loam; well-developed platy structure; occasional clusters of faecal material. Sparse roots. Moderately distinct boundaries to top and bottom.

195-260 cm   Reddish yellow (dry 7.5YR 7/6; wet 7.5YR 5/6, strong brown); very firm, silty clay; weak subangular blocky structure with occasional to common voids and faecal pellet clusters; one or two root pseudo-morphs (slightly cemented). Very sparse roots.

260-270 cm   Reddish yellow (slightly moist 7.5YR 6/6; wet 7.5YR 5/6, strong brown); very firm silty clay loam; sparse calcium-carbonate filaments; coarse subangular blocky structure.

Because artefacts or archaeological deposits are absent, the sequence can only be assessed chronologically by reference to levels of soil development. Weak pedogenesis in the form of development of blocky structure, biogenic voids and calcium-carbonate filaments suggests episodes of moderate stability at 10-80 cm, 115-170 cm and 195-270 cm. Conversely, the presence of a platy structure, particularly with fine sand on the plate faces (i.e. at 80-115 cm), suggests that sedimentary aggradation of silts and fine sands was greater than the rate of soil formation, hence the original sedimentary structure was preserved. A second platy horizon from 170-195 cm may also have accumulated in a similar manner. The platy horizons aggraded with a low-energy silt-plain environment subject to frequent flooding which probably limited the areas of valley bottom soil for agricultural use (M. Mulders, pers. comm.). Aggradation appears to have occurred at uneven rates with the pedogenic horizons representing episodes of slower or zero accumulation. Although these cannot be dated absolutely, with reference to Gile et al.'s (1966) carbonate build-up stages, these episodes must have been significantly shorter than 3500 years and probably no more than a few hundred years each.

Similar conclusions could be drawn from other soil profiles at 29, 30, 31 and 32, in the plain to the east of Sabi Abyad (fig. 1.2). The only obvious difference was at 32 where more well-developed soil structure and calcium-carbonate soft concretions at depths of 1.5-2.0 m imply that aggradation rates were lower to the southeast, towards the margins of the terrace/plateau lands. Only at 88, to the south of Hammam et-Turkman village, could high-energy gravel of probably Pleistocene date be recognised. This medium-coarse, subrounded and subangular gravel, at a depth of circa four metres, was overlaid by a blocky clay loam with a well-developed horizon of soft calcium carbonate concretions at 2.5-3.0 m. Above this, the 2.5 m of reddish-brown blocky clay loam suggests a steady but slow aggradation over a period in which the formation of soil structure in the top and subsoils proceeded in equilibrium with the rate of aggradation.

Only at 39, immediately west of Tell Sabi Abyad, was there any archaeological material in the section. Here, in a 170 cm deep pit, sherds (probably Middle Assyrian, ca. 1260-1200 B.C.) occurred at 110 and 140 cm depth. Again the soil profile comprised uniform silty clays with little evidence of horizon development.

(c) Borehole immediately southeast of Tell Sabi Abyad. From base to top this comprised a basal fine-medium gravel with a sparse silt/clay matrix overlain by a buried brown soil with a well-developed blocky structure (ca. 20-22 m). This was overlain from 20-7.3 m by a thick accumulation of rather indeterminate strong brown (7.5YR 5/6 wet) sandy clay or loam. A possible stable episode is represented by a firm silty clay with nests of gypsum crystals between 13-11 m. Although occasional gravel was evident through this unit, the only deposit suggestive of fluvial activity was from 11-10 m, immediately above the stable horizon; this may have resulted from localised deposition of gravel in a minor wadi or alluvial fan. The surface of the pre-existing natural plain is represented by the reddish-yellow firm clay loam (7.3-4 m) which exhibits minor calcium-carbonate concretions and occasional gypsum crystals at a depth indicative of weak soil development. Finally, the uppermost four metres comprise a dark brown to dark yellowish-brown (10YR 4/3-4/4) clay loam containing sparse charcoal flecks and occasional stones. This layer, which appears to be wash from the tell, supports the observation made by excavation that the occupation deposits run well below the level of the plain.

(d) Section exposed in side of excavated trench in the aceramic site of Sabi Abyad II (BS 190). Note: base of occupation (i.e. 0 m here) is 1.2-1.5 m below the level of the adjacent fields (fig. 1.5).

0-40 cm	Strong brown (7.5YR 5/6 wet) silty clay, slightly blocky with fine vertical and horizontal cracks. Probably aggraded silt plain but including minor contaminants from human occupation.
40-86 cm	Strong brown (7.5YR 5/8 wet), but appearing reddish-brown, silty clay; occasional needle-shaped or flat gypsum crystals 2-5 mm in length. Low-energy aggraded silt plain with secondary gypsum accumulation.
86-115 cm	Strong brown (7.5YR 5/8 wet), drying rapidly to reddish-yellow (7.5YR 6/6, but appearing conspicuously lighter), silt loam with occasional off-white soft calcium carbonate concretions 2-5 mm in diameter. Buried Bca horizon of stable soil profile.

115-194cm   Below merging boundary at 115 cm, soil matrix continues as for the layer above but without the calcium carbonate concretions. Towards base of exposure this becomes a yellowish-red (5YR 4/6 wet), silty clay.

The base of occupation, being 1.2 to 1.5 m below plain level, suggests that there has been sedimentary aggradation around the tell approximating to this figure. This is significantly lower than the aggradation estimated from the excavations at the main mound of Sabi Abyad (ca. 4 m), which implies that sedimentation has increased towards the axis of the valley of the Nahr Slouq, that is towards the southeast. The presence of the stable subsoil horizon 86-115 cm below the base of occupation suggests that this site was not developed upon a permanently dry stable soil, but upon a slowly aggrading silt plain.

Taken together, the above profiles suggest that the valley of the Nahr Slouq adjacent to the site of Sabi Abyad has been subjected to steady, low-energy silt-plain aggradation which has formed a wedge of sediment thickening from ca. 80 cm of post-Uruk deposition near Tell Hajiran (figs. 1.4 and 1.5) to around four metres adjacent to the main mound at Sabi Abyad. To the northwest, sedimentation was evidently less. Although occasional episodes of stability are evident in exposed sections, the elapsed time was nowhere sufficient to produce well-developed $CaCO_3$ horizons comparable to those on the adjacent plateau-steppe. This impression of aggradation within the Nahr Slouq plain is reinforced by the absence of field scatters and hollow ways from this area (see below) as well as by the virtual filling in of a relict meandering wadi channel to the southeast and south of Sabi Abyad. It can be suggested that in these areas with a low rate of soil-profile development (horizontal lines on fig. 1.4), sedimentation has led to the gradual obliteration of landscape features that would otherwise be recognisable if low rates of sedimentation had prevailed. This process could therefore easily have obscured minor prehistoric sites as well.

The Cultural Landscape

Site distribution

Because the Balikh valley has already been surveyed by P.M.M.G. Akkermans, no attempt was made at systematic site survey, and instead we concentrated upon evaluating the context of known sites and on recording landscape or off-site features within the physical environment. However, before describing the landscape and off-site features it is necessary to summarise the general distribution of sites within the bounds of figure 1.1 (from Akkermans 1993:138ff and other data supplied by Akkermans). Additional sites recorded (Sites 1-39), together with brief observations on Balikh survey sites revisited which deserve additional comment, will be described elsewhere. Although landscape survey did not increase the numbers of known settlements in most areas, survey on foot along the banks of the Balikh did, because adjacent to the river sites did not register so well on aerial photographs and could only be recognised by field walking.

By the Pre-Pottery Neolithic (or, in local terms, Balikh I period, ca. 7500-6000 B.C; cf. Akkermans 1993:111-12), the area around Sabi Abyad was occupied by at least the following sites: Sabi Abyad (mounds BS 190-192), Tulul Breilat (BS 161-5), Tells Damishliyya I and II (BS 177 and 178) and probably Tell Eftaim (BS 212). Although occupation may have thinned slightly, occupation during the early Pottery Neolithic (Balikh II) apparently persisted at Sabi Abyad (BS 189), Tulul Breilat (BS 161-62) and Tells Damishliyya I-II (BS 177-78). Settlement of the transitional stage to Halaf and full Halaf (Balikh III) occurs at Sabi Abyad (BS 189 and 192), Haramie (BS 168), Tell Hammam et-Turkman (BS 175), Tells Damishliyya I-II (BS 177-78), Khirbet esh-Shenef (BS 170) and the newly discovered Site 1. Some degree of centralisation had probably taken place by Ubaid times (Balikh IV) when settlement appears to have been concentrated at Tells Hammam et-Turkman and Haramie.

Tell Hammam et-Turkman functioned as the main Late Chalcolithic and Early Bronze Age (Balikh VI) centre, while a secondary place existed at Tell Eftaim (BS 212; Curvers 1991). Interestingly, a tiny Late Uruk site with southern Mesopotamian pottery types was discovered overlooking the Balikh ca. 1.5 km south of Tell Hammam et-Turkman, a site which, although rich with remains of 'local' type (Akkermans 1988), has yielded no southern Uruk materials. The position of the Uruk site (Site 7 on fig. 1.2) a short distance from a hollow way route is in keeping with equivalent small Uruk sites recorded near Titrish Höyük (Algaze et al. 1992, site 9) and in the northern Jezirah of Iraq (Wilkinson 1990, sites 75 and 139). During the Early Bronze Age rural settlements were rare, one of the few examples being the small mound BS 305, near Khirbet esh-Shenef. The marked nucleation and associated decrease in the number of sites during the Bronze Age may explain the high visibility of prehistoric settlements in this area, which unlike in the eastern Jezirah of Syria and Iraq, are not necessarily obscured by overlying layers of Bronze Age and Iron Age date.

Occupation continued at Tell Hammam et-Turkman during the second millennium B.C. (Balikh VII and VIII) but ceased by the second half of the millennium, by which time a number of other settlements were occupied, among them BS 186, BS 211 (Tell Jital), BS 195 and perhaps Tells Eftaim (BS 212) and Zkero (BS 152). Of particular interest is the small Middle-Assyrian (Balikh VIII) occupation at Tell Sabi Abyad which may have been positioned near the westernmost limit of the Middle-Assyrian empire. Although a large number of Iron Age and later sites are present (including late Hellenistic and Roman levels at Tell Hammam et-Turkman), the general distribution of settlement awaits final analysis. However, by the late Roman and early Islamic periods (ca. 4th-10th centuries A.D.) settlement was dispersed with small sites at Site 2, Hammam et-Turkman village (BS 194 and 195), BS 199 and Haramie (BS 168). This dispersal may have been partly associated with the construction of the Nahr al-Abbara canal system which appears to have come into use around this time. A similar dispersal of settlements was recorded along the banks of the Balikh river, many of which were recorded for the first time by the landscape survey. These sites, which included a significant number of Iron Age, Hellenistic, Roman and early Islamic settlements, appear to represent a dispersal of small villages and farmsteads away from Tell Hammam et-Turkman after its demise in the Late Bronze Age. Further details on this pattern of settlement will be contained in a future report.

Although there is no evidence that the Balikh valley was fully occupied during the early Islamic period, land-use intensity appears to have been high (see below) and there is even a sign of another tier of settlements located within the fringing plateau and terraces. These sites, i.e. Medinat al-Far, BS 172 as well as Sites 8, 9 and 10, were all located within unirrigated but still cultivable terrain. In such a position they appear to have been partly sustained by rain-fed cultivation, but were equally in a climatically marginal location (see discussion below). Clearly this situation did not last for long and there was a significant decline in settlement numbers after the Abbasid period.

Cultural and landscape features

Although multi-period, the bulk of the cultural features within the landscape probably date from the later phases of settlement, so unfortunately at present there is little landscape evidence that bears directly upon the prehistoric occupations of the Balikh I to IV periods.

Typically, canals should be traceable as linear depressions along which occur elongate mounds of upcast derived from the excavation of the original cut and subsequent cleaning out. Ideally a complete system should be present, with a water source (usually a spring, wadi or perennial stream), water distribution canals which dispersed water to the fields from the trunk canal, and perhaps even sluices. Obviously the canal should have been constructed at an even grade sloping consistently downwards unless there is good reason to suggest that tectonic activity might have caused warping or dislocation of the system.

Two apparently early canal systems were identified in 1992: the first a large complex system paralleling the Balikh river, and the second a less securely identified feature downstream of Medinat al-Far. In addition summary details are given here of a major canal which was identified in 1993 between Tells Sahlan and Hammam et-Turkman.

Late Roman to Islamic canals. The Nahr al-Abbara today forms a narrow, meandering ditch running through or alongside a broad greyish soil mark. At intervals occasional distributary-like channels branch from it. The sinuous trace of the ditch is more like that of a river, but the presence of distributaries in this non-deltaic environment is not. Also, its position along the highest part of the terrace contrasts with that of the Balikh, which occupies a course along the lower part of the valley.

Although possessing a channel, the Nahr al-Abbara is dry today. According to local people, however, it did conduct water before modern overpumping lowered the water table. The original feature is represented by a broad soil mark some five to eight metres wide, which spreads well beyond the narrow recent channel. Forming a sparse scatter on the grey clay soil are occasional small fragments of limestone, and less frequently pottery. The soil mark contrasts with the soils reddish-brown hued of the adjacent plain above which it is often raised as a low levee. Occasional groups of two or three large limestone blocks with a 0.5-1.0 m long axis occur every 0.5 or 1.0 km (X on fig. 1.2). These may derive from installations constructed to divert flow into secondary distributary channels. In addition, occasional large fragments of basalt querns occurred at intervals along the canals. Although these were mainly saddle querns, one or two large pieces of rotary quern were collected at 71 (cf. fig. 1.2). The size of the quern fragments (usually 30% or more of the quern is preserved) suggests that these did not arrive as the result of manuring with settlement waste, and the absence of associated habitation debris suggests that the querns were used approximately where they were found. Finally, in addition to sherds (often abraded) within the grey channel deposits, spreads of small sherds (field scatters) were common across the terrain adjacent to canals.

The grey chemically-reduced soil mark probably results from prolonged waterlogging, which suggests that the feature represents some form of channel or canal and its deposits. The original channel subsequently became replaced, after frequent flooding, by the shallow sinuous feature that developed within the clogged-up channel. Upcast banks are rare, being limited to the area below Haramie (BS 168) and in the vicinity of Tells Jital and Eftaim (BS 211 and BS 212). Nowhere, however, were there soil banks of obvious antiquity and it is suggested here that the original features, as is common in southern Mesopotamia, were blown away as silt-clay aggregates, were eroded by flow along the channel or were obscured by alluviation. The lack of an obvious cut channel and associated upcast mounds may result from the accumulation of sediments both within the channel and on the plain to either side, which would have obscured the morphology and resulted in a virtually flat cross-profile. The canal was traced intermittently to its source on the Balikh at Tell Sahlan where a dam blocks the Balikh. The masonry dam, 2 m high and 1.25 m wide, is equipped with five small culverts to allow flood waters to escape. It evidently intercepted the Balikh flow, directing some down the Nahr al-Abbara and allowing the base flow through the culverts to continue down the Balikh. Extra high discharges flowed over the reinforced spillway. Although according to local informants, this dam seems to be of 20th century construction, it may have replaced an earlier feature.

The field evidence suggests that a complete canal system extended from a source on the Balikh, probably near Tell Sahlan, for at least 20 km downstream to a point downstream of Tell Zkero (BS 152). The feature follows close to the crest of the lowest Balikh terrace which thus allowed distributary channels to be constructed away from the trunk canal. Habitation sites are rare along the Nahr al-Abbara, but the early Islamic sites BS 171, BS 200 and Sites 2 and 4 are alongside, and may be contemporary with the system. Elsewhere, the presence of surface scatters of pottery dated to between the 4th and 10th centuries A.D. associated with the channel sediments and strewn over adjacent fields (e.g. 44 on fig. 1.2), supports a date within this time range. The presence of basalt querns along various branches of the system suggests that crop processing may have gone on alongside the canals. It may therefore be tentatively suggested that cereals were brought from the fields to the canal banks where milling took place prior to distribution along the canal network. Although flour may have been produced, the presence of copious water for soaking grain suggests that instead a form of crushed wheat or *burghal* may have been produced at these milling points. The presence of field scatters suggests that irrigated lands were also intensively cultivated and manured.

The second system is a subtle and ambiguous feature extending southwest from the major Islamic site of Medinat al-Far. Today the only extant feature is a straight cut channel raised upon a very low silt levee, which conducted flow from the Nahr Slouq, near BS 186. Both the straight cut and the Nahr Slouq are dry as are a number of small channels that fan out from the straight cut (e.g. 5 and 6 on fig. 1.2). This system showed no sign of being of great antiquity and it may be of recent date. Unlike the Nahr al-Abbara, there are no associated artefacts, stones, soil marks or field scatters. However, its association with Medinat al-Far suggests that it may be early Islamic in date; it is unlikely to be any earlier. Irrespective of its date, this system may have been partly responsible for the later stages of the above mentioned silt and clay aggradation on the plain to the east of Sabi Abyad.

The Tell Hammam et-Turkman canal system. This large but undated system, which was discovered during the 1993 field season, comprises two segments, the upper near Tell Sahlan measuring five kilometres in length and the lower near Tell Hammam et-Turkman being some two kilometres long. Although separated by a gap of some six kilometres, the scale of these two features and their channel morphology suggest that they originally belonged to the same feature, the central sections of which have been removed by riverine erosion. A measured section near site BS 242, between Tells Sahlan and Eftaim, indicates a width of the filled-in channel of some 13-15 m (fig. 1.6). This measurement, however, being for the filled-in channel base, probably overestimates the width of the actual channel. Nevertheless, the original canal must have been of a scale comparable to that of the Balikh in the early 20th century, which suggests that it was probably capable of conducting much or all of the flow of the Balikh. The presence of Hellenistic occupation on top of a possible

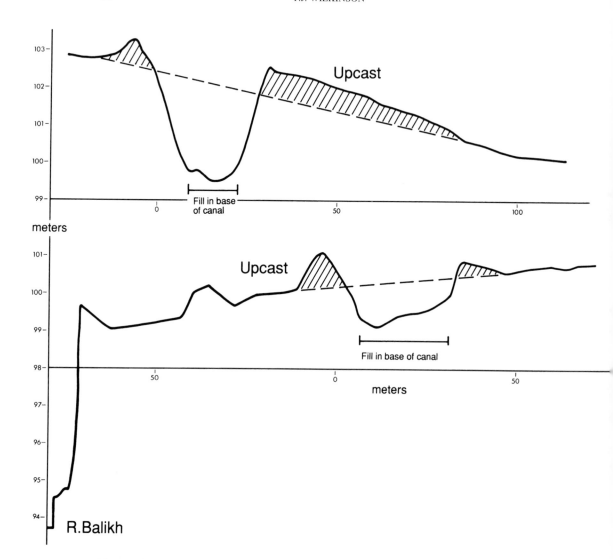

Figure 1.6. Surveyed profiles across major canal between Tell Sahlan and Tell Hammam et-Turkman.

mound of spoil cast up from this canal (Site 16) suggests a pre-Hellenistic date, and Islamic occupation within the canal void at BS 249 suggests a *terminus ante quem* of early Islamic date.[2] This canal would have been capable of diverting much or all of the Balikh flow and would thus have caused considerable problems for settlements located downstream.

[1] Note that excavation in 1994 demonstrated that the canal was in use between approximately the 3rd/2nd century B.C. and the 6th century A.D.

Hollow ways. Of the linear features that are recognisable around Sabi Abyad (cf. figs. 1.1 and 1.2), most occur on the drier fringing terraces and plateaus where water sources are absent and there is no evidence of water flow along the features or of any upcast.

These broad linear features can be compared with similar hollows and vegetation lines recorded elsewhere in the Jezirah. Such features, although vague and ill-defined on the ground, are usually more obvious on aerial photographs where they can range from broad dark linear features to narrow lines. Some of the latter are probably traditional tracks whereas the broad features, rather than relating to the modern pattern of the settlements, tend to link or radiate from archaeological sites. Only the broad features and those narrower features that relate to archaeological sites are indicated on figures 1.1 and 1.2. Field checking indicates that the features vary between extremely shallow hollows (e.g. 83 and 84 on fig. 1.2) through moderately shallow hollows, 20-30 cm deep, sometimes with vegetation marks (57, 58 and 59), to, less commonly, broad deep valleys up to 1.3 m in depth (176[3]). Other features on the other hand are virtually undetectable on the ground and must have shown up on the aerial photographs by virtue of their vegetation which has now been eradicated by ploughing. From the absence of upcast and relict water-logged sediments and their tendency, in some cases, to run up and down over low rolling hills, with the exception of 176, these features are clearly not ancient canals. This impression is reinforced by the total absence of water sources along them. Where such features occur elsewhere in the Jezirah they can be interpreted as being the traces of former roads or tracks that have become compacted and partly worn away by the continued passage of humans and animals (Wilkinson 1993). This constant traffic concentrates overland flow resulting in further erosion, which in turn is reinforced by the blowing away of dust stirred up by passing traffic. The large size range of these features suggests that erosional effects vary significantly depending upon the local geomorphology and pattern of drainage, hence linear hollows that coincide with natural runoff systems can be eroded very rapidly, whereas others on flat terrain away from any obvious drainage net may only erode by wind action.

The following pre-modern routes can be suggested (cf. figs. 1.1 and 1.2):

(a) A major system running northwest-southeast to the northwest of Medinat al-Far.

(b) A narrow north-south feature north of early Islamic Medinat al-Far, which continues as a broader feature to the south of BS 186 to the large contemporaneous site of Khirbet al-Amber (BS 172), after which it runs south and southwest towards BS 307. An early Islamic *khan* or similar structure (60) at BS 172 (cf. figs. 1.1 and 1.7) reinforces the impression that this linear hollow is a route, which probably followed the east side of the Balikh valley between Raqqa and Harran.

---

[3] Re-survey in 1995 with Dr C.-P. Haase suggests that the feature at 176 was a canal distributing water from the Nahr al-Abbara to a little south of Medinat al-Far.

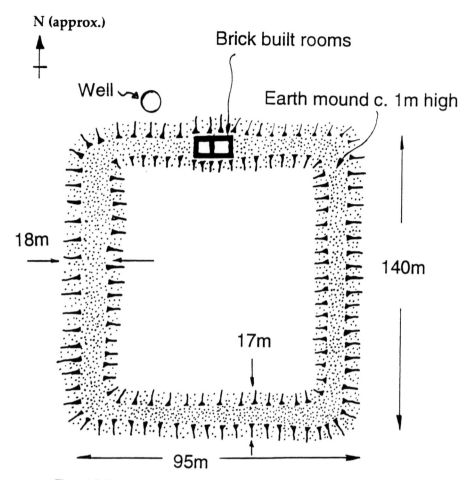

Figure 1.7. Early Islamic *khan* at point 60 near Khirbet al-Ambar (site BS 172).

(c) Two north-south features running south from Tell Hammam et-Turkman, the eastern one running towards BS 152 and the western one towards the early Islamic Site 8.

(d) A north-south feature diverging to the west of Site 8 and ultimately leading to the northwest. This feature which has only Iron Age sites along it (with perhaps a minor component of Late Bronze Age settlement) can be traced to the south towards Site 38, a major Iron Age site. This hollow way may therefore represent an Iron Age, perhaps Late Assyrian, route system leading northwards towards the Harran plain.

(e) In addition, several shorter features can be identified as follows: three very slight radial features to the west of Tell Hammam et-Turkman; a possible east-west feature running to the west of Tulul Breilat (BS 161-5); two broad features focusing on Tell Zkero (BS 152); a substantial but short feature on a west-north-west orientation about one kilometre north of Hammam et-Turkman village (16 on fig. 1.2).

These features are difficult to trace on the ground, and without aerial photographs many would be virtually invisible. Their presence suggests that major north-south route systems have existed at various times on both the east and west sides of the Balikh valley, and it seems likely that the large sites of Medinat al-Far, Khirbet al-Ambar and Site 38 all developed on major ancient routes. However, unless specific dating evidence is associated with these hollows they should be regarded as multi-period. This is especially so for features associated with multi-period sites such as Tell Zkero (BS 152) and Tell Hammam et-Turkman.

Field scatters. During the 1992 field season, off-site sherd scatters were plotted (fig. 1.2) and were supplemented by quantitative counts at selected localities in 1993. The 1992 qualitative assessment indicated that moderate-density scatters of small battered sherds were noticeably present on the lowest Balikh terrace between the distributary channels of the Nahr al-Abbara and were especially dense to the north in the vicinity of Tell Jital (BS 211). These scatters commonly include sherds of late Roman and early Islamic type and their consistent presence along this system suggests that they might be associated with irrigation that took place at that time. Although field scatters are also present on the dry and unirrigated fringing terraces and plateaus, these are sparser and more localized, mainly being present west of Tell Hammam et-Turkman and Tell Zkero and at lower densities near Medinat al-Far.

Such scatters are not associated with significant evidence of in-situ occupation refuse, building foundation stones, etc., and are probably the result of manuring in antiquity with settlement-derived refuse (Wilkinson 1982). The scatters, if they are indicators of past intensive cultivation and manuring, are particularly important for the following reasons. First, they indicate that intensive cultivation occurred along the Nahr al-Abbara, which suggests that the area formed part of an agricultural system which entailed irrigation and manuring (as well as crop processing) during the late Antique period. Second, those scatters to the west of Tell Hammam et-Turk-man, which were quantitatively assessed in 1993, are too elevated to have been irrigated from any existing water sources and are almost certainly related to rain-fed cultivation. Similar high-density scatters to the east of Tell Hammam et-Turkman may either relate to dry farming or to irrigation from the Nahr al-Abbara. In addition, during the 1993 field season significant off-site 'field scatters' were observed on fields on the Balikh flood plain around Tell Zkero as well as downstream to the south of Tell as-Sawwan. Such scatters, which frequently occurred at densities of over 100 sherds per 100 sq. m, appear to be concentrated on the lower terrain, i.e. most conveniently watered from gravity canals. Adjacent cultivated terrain, only slightly more elevated, appears to have exhibited much sparser scatters and probably did not receive irrigation water. Sherd scatters may therefore be used to differentiate between irrigated and rain-fed cultivation, and thus may help to establish the former limit of rain-fed cultivation.

Discussion

Soil and landscape mapping allowed the area to be divided into a zone of long term rain-fed cultivation to the north of Tells Zkero and Hammam et-Turkman. Further south, especially in the region of Tell Mounbatah and Tell as-Sawwan, sites were absent from the steppe away from ancient water courses or the Balikh, but abundant evidence for irrigation occurred in the form of very dense sherd scatters associated with traces of canals. Although at this stage it is only possible to sketch the relative importance of irrigation versus rain-fed cultivation, a number of points can be made. The fringing plateaus and terrace to the north of Tell Zkero would have fluctuated between rain-fed cultivation and steppe, but only around major sites, for example Tells Zkero and Hammam et-Turkman, is there any evidence of significant intensive cultivation in the form of off-site field scatters. The irrigated zone, to judge from the distribution of traces of irrigation canals and high-density 'field scatters' on flood-plain soils, appears to have been mainly downstream of Tell Zkero, especially around Tells Mounbatah and as-Sawwan, but also penetrated northwards into the rain-fed belt as a re-entrant extending perhaps as far north as Tell Sahlan. Thus the approximate limit of viable long-term rain-fed cultivation appears to lie in the vicinity of Tell Zkero.

Having treated formal irrigation systems and rain-fed cultivation, there remains a broad category of cultivation which was potentially dependent upon soil moisture enhancement from flooding. The soils of the fringing terraces and plateaus, being moderately well-drained, are susceptible to drought and if cultivated are more likely to incur crop failure in dry years. Areas of water spreading and episodic flooding located where side wadis debouch onto the lowest terrace or along the Nahr Slouq would, on the other hand, receive a slight surplus of water. Although not constituting formal irrigation this factor would raise crop yields and prevent failure during driest years. The best evidence for an annual flooding regime comes from the soil sections on the plain of the Nahr Slouq, which demonstrate that aggradation as a result of low-energy overbank flooding has been a characteristic feature of the lands adjacent to and upstream of Sabi Abyad from before the aceramic Neolithic (see above). Consequently this land would have provided either good grazing or favourable conditions for crop cultivation due to supplementary additions of run-off water. Unfortunately spring floods could also result in the destruction of crops. However, the replacement of fields around the margin of flooding, or the construction of bunds to divert the late spring floods, would have provided the benefits of enhanced moisture levels without the problem of destructive flooding. Not only would Neolithic Sabi Abyad have benefited from such valley-bottom lowlands, the presence of the Nahr Slouq, which ultimately derived its water from springs (now dry) at Slouq a short distance to the north, may also have provided a perennial source of water.

The question of marshes posed by Akkermans (1989:131) remains ambiguous. No soil profiles examined during the 1992 and 1993 field seasons showed even a hint of former marsh development. Although the gilgai/Tabra basins of the lowest Balikh terrace must have been associated with episodic flooding and perhaps marsh development, such features may not be ancient. Like similar features in Iraq they may have developed from flood basins adjacent to irrigation canals. The discovery of the early Halaf Site 1 conflicts with the view that no prehistoric sites are found on the plain west of the village of Hammam et-Turkman (Akkermans 1989:131). Rather than being in an area of marsh, this site again may have benefited from either the moisture enhancement effect of a debouching side wadi (i.e. the valley immediately northeast of Site 1 on fig. 1.2) or the course of an ancestral Balikh river. The latter is suggested by the presence of a shallow valley system feeding into the ephemeral Wadi al-Khedr which leads southward towards the Breilat sites and Mafraq Slouq. Although requiring further verification by borehole evidence, traces of such a palaeochannel were found to the north of Tell Mounbatah as well as immediately south of Tell as-Sawwan, where it appears to have flowed after following a course between the major prehistoric sites of Tells Mounbatah and as-Sawwan. Such a channel may represent a former course of the Balikh river. However, the presence of an early river channel immediately east of Tell Hammam et-Turkman (see above) suggests that such a river cannot have conducted the entire drainage of the valley. Clearly before such an ancestral early Holocene Balikh can be accepted, confirmation will be required from additional field work.

The most conspicuous landscape features recorded during the 1992 field season are those of the early Islamic period. Although the Nahr al-Abbara was not necessarily constructed during the early Islamic period, it appears to have been in use then. The existence of this feature may therefore shed some light on the early Islamic geography of the area which includes the major sites of Medinat al-Far and Khirbet al-Ambar along a north-south hollow way route as well as a similar west-bank route system with a minor Islamic site (Site 8) alongside. The location of Medinat al-Far a little to the east of the Balikh between Harran and Raqqa suggests that it may be Hisn Maslama as mentioned by Yaqut (Le Strange 1905:105; for discussion see Bartl 1994). According to Yaqut this settlement lay about one mile and a half from the Balikh from which water was conducted via a canal to a fortress to fill a cistern and also to irrigate the adjacent lands. It is,

however, clear from the topography of the area that the Nahr al-Abbara could not
have supplied Medinat al-Far directly (cf. fig. 1.2). Similarly, the proposed canal
system downstream of Medinat al-Far did not receive its water from the Balikh.
Therefore if taken literally, Yaqut's description does not match well with the field
evidence as it stands. However, there is a general association because Medinat
al-Far lies only a short distance to the east of the Balikh and almost certainly
some of its *lands* were watered by a canal from the Balikh (i.e. the Nahr al-
Abbara). Without further field research it is not possible to resolve such points of
Islamic geography.

In spite of the ambiguous historical geography, it is clear that Medinat al-Far, its
sister settlement at Khirbet al-Ambar and the associated *khan* must have developed
on the route between Harran and Raqqa within marginal dry-farmed lands to the east
of the Balikh. Although there is a sparse field scatter suggestive of former manuring
in the immediate vicinity of Medinat al-Far, the presence of well-developed sherd
scatters along the Nahr al-Abbara system suggests that the centre of gravity of cultivation, particularly intensive cropping, was located some three kilometres to the
west of Medinat al-Far along this canal. The location of such major town development away from the centre of food production suggests that the presence of the route
was a more important determinant of early Islamic settlement than the location of
agricultural lands.

CHAPTER 2

THE EXCAVATIONS: STRATIGRAPHY AND ARCHITECTURE

MARC VERHOEVEN and PETER KRANENDONK
with a contribution by NICO ATEN

Introduction

The main area chosen for our prehistoric investigations is the relatively low and gently sloping southeastern portion of Sabi Abyad. The emphasis has been on broad-scale exposure of the Halaf occupation levels and their immediate predecessors to obtain an insight into late Neolithic settlement organisation and developments in the use of space. These broad-scale, horizontal excavations were conducted primarily in 9 × 9 m squares, designated from west to east with capital letters and from north to south with cardinal numbers (fig. 2.1). In many cases the squares were divided into smaller units during excavation for better stratigraphic and/or areal control. The one-metre-wide section baulks between the excavation units were repeatedly removed in order to solve particular stratigraphic problems or to obtain coherent architectural plans. Deposits from a selected number of floors, rooms, hearths, etc., were sieved and/or flotated. So far, the remains of prehistoric occupation have been unearthed in 17 squares, viz. O13-O14, P11 to P15, Q12 to Q15, R11 to R14, S12 and S13, covering an area of about 1270 m².

Earlier strata of settlement were sampled on a limited scale in various stepped-trench operations. Judging from the ceramic assemblage and some radiocarbon dates, the earliest levels uncovered at Sabi Abyad date from around 5700 B.C., whereas the youngest date from ca. 5000 B.C. (uncalibrated). Natural soil has been reached in trench P15 at a depth of four metres below present-day field level. Apparently, the surroundings of the site have witnessed a considerable accumulation of aeolic-fluviatile deposits in the course of time, which has hidden part of the mound from view (see chapter 1). Prehistoric occupation levels have also been reached on a restricted scale in operations carried out on the top and on the northeastern part of the site (fig. 2.1). However, the results of the soundings in these areas await further analysis and have, consequently, not been included in the present study. This chapter intends to give a detailed account of the stratigraphy and architecture of the southeastern area of Sabi Abyad (a first account has been published by, e.g., Akkermans 1989b, 1993:45-68; Akkermans and Le Mière 1992).

The stratigraphical sequence strongly varied from trench to trench, due to a different use of space for various activities. Per square of excavation, a number of strata were recognised, each characterised by consistent soil characteristics or coherent architectural features. Most strata were subdivided on the basis of (minor) differences in the nature and sequence of the depositions and constructions. The strata themselves were regrouped into 11 main levels of occupation. These levels emphasise the overall relationships between the various trenches and delineate coherent building phases. So far, the earliest levels 11 to 7 have mainly been reached in a narrow trench (P15) 9 m long and 2 m wide along the southern slope of the southeastern mound. The topmost levels 6-1 have been investigated in broad horizontal exposures, up to 800 m². All strata and levels have been numbered in order of excavation (i.e. from the top downwards) but will be discussed in order of accumulation (i.e. from the earliest to the last).

When relating the various levels to our main periods attested on the southeastern mound, i.e. Balikh IIA-C, IIIA and IIIB (see Foreword), it appears that (a) level 11 represents the final part of the Balikh IIA period, (b) levels 10-7 belong to the Balikh IIC period, (c) levels 6-4 are part of Balikh IIIA (Transitional period) and (d) levels 3-1 represent Balikh IIIB (Early Halaf).[1] This correlation between level and period was initially based on developments in pottery typology and technology but is strongly supported by other categories of artefacts as well (Akkermans 1993:50).

Generally, the southeastern part of Sabi Abyad has given evidence of a continuous sequence of late Neolithic occupation (Akkermans 1987a, 1987b, 1989c, 1993); there seems to be no major hiatus in settlement, except perhaps between the lowest levels 11 and 10. The former level consisted of a compact and rather homogeneous, waterlogged deposit, greyish in colour. Hardly any clear-cut micro-stratigraphy was recognised, which points towards a rapid rate of deposition, uniform in nature. In contrast, the subsequent level 10 mainly consisted of greyish to orange-brown layers of domestic refuse, which was most likely dumped over a considerable period of time (cf. fig. 2.3). Not only the stratigraphic evidence but also the considerable differences in ceramics and other material-culture assemblages from both phases seem to indicate a break in occupation. The level 11 pottery differs very much from that of the subsequent level 10 and shows close similarities to the ceramics from the nearby sites of Tell Assouad and Tell Damishliyya (Cauvin 1972; Le Mière 1979; Akkermans 1986/87, 1988a). The latter sites were both deserted around 5800/5700 B.C., as part of a general trend towards community abandonment in the Balikh region at this time (cf. Akkermans 1993:115); most likely a similar date should be attributed to level 11 at Sabi Abyad. The duration of this possible gap between levels 11 and 10 is hard to establish at present, but can hardly have exceeded 200 or 300 years. Survey evidence from the Balikh valley has made it clear that the local trend of site desertion came to a halt around the middle of the 6th millennium B.C. or slightly afterwards, and was followed by an attempt to recolonise gradually the lands earlier abandoned (ibid.).

---

[1] Balikh IIB levels have not yet been attested on the southeastern mound (see Foreword).

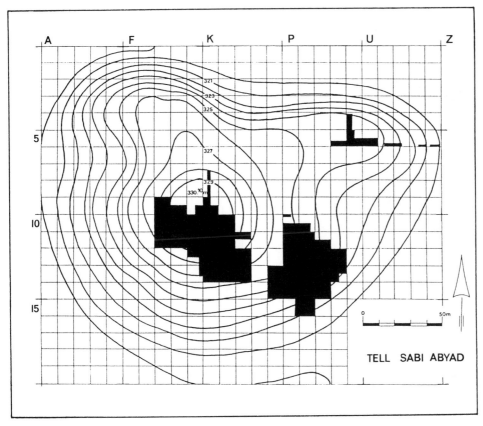

Figure 2.1. Contour map of Tell Sabi Abyad with the areas of excavation.

The Prehistoric Sequence

Level 11

So far, this has been the earliest level excavated at Tell Sabi Abyad. Most likely, it dates from the later Balikh IIA period, i.e. around 5700 B.C. The level was reached in the northern half of trench P15 over an area of 4.50 × 2.00 m only, at a depth of ca. 4.50 m below the level of the surrounding fields. The level was situated directly upon the virgin soil, which appeared as a compact orange-brown loam devoid of artefacts or other finds (fig. 2.3).

Stratigraphy

Level 11 equalled stratum 11 in trench P15, which has been divided into two substrata: 11B and 11A (fig. 2.3). Stratum 11B was represented by a horizontal layer or, perhaps, a pavement of pebbles and cobbles on virgin soil (fig. 2.3, feature AI). Stratum 11A consisted of two deposits of more or less the same character and consistency accumulated upon this stone layer. The lower deposit, ca. 30-40 cm thick, consisted of very hard, brown-grey loam, containing charcoal particles. The upper deposit had a brown colour and was between 20 and 60 cm thick. This layer was disturbed by pit AG, sunk from level 8. Both depositions were laid down virtually horizontally. The homogeneity of both deposits suggests that they accumulated within a rather short period of time.

Architectural features

The virgin soil in the northeastern part of trench P15 was disturbed by a shallow depression partly hidden in the east section (cf. fig. 2.3). This feature was oval in shape, over 95 cm in diameter and ca. 25 cm deep. The depression was filled with a compact and very hard, brownish-grey loam. This feature may represent either a man-made pit or a natural depression.

The depression and the surrounding virgin-soil surface were covered by a stone layer or pavement ca. 10 cm thick (feature AI). This pavement consisted of blackish-grey pebbles (each ca. 2 cm wide and ca. 6 cm long) and cobbles (ca. 6 cm wide and ca. 15 cm long).

Level 10

So far, level 10 has been reached over a limited area in trench P15 only. Most likely, this level fits in the Balikh IIC period and dates from around the middle of the 6th millennium B.C. It was separated from level 11 by a sherd layer.

Stratigraphy

Level 10 consisted of strata 10 and 9 (fig. 2.3). Stratum 10 was divided into two substrata: 10B and 10A. Stratum 10B consisted of a layer of sherds (fig. 2.3, feature AH), covered by the stratum 10A deposit built of four loamy layers, greenish-grey to grey-brown in colour and containing charcoal particles and lime spots (particularly the topmost layer showed numerous lime spots). Stratum 10A gently sloped to the south and varied in thickness from about 60 cm in the north of trench P15 to about 10 cm in its southern part. In addition to the stratum 10B sherd pavement, another layer of sherds was found in the second-lowest stratum 10A deposit, although this layer was not as firm as its 10B counterpart. Moreover, it was found only in the extreme north of trench P15.

Stratum 9, above stratum 10A, consisted of several layers and 'patches' of very hard, orange-brown loam, intermingled with charcoal parts and limespots. Like the former stratum, this stratum 9 sloped towards the south and varied considerably in thickness, from about 20 cm in the northern part of trench P15 through about 60 cm in its central part to 10 cm in its southern part. Strata 10-9 were both disturbed by pit AG sunk from level 8 (cf. fig. 2.3).

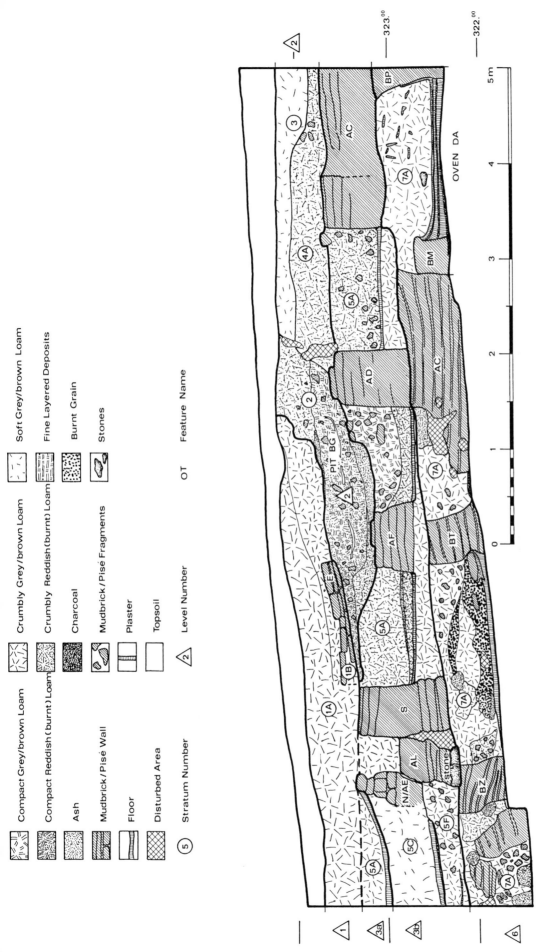

Figure 2.2. West section of square Q13.

Legend:

Compact Grey/brown Loam

Compact Reddish (burnt) Loam

Ash

Mudbrick/Pisé Wall

Floor

Disturbed Area

⑤ Stratum Number

Soft Grey/brown Loam

Fine Layered Deposits

Burnt Grain

Stones

Crumbly Grey/brown Loam

Crumbly Reddish (burnt) Loam

Charcoal

Mudbrick/Pisé Fragments

Plaster

Topsoil

△2 Level Number

OT   Feature Name

Q13 : WEST SECTION

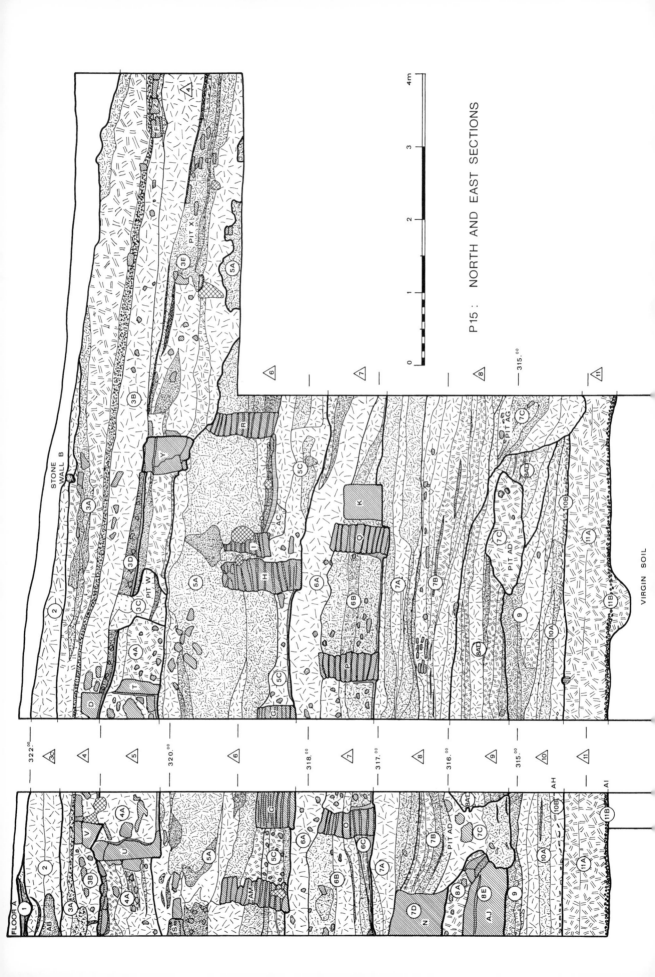

P15 : NORTH AND EAST SECTIONS

Architectural features

The sherd pavement (feature AH), ca. 5 cm thick and built of rather small (diameter ca. 8 cm) coarsely made ceramics, was the only architectural feature ascribed to level 10. In the northern part of the trench, the pavement seemed to have been disturbed; it had been partially removed or reduced in sherd density. No other features have been ascribed to stratum 9.

Level 9

Level 9 is part of the Balikh IIC period and dates from slightly after the middle of the 6th millennium B.C. So far, this level has been exposed only in trench P15 over an area of 4.50 × 2.00 m. It is the first level with clear evidence of architectural features, viz. parts of a wall and a small oven (fig. 2.4).

Stratigraphy

Level 9 equalled stratum 8 in trench P15, subdivided in strata 8E to 8A.[2] The lowest stratum 8E was represented by the construction of wall AJ and its associated floor level. The next stratum 8D consisted of several grey-brown and orange-brown, loamy and crumbly deposits varying in thickness between ca. 10 and 20 cm, which accumulated around wall AJ (cf. fig. 2.3). Charcoal particles and lime spots occurred commonly. Stratum 8D (particularly its upper part) contained orangey-brown and irregularly-shaped mud blocks, probably representing building debris. Stratum 8C represented an oven (AF) and its floor level (cf. fig. 2.4). A black ash layer ca. 3 cm thick was found on the oven floor which in turn was covered by a deposit of orange-black mud fragments and dark ashes ca. 14 cm thick. Numerous very thin, orange and black, ashy lenses up to ca. 30 cm thick accumulated around the oven. Most likely, this deposit was oven waste from its various periods of use. Stratum 8B consisted of numerous tiny debris layers which covered oven AF. The various layers, each ca. 10 cm thick, gradually sloped to the south. They were orange-brown, dark-brown and greenish-grey in colour, and either hard or crumbly in consistency. The various layers added up to a thickness of ca. 70 cm. Many of the layers gradually changed colour from greyish-brown and orange-brown to dark brown or greenish-grey when they started sloping towards the south. Many layers contained orange-brown and dark-brown mud fragments, most probably representing building debris. Most layers were intermingled with charcoal particles and/or limespots. The topmost stratum 8A consisted of a ca. 30 cm thick deposit of dark and orange-brown, loamy layers, which contained numerous orange-brown mud fragments, charcoal particles and lime spots. Stratum 8A consisted for the larger part of debris having descended from the collapsed upper part of the stratum 8E wall(s).

---

[2] In the western and southern part of trench P15 the various substrata could be clearly distinguished. In the east, however, the distinction between these strata was unclear; on fig. 2.3 the subdivisions of stratum 8 are therefore not indicated.

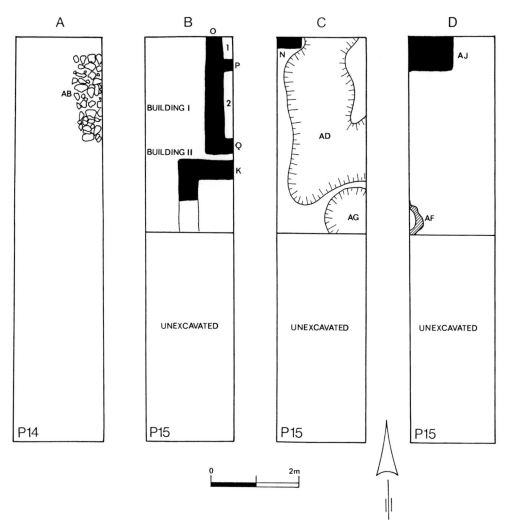

Figure 2.4. Architectural remains in the test trench along the east section of square P14 and in trench P15. A and B: level 7. C: level 8. D: level 9.

Architecture and related features

Two architectural features have been ascribed to level 9, viz. wall AJ and oven AF. Wall AJ was largely hidden in the north and west sections (figs. 2.3 and 2.4). The wall stood to a height of about 80 cm, and was at least 1.10 m long and 92 cm wide. It was built of compact layers of beige-brown loam, each ca. 10 cm thick. These layers were joined by a dark grey-brown mortar ca. 4 cm thick. The south face of wall AJ was hollowed out, probably due to erosion. The east face had been disturbed by the level 8 pit AD.

The circular or oval oven AF, built upon the stratum 8D deposits around wall AJ (fig. 2.4), was at least 67 cm in diameter and stood to a height of ca. 4 cm. The floor of the oven was made of hard-burnt, black-coloured loam ca. 2 cm thick. The oven wall was about 3 cm wide, and made of solid reddish-brown clay. The oven was embedded in a very hard, orange-brown loam coating ca. 20 cm wide and preserved to a height of 28 cm. This loam coating must have served to protect the oven.

Level 8

Level 8 is part of the Balikh IIC period and is dated at around 5300 B.C. So far, it has been traced in a very restricted part (4.5 × 2 m) in trench P15 only. Level 8 showed evidence of a compact wall and two large pits (fig. 2.4).

Stratigraphy

In trench P15, level 8 was represented by stratum 7, which can be divided into four substrata: 7D-7A (fig. 2.3). Stratum 7D consisted of wall N with its associated floor level. Two large pits (AD and AG), dug shortly after the construction of wall N, represented stratum 7C. Subsequently, a considerable amount of debris layers accumulated around wall N and in pits AD and AG (now out of use): stratum 7B. This deposit as a whole gently sloped in a southern direction, and varied in thickness between 0.50 and 1.00 m. The various layers varied between 4 and 20 cm in thickness. The layers were either hard or crumbly in consistency, and grey-brown, orange-brown and greenish-grey in colour. The topmost part of stratum 7B contained fragments of orange-brown mud, probably representing building debris. Most layers were intermingled with charcoal particles and limespots. The stratum 7B fill and the lower features were eventually covered by stratum 7A, which was represented by a greyish-brown, loamy deposition ca. 30-50 cm thick, containing numerous charcoal particles and limespots.

Architecture and related features

Wall N (fig. 2.4) was made of very hard, orange-brown pisé. The wall was largely hidden in the north and west sections. It was at least 70 cm long and 25 cm wide, and stood to a height of ca. 80 cm. The wall base was slightly disturbed by pit AD (cf. fig. 2.3). The floor associated with the wall sloped towards the south. Two large pits, AD and AG, were sunk into this floor. Pit AD was a very large, oblong feature, with an irregularly shaped cross-section and a flattened base. It was ca. 1.00 m deep, at least 3.80 m long and 1.50 m wide. The pit had a rather homogeneous fill: grey-brown loam mixed with orange-brown and grey-brown mud fragments, which, perhaps, represent discarded building material. In addition, the pit contained a rather large number of sherds, animal bones, flint and obsidian implements, fragments of pestles and mortars, bone awls, pierced discs, etc. Pit AD heavily disturbed the lower level 9 and even the topmost part of level 10.

The large pit AG, situated immediately south of pit AD, was circular in shape and had a more or less V-shaped cross-section. This feature was partly hidden in the south and east baulks. It was ca. 1.90 m in diameter, and about 1.20 m deep. Unlike pit AD, pit AG showed a clear stratigraphy (seven deposits could be recognised; fig. 2.3), indicating a gradual accumulation of debris and, in addition, a rather long period of use. The various deposits had a soft consistency and a dark-brown or greenish-grey colour. The lower three deposits showed numerous thin, black and ashy lenses, while the upper three deposits yielded orange-brown mud fragments, probably representing discarded building material. Pit AG contained numerous sherds, lithic artefacts and, in particular, rather large animal bones.

Level 7

Level 7 is the final Balikh IIC level, dated at around 5250/5200 B.C., and was exposed both in the northern half of trench P15 and in a test trench two metres wide along the east section of square P14. In the latter square fragments of a stone wall appeared. Trench P15 gave evidence of parts of two rectangular buildings (fig. 2.4). In addition, level 7 remains were uncovered in very restricted areas in squares P12, Q14 and R14.

Stratigraphy

In trench P15, level 7 was represented by strata 6C to 6A (fig. 2.3). Stratum 6C consisted of the remains of two rectangular buildings (I-II). Stratum 6B, found in and around the stratum 6C structures, represented a ca. 80 cm thick deposition of dark-brown loam, reddish wall debris, ashes and charcoal particles; this debris was clearly affected by fire. Building II contained a series of debris layers sloping south-wards. Finally, stratum 6A covered the lower features and their fill accumulation. Stratum 6A, sloping towards the southeast, was a ca. 40 cm thick layer of soft, greyish-brown soil, mixed with cobbles, ashes and charcoal particles. The stratum 6C building II must still have stood to some extent and was still visible as a shallow depression. This depression contained a concentration of flint and obsidian artefacts.

In the neighbouring square P14, level 7 was represented by strata 11 and 10 (cf. Akkermans 1989b:23-24). Stratum 11 was marked by a stone wall (AB) and a related deposit (cf. fig. 2.4). The stone structure was surrounded by ashy loam, in its turn covered by a lens of grey loam ca. 4 cm thick. Stratum 10 in square P14 was an accumulation of dark loam ca. 35-50 cm thick and mixed with ashes and both burnt and unburnt wall fragments. Two substrata were distinguished, the upper separated from the lower by a 4-8 cm thick layer of greyish loam (probably a floor; ibid.:24).

In square P12, level 7 was represented by stratum 9, the earliest layer thus far reached in this square. Stratum 9 has been exposed in the southern half of the square

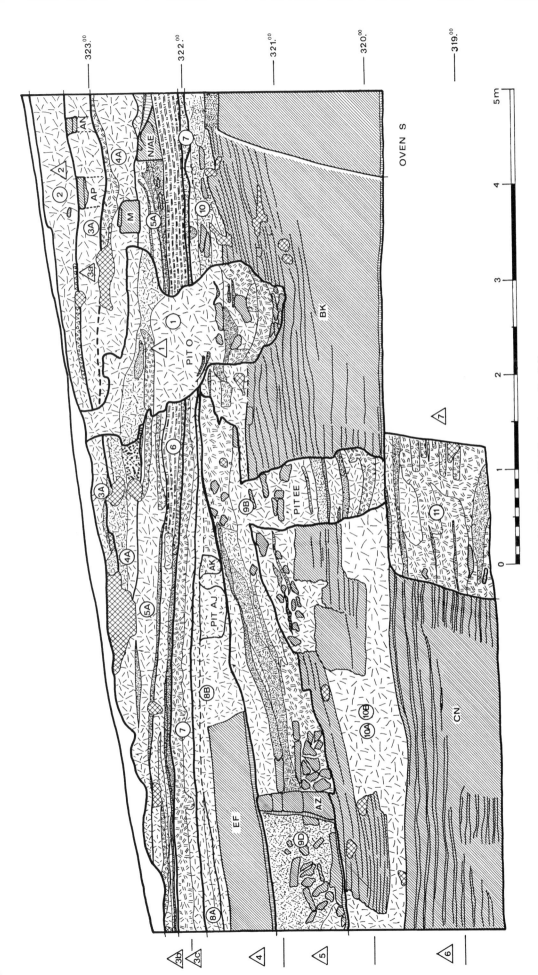

Figure 2.5. West section of square Q14 (legend: see fig. 2.2).

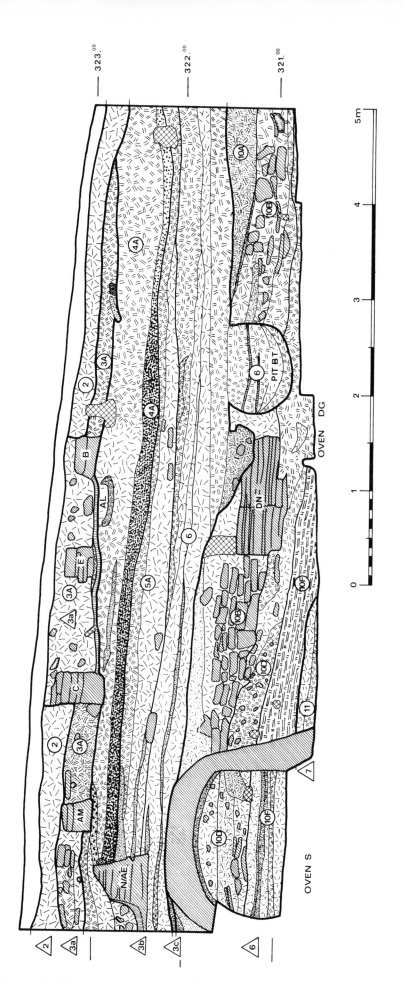

Q14: NORTH SECTION

Figure 2.6. North section of square Q14 (legend: see fig. 2.2).

only (which was excavated somewhat deeper than the northern half), and consisted of a greyish-brown loam deposit, ca. 30 cm thick, intermingled with limespots. Lenses of charcoal and ashes each ca. 2 cm thick were encountered at various places. In the southwestern part of square P12, the upper part of the deposit consisted of dark grey loam, intermingled with charcoal particles.

In square Q14, level 7 was represented by stratum 11 (cf. fig. 2.5), which included the remnants of a deposit of various grey and loamy debris layers ca. 1.10 m thick.

In square R14, level 7 was represented by stratum 5. This deposit was only reached in the north of a narrow trench (1.00 m wide) along the east section. Stratum 5 was a hard and very loamy, greyish deposition, at least 30 cm thick. Two pits (AQ and AR) in the northern part of square R14 have been ascribed to stratum 5.

Architecture and related features

In trench P15, two rectangular buildings were erected next to each other upon the lower, level 8 remains (fig. 2.4). The building I walls (features O, P and Q; figs. 2.3 and 2.4) were preserved to a height of about 80 cm. Wall O was oriented north-south and at least 2.80 m long. Wall P could be traced over a distance of only 35 cm. This wall was oriented east-west and divided building I in at least two rooms. Wall Q, too, could be traced over a distance of about 35 cm only. The various walls were built of pisé, which was laid down in two layers: first a grey loam layer ca. 5-8 cm thick, which was followed by a somewhat lighter-coloured grey layer 2-4 cm thick. Only the bases of walls O, P and Q showed traces of mud plaster ca. 2 cm thick (cf. fig. 2.3). The floor level associated with building I was made of hard-tamped grey-brown clay ca. 4 cm thick.

Wall K of building II was at least 1.35 m long and ca. 40 cm thick. This wall was oriented east-west and was standing perpendicularly to another wall running north-south. The latter was ca. 90 cm long and ca. 40 cm thick, and contained a doorway ca. 50 cm wide. Both walls stood to a height of ca. 60 cm. They were built of pisé comparable to building I. Plaster was not detected on the walls. The floor of building II was very eroded and hardly recognisable.

The stone wall AB found in square P14 perhaps served as a foundation for a clay wall. The NNW-SSE oriented and carefully constructed feature was built of large hewn boulders, up to 40 cm in length. The wall was about 2.20 m long and at least 80 cm thick (the exact width could not be established; part of the wall was hidden in the east baulk). Remarkably, the wall had a step-like construction (Akkermans 1989b:24-25).

In square R14, two possibly oval pits (AQ and AR) have been ascribed to level 7. The pits were found next to each other in the northwest of square R14; parts were hidden in the north section. Both pits were hardly 20 cm deep and measured at least 50 × 75 cm. They were filled with red and black burnt loam, containing some sherds and animal bones. Two wall fragments, each ca. 1.00 m long and about 35 cm wide, appeared to the east and west of the pits. It seems that these features were constructed of dark grey and red pisé layers.

Level 6

Level 6 is the earliest of the so-called Transitional or Balikh IIIA levels, and is dated at ca. 5200/5150 B.C. Two radiocarbon dates are available, both taken from building II. One sample (GrN-19367) stems from the vast quantity of burnt cereals found on the floor in room 14 and has yielded a date of 7075±25 BP, the other (GrN-19368) has been taken from charcoal found on the floor in room 7 and has given a date of 7100±60 BP. Level 6 yielded a series of well-preserved structures which had all been heavily affected by a violent fire: the so-called Burnt Village.[3] So far, eight rectangular and multi-roomed buildings (I-V, X-XII), four circular structures (VI-IX) and a number of ovens have been unearthed (fig. 2.7). Vast quantities of in-situ finds have been recovered from the various burnt structures, including ceramic and stone vessels, ground-stone implements, flint and obsidian tools, human and animal figurines of unbaked clay, labrets, axes, jewellery and hundreds of clay sealings with stamp-seal impressions.[4]

Stratigraphy

So far, level 6 has been exposed in squares P12 to P14, Q12 to Q15, R11 to R14, S12-S13 and trench P15 (figs. 2.2, 2.3, 2.5-2.7, 2.16 and 2.30). Apart from some tholoi and one rectangular structure (building XII), all level 6 buildings were heavily affected by an intense fire which penetrated the walls throughout and which caused a considerable accumulation of orange to brown crumbly loam, wall fragments, dark ashes and charred wood in the buildings (fig. 2.9). The burnt material was restricted to the various buildings; the deposit was virtually absent in the open areas or courtyards between these structures.

In square P12, level 6 was represented by strata 8D-8A. The stratum 8D features consisted of a number of rectangular rooms in the northeast of square P12, which were part of the large building XII. This structure did not seem to have been affected by the fire. Stratum 8C consisted of dark or greyish-brown loamy room fill. The fill found in the upper part of room 7 in building XII contained numerous lime spots, whereas the lower room fill was devoid of these elements. The thickness of the various fill layers was approximately 30 cm (actually, most walls in square P12 were preserved to this height only). Stratum 8C consisted of the construction of a rectangular pit (AS). The subsequent stratum 8B was represented by the characteristic orange-brown, soft and ashy layer which was the result of the fire that had largely destroyed the level 6 settlement. The deposit, ca. 20 cm thick, was only found in small areas in the southeastern and the northeastern part of square P12. Occasionally, stratum 8B material seems to have been present above the eroded remnants of building

---

[3]   The present level 6 discussion is a modified and expanded version of an article published earlier in *American Journal of Archaeology* (Akkermans and Verhoeven 1995).
[4]   A detailed spatial analysis is underway (Verhoeven, in prep.).

XII. Also in the neighbouring square Q12 some building XII wall stubs were covered by the burnt layer. Apparently, building XII was already out of use and decaying at the time of the fire (consequently, the burnt debris material in square P12 must have been deposited secondarily). Finally, the various features and their related debris layers were covered by a homogeneous, orange-brown loam deposit ca. 10-15 cm thick, representing stratum 8A. Three pits (AC, AM and AP) have been attributed to stratum 8A.

In square P13, level 6 was marked by strata 11D-11A. Stratum 11D comprised large portions of the rectangular, multi-roomed buildings II, X and XI and the circular oven DA. Initial accumulation of debris in building X (room 1), building XI (rooms 1-3, 5-7 and 9) and in the open area immediately north of these structures has been designated stratum 11C. The debris in these various areas consisted of greyish-brown, crumbly loam, containing wall fragments, ashes and charcoal particles. The deposits varied between ca. 10 and 20 cm in thickness. Stratum 11B consisted of the distinctive orange-brown, burnt loam and the grey-black ashes which were the result of the violent fire destroying the level 6 settlement. Generally, stratum 11B in square Q13 was about 60 cm thick. Interestingly, rooms 1 and 5 in building XI, room 1 in building X and the oven DA were virtually untouched by the fire (consequently, hardly any traces of stratum 11B material have been found in these areas). Finally, stratum 11A stood for a period of debris accumulation following the fire. This debris was only encountered in the open area to the north of buildings X and XI, where it accumulated up to 40 cm upon the lower stratum 11C layer. Stratum 11A consisted of compact and soft light brown soil. Occasionally, the soil was intermingled with ashes near the burnt areas. Elsewhere, the level 6 wall stubs were immediately covered with level 3 buildings; apparently, stratum 11A was removed here.

In square P14, level 6 was represented by stratum 9. Two walls (W and X) were found, both surrounded by dark ashes and fragments of, possibly, mud bricks (cf. Akkermans 1989b:24-25).

In square Q12, stratum 8D showed the construction of the western portion of building I (this structure was largely situated in the neighbouring square R12), part of building XII, the round oven (AR) and pit (AQ) and the large tholos IX. The subsequent stratum 8C represented the first period of debris accumulation in and around the lower architectural features. It consisted of rather granular brown and grey-brown loam, containing wall fragments (particularly in the southern part of square Q12) and, occasionally, limespots. Stratum 8C materials were not encountered in rooms 10 and 11 of building I; apparently, these areas were kept clean until they were finally ruined by the fire (stratum 8B). Generally, the stratum 8C debris layer was ca. 60 cm thick, except for the large tholos IX where it reached a thickness of ca. 10-20 cm only. Building XII and parts of building I (rooms 12-13) seem to have been already in a ruined state, while the other areas were still in use. The distinctive orange-brown or black, ashy deposit, which resulted from the fire, was designated stratum 8B. The fire only destroyed the features in the southeastern part of square Q12. Like elsewhere, the lower part of the deposit consisted of a ca. 10 cm thick soft, black and ashy layer in which most finds were concentrated. In building I, rooms 10-11, the burnt deposit was situated directly upon the floors. However, the area between building I and tholos IX yielded a thick accumulation of stratum 8C debris instead of burnt stratum 8B material; apparently, the accumulation of debris went along different lines in different areas. In tholos IX, the burnt stratum 8B debris, situated somewhat above the floor, was largely concentrated in the eastern half of the structure. The debris in the western half of the tholos was less homogeneous and partly mixed with later, stratum 8A deposits. Many fragments of the tholos wall were found in the fill. Eventually, the ruined architecture in the eastern part of square Q12 was covered by a red-brown and granular loam accumulation, representing stratum 8A (this deposit was only encountered above rooms 10-11 of building I).

In square Q13, level 6 was represented by strata 7G-7A. The lowest stratum 7G showed the construction of the rectangular, multi-roomed building II and the oven S (which was for the larger part situated in square Q14; cf. figs. 2.5 and 2.6). Oven S remained in use during the entire level 6 period. However, several other ovens (CR, CS and BQ, see below) found around our feature S seem to have replaced each other rather rapidly. Stratum 7F consisted of the loamy debris which accumulated between the floor level associated with the stratum 7G architectural features and the two ovens (CR and CS) ascribed to stratum 7E. This debris included a series of orangey-brown to grey-brown, hard or crumbly loam layers ca. 25 cm thick. Stratum 7E contained the ovens CR and CS and their associated floor. The fill material in and around both ovens was designated stratum 7D. The ovens contained crumbly, orange-brown loam, with ash pockets and charcoal particles. A greyish loam accumulation ca. 20 cm thick was found around the ovens. Stratum 7C comprised the ovens BQ and DA, situated south and north of building II, respectively. Oven BQ was placed upon the lower, stratum 7D ovens CR and CS. Debris which eventually accumulated around building II and the other features represented stratum 7B. This stratum, which was mainly found around oven DA, was characterised by an accumulation of crumbly, brown-grey loam up to 15 cm in thickness. Finally, stratum 7A comprised the characteristic burnt deposit (cf. fig. 2.2). This deposit accumulated to a maximum thickness of ca. 80 cm in square Q13.

In square Q14, level 6 was represented by stratum 10, which has been divided into strata 10G-10A (figs. 2.5 and 2.6). Buildings III-IV and the ovens S and DG have been ascribed to stratum 10G. Interestingly, building IV was founded ca. 1.20 m below building III, due to the fact that the level 6 settlement was built in terraces (cf. fig. 2.5, walls CN and BK). Debris which accumulated during the use of these features was termed stratum 10F. At some places this debris, consisting of grey and red-brown loam, reached a thickness of ca. 60 cm. Stratum 10E was represented by oven CS, part of which was also present in the southwest of square Q13 (stratum 7E, see above). The various features in square Q14 were surrounded by a ca. 20 cm thick layer of grey-brown loam: stratum 10D. In the north of square Q14, a single wall had been constructed upon the stratum 10D debris. This wall DN, largely hidden in the north section, has been ascribed to stratum 10C (cf. fig. 2.6). The debris material which resulted from the fire has been termed stratum 10B. Stratum 10B also included the unburnt debris found in building IV (rooms 1 to 4), the northeastern part of building III and the various ovens in the north of square Q14, which were all spared from the fire (fig. 2.9). As in the other squares, the burnt stratum 10B material consisted of orange-brown loam and grey-black ashes. Occasionally, fragments of charred roofbeams were found. Three wall fragments, each ca. 4.00 m long and ca. 30 cm thick and consisting of reddish-brown, unburnt pisé, were found in the west of square Q14, i.e. above the lower walls of building IV. Most likely, these fragments represented the collapsed upper part of the southern facade of building III, which was located at the margin of the terrace immediately north of building IV. Generally, the stratum 10B material reached a thickness of about 60 cm. Stratum 10A was the topmost level 6 deposit in square Q14 and consisted of crumbly red loam. The stratum had an average thickness of ca. 40 cm.

In square Q15 and trench P15, strata 5D-5A represented level 6 (figs. 2.3 and 2.16). Building IV was erected at the very beginning of the level 6 period; this structure has been ascribed to stratum 5D. The next stratum 5C contained a ca. 50 cm thick accumulation of debris south of building IV. This debris consisted of grey-brown loam intermingled with reddish-brown pisé fragments. Stratum 5C debris was also encountered in room 10 of building IV; here ca. 30 cm of grey-brown loamy layers accumulated. Apparently room 10 had been abandoned, when the other rooms were still in use. In the area south of room 10, pit AC had been sunk into the upper part of the stratum 5C debris (cf. fig. 2.3). Upon this pit and upon stratum 5C debris, another multi-roomed building, V, had been erected, which represented stratum 5B. The characteristic orange-brown or black, ashy burnt debris has been attributed to stratum 5A. This material had accumulated directly upon the floors of all rooms of building V and most rooms of building IV. In the open area or, perhaps, courtyard east of building V, the burnt debris was present along the walls of the building only. In trench P15, on top of the stratum 5A remains, a wall (S) had been raised, which was partly hidden in the north section (cf. fig. 2.3).

In square R11 (of which only the southern half has been excavated), level 6 was represented by stratum 3, consisting of compact and rather homogeneous, brownish-grey loam. No architectural features could be attributed to stratum 3.

In square R12, level 6 was represented by stratum 3, which has been subdivided into strata 3C to 3A. The lowest stratum 3C referred to the construction of the rectilinear, multi-roomed building I with the two circular ovens T and M (building I was also found in the neighbouring square R13). Several layers of grey-brown loam accumulated (in some places up to ca. 30 cm) in and around building I: stratum 3B.

Finally, the debris resulting from the fire was termed stratum 3A. Rooms 5-7, 9 and part of room 8 (see below) were not affected by the fire; these rooms seem to have been filled in with a crumbly grey-brown loam, representing stratum 2 (see below).

In square R13, level 6 was represented by strata 3F to 3A. The lowest stratum 3F comprised the construction of building I and the tholoi VII-VIII. The subsequent strata 3E to 3A could only be distinguished in building I, rooms 1 and 2, and to a limited extent in tholos VIII. Indeed, debris accumulated in the other areas, as well, but here the various strata could not be separated with any certainty. In building I, rooms 1-2, stratum 3E consisted of a 10-20 cm thick deposition of grey-brown loam upon the lower stratum 3F floor. Stratum 3D showed the construction of new floors in building I, rooms 1 and 2, and in the nearby tholos VIII. The southern entrances in building I were now blocked with loam, but the stratum 3F oven T in the north-west corner of room 2 remained in use. A free-standing wall was built immediately east of tholos VIII. Rooms 1 and 2 were finally abandoned during stratum 3C times, as shown by the accumulation of pisé wall fragments and loam upon the lower stratum 3D floors. The child burial (SAB91-B1) found in oven T in room 2 has also been ascribed to stratum 3C. Stratum 3B consisted of the characteristic burnt material (ca. 50 cm thick) which covered stratum 3C. The burnt deposit was restricted to building I, rooms 1-2; the tholoi VII-VIII and the open area or courtyard east of building I showed no traces of the fire. Finally, stratum 3A was a ca. 10-15 cm thick deposit of grey-brown loam, which accumulated in the courtyard after the fire. Two pits (AB and AC) were sunk into the stratum 3A debris.

In square R14, level 6 was represented by stratum 4. It was found in the north of the narrow test trench dug along the east section. Stratum 4, steeply sloping towards the south, consisted of unburnt, greyish-brown loam.

In square S12, level 6 comprised stratum 3, which has been divided into three substrata: 3C to 3A. The northern part of building VI (rooms 5-7) and its associated floor have been ascribed to stratum 3C. The subsequent stratum 3B consisted of a ca. 10-15 cm thick deposit of grey-brown loam, laid upon the floor of building VI and its immediate surroundings. Stratum 3A was represented by the well-known burnt deposit, which accumulated to a thickness of ca. 60 cm in rooms 5 to 7 of building VI.

In square S13, level 6 was represented by strata 3B and 3A. Stratum 3B consisted of rooms 1-4 of building VI. Stratum 3A consisted of the burnt deposit up to 80 cm thick which was found in these rooms.

Architecture and related features

So far, the level 6 or Burnt Village remains, partially standing to a height of 1.40 m, have been excavated over an area of about 800 m² (fig. 2.7). The settlement was built in terraces: part of the mound had been dug away along the slope, and the floors, walls, etc., of the houses low on the slope were founded about two metres below those of the buildings somewhat higher on the mound. Consequently, it

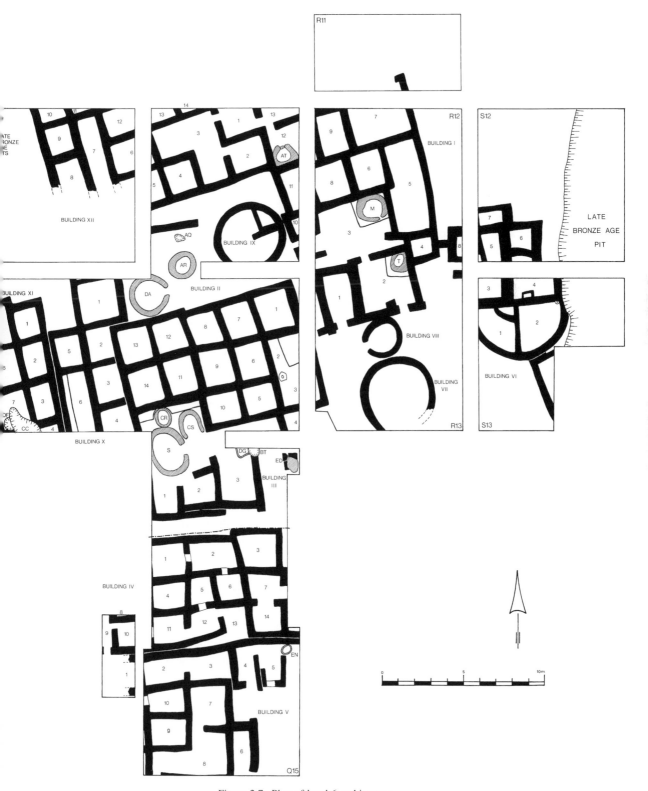

Figure 2.7. Plan of level 6 architecture.

appears that the floors of the upper houses must have been more or less on the same level as the roofs of the lower-situated houses; one could easily walk onto these roofs (cf. figs. 2.14 and 2.15). Actually, we have some evidence that this was indeed the case and that various kinds of activities were carried out on the roof (see below).

So far, the Burnt Village is represented by eight rectangular, multi-roomed structures (buildings I-V, X-XII) and four circular ones (the so-called tholoi; buildings VI-IX). In addition, ten ovens were unearthed in and between the house remains. The dimensions of the rectangular buildings seem to have varied between ca. 90 and 120 m². Generally speaking, the houses of the Burnt Village were originally built along very regular lines and closely attached to each other (cf. fig. 2.13), although all kinds of renovations and reconstructions took place in the course of time. Some houses seem to have had more than one floor (each consisting of hard-tamped loam layers ca. 1-3 cm thick), of which only the upper one has been exposed so far. Basically, the oblong structures seem to have been divided into three rows or wings, each of which consisted of a series of small rooms. Some of these houses had 15 or more rooms, all very small and varying in size between about 3 and 5 m².

The generally 40 cm wide walls of the level 6 buildings were simply founded on earth and were all built of pisé, laid down in layers of various colours and, most likely, various consistency. The order was always the same: a grey, 2 or 3 cm thick loam band followed by an orange-brown, ca. 2-4 cm thick deposit, in its turn covered by a buff layer, about 6-8 cm thick, etc. Apparently, various sources of clay were in use, which each must have had different qualities. Certainly the alternating banding did not have any 'decorative' meaning, for the walls all seem to have been covered with mud plaster. The use of pisé instead of mud bricks for construction purposes is remarkable when considering the fact that mud bricks have a much longer history of use in the Balikh region.[5]

Circulation through the various buildings was of a somewhat peculiar nature. Indeed access to most rooms seems to have been made possible by a series of rather narrow doorways but, interestingly enough, circulation was not always continuous. The best evidence in this respect comes from our well-preserved building IV. Here it appeared that rooms 9 to 13 were linked by doorways in a linear pattern; in addition, this chain of linked rooms gave access to room 5 and, possibly, room 6 (fig. 2.7). However, these southern and central rooms did not give access to the northernmost and eastern series of chambers, i.e. rooms 1 to 4, 7 and 14 (moreover, these rooms were not all linked to each other either). Apparently, one could not simply enter this building IV through a central or main gate and subsequently walk through the entire structure; in order to reach a particular room or wing of rooms one

---

[5]   Mud bricks were the main buiding material at Tell Damishliyya and Tell Assouad, both dated in the late 7th to early 6th millenium B.C.; Akkermans 1986/87, 1988a; Cauvin 1972. At Sabi Abyad, mud bricks seem to have been introduced in the Transitional period, i.e. around 5200/5100 B.C.

Figure 2.8. Porthole between rooms 5 and 12 of building IV, level 6 (view from the south).

had to return and take another main entry. In some instances this even meant that one had to leave the building and had to walk not only around the building itself but also around the closely attached, neighbouring structures, which, indeed, seems a most unpractical and wearying procedure. In this respect, one wonders whether the present passages should be considered of secondary importance and whether the main access to the various rooms was actually organised in a wholly different manner, i.e. from the roof of the building. We do know that the roof of some structures was used for various kinds of activities, but the most convincing evidence in this direction was found in the fact that some rooms did not have a doorway at floor level and, consequently, were not linked to any other room at all; of necessity, these rooms must have been accessible from a higher level only.[6] Moreover, when taking into account that building IV stood immediately next to buildings III and V, it appears that the rooms on the ground floor of building IV must have been very dark; an opening in the roof may have provided not only access but the necessary light and air as well.

[6] Actually, the same holds for some rooms in buildings I-II, V, X-XII. However, in the case of buildings I-II and X-XII, the general absence of doorways may partially be due to the rather poor state of preservation of the various walls.

If in the case of building IV the roof indeed provided the main entry, the various doorways at floor level may have been of lesser importance, perhaps constructed in a somewhat random manner according to need. Many rooms seem to have had doorways of such restricted size (diameter ca. 50 cm) that one had to crawl through them on hands and knees. These 'portholes', earlier reported from sites like Bouqras, Umm Dabaghiyah, Beidha, Abu Hureyra and Ganj Dareh (see e.g. P.A. Akkermans et al. 1983; Smith 1990), were all situated at a somewhat higher level in the wall and had a rounded, almost 'arched' superstructure (cf. fig. 2.8). No traces of wooden jambs have yet been found, which suggests that these doorways were simply hewn out of the already existing walls. Portholes were also attested in building V and were most likely originally present in the other buildings as well.

On the other hand it appeared that building IV originally had at least two main entrances at floor level, both located in the south: one in room 9, the other in room 13. The one in room 13 was blocked when building V was enlarged by the construction of rooms 3 to 5 at a certain point in time. Moreover, some chambers definitely had normal doorways, usually ca. 50 cm wide. The same actually holds for the other structures of the Burnt Village. In two cases (the doorway between rooms 2 and 3 in building II and the entrance to tholos VI) a pivot-stone was present, indicating that this passage was originally closed by a wooden door. Normal doorways at floor level also gave access to building I (rooms 1-2) and were further encountered between, e.g., rooms 12-13 of building I and rooms 1 to 3 of building XII. Apparently, access to the level 6 houses was gained in a variety of ways.

Apart from some tholoi, all level 6 structures were heavily affected by an intense fire which penetrated the walls throughout and which caused a considerable accumulation of orange to brown, crumbly loam, wall fragments, dark ashes and charred wood in the buildings (fig. 2.9). The lowest, ca. 10 cm thick part of these deposits, directly situated on the floors, virtually always consisted of fine and powdery, black ashes; most likely, these ashes were the burnt residue of the roof cover (reed mats). The common occurrence of charred beams and hard-burnt loam fragments with impressions of reeds and circular wooden poles in the various houses reveals that the roofs were all made in the same way: wooden rafters were placed at regular intervals and covered with reed mats, in their turn covered by a thick mud layer (cf. fig. 2.15).

Building I. Building I was oriented NE-SW, at least 12.50 m long and 9.50 m wide. Excavation has so far shown that it consisted of 13 rooms constructed around a large, central room or, perhaps, courtyard (area 3; cf. fig. 2.7). The southernmost series of rooms (1-4 and 10-11) was heavily affected by fire and filled with ashes, but the other rooms had been left undisturbed. These rooms may have been already out of use when the fire started; we do have some, admittedly poor, evidence that the 30-60 cm thick accumulation of grey to brown loam (undoubtedly wall debris) found in these rooms preceded the deposition of ashes and other burnt materials (cf. the

Figure 2.9. The level 6 settlement: the area affected by the fire (dotted).

earlier discussion on the level 6 stratigraphy). On the other hand, it may also be the case that the fire stopped for one reason or another, and that these rooms were simply left to the elements.

Doorways were recognised in the case of rooms 1-2 (marked by small buttresses) and rooms 12-13. No passages were found in the other areas, probably largely due to the rather poor state of wall preservation (some walls stood to a height of only 20 cm). Room 1 was accessible only from the open area or courtyard south of building I, whereas room 2 could be entered both from the south and the north (cf. fig. 2.7).

A rounded, beehive-shaped oven (T), about 75-80 cm in diameter and built of pisé, was found in the northeastern corner of room 2. The interior showed a ca. 6 cm thick mud plaster. The oven wall stood upon a low mud platform, measuring ca. $1.40 \times 1.20 \times 0.20$ m; the hard-burnt interior base of the oven was sunk to a depth of about 35 cm into this platform. A circular pit ca. 55 cm in diameter and sunk to a depth of ca. 10 cm was found immediately southwest of the oven T. The pit showed a mud plaster and was filled with ashes. Probably it served as a container for cleared-out, hot ashes from the oven.

The find of an infant burial (SAB91-B1; see also the contribution by N. Aten, below) in this oven, unfortunately rather poorly preserved, was surprising. The dead child was lying upon a ca. 10 cm thick layer of brown loam; a similar deposit, in its turn followed by burnt debris, was found on top of the skeletal remains. The dead infant was oriented NNE-SSW and was lying on its back, with the head towards the southwest, the legs spread and the right arm in a flexed position. A small bowl seems to have been placed at the feet of the child, perhaps as a burial gift.[7]

Another oven (M), similar to the one in room 2, was uncovered in the court area 3 of building I. This oven was ca. 1.90 m in diameter but preserved to a height of only 10 cm. It had a 20 to 40 cm wide clay wall, lined on the interior with a ca. 8 cm thick mud plaster. An opening or ventilation hole, 25 cm wide, was present in the southeast. The oven stood upon a low mud platform measuring $1.80 \times 1.60 \times 0.20$ m. Intensive domestic use of the area around this oven was demonstrated by the presence of considerable quantities of artefacts of various kinds (ceramics, stone mortars and pestles, bone awls, clay sling missiles), apparently all in situ.

Another oven (AT) was found in the southwestern corner of room 12. This oven was horseshoe-shaped, with a ca. 50 cm wide opening on its northern side. The opening was blocked with a rectangular piece of grey compact loam. The oven wall was constructed of grey pisé and ca. 30 cm thick. The interior wall face was covered with red-burnt mud plaster ca. 5 cm thick, whereas the floor was black-coloured and thoroughly fired.

On the floor in the southeastern corner of room 8, three vessels were found in situ. A large but brittle, red-painted and incised bowl was found lying upside down,

---

[7] It remains doubtful whether this is truly the case: the bowl was found on the oven floor, below the loam layer upon which the dead child had been laid.

covering a jar solidly painted red. Next to these vessels stood a rather coarsely finished pot with a low neck.

The stone construction found in the northern part of room 5 was rather curious
and is as yet unexplained. It consisted of cobbles and gypsum boulders, carefully
placed in line with the surrounding mud walls. The stones seemed to constitute a
kind of platform, ca. 3.50 m^2 large and about 30 cm high.

A series of rooms directly northwest of building I has been termed building XII
(fig. 2.7) but it is not excluded that these rooms were originally part of building I; if
so, building I constituted an extremely large, L-shaped structure. It was noticed that
the southern wall of room 2 of this structure is connected to building I; in addition,
room 1 of building XII and room 13 of building I were connected by a small doorway. On the other hand, it appeared that the rooms of building XII were all of more
or less the same shape and dimensions, whereas the various rooms of building I were
less coherent in this respect. Moreover, household features have been found to be
wholly absent from building XII so far, whereas three ovens were present in building I. At present, we feel that buildings I and XII were separate structures.

Building II and the oven area III. Building II, like building I oriented NE-SW, has
been completely excavated. It was 12.00 m long and 7.75 m wide. The structure consisted of 14 small and square rooms arranged in three rows. The rooms were
virtually identical in size, measuring ca. 1.75 × 1.75 m (cf. figs. 2.7 and 2.14). Its
very regular layout stood in sharp contrast with building I and may suggest that both
features served different purposes. Domestic installations other than a low platform
in room 2 were absent from building II but have been found in area III along the
southern facade. Originally, buildings II and III were considered to represent two
separate structures, with building III subsidiary to building II (cf. Akkermans and
Verhoeven 1995). However, it now appears that both structures form part of the
same, basically L-shaped building (cf. figs. 2.7, 2.14 and 2.15).

The rooms of building II were all very restricted in size and one wonders whether
they were truly used for living. Actually, the finds in these rooms suggest that
storage and related activities were their main fuction. Storage seems to have been
pursued along various lines. The considerable quantities of charred grain found in
building II, particularly in its westernmost rooms (11, 12 and 14; in addition, some
grain was found in room 7) suggests that cereals were stored in bulk. In room 14 the
grain lay almost knee-high and was surrounded and partly covered by a layer of ashy
white fibrous material of vegetable origin. Other products seem to have been stored
in large ceramic vessels, placed in small groups in various rooms, or in containers
made of more perishable material, i.e. baskets and sacks. The abundant presence of
the latter types of containers has been proved by the reverse of the numerous sealings found in building II (and in building V). Particularly baskets seem to have been
used in massive numbers (see chapter 5).

Figure 2.10. In-situ finds upon the floor of room 6 of building II (level 6).

The common occurrence of grinding slabs, mortars and pestles on the floors of some rooms suggests that cereal or food processing took place in building II as well. The low and rectangular feature found in the northeast corner of room 2 may have served as a working-platform. It was built of hard brown loam and measured about 1.60 × 1.25 × 0.20 m. The top surface was slightly concave with rounded edges.

The finds in room 6 were most remarkable. In contrast with the sparse artefactual remains other than ground-stone tools and pottery in most other areas of building II, this room 6 yielded hundreds of small objects of all kinds, e.g. ceramics, stone bowls and axes, bone implements, labrets and clay figurines of both women and animals (cf. fig. 2.10). Most exciting, however, were the more than 150 clay sealings with stamp-seal impressions and the small tokens, which point to a very early but well-developed system of recording and administration (cf. chapter 5). Apparently, this room 6 was not used for common domestic activities or storage in the usual sense but instead served as a kind of 'archive'. Rooms 1 and 7, situated immediately north and northeast of room 6, also gave evidence of small objects such as sealings, tokens, jar stoppers, etc., albeit in much smaller numbers. A similar hoard of sealings and tokens was found in building V, situated somewhat lower on the mound.

Unfortunately, no evidence for doorways has been found in building II apart from the passage between rooms 2 and 3. A small pivot-hole ca. 13 cm in diameter and 7 cm deep was hollowed out in a rounded loam boulder, suggesting that this doorway was once closed by a wooden door. In all other instances the walls (which, admittedly, stood to a limited height only) were uninterrupted, and apparently these rooms were accessible either through a passage situated at a higher and now eroded level in the wall (i.e. portholes) or from the roof of the building.

The area immediately to the south of the main building gave evidence of some rooms and of a series of ovens of various sizes and layout, which had all been constructed within a walled enclosure (area III; cf. figs. 2.7 and 2.15). It remains doubtful whether this area was originally roofed. The oven area III measured ca. 7.00 × 3.50 m and its walls still stood to a height of about 80 cm (the western wall BK, however, was preserved to a height of ca. 1.80 m!; cf. fig. 2.5). It consisted of three rooms, all accessible from the north. Most likely these rooms were related to the nearby ovens and served subsidiary purposes, e.g. the storage of fuel and the preparation of food products. The latter is indicated by the presence of pestles and mortars in rooms 2 and 3. Other domestic activity is illustrated by some bone awls and spindle whorls in these areas.

The ovens, concentrated in the area in front of rooms 1-2, were not conceived and raised at a single point in time but built in at least three stages. Apparently, when an oven went out of use for some reason or other, the feature was levelled and a new installation constructed. The largest oven (S), however, seemed to have been used continuously for a considerable period of time. This impressive, beehive-shaped feature stood to a height of almost 1.50 m, with its vaulted roof still partly intact (cf. fig. 2.6). The oven was oval in shape and had a maximum diameter of 2.90 m. Its wall was ca. 35 cm wide and constructed of layers of orange-brown clay, heavily tempered with straw. The interior was considerably sooted. Cross-sections revealed that the heat had penetrated the wall up to 4 cm, thereby gradually colouring the burnt part from orange-brown into black. The oven was accessible through a tapering opening in the east, ca. 70 cm wide at its base, and contained five floors of hard-tamped, burnt loam, varying in thickness between 2 and 7 cm and all sloping towards the south. The various floors were separated from each other by means of layers of grey and black ashes. Upon the upper floor orange-red and grey-brown loam had accumulated, most likely part of the collapsed superstructure. The lowest floor was laid against a ca. 10 cm wide, protruding strip of clay which ran along the inner facade and, possibly, below the oven wall. Perhaps this strip of clay and the earliest floor were part of an older oven which was incorporated in oven S at a certain time. On the other hand the clay strip may also have served to strengthen the base of oven S.

Two other types of ovens were constructed immediately to the north and the northeast of oven S. A horseshoe-shaped oven or hearthplace (CS) was ca. 1.75 m

Figure 2.11. Child burial below the floor of room 10 of building II (level 6).

long and 1.35 m wide. Its wall was ca. 20 cm thick and made of orange-brown clay. Like oven S, this feature had been used intensively: seven floor levels were recognised, each ca. 1 cm thick and made of hard-burnt clay. When this hearthplace went out of use, a circular *tannur*-like oven (BQ), ca. 75 cm in diameter, was built upon its remains. Another *tannur* (CR), about 100 cm in diameter, stood to the west. Oven CR had a ca. 25 cm thick wall constructed of orange-brown compact loam.

Some other ovens, again of various shapes and sizes, were found elsewhere in front of building III and in the open area to the east of it. A small keyhole-shaped oven (DG), measuring ca. 75 × 35 cm, was present in the north of room 3, built against the eastern wall. It was raised of ca. 3 cm thick coils of hard, orange-brown clay. Part of the oven (and of the associated eastern wall of room 3) was disturbed by a pit (BT) sunk from an upper level of occupation. Another oven or hearth-like construction (ED), more or less square in layout and measuring 1.10 × 1.00 m, was found in the open area to the east of building III. It consisted of a shallow pit, whose edges seem to have been lined with mud bricks. The interior of the pit was paved with fragments of a large ceramic vessel. Most sherds had undergone secondary firing and were covered with fine charcoal and ashes.

Finally, attention is drawn to a well-preserved child inhumation (SAB92-B1; cf. the contribution by Nico Aten, below) found just along the northern wall and below the floor of building II, room 10 (actually, the floor was renewed after interment). The dead child was lying on its right side in a tightly flexed position in a shallow pit ca. 45 cm in diameter and 22 cm deep (cf. fig. 2.11). The body was oriented east-west (atlas to sacrum), with the head facing south. No burial gifts were found.

Building IV. The remains of the east-west oriented building IV, partially standing to a height of 1.40 m, were (with building V) among the best preserved of the Burnt Village (fig. 2.12). Building IV measured at least 11.00 × 7.00 m and consisted of minimally 14 rooms. As in building II, these rooms were arranged in three rows (cf. figs. 2.7 and 2.14). The building was heavily affected by fire except in the northernmost series of rooms 1 to 4. Whereas most rooms were entirely filled with ashes and other burnt building debris, the latter areas gave evidence of loam only. Interestingly, some of the walls in these northernmost rooms leaned over severely to the north and east, probably due to the pressure of the collapsed upper walls and roof covering.

Most rooms seem to have had normal doorways but portholes were found as well (cf. fig. 2.8). Some rooms did not have a passage at floor level at all and were apparently accessible from the roof. In terms of passage, the construction of building V, immediately to the south of building IV, must have had a considerable impact: it blocked the main entrance in room 13 to building IV (and, perhaps, the one in room 9 as well) and so passage must have shifted to another area.

The function of building IV remains somewhat enigmatic. In terms of shape, size and room partitioning, the structure closely resembled the nearby building II which seems to have served largely for storage and food processing. Similar activities may have been pursued in building IV. The absence of ovens, bins or other domestic installations may point in this direction. Other evidence is provided by the finds in the small room 6 in the centre of the building, which yielded eight jar necks standing upside down on the floor and placed along the eastern wall. Most likely, they originally served as potstands. The necks, which mostly still had part of the shoulder of the original vessel for proper placement, were about 10 cm high except for one which had a height of 18 cm, and all were ca. 10 cm in diameter. Two of them were painted, two others incised.

Actually, most finds in building IV stem from the large room 2 (measuring ca. 2.70 × 1.70 m) in the north wing of the structure. Pestles and grinding slabs were found in considerable numbers on the floor in this area, as were some ceramics, clay labrets, pierced discs made of sherds and a flint nucleus. As in building II, the heavy ground-stone tools illustrate the processing of food products or other raw materials and the manufacture of various kinds of artefacts.

Pit AC had been sunk in the open area south of room 10. This pit is ca. 40 cm in diameter and ca. 20 cm deep. It was filled with grey-brown loam, containing charcoal particles. Part of pit AC was disturbed by building V, which was erected upon it (cf. fig. 2.3).

Figure 2.12. The Burnt Village: the well-preserved house remains in squares
Q13 to Q15 (view from the south).

To the west of building IV (in square P14), an east-west oriented wall (W) stood
perpendicularly to another wall (X). The former wall was built of one row of possible mud bricks, the latter of two rows. The bricks of both walls measured about
35/45 × 35 × 8/10 cm. Around the walls a ca. 40 cm thick accumulation of ashes and
mud-brick debris was found. Most likely, these ashes, etc., resulted from dumping
activities and not from a fire on that spot; walls W and X showed no signs of burning (Akkermans 1989b:24-25).

Building V. Building V measured at least 10.50 × 8.00 m and consisted of ten rooms of varying dimensions so far.[8] The structure suffered severely from the fire that swept over the village and all rooms were filled in with ashes and other burnt building debris. The walls were generally preserved to a height of about 1.00 m but stood much lower in the heavily eroded westernmost area 1. Fragments of charred wooden poles ca. 10 cm in diameter and up to 1.50 m long (undoubtedly part of the roof cover) were found in various rooms as were burnt impressions of reeds. Roof remains were most clearly recognised in rooms 2 and 3: these oblong chambers were originally covered by north-south oriented timbers laid at regular intervals and a thick layer of reeds oriented east-west. The reeds were subsequently covered with a thick layer of mud.

Basically, building V seems to have consisted of room 2 and rooms 7 to 10. The other parts (rooms 3 to 6) were added to the main structure at a somewhat later stage. The walls of this added part were not bonded with those of the original structure but abutted them instead. Moreover, some rooms (3 to 5) were raised upon debris which had accumulated in the open area or court in front of both buildings IV and V and blocked the southern doorway of the former structure. The various rooms had either normal doorways (chambers 2-8) or portholes (room 10). Direct access to room 2 was blocked when the neighbouring rooms 3 to 5 were constructed; apparently, access to this room 2 (and to the newly built room 3) now shifted to the roof. Room 9 in the centre of building V yielded no passage at floor level either and must also have been accessible from the roof only.

No domestic installations were found in building V except in room 5. Here a small *tannur*-like oven (EN) appeared, ca. 70 cm long and 50 cm wide. Its wall was about 1-2 cm wide. The oven base was plastered with sherds. The oven was somewhat peculiarly located in what originally may have been a passage from this area 5 to either the courtyard or another room situated further east. In addition to this oven, room 5 contained a large limestone mortar partly sunk into the floor. By means of a lining of stones, this mortar was solidly crammed into the floor. Pestles and grinding slabs were found in considerable quantities, as were large numbers of animal bones on the floor, including the jaws of both bovids and caprines. Grinding equipment was also encountered in other rooms but it was rare or completely absent from rooms 2, 3 and 9, i.e. the areas accessible from the roof only. The presence of some large ceramic vessels in room 3 may indicate that at least some of these closed chambers were used for storage, this in contrast with the easily accessible rooms around the court which mainly seem to have served for the daily preparation of food.

The most noteworthy finds came from rooms 6 and 7. Here, in addition to ceramics and various kinds of stone tools, hundreds of small objects of sun-dried clay were found, including jar stoppers, sling missiles, figurines, tokens and sealings which

---

[8] Undoubtedly, more rooms can be found in the areas further west and south.

usually carried stamp-seal impressions. These finds closely resemble those in room 6 of building II. In room 7 of building V the clay objects were mainly found on or just above the floor but in the case of the nearby room 6 this seems to hold for part of the finds only; many objects appeared in the dark ashes and other room fill high above the floor. In this respect, it may well be that the various objects in room 6 had originally been placed on shelves or the like along the walls and had subsequently fallen down. It may also be the case that the objects fell from a much higher level, i.e. from the roof. The latter definitely seems to hold for a number of pestles and grinding slabs found in the upper part of the room debris, ca. 70 cm above the floor and, most importantly, above some charred timbers which must have been part of the roof construction.

In addition to this possible domestic use, it seems that some sort of ritual activity was practised on the roof of building V. Eleven large and rather curiously-shaped clay objects were found in the fill of the house, sometimes high above the floor and amidst the charred roof beams and the impressions of reed mats; in view of their position, these heavy objects must originally have stood on the roof and fallen down when the building collapsed. Most likely, these objects had ritual implications (a detailed discussion of these items is given in chapter 8). Interestingly, in the fill of room 7 and amidst some of these 'ritual' objects, the skeletal remains were found of two adults (burials SAB92-B3 and B4; cf. the contribution by Nico Aten, below), with the bones completely crushed and burnt. These persons, too, must have fallen down from the roof.

Building X. Building X was a rather narrow, NW-SE oriented structure (cf. fig. 2.13) measuring ca. 10 × 5 m. It was composed of two rows of rectangular rooms (nos. 1-6, cf. fig. 2.7). Unfortunately, the building was preserved to a limited height only (i.e. 30 cm at the most). There can be little doubt that building X was raised at a somewhat later time than its neighbours; it seems to have been constructed in what originally must have been an open area or, perhaps, alley between buildings II and XI. The walls of building X were positioned against the exterior facades of the other structures (fig. 2.13). In the case of rooms 2 and 3, it appears that the interior division walls stood against the outer facade of building II; apparently, the exterior wall of building II served to bound building X as well, thus suggesting a close relationship between both structures.

Room 1 was a relatively large square area, measuring ca. 2.30 × 2.30 m. Room 6 was rectangular in plan and measured ca. 3.50 × 1.50 m.[9] The other rooms all represented small rectangular compartments, each measuring ca. 1.80 × 1.50 m. All rooms except room 1 had been affected by the fire. An unroofed area was present

---

[9] However, it cannot be excluded that originally room 6 was divided into two smaller compartments (cf. rooms 3-4).

Figure 2.13. Level 6 buildings X and XI in square P13.

north of room 5, whereas traces of yet another room seem to be present north of room 1, largely hidden in the section baulk. So far, no evidence of this additional room has been found in the neighbouring square P12 (perhaps due to slope erosion).

A thin layer of burnt grain was found on the floor of room 4. Like in room 14 of building II, the grain had been covered by ashy, white fibrous material of vegetable origin. Small amounts of charred grain were also found on the floor of room 6. A low and narrow bench (ca. 40 cm wide and 20 cm high) had been constructed along the western wall of this room. In none of the other buildings has a similar bench been found.

Building XI. The NW-SE oriented building XI (cf. fig. 2.13) measured at least 9 × 5 m and consisted of at least three rows of rectangular rooms (nos. 1-9; fig. 2.7). The eastern row consisted of four rooms (nos. 1-4) which each measured ca. 2.00 × 1.25 m, whereas the central series of rooms (5-7) each measured about 2.00 × 1.75 m. The central row of rooms protruded slightly to the north when compared with the eastern wing (cf. fig. 2.7). Similar protrusions were found along the north facade of building II (north of room 12), the west facade of building I (west of room 10) and the north facade of building IV (north of room 3). The floors yielded a variety of objects such as ceramics, ground-stone tools and bone implements, apparently all in situ. Rooms 4 and 7 were partly disturbed by a kiln and a pit sunk from level 3.

Building XI seems to have been less heavily affected by the fire than the other level 6 structures. The northern rooms 1 and 5 were not touched at all; their walls were unburnt and they were filled with grey-brown loam instead of the orange-brown burnt material.

Building XII. Building XII was a large, NE-SW oriented structure, very regular in layout and measuring at least 13 × 8 m. The building consisted of at least 14 small rooms (fig. 2.7). The southwestern part of the building had been heavily affected by slope erosion. The building seemed to be closely associated with the neighbouring structure I; actually, it is not excluded that building XII was originally integrated within building I (see above).

Three types of rooms could be distinguished: (a) small square rooms, each measuring ca. 1.50 × 1.50 m (nos. 4, 9 and 12), (b) larger rectangular rooms, each measuring ca. 2.00/2.30 × 1.50/1.75 m (nos. 1-2, 5-6) and (c) a narrow rectangular compartment measuring ca. 4 × 1 m (no. 7). Room 3 is L-shaped but most likely it originally consisted of three separate, rectangular chambers (the walls in this area were very eroded). The eastern rooms 1-3 were connected by small doorways at floor level, each ca. 50 cm wide. No other entrances have been found, most likely due to the rather poor state of preservation of building XII.

Generally, the walls were constructed of pisé but the southern wall of rooms 2-4 seem to have been constructed of large, almost square mud bricks measuring ca. 45 × 40 × 10 cm. Bricks were used in only one other case in the level 6 settlement, i.e. the construction of walls W and X in square P14. Most walls carried a ca. 1 cm thick mud plaster. However, the interior wall faces of room 7 were coated with a ca. 1 cm thick white plaster (most likely calcite; cf. Rehhoff et al. 1990). Floors were made of tamped loam, except in room 8: the slightly sloping floor was built of coarsely made sherds, covered by a layer of white plaster ca. 1 cm thick.

Building XII seems to have been abandoned before the start of the devastating fire (similar to the northern part of building I). The wall stubbs, which stood to a height of maximally 60 cm, were mainly surrounded by grey-brown wall debris instead of the burnt materials (cf. the above discussion on the level 6 stratigraphy). Hardly any in-situ finds have been recovered from building XII.

A series of pits (AC, AM, AP and AS) seems to have been sunk in the open area or courtyard of building XII shortly after its abandonment. Pit AS had a rectangular outline and was ca. 1.25 m long, 0.60 m wide and at least 15 cm deep. The pit was filled with grey loam intermingled with charcoal particles, whereas its base was covered with coarse sherds and some large animal bones. Feature AC represented a rather large pit, partly hidden in the north section of square P12. This pit was oriented east-west. It was at least 5 m long, 1 m wide and 0.30 m deep. Pit AC was filled with soft brown loam, covered by some thin grey lenses, which in turn were followed by light-greyish loam. Pit AM represented a small irregular depression,

Figure 2.14. Axonometric reconstruction of the level 6 settlement.

measuring ca. 1.00 × 0.40 m with a depth of about 15 cm. The pit was filled with burnt loam and charcoal. Finally, the rectangular pit AP measured ca. 1.00 × 0.60 m, with a depth of at least 10 cm. The pit was filled with grey-brown loam and charcoal.

Wall AV in square Q12 was situated immediately south of rooms 2 and 3. This pisé wall stood in a ramshackle state and has been exposed to a limited extent only. It is ca. 4.50 m long and 40 cm thick. It is not excluded that wall AV originally formed part of building XII.

The circular buildings VI-IX. In addition to the rectangular structures, four circular buildings or tholoi were found (fig. 2.7). The largest one was building VI, situated to the east of building I. It had an interior diameter of about 5.75 m and was divided into a series of smaller compartments. Some very small rectangular

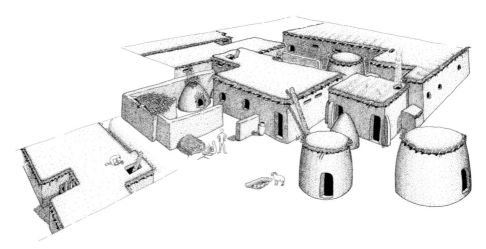

Figure 2.15. Artistic reconstruction of the level 6 village.

rooms (5 to 8) seem to have been added to the circular chamber at a somewhat later date. Another rectangular structure could be found immediately south of the tholos. It had been partly destroyed by a large pit sunk from a late second millennium layer of occupation.

The main entrance to tholos VI was found in the northeast corner of compartment 2. This doorway had a low, clay threshold and contained a stone door-socket, indicating that the passage was originally closed by a wooden door. No other doorways were recognised, perhaps due to the fact that the walls stood to a very limited height only, i.e. about 20 cm.

The presence of some pestles, spindle whorls, loomweights and bone awls in the main compartments 1, 2 and 4 suggests that these areas served for common domestic activities such as food preparation or cloth manufacture. Other evidence pointing in this direction is provided by the small and low, rounded bin made of clay slabs found in the northeast corner of compartment 1, and the ca. 15 cm deep basin found along the wall in area 4. The basin was rectangular in plan and measured about 45 × 30 cm. Its interior facades carried a ca. 1-1.5 cm thick mud plaster covered by a thin white coating. The other rooms (3 to 8) were each very restricted in size and can hardly have served purposes other than storage. The sole exception may have been room 8, added to the tholos at a somewhat later stage. This area appeared to have been built upon the remains of a large but levelled oven; the hard-burnt oven floor, however, was incorporated and re-used in the newly constructed room 8. In this respect, room 8 perhaps should be seen as a modification of the earlier existing oven.

Two other circular structures (VII-VIII) were found in the open area to the southwest of tholos VI. Building VII had an interior diameter of about 4.0 m and stood to a height of ca. 70 cm. Its wall, thickly white-plastered on the exterior facade, curved slightly inwards already at floor level, thus suggesting a domed superstructure. The southeastern part of the tholos was disturbed by later building activities.

Tholos VIII stood immediately to the north of building VII but was much smaller in size: it had an interior diameter of ca. 1.75 m only. The structure was preserved to a height of ca. 80 cm and was accessible through a ca. 50 cm wide doorway in the western facade. This small tholos seems to have been in use for a considerable period of time: at least five superimposed floor levels of tamped loam were found, each separated from the other by a series of thin and compact grey-brown layers of loam. The lower floors all sharply inclined towards the west, i.e. to the entrance of the building; the topmost surface, however, had been levelled. Evidently, the construction of a new floor in the tholos was related to a heightening of the open area or courtyard around the structure. Considerable quantities of domestic debris, ultimately up to about 80 cm in height, must have been deposited deliberately in this court, requiring a continuous modification of the undulating area and the associated structures. Tholos VII gave evidence of only one floor and must have stood in a ramshackle state or even been buried deeply below later debris when the small tholos VIII was still in use.[10]

After the fire, the remains of tholoi VII and VIII were eventually covered by grey-brown loam (stratum 2A in square R13). Two lime-plastered pits (AB and AC) were sunk into this loam deposition. Pit AC, located east of the tholoi, had a rectangular shape and rounded walls. This pit was oriented north-south and was ca. 90 cm long, about 60 cm wide and only ca. 3 cm deep. The circular pit AB, cutting tholos VI in the south, had a diameter of ca. 60 cm and a depth of about 20 cm. It was filled with ashy material.

The fourth tholos (IX) stood in the courtyard between buildings I, II and XII (more or less against the exterior facade of building I; cf. fig. 2.7).[11] The tholos had an interior diameter of ca. 3.50 m and still stood to a height of ca. 50 cm. The entrance was hidden in the section baulk between squares Q12 and Q13. Tholos IX seems to have been divided into two compartments, the smallest measuring ca. 100 × 80 cm. The steeply southwards sloping floor was made of tamped loam, covered by a thin white plaster. The walls of tholos IX were straight; most likely the structure had a flat roof instead of a beehive-shaped superstructure. Fragments of hard-burnt loam with impressions of reeds and circular wooden poles made it clear that this roof was made of wooden rafters covered by reed mats, in their turn covered by a thick mud layer (cf. the rectangular buildings). Actually, it seems that these flat

---

[10] Clearly, the height of the court did not only affect the tholoi. It is recalled that the entrances and floors of rooms 1 and 2 of the neighbouring building I were raised as well.

[11] Earlier, a circular structure immediately north of building II was thought to represent a tholos and termed building IX (Akkermans and Verhoeven 1995). Continued fieldwork, however, has made it clear that this structure is a large, beehive-shaped oven instead of a tholos. This feature has been re-named oven DA.

roofs made of reeds and timber (i.e. highly inflammable materials) accounted for the burning of some of the level 6 tholoi; the unburnt circular structures all seem to have had a beehive-shaped, clay superstructure.

Interestingly, only the eastern half of the tholos was affected by the fire; here the wall was burnt throughout and surrounded by burnt debris. The building yielded a considerable number of in-situ objects, such as grinders and pestles, bone tools, sling missiles, figurines and some tokens.

It is not excluded that tholos IX was raised upon the remains of an earlier circular structure with a more or less similar diameter (the rapid replacement of tholoi was a common practice in the Early Halaf levels of occupation at Sabi Abyad; cf. Akkermans 1989b:59-66). Some evidence was found of poorly preserved wall remains ca. 10 cm high. A circular hearth ca. 40 cm in diameter and ca. 10 cm deep was present, as well as a small square platform made of nine rounded stones (each ca. 6 cm in diameter). South of these features, a shallow, circular pit was found, which was ca. 30 cm in diameter and at least 10 cm deep. Large animal-bone fragments were scattered around this pit.

Two circular ovens were found in the southwestern part of the courtyard (measuring ca. 11.00 × 7.50 m) between buildings I, II and XII (fig. 2.7). Both features were unaffected by the level 6 fire. The beehive-shaped oven DA stood in the southwestern corner of the courtyard (fig. 2.2). It had an interior diameter of ca. 2.00 m and stood to a height of ca. 40 cm. Its wall was ca. 40 cm thick and was constructed of compact grey pisé. The exterior facade was covered by a mud plaster. The interior gave evidence of a twice-renewed, hard-burnt mud plaster, ca. 4-8 cm thick on both floor and wall. The oven was accessible from the east through a narrow, ca. 50 cm wide opening at floor level. The fill consisted of brown-grey and orange-brown loam, intermingled with some charcoal parts and wall-plaster fragments.

Oven AR, standing next to oven DA, had an interior diameter of about 1.00 m and stood to a height of ca. 80 cm. The oven was beehive-shaped and built of compact, grey-brown pisé layers, each ca. 40 cm wide and 8 cm thick. The layers were joined by a granular brown loam. The oven wall stood upon a 4-10 cm thick floor or platform of compact brown loam. The interior oven face carried a 2-4 cm thick, brown mud plaster. An opening has not been found, due to the poor state of preservation. The lower part of the oven was filled with grey loam, mixed with soft charcoal, ashes and some red-brown, burnt loam fragments. The upper fill consisted of soft grey loam, intermingled with collapsed fragments of the oven wall. A low bench abutted oven AR to the east. The bench was ca. 40 cm high, 60 cm long and 30 cm wide, and constructed of grey layers of pisé.

Immediately north of oven AR a small, oval and quite shallow pit was present. This pit AQ measured ca. 40 × 30 × 20 cm, and showed a ca. 5 cm thick, red-burnt mud plaster. It was filled with soft, grey and black ashes. It is suggested that pit AQ served as a container for cleared-out ashes from oven AR.

A NE-SW oriented wall was found ca. 1.25 m north of oven AR. Perhaps this wall served as the boundary of an activity area around ovens AD and AR, and, at the same time, it may have enclosed the courtyard. The entrance to the court may have been the shallow passage between this wall and the opposite building XII.

Level 5

Level 5 is part of the Transitional or Balikh IIIA period, and dates at around 5150 B.C. Level 5 remains were traced over an area of about 280 m^2 in trenches P14, Q14, R14, P15 and Q15. Two rectangular buildings found in squares P12 and Q12 may also belong to level 5, but this can as yet not be decided with certainty. For matters of convenience, these structures are dealt with in the level 4 discussion. The central squares P13 to S13 have yielded no level 5 (and, in addition, hardly any level 4) remains due to the levelling of the mound and the removal of earlier strata of occupation in Halaf times (in these areas level 3 structures were laid immediately upon the lower level 6 remains; cf. fig. 2.2).

Level 5 was mainly represented by the large rectangular, multi-roomed building I in squares Q14, P14, Q15 and trench P15 (fig. 2.17). Parts of another structure (building II) were recovered in square R14 and in the southeast of square Q14.

Stratigraphy

In square P14, level 5 is represented by stratum 8, excavated in 1986 in the southern part of a narrow trench along the east section (Akkermans 1989b:25). Stratum 8 consisted of two walls (Y and Z), which represented the northwestern corner of room 1 of building I. The junction of the walls was marked by buttresses. A small oblong oven or fireplace (AA) was reported immediately west of walls Y and Z.

This building was also found in trench P15, where stratum 4B gave evidence of the southwestern corner of room 1. Like the northwestern corner in square P14, the junction of the walls (which still stood to a height of ca. 1 m) was indicated by two buttresses. The subsequent stratum 4A in trench P15 yielded debris, which accumulated in and around room 1 of building I after its abandonment (cf. fig. 2.3). Room 1 was filled with grey-brown loam and, occasionally plastered, wall fragments. Grey or red-brown loam accumulated to a thickness of about 60-80 cm in the area around room 1. Various thin ashy layers were found on top of this debris.

In square Q15, level 5 is represented by stratum 4, which has been divided into five substrata, i.e. 4E-4A (fig. 2.16). Stratum 4E marks the initial construction of building I. During a short period of use, some debris, representing stratum 4D, accumulated around the building and some floors were replaced by new ones. This deposition had a maximum thickness of ca. 40 cm. Stratum 4C consisted of a comprehensive extension of the stratum 4F building I. A series of new walls was raised, and a number of domestic installations were constructed (ovens O, AT, AZ, BD, hearths

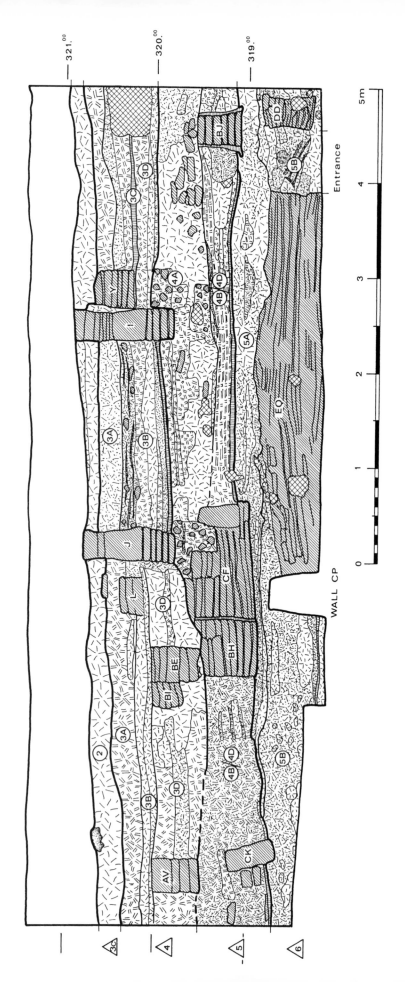

Q15 : SOUTH SECTION

Figure 2.16. South section of square Q15 (legend: see fig. 2.2).

W, BZ and CD, basin BW, pit BE). Subsequently the building went out of use, and again debris accumulated in its rooms: stratum 4B. This stratum 4B debris consists of compact, red-brown loam mixed with grey and red-brown wall remains and a number of ash lenses. At some places stratum 4B reached a thickness of 70 cm. Finally, strata 4E-4B were covered by a 20-60 cm thick layer of grey and red-brown loam, containing some ash lenses and numerous charcoal particles: stratum 4A. The stratum 4A debris stems both from the dumping of refuse and the deterioration of the strata 4F and 4D walls.

In square Q14, level 5 is represented by strata 9E-9A (fig. 2.5). The lowest stratum 9E (equated with stratum 4E in square Q15) contained the northern part of building I and parts of another building (II). Debris related to the stratum 9E features has been termed stratum 9D. This deposition consisted of grey and red-brown loam and ash lenses, intermingled with charcoal particles and limespots, which reached a thickness of 30 cm at the most. Stratum 9C gave evidence of the extension of the stratum 9E architecture (cf. stratum 4C in square Q15): new walls had been added to the already existing structures. After the building went out of use, the various rooms and outdoor areas gradually filled in with debris from collapsing walls and domestic refuse up to ca. 1.00 m in thickness: stratum 9B (= stratum 4B in square Q15). This thick deposition consisted of grey and red-brown loam, with charcoal particles and grey ashes. Finally stratum 9A, a red-brown, crumbly loam deposit, covered the lower strata in square Q14.

Remains of level 5, unfortunately rather eroded and hard to define, were also encountered in square R14. So far, the stratigraphy in this square is only partly understood due to the poor state of preservation of the various features. Provisionally, level 5 is represented by strata 3F to 3A. The lowest stratum 3F comprised various walls, which were all part of building II. The subsequent stratum 3E was exposed only in a narrow trench along the east section of square R14 and represents the accumulation of debris material upon the stratum 3F floor. The deposition consisted of hard, grey loam, probably originating from the collapsed walls. In the northern part of the trench, stratum 3E consisted of hard to granular, orange-red loam, about 30-70 cm thick. Both depositions sloped steeply towards the south. Stratum 3D is represented by the construction of an oven (AN) in room 2 of building II. Stratum 3C, then, consists of debris which accumulated in and around the oven. In the eastern part of square R14, this stratum 3C debris consisted of an up to 60 cm thick layer of hard or crumbly, red-brown and red-black loam. Like stratum 3E, stratum 3C steeply sloped southwards. Various features were sunk into the stratum 3C debris layer: basin AA, hearths T, AH, AI and AM. These features were constructed around the wall stubs of building II (perhaps the stubs acted as wind shields) and represent stratum 3B. Finally, stratum 3A debris surrounded and covered the earlier level 5 features. This debris mainly consisted of orange-red and grey-black loam, which came from the collapsed stratum 3F walls. This very hard material accumulated to a thickness of up to 50 cm in the south of square R14. In the northwestern part of the square some stratigraphy within this rather homogeneous deposition is indicated by a series of southward-sloping, either soft or hard, loamy lenses varying in thickness between 5 and 20 cm.

Architecture and related features

Building I, oriented N-S, measured at least 13.00 × 11.00 m, but large parts of the structure are still hidden from view. Building I consisted of at least 15 rooms, ranging in size from 1.00 × 0.75 m (room 5) to 5.00 × 3.50 m (room 14; fig. 2.17). The walls of the northernmost series of rooms (nos. 1-5) were well-preserved and stood to a height of 1.10 m (cf. fig. 2.5, wall AZ, and fig. 2.18). However, in other areas the walls were preserved to a height of 0.70 m at the most (figs. 2.16 and 2.19). The walls were each ca. 25-50 cm thick and built either of compact grey pisé or grey mud bricks measuring ca. 40 × 35/30 × 8 cm. The bricks were joined by a 1-3 cm thick red-brown mortar. Most walls were bonded, but the northern wall of rooms 7-8 abutted the southern wall of rooms 3 to 5. This may indicate a (slight) chronological distance between the northern series of rooms (1-5) and the other parts of building I. Small buttresses were commonly found, mainly at the junction of walls. Some were found along the interior wall faces, where they served both as wall reinforcements and as room divisions (e.g. in rooms 2, 4-5, 8, 14-15). The interior wall faces of some rooms (i.e. nos. 1-7, 14) carried an orangey-brown mud plaster ca. 0.5-1.5 cm thick, in its turn covered by a white plaster ca. 0.2 cm thick.

The carefully made floors in the northern rooms 1 to 5 consisted of a very compact, orange-brown loam, containing numerous lime spots which gave the floors a glittering appearance. The floors in the other rooms were simply made of a layer of tamped, red-brown loam, covered by two thin grey layers, of which the upper contained numerous lime spots. These floors were ca. 1-1.5 cm thick. Most surfaces appeared to have been renewed several times; in some instances, three superimposed floors were recorded. Most floors (and walls) simply followed the course of the tell slope but in the southern rooms 10-12 and 15 the floors were raised, apparently to produce a plane surface on the sloping tell. The thresholds between the various rooms acted as small steps.

The rooms were connected by doorways ca. 50 cm wide. Various entrances (particularly those in the southern part of building I) were marked by low thresholds, each ca. 8 cm high and made of compact grey loam. The doorway between rooms 1 and 3 was marked by a pivot hole for a wooden door. This ca. 10 cm deep, rounded depression was sunk into a small rectangular platform (BA) of red-brown loam. Feature BA measured ca. 40 × 50 cm and was 10 cm high. A small, so-called porthole enabled the passage between rooms 3 and 4 (see the earlier discussion on level 6 entrances). This feature, situated about 20 cm above floor level, was only ca. 40 cm wide. In section it was square with rounded edges. The sides of the opening

Figure 2.17. Plan of level 5 architecture.

were coated with a ca. 10 cm thick, orange-brown mud plaster, in its turn covered by a very thin white plaster. The northern rooms 1 to 5 (fig. 2.18) seem to have been accessible from the east, via the open area (court) 16 and room 7. However, the port-hole between rooms 3 and 4 hardly allowed regular passage. In this respect, it is not excluded that the northern series of rooms could also be entered from the west, through an entrance to room 1 which is still hidden in the section baulk between square P14 and trench P15 (cf. fig. 2.17). Rooms 7, 11, 12 and possibly 6 could only be reached from the east. The other areas (8-10, 13-15) were probably accessible only from the west (rooms 13 and 14 perhaps from the south).

In the northwestern corner of room 6 the small keyhole-shaped oven AZ was found, measuring ca. 90×45 cm and preserved to a height of about 20 cm. The oven wall, curving inwards towards the top, seems to have been built of coils of red-brown loam, each ca. 4 cm thick and wide. The oven fill consisted of grey ashes.

Hearth BZ was found in the northern part of room 14, in front of the doorway between rooms 10 and 14. The hearth is more or less circular and has a diameter of ca. 70 cm. It was sunk to a depth of about 10 cm. Its wall carried a ca. 10 cm thick red-brown loam coating, heavily affected by fire. The rather curious location of hearth BZ may suggest that it was constructed when rooms 10 and 14 had both lost their original function.

Various household structures such as ovens and hearths were constructed in the courtyards around building I. West of room 1, a small oblong structure (AA) with rounded corners and raised to a height of ca. 30 cm was found. Its length was ca. 75 cm (however, part of the structure was hidden in the south baulk of square P14), while its width was ca. 42 cm. Feature AA was filled with dark ashes, and it had ca. 2 cm thick burnt mud walls; most likely, this feature served as an oven or fireplace (Akkermans 1989b:25).

In courtyard 16, ovens AT, BD and hearth CD were constructed along the eastern facade of room 14 (cf. figs. 2.17 and 2.19). Oven AT was more or less oval, ca. 1.35 m long and 0.65 m wide. It was preserved to a height of 45 cm. The 4 cm thick oven wall, curving inwards towards the top, was built of reddish-brown loam. The oven was filled with dark ashes and loam fragments; in addition, it contained a small amount of burnt grain. Immediately south of oven AT, the small oven BD had been erected. Oven BD was more or less rectangular in outline, and measured ca. 40×50 cm. The 1.5 cm wide wall stood to a height of ca. 45 cm. The oven was filled with ashes. Southeast of oven BD, the triangular hearth CD was sunk to a depth of ca. 20 cm into the floor. The pit had a hard-burnt, ca. 2 cm thick coating of red-brown loam. The pit contained ashes and a rather large amount of burnt grain. Ovens AT and BD seem to have been erected when hearth CD was already out of use.

Another series of domestic features was found in the neighbouring areas 8 and 15. Most likely, these areas were not roofed but instead represented a small courtyard open to the elements. An oval oven (O) was partly incorporated into the wall dividing

Figure 2.18. Level 5: rooms 1-5 of building I.

Figure 2.19. Level 5: rooms 7-16 of building I.

Figure 2.20. Child burial below the floor of room 12 of building I (level 5; view from the south).

areas 8 and 15 (cf. fig. 2.17 and 2.19); apparently, this wall had lost its proper meaning at the time of construction of oven O. The oven measured about 1.35 × 0.75 m, and stood to a height of ca. 30 cm. It had a ca. 2 cm thick wall of red-brown loam. The floor of the oven was covered with small, irregularly-shaped stones with traces of burning. Oven O was filled with ashes and charcoal. Immediately west of oven O, the lime-plastered basin BW was found. This basin had a circular outline and was ca. 65 cm in diameter. It was partly cut by the division wall between areas 8 and 15; apparently, it preceded the construction of this wall.

In area 15, fireplace W was built against two short walls which stood perpendicularly to each other. Fireplace W consisted of a platform, more or less rectangular in shape and measuring ca. 1.20 × 0.80 × 0.20 m. It was built of red-brown mud bricks measuring ca. 25/30 × 15 × 8 cm. Over an area of ca. 0.75 × 0.50 m these bricks were partly covered with an oval, red-burnt layer of clay, ca. 5 cm thick, which seems to have served as the baking plate. Next to this fireplace, a small circular pit (BE) ca. 55 cm in diameter was found. The sides of this pit were red-coloured, due to burning. Most likely, it served as a container for cleared-out, hot ashes from fireplace W.

The oblong and narrow pit EE was the only feature in the court north of building I. Partly hidden in the western section baulk of square Q14 (fig. 2.5), it was at least

Figure 2.21. Pottery found in the level 5 child burial.

4.25 m long and ca. 70 cm wide. It reached a depth of ca. 1.50 m. The pit fill consisted of various depositions of crumbly grey-brown loam and layers of grey ashes and charcoal. Large amounts of domestic refuse were recovered from the feature.

Interestingly, a child inhumation (SAB92-B2; cf. the contribution by Nico Aten, below) was found immediately below the floor of room 12 (and partly below its doorway). The dead child was lying in a shallow, oval pit ca. 1.40 m long, 1.00 m wide and approximately 25 cm deep. The pit was partly lined with mud bricks and a loam band ca. 20 cm wide. The skeletal remains were oriented east-west, with the head placed in the east, facing south (fig. 2.20). The child was positioned on its right side, in a tightly flexed position (both legs and the right arm were flexed; only the left arm was extended). The child was accompanied by various grave goods (cf. fig. 2.21; see also chapter 3, figs. 3.20, no. 2, 3.22, no. 12, 3.25, no. 11). It carried a bracelet on its right arm, consisting of ten cilindrical bone beads, either concave or convex at the short ends, allowing a proper connection of the various beads. Below the skull (crushed due to the pressure of later deposits), eight circular beads were found, all made of rockcrystal. Most likely, these beads were part of a small necklace. Near the right arm a small piece of red ochre, a small cilindrical piece of black pigment (unidentified) and a triangular pottery sherd were found. In addition, a low and wide, painted bowl was situated at the head. Two jars with flaring necks and rounded bases were found near the lower spine. The largest of these vessels was burnished, red-painted and incised. The other jar was painted.

Attention is also drawn to the discovery of 56 transverse flint arrowheads in the southeast of room 14 (cf. chapter 4). The arrowheads were all found together and seem to have been simply left on the floor; they are not related to any feature. In addition, some small lumps of red ochre were found among the projectiles.

Another rectangular building has been found to the northeast of building I. This building II was oriented east-west and consisted of at least four rooms (fig. 2.17). So far, this structure has been excavated to a limited extent only; particularly its southern half awaits excavation. Building II was accessible from a small court in the west. Here a ca. 35 cm wide doorway gave entrance to room 1, which measured at least 4.50 × 2.00 m. The walls bordering room 1 stood to a height of about 1.10 m and were constructed of square mud bricks, each measuring 30 × 30 × 12 cm. The exterior wall facades lacked any traces of plaster, but the interior gave evidence of a ca. 1 cm thick, orangey mud plaster, in its turn coated with white plaster ca. 0.2 cm thick. The floor of the room showed a similar plaster ca. 4-6 cm thick. The next room 2 was accessible from the west through a large, ca. 70 cm wide doorway. The room measured at least 2.50 × 1.20. The interior wall faces carried a 3-7 cm thick orange mud plaster, which was covered with a ca. 0.2 cm thick white plaster. A similar plaster was found at the exterior face of the western wall of room 2.

A large oven (AN) was constructed in the northern half of room 2. The oven blocked the western entrance of the room; consequently, it must have been raised some time after the initial construction of room 2. The oven was horseshoe-shaped and measured ca. 1.40 × 1.20 m. It still stood to a height of about 50 cm. The 20-30 cm thick oven wall was made of compact brown loam and stood against the room walls. The oven wall curved inwards about 30 cm above the floor. In the south a 60 cm wide opening was present. Grey ashes were found in front of this opening (most likely, these ashes represent cleared-out oven debris). The floor of the oven was made of tamped loam, and cracked and black-coloured due to the fire. The interior carried a ca. 1 cm thick, red-burnt plaster. Oven AN was filled with brown loam, including a rather large number of (unburnt) animal bones. Clearly, this fill has nothing to do with the primary use of the oven, but was deposited at a stage when the oven was already out of use.

Rooms 3 and 4 have been exposed to a very limited extent only. The northern facade of these rooms slightly extended northwards when compared with room 2; building II apparently had a 'stepped' northern facade.

Four hearths (T, AH, AI and AM) and a basin (AA) were constructed at a time when building II had already been deserted and debris had accumulated in it to a considerable extent. Hearths AI, AH and AM were situated among the wall remnants of building II. Most likely, the wall stubs protected these hearths against the wind (cf. fig. 2.17). All hearths were oval in shape and quite shallow (maximum depth: ca. 15 cm). They were filled with grey and black ashes, occasionally containing a few small pieces of charcoal. Feature T, situated in the northwestern part of square R14, represented a small oval hearth measuring ca. 60 × 23 cm. Hearth AI had more or less the same dimensions, i.e. 50 × 30 cm. Hearths AM and AH measured ca. 90 × 60 cm and 100 × 40 cm, respectively. Finally, basin AA had a diameter of ca. 60 cm. It was sunk to a depth of ca. 5 cm only. The interior carried a ca. 2 cm thick, red-brown mud plaster, which was covered with a ca. 2 cm thick, white plaster. Basin AA seems to have been repeatedly re-plastered, suggesting intensive use.

Level 4

Level 4 is the final stage of the Balikh IIIA period and is dated at about 5150-5100 B.C. Level 4 is represented by a large tholos with an antechamber, and a small rectangular building containing a large keyhole-shaped kiln (fig. 2.22).[12] Two rectangular, multi-roomed buildings (I-II) found in the northern squares P12 and Q12 (fig. 2.24) belong to either level 4 or level 5; they are included in the present level 4 discussion for matters of convenience.[13] No level 4 or 5 remains were found in the central squares P13, Q13, S13, due to the levelling of the tell in Early Halaf, level 3 times (cf. fig. 2.2).

Stratigraphy

In square Q14, stratum 8 is ascribed to level 4. This stratum is divided in three substrata: 8C to 8A. Stratum 8C is represented by the construction of a small multi-roomed building, the large keyhole-shaped kiln R and the five ovens V, W, AE, AF and AG. Stratum 8B is represented by an accumulation of debris in and around these architectural features. It consisted of a ca. 20 cm thick, rather homogeneous deposit of crumbly grey-brown loam, intermingled with mud-brick fragments and soft grey ashes. Three pits (AA, T and U) in the southwest of square Q14 have been sunk into this debris accumulation. The subsequent stratum 8A consisted of a ca. 10 cm thick layer of crumbly red-brown loam. Two pits (AJ and AK) are ascribed to stratum 8A.

In square P14, level 4 is represented by stratum 7, which is divided into two substrata: 7B and 7A. During the 1986 campaign, three walls (T, U and V) were ascribed to stratum 7B (Akkermans 1989b:25, 28). These walls are part of the small

---

[12] With regard to the earlier published level 4 plans (cf. Akkermans 1993:53 and fig. 3.11; Akkermans and Le Mière 1992:5 and fig. 3) the present plan differs slightly. Added are ovens D, F, G, H, L, M, O and S, hearth AJ and pit X in square R14, oven AG and pits U and T in square Q14, pits W and X in trench P15, and pits AG, AH, AI, BB, BF and BG in square P14. Three pits and some walls northeast of the large tholos in square Q15, earlier ascribed to level 4, have been relocated to other levels: the walls and the one pit in square Q15 have been assigned to level 5, whereas two pits (AI and AH) in square Q14 have been ascribed to level 3B.

[13] Initially, Akkermans (1993:52-56) ascribed these buildings to level 4.

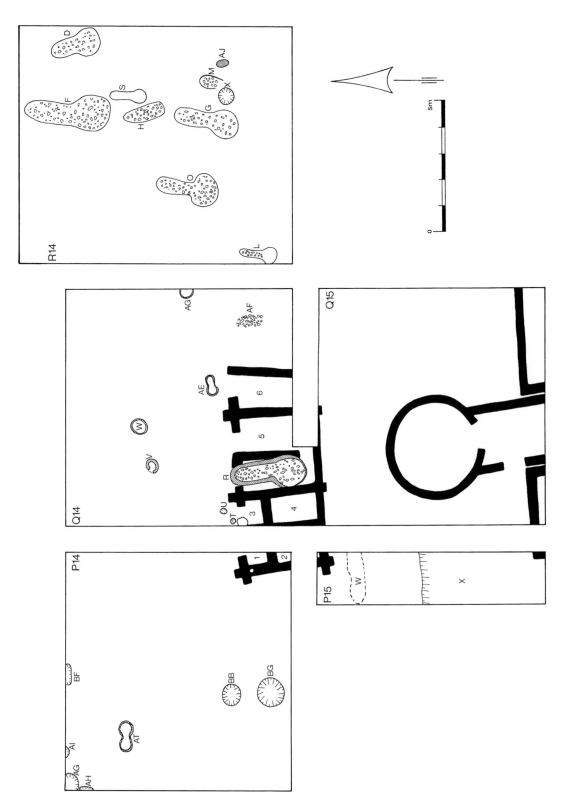

Figure 2.22. Plan of level 4 architecture.

multi-roomed structure which is largely situated in square Q14 (stratum 8C). Subsequent excavations in 1988 yielded other stratum 7B features, including a thin mud surface, wall fragments and an eight-shaped oven (AT). Following Akkermans (1989b:25-28), the debris surrounding the multi-roomed building and the features in square P14 have also been designated stratum 7B. Finally, stratum 7A represents a period of local erosion, following the collapse of the stratum 7B features. This stratum represents a ca. 30 cm thick brown loam deposit. Various pits can be ascribed to stratum 7A: features AG, AH, AI, BB, BF and BG.

In trench P15 and square Q15, level 4 is represented by stratum 3, which has been divided into five substrata: 3E-3A (figs. 2.3 and 2.16). The lowest stratum 3E comprised a tholos with an antechamber (cf. fig. 2.16; walls I and J), and the southern facade of the multi-roomed structure mentioned above (fig. 2.22). In the southeastern part of square Q15, traces of another building were found (cf. fig. 2.16; walls AV, BI and BE). In trench P15, the large pit X has been attributed to stratum 3E. Eventually, stratum 3D debris material accumulated upon the surface surrounding the stratum 3E tholos. In trench P15, stratum 3D consisted of a ca. 10 cm thick layer of grey-brown mud-brick debris and grey ashes. Stratum 3D in square Q15 is represented by a 20-50 cm thick deposit of compact and crumbly grey-brown loam. The subsequent stratum 3C consists of the construction of two annexes flanking the stratum 3E tholos. They were built upon the stratum 3D debris (fig. 2.16, walls Y and L; note that the eastern annex was erected upon the stratum 3E building in the southwestern part of square Q15). In addition, an elongated pit (W) in the north of trench P15 has been attributed to stratum 3C. In stratum 3B times, the tholos and its annexes went out of use. A rather homogeneous deposit (ca. 40-50 cm thick) of hard red-brown loam, containing mud-brick fragments and ash spots, accumulated in the area outside these structures. The interior of the buildings was filled with a number of thin layers of grey and black ashes and grey-brown mud-brick debris. The upper stratum 3A, sloping towards the south, closely resembles stratum 3B. In the north of square Q15, stratum 3A materials covered the architectural remains, while in the south stratum 3A debris accumulated between the walls of the antechamber and the annexes of the tholos. Stratum 3A was a hard red-brown loam deposit intermingled with wall debris and grey ash lenses. The thickness of this deposit varied between ca. 15 cm and 50 cm. The topmost part of stratum 3A consisted of a ca. 10 cm thick layer of dark ashes and burnt grain. In square Q15, five pits (pits G, H, AB, AC and AD) and two small eight-shaped ovens (AF and AG) are ascribed to stratum 3A. In trench P15 no features have been associated with stratum 3A.

In square R14, strata 2D-2A represent level 4. Several walls (which do not seem to be part of a coherent structure) and a kiln (AO) have been attributed to stratum 2D. Debris found around the few stratum 2D walls has been termed stratum 2C. This ca. 40 cm thick deposit mainly consisted of hard, brown or orange-red loam. A series of kilns (D, F, G, L, M, O, and S) represent level 2B. They were sunk into the lower stratum 2C deposit. Furthermore, a pit (X), a hearth (AJ) and the oblong oven H can be assigned to this stratum. Finally, stratum 2A represents the last phase of level 4 debris accumulation in square R14. This stratum consisted of a rather granular, brown to dark-brown loamy deposit which had been laid down in and around the various (stratum 2B) kilns, and upon the stratum 2C deposition and the eroded stratum 2D walls. In the eastern half of square R14, the distinction between strata 2C-2A was unclear and can therefore not be defined precisely. Strata 2C and 2A are absent from the northernmost two metres of square R14: here stratum 1A (ascribed to level 3B) lies directly upon stratum 3A (ascribed to level 5). The average thickness of stratum 2A is ca. 20 cm (occasionally, it is up to 50 cm thick).

In square R13, level 4 is represented by strata 2B and 2A. Stratum 2B is marked by an oblong oven (V) only. Stratum 2A consisted of the fill in this feature, as well as a ca. 10 cm thick accumulation of crumbly red-brown loam, occasionally containing limespots, found around the oven.

Buildings I and II in the northern squares P12 and Q12 may belong to either level 4 or level 5; they have been included in the present level 4 discussion for matters of convenience (cf. Akkermans and Le Mière 1992:5-8; Akkermans 1993:52-56). These buildings comprise stratum 7B in square P12 and strata 7C/7B in square Q12. In addition, an oven (BD), a hearth (BO) and a pit (AJ) have been ascribed to stratum 7C in square Q12. In the Early Halaf period (level 3C) the remains of these features were levelled to enable the construction of a stone wall and a terrace. This levelling of the area presumably accounts for the limited height of the various level 4 or 5 structures. Stratum 7A consisted of the debris which was the result of the collapse of buildings I-II. This debris consisted of a ca. 40 cm thick deposition of grey-red loam, which, moreover, in square P12 contained a large amount of wall fragments (this in contrast with square Q12, where hardly any wall fragments occurred).

Architecture and related features

The main level 4 feature is the large tholos in square Q15 (fig. 2.23). This structure was rather well-preserved, although some parts had been disturbed by pits sunk from later phases of occupation. The tholos walls still stood to a height of ca. 30-70 cm.

The tholos consisted of two rooms, one circular and one rectangular. The circular part had an interior diameter of ca. 3.25 m, whereas the antechamber was ca. 2 m wide and at least 3 m long. The walls were built of red-brown mud bricks of various size. The circular room was built of small, more or less square bricks measuring ca. 25 × 25/30 × 8/10 cm. The walls of the antechamber were raised of rectangular bricks measuring ca. 40/45 × 30/35 × 8/10 cm. The exterior and interior wall faces carried a grey mud plaster ca. 2.5 cm thick. The floors were made of tamped loam ca. 3 cm thick. A doorway in the western wall of the antechamber, which was 80 cm wide, served as the main entrance to the building. The circular room could be entered from the antechamber through a ca. 1 m wide doorway. This entrance had a

Figure 2.23. The large tholos in square Q15, level 4 (view from the south).

low mud-brick threshold. Most likely, the tholos had a flat roof (no traces of walls curving inwards or dome-like constructions were found; (cf. Akkermans 1989b:59-66; see also Akkermans 1993:54-55).

The antechamber was flanked on both sides by rectangular mud-brick buildings, only small parts of which have been excavated so far (fig. 2.22). The walls of these auxiliary structures were very eroded, ca. 32-35 cm wide and preserved to a height of ca. 15 cm only. No traces of wall plaster were found. These annexes seem to have replaced another rectangular mud-brick building near the tholos, parts of which were

found in the southeastern corner of square Q15. This structure measured at least
3.00 × 3.00 m, and stood to a height of ca. 40 cm. It consisted of at least three small
rooms. The walls were raised of grey-brown, square mud bricks measuring ca.
25/30 × 25/30 × 8/10 cm.

The irregularly shaped pit W (largely hidden in the section baulk between trench
P15 and square Q15; figs. 2.3 and 2.22) was sunk into the floor associated with the
annexes. The pit was at least 3.2 m long, ca. 0.5-0.7 m wide and up to 0.7 m deep.
It was filled with grey mud-brick debris, intermingled with ashes, charcoal particles,
some animal bones and sherds. At a time when this pit had already been largely
filled in, another small pit (depth ca. 30 cm), filled with grey-black ashy material,
was sunk into it. In the south of trench P15, a large oblong pit (X) was sunk from the
floor level related to the large tholos. This pit is at least 5 m long, 2 m wide and 1 m
deep. Pit X was filled with mud-brick debris, loose soil of various colours, charcoal
and ashes (cf. fig. 2.3). In the upper pit fill an irregularly shaped and poorly
preserved fireplace was present. Large quantities of sherds and animal bones were
recovered from pit X, as well as numerous flint artefacts and other stone objects.
Most likely, pit X should be regarded as a refuse-pit.

North of the tholos, a small rectangular structure was erected (fig. 2.22). The east-
west oriented building measured ca. 8.20 × 3.80 m and consisted of six rooms. The
walls of the building were rather poorly preserved, i.e. to a height of ca. 30 cm only.
Interestingly, some walls (most noteworthy the southernmost wall of the building)
were made of grey or reddish-brown pisé, whereas others seem to have been built of
red-brown mud bricks measuring ca. 40 × 40 × 6/8 cm. The bricks were joined by a
grey mortar. Apart from the easternmost wall of the building, all walls were marked by
buttresses at their edges. The exterior wall faces seem to have been white-plastered.

The small rooms 1 and 2 measured ca. 1.10 × 0.75 m and 1.60 × 1.25 m, respectively. Room 1 could be entered both from the north and from the west. The western
entrance had a mud-brick threshold carrying a door socket (cf. Akkermans 1989b: 25,
28). The entrance to room 2 has not yet been found; most likely, it was situated in the
baulk between trench P15 and square Q15. Room 3 was very small and measured only
0.80 × 0.70 m. It was accessible through a relatively wide (60 cm) entrance in the north
facade of the building. This doorway was marked by a large limestone boulder. Two
small, circular pits (T and U) were located immediately in front of the entrance. The
rectangular room 4 measured ca. 1.75 × 1.00 m. It yielded no evidence of an entrance
at floor level; the doorway to this room must have been situated at a higher elevation
in the wall or perhaps even on the roof of the building (cf. the level 6 architecture). The
square room 5 measured ca. 2.75 × 2.75 m, and was accessible through a ca. 75 cm
wide door opening in the north facade. A large keyhole-shaped kiln (R) had been constructed in the western half of room 5 (see below). The oven was protected by a wall,
which at the same time may have served for room partitioning. Room 6 was a narrow
room measuring about 2.75 × 1.25 m with an entrance ca. 80 cm wide in the north.

In square R14, level 4 can be divided into an early and a late phase (represented by strata 2D-2C and 2B-2A, respectively). The late phase is mainly represented by ovens and kilns (see the separate section below) and can be equated with the tholos and the other features in squares Q14-Q15. The early phase, however, has no counterparts in the latter areas. The early phase in square R14 (strata 2D-2C) consists of parts of some highly eroded walls in the southwest and east. These walls were ca. 30-40 cm wide and constructed of compact reddish-brown pisé, including grey-black clay bands each ca. 10-50 cm long and 15 cm thick. The walls stood upon a ca. 4 cm thick floor of greyish-brown, tamped mud. So far, these features do not present a coherent structure. In addition to the walls, a circular oven (AO; largely hidden in the western section baulk of square R14) has been ascribed to the early phase. Oven AO was sunk to a depth of 75 cm from the floor level associated with the pisé walls. The oven was bell-shaped in section and was 1.00 m wide at the base. The base was covered by a ca. 5-15 cm thick deposit of soft grey-black ashes, which was followed by a layer of heat-cracked cobbles. In turn these stones were covered with grey-black loam, containing fragments of red-burnt loam. This fill closely resembled the debris found in the various keyhole-shaped kilns of the late phase of level 4 (see below). It is not excluded that oven AO represents the circular part of a keyhole-shaped kiln of which the long-drawn part is still hidden in the section baulk.

In square P14, fragments of a wall and an eight-shaped oven (AT) appeared. Both features are associated with a ca. 1 cm thick, greyish floor of tamped loam, which was only fragmentarily preserved. The wall was oriented east-west and preserved to a height of one brick (ca. 8 cm) only. Oven AT will be discussed below in association with the other ovens and kilns.

Level 4 or 5 features were also unearthed in the northern squares P12-Q12 (see the discussion on level 4 stratigraphy above). In square Q12, the remains were found of a multi-roomed, rectangular building, oriented east-west and measuring ca. 8.00×6.00 m (building II; fig. 2.24). The walls were built of mud bricks each measuring ca. $35/30 \times 25 \times 6$ cm. This structure had been raised in two stages upon the lower, burnt level 6 debris. The earliest stage of construction comprised the rather large room 1 in the southwest of square Q12. The walls defining this room were partly preserved; the southern walls seem to have been removed when the level 3C stone wall was constructed (see below). Room 1 measured ca. 4.50×1.75 m. It carried a hard-tamped, repeatedly renewed mud floor. A doorway ca. 1.00 m wide gave access to the room from the north.

The second building-stage started with the blocking of the main rooms' entrance with mud bricks. Access apparently changed, for the room remained in use. A stone mortar was sunk into the floor, solidly crammed with a lining of animal bones. Around this mortar, some small objects were found in situ, including three broken but restorable ceramic vessels, a pierced disc, two spindle whorls and two bone awls. In addition to the blocking of the passage, seven very small rooms were constructed,

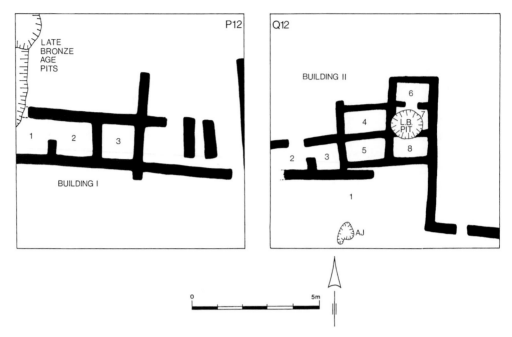

Figure 2.24. Plan of level 5 or 4 architecture in squares P12-Q12.

varying in size between ca. 1.00 × 1.00 m (room 3) and 1.75 × 0.75 m (room 4). The walls were built of small mud bricks, each measuring ca. 30 × 25 × 6 cm, and stood to a height of two bricks only. Plaster was only found on the exterior of the eastern-most wall. The latter wall was bonded to another, east-west oriented mud-brick wall, which had a very small (width: ca. 35 cm only), white-plastered passage. Some of the small rooms were accessible through doorways ca. 50 cm wide, but others lacked any trace of passage at floor level (apparently, these areas were accessible through a higher elevation in the walls or from the roof). However, if mud-brick thresholds were in use (commonly attested at Sabi Abyad), more entrances at floor level may be considered, particularly when taking into account the very restricted height of the walls.

Another rectangular structure was found in the neighbouring square P12. This building I comprised three small rooms (varying in size between ca. 1.25 × 1.25 m and 1.50 × 1.25 m) but originally more rooms must have been present (parts were disturbed by erosion and a large, Late Bronze Age pit (cf. fig. 2.24). The structure was at least 8.50 m long and ca. 2.20 m wide. The walls were ca. 40 cm wide and preserved to a height of ca. 20 cm only, i.e. one or two bricks (however, individual mud bricks could not be distinguished). Traces of white plaster occurred only on the exterior faces of the east-west oriented walls north and south of room 1. Rooms 1-2 had doorways ca. 50 and 75 cm wide, respectively. No entrance at floor level could be discerned in the case of room 3; this area may have been accessible from an higher elevation. East of room 3, two short, north-south oriented mud-brick walls stood next to each other. Both walls were ca. 1.50 m long and 35/45 cm wide. The wall faces showed evidence of white plaster. The function of these walls is as yet unexplained.

Ovens and kilns. Ovens and kilns were found in considerable numbers (fig. 2.22): nine keyhole-shaped kilns (D, F, G, L, M, O, R, S and AE), three rounded ovens or *tannurs* (V, W and AG), three eight-shaped ovens (AF, AG, AT), three oblong ovens (H, V and AF) and one hearthplace (AJ).

The keyhole-shaped kilns each consisted of a narrow but elongated absidal part, which probably served as the combustion chamber, and a more or less circular part, which acted as the heating chamber. All kilns were oriented roughly north-south, except for feature AE which was oriented WWS-NEE. The features varied considerably in size. The circular heating chambers varied in diameter between ca. 1.50 and 0.50 m, whereas the longdrawn combustion chambers varied between 1.75 and 0.75 m in length and between 0.90 and 0.30 m in width. The kilns were all sunk into the ground. The largest specimens were sunk to a depth of ca. 1.00 m at the most, whereas the smaller specimens were sunk to a depth of ca. 0.30-0.45 m. Often, the circular chamber was sunk slightly deeper than the longdrawn part. In some cases, both the heating chamber and the combustion chamber had simple straight walls, but in other instances the combustion chambers widened from top to base, whereas, in contrast, the heating chambers widened from base to top. The kiln interior carried a straw-tempered, red-burnt and black-sooted mud plaster ca. 2.5 cm thick. The heat penetrated the walls to a very limited extent; apparently, the temperatures reached in the kiln were not very high.

The floors of the kilns simply consisted of tamped mud. Blackened and fire-cracked stones (5-20 cm in diameter) were found on the floor in all ovens except feature S. In some kilns (D, F, G, O and R) these stones appeared in both the heating chamber and combustion chamber, but in others they were found only in the latter chamber (L, M). Most kilns had only one layer of stones, but kilns L and O yielded three layers. In all cases, the stones were situated on top of a thin layer of charcoal and ashes on the floor; apparently, they were laid upon the fuel (wood and shrubs) and served to retain the heat. The upper kiln fill usually consisted of fragments of red-burnt loam (possibly the remains of the collapsed superstructure) and ashy, black or grey-brown soil intermingled with limespots and charcoal particles.

Evidence of some sort of superstructure was preserved only in the case of kiln L. This feature seemed to have had a dome-shaped circular chamber, whereas the elongated combustion chamber was arched. The roof seems to have been made of loam coils ca. 2 cm thick. The kiln must have been accessible through an opening in the roof construction (the other parts were sunk below floor level).

All kilns stood in the open air, except kiln R which was built along the wall in the central room of the small rectangular structure in square Q14 (cf. fig. 2.22). Immediately east of the kiln, a 2.60 m long wall made of more or less square (25 × 25 × 6/8 cm) mud bricks was found. This wall probably served to protect the kiln and not to support the roof.

The function of these keyhole-shaped kilns is far from clear. Most likely they were used for the roasting or drying of meat and cereals, placed upon the heated stones (Helbaek 1964:402; Van Loon 1968:269; Hole 1977:88-90; Morris 1979:5ff; Akkermans 1989b:72; see also Molist 1986). It is unlikely that they were used for the manufacture of ceramics, since (a) wasters were not attested in or around these features, (b) only limited temperatures were reached in the kilns, and (c) the shape and construction of the kilns is hardly suited for the production of pottery (cf. Akkermans 1989b:71). The clustering of kilns and other heating facilities, all more or less contemporary, points towards the presence of a specialised, outdoor activity area along the southern slope of Tell Sabi Abyad. Close parallels to the keyhole-shaped kilns of Sabi Abyad have been found in the Halafian levels at Yarim Tepe II (Merpert et al. 1976:47, 1978:40; Munchaev and Merpert 1981:166ff and Fig. 48).

In addition to the keyhole-shaped kilns, some *tannur*-like ovens were found in square Q14 (V, W and AG). These ovens were oval or circular in shape, between ca. 50 and 70 cm in diameter and had ca. 2 cm thick clay walls, burnt along the interior. The ovens were preserved to a height of ca. 20 cm. They were filled with grey ashes, intermingled with charcoal-particles and grey-brown loam. It is generally accepted that these *tannurs* were used for bread baking (cf. Aurenche 1981:251).

Two eight-shaped ovens (AF and AG) were found next to each other in square Q15. Both were north-south oriented and virtually identical in size, i.e. ca. 95/100 cm long and 40/45 cm wide. The (burnt) walls were made of clay coils ca. 2 cm wide. Both ovens were filled with ashy material. Another eight-shaped oven was found in the northwest of square P14.[14] This oven AT was ca. 100 cm long and 50 cm wide, and sunk to a depth of ca. 12 cm. The sides carried a red-burnt mud plaster ca. 5 cm thick. The oven was filled with grey and black ashes, including charcoal particles.

Three oblong ovens (H, V and AF) were found. Oven H was oriented NW-SE and situated between the keyhole-shaped kilns G and S in square R14. Oven H was ca. 1.60 m long and 0.50 m wide, and sunk to a depth of about 40 cm. The sides were covered with a ca. 2 cm thick plaster of red-burnt clay. The oven floor was covered with a layer of burnt stones upon a thin layer of ashes and charcoal; apparently, this feature was used in a similar way as the keyhole-shaped kilns. However, oven H differed from the kilns both in shape and orientation. The next oven V,

---

[14] Earlier, this feature was thought to represent a keyhole-shaped kiln (Akkermans 1993:53 and fig. 3.11; Akkermans and Le Mière 1992:5 and fig. 3) but closer examination revealed that it is an eight-shaped oven.

located in square R13, was a more or less oval feature oriented north-south and measuring about 70 × 45 cm. The oven had a ca. 2 cm thick clay wall with traces of firing.
Traces of another oblong oven (AF) were found about 1.50 m east of the small 'oven
building' in square Q14. This feature was ca. 1.10 m long and 0.50 m wide. Its wall
was made of red-burnt clay and ca. 2 cm thick. The oven was filled with rounded
quartsite pebbles (each ca. 6 cm in diameter); however, these stones showed no
traces of firing and must have been laid in the oven when it was already out of use.

A small oval-shaped hearth (AJ) was found east of kiln M in square R14. The
hearth was ca. 50 cm long and 25 cm wide. It was sunk to a depth of about 10 cm.
It was more or less hemispherical in cross-section, and filled with soft black and
grey ashes.

In the northern square Q12, the circular oven BD, ashpit AJ and hearth BO can
probably be ascribed to level 4. Oven BD was preserved only to a height of 20 cm.
The circular oven was ca. 2.00 m in diameter and built of mud bricks ca. 30 cm
wide. Its floor consisted of a 2-4 cm thick layer of black coloured, hard-burnt loam.
The interior carried a ca. 1 cm thick mud plaster, which was reddish-coloured due to
the firing. Upon the floor, a thin layer of grey-black ashes and some collapsed mud
bricks was followed by a soft, grey ashy fill. The small, irregularly shaped pit AJ
was found next to oven BD. It was ca. 90/70 cm in diameter and ca. 15 cm deep. The
interior was covered with an up to 5 cm thick, orange-red mud plaster. The pit was
filled with soft grey and black ashes, which probably stem from oven BD; most
likely, the pit served as a container for the smouldering ashes taken out of oven BD.

East of oven BD, a hearth (BO) with a diameter of ca. 1.00 m was sunk to a depth
of ca. 30 cm. Its base had a ca. 5 cm thick, red-coloured and hard-burnt mud plaster.
The hearth was filled with soft black and dark-grey ashes. Immediately west of this
hearth, a platform was found (although largely hidden in the section baulk between
squares Q13 and Q12). This platform was 1.40 m long and constructed of four long-
drawn strokes of brown, compact clay, each ca. 10 cm thick.

Pits. In addition to the kilns and ovens, a large number of pits has been ascribed
to level 4. In square Q15, five circular pits (G, H, AB, AC and AD)[15] were sunk
from the topmost level 4 surface (i.e. stratum 3A; the level 4 buildings were already
out of use). Pit G is ca. 1 m in diameter and ca. 30 cm deep. Several small stones and
some sherds were found at its base. Upon these stones and sherds, several thin
layers of very fine, red-brown loam had been laid. Pit G partly disturbed the wall of
the large tholos. The shallow pits H and AB were both filled with soft grey ashes.
Pit H is ca. 1 m in diameter and only 3 cm deep. Pit AB had more or less the same
depth as the former but was ca. 60 cm in diameter. Both pits were filled with ashes;

---

[15] These features in square Q15 are not illustrated on the level 4 plan on which the tholos is depicted;
they were constructed when the level 4 tholos in square Q15 was already largely covered with debris,
and are therefore out of place in this drawing.

perhaps both served as simple (unlined) hearthplaces or firepits. The next feature AC was about 1.10 m in diameter and ca. 12 cm deep. It contained hard, brown loam with pebbles, sherds, animal bones and some flint implements. Finally, pit AD was ca. 75 cm in diameter and only about 3 cm deep. It was filled with brown loam.

In square P14, six pits (AG, AH, AI, BB, BF and BG) were sunk into the court-yard west of the small rectangular building. These pits were all partly hidden in the west or north section baulks (cf. fig. 2.22); consequently, their shape and dimensions cannot be precisely established. Most seem to have had more or less flat bases and straight sides. Pit AG was minimally 60 cm long and 50 cm wide. Its depth was ca. 50 cm. The pit was filled with dark ashes, containing charcoal particles. The base carried stones of various sizes. Pit AH, partly cut by pit AG, was minimally ca. 70 cm wide and 50 cm deep. Its lower part was filled with dark ashes, whereas the upper part (upper 30 cm) contained orange-brown, burnt loam. Pit AI was at least 25 cm wide and 25 cm deep. This feature may have been a basin, for its wall was covered with white plaster (cf. Akkermans 1989b:72). Pit BF was minimally 60 cm wide and 60 cm deep. The pit was filled with burnt orange-brown mud-brick debris and dark ashes. The next pit BG had a diameter of ca. 1.00 m, whereas pit BB was ca. 70 cm in diameter and ca. 18 cm deep. The latter pit was filled with orange-brown mud-brick debris and some sherds, animal bones and flint artefacts.

The three pits in square Q14 all appeared in the southwest corner. Pit AA was at least 75 cm long, 60 cm wide and 15 cm deep. The sides of the pit were straight, while its base was more or less flat. Pit AA was filled with orange-brown loam con-taining some sherds, animal bones, cobbles and charcoal particles. About 2.00 m north of pit AA, two very small pits (T and U) appeared. Both features were filled with soft grey ashes and charcoal. These pits were ca. 15 and 25 cm in diameter respectively, and both were 10 cm deep.

Square Q14 yielded two pits (AJ and AK), both recognised while the west section was being drawn (fig. 2.5). The pits were ca. 60 and 20 cm wide, respectively, and both were 30 cm deep. Both pits showed straight sides and a flat base. They were filled with grey-brown loam.

Finally, pit X in square R14 was ca. 60 cm in diameter and about 15 cm deep. Its fill consisted of grey-brown loam.

Level 3

Level 3 at Sabi Abyad started with the partial levelling of the mound and the removal of earlier strata of occupation to a considerable extent (the central squares Q13, P13, S13 and parts of square R13 yielded no level 5 or 4 features, due to level 3 levelling activities; in these areas level 3 features were found immediately above level 6 occupation remains; cf. fig. 2.2). Settlement contracted more and more to the highest parts of the mound. However, the slopes were not wholly deserted.

Level 3 is part of the Early Halaf or Balikh IIIB period, and is dated at around 5100-5050 B.C. Level 3 has been divided into three closely related sublevels, i.e. 3C to 3A. The earliest level 3C is represented by an impressive stone wall. In level 3B times this wall was incorporated into the large, multi-roomed building I. This building is associated with a series of circular structures (tholoi) and other features. Level 3A starts with the construction of the small rectangular building IV south of the main building I (however, the latter structure remained in use, although parts of it were in a ramshackle state). So far, the generally well-preserved level 3 remains, which occasionally stood to a height of about 1.50 m, have been traced over an extensive area, i.e. around 875 m².

Level 3C

Stratigraphy

Level 3C starts with the construction of a large stone wall in squares P12, P13, Q12 and Q13 (fig. 2.25). This feature has been ascribed to stratum 6 in squares P12, Q12 and Q13, and to stratum 10A in square P13. In square Q13, the stone wall was built immediately upon the level 6 remains. In square P12, the wall partly stood upon level 4 or 5 remnants.

In the northern half of square P13, the stone wall stood upon two foundation layers, both laid upon the lower, level 6 wall stubs in order to create a horizontal base. The lowest layer, representing stratum 10C, consisted of a compact, orange-brown loam deposition up to 40 cm thick. The other, stratum 10B layer consisted of compact grey-brown mud-brick debris ca. 10-12 cm thick.

In square Q14, stratum 7 has been ascribed to level 3. This stratum 7 could be divided into two almost identical deposits, viz. a lower, ca. 10 cm thick deposit of red-brown crumbly soil, which was followed by a hard, grey-brown loam layer, ca. 10 cm thick. Stratum 7 is largely absent from the northeast part of square Q14.

Stratum 2 in square Q15 and trench P15 is closely related to stratum 7 in the neighbouring square Q14. Stratum 2 showed two bonded stone walls (or, perhaps more correctly, foundation walls) immediately below the top soil. So far, no floor has been associated with these stone walls; it is not excluded that they belong to another, now largely eroded level of occupation.

Architecture and related features

Level 3C is represented by impressive architecture: in squares Q13, P13, P12 and Q12 parts of a huge stone wall appeared, which could be traced over a distance of at least 18 m. The wall was oriented more or less east-west. In square P12, the wall seemed to be leaning slightly towards the south, but the most curious feature is the heavily enforced and almost tower-like projection in square Q13 (cf. fig. 2.25). The wall was constructed of several rows (five at the most) of roughly hewn, gypsum boulders, each measuring ca. 35 × 35 cm (these stones probably came from the Pleis-tocene terraces at a distance of 5-10 km east of Sabi Abyad). The width of the wall varied between 0.75 and 1.75 m. It partly stood to a height of 1.20-1.50 m, which is probably its original height (the closely related, level 3B mud-brick building was founded on it). Definitely, this stone wall was not sunk into the tell, as shown by an exterior facade plaster and the presence of the large mud-brick building built against this facade soon after the construction of the wall. The southern, exterior facade was carefully finished: the stones had been hewn regularly to create a smooth, more or less straight surface and subsequently a ca. two cm thick layer of mud plaster was applied, in its turn covered by a thin (ca. 2-3 mm) white coating. In contrast, the interior was roughly executed, with the wall becoming increasingly narrow towards the top, and completely filled with loose and rather clean, reddish-brown soil.

Akkermans (1993:57) suggested that this wall served as a kind of retaining wall supporting a terrace on the top and along the northern slope of the southeastern mound. The north-south oriented parts then may have served as 'grips', clamping the support wall into the terrace and strengthening it to withstand the terrace's lateral thrust. If a terrace was indeed present in the northern squares, it must have been one of exceptional size, and enormous amounts of earth must have been brought in for its construction. This fill must have been largely extracted from level 6 deposits in view of the ceramics found in it.

Stone constructions were also unearthed in the southern squares Q15-P15, although these features seem to represent foundations instead of retaining walls (traces of mud brick were found on the top of the stones). Two walls, each built of one row of roughly hewn gypsum stones (each measuring ca. 45 × 25 × 15 cm) stood perpendicularly to each other (cf. fig. 2.25). The walls seemed to bound an area of at least 6.75 by 2.00 m, which was disturbed by erosion and a Late Bronze Age pit. The walls were surrounded by a crumbly, grey-brown loam layer ca. 20 cm thick containing limespots. A small circular, bell-shaped pit[16] (D) had been sunk into this deposit. The pit was ca. 20 cm deep and about 40 cm in diameter at its base. It carried a white plaster ca. 2 cm thick along its interior. Pit D was filled with grey-brown loam containing animal bones, some sherds and a few flint artefacts. In addition to the pit, parts of a small, more or less rectangular (minimal size 80 × 80 cm) pavement (EW) made of stones and sherds appeared in the northwest of square Q15, while traces of a circular (diameter ca. 50 cm), very shallow fireplace, rich in ashes, were found along the east section of trench P15. Finally, in the northwestern corner of trench P15, a ca. 60 cm long, oblong and shallow (about 30 cm deep) pit appeared. This pit (AB) was filled with soft grey ashes (cf. fig. 2.3).

In square Q14, four very small circular and shallow pits had been sunk into the stratum 7 deposit. These pits were all ca. 10 cm in diameter and ca. 6 cm deep. All

---

[16] Bell-shaped pits at Sabi Abyad and their possible use have been discussed in detail elsewhere (Akkermans 1989b:73).

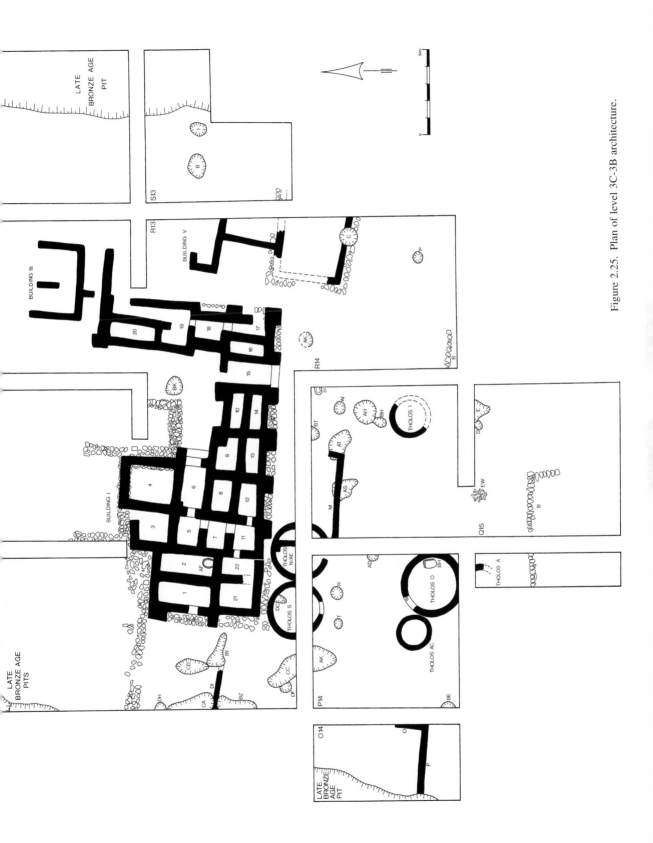

Figure 2.25. Plan of level 3C-3B architecture.

carried a white plaster ca. 1 cm thick. Three of these pits were situated in a linear sequence at short intervals in the southwest of square Q14. All were sunk in an open area not related to any architectural features. The function of these pits remains unknown.

Level 3B

Stratigraphy

During the 1986 season of excavation, level 3B remains were encountered in squares O14 (stratum 3), P13 (stratum 6) and P14 (strata 6 to 4). These strata have been extensively dealt with in an earlier report (Akkermans 1989b:28-36, 38, 54) and will be only shortly commented upon here. Subsequent excavations in 1988 and 1991 have revealed level 3B features in trench P15 (stratum 1), squares Q12 (stratum 5B), Q13 (strata 5G-5C), Q14 (strata 6, 5C to 4A), Q15 (stratum 1), R12 (strata 1C-1B), R13 (strata 1C-1B), S13 (stratum 2C), R14 (stratum 1B) and, possibly, S12 (stratum 2) and R11 (stratum 2). Finally, the 1993 campaign has yielded another series of level 3B strata in square P13, viz. strata 9B to 6A.

In square O14, stratum 3 was characterised by two mud-brick walls (O and P) standing perpendicular to each other (Akkermans 1989b:54).

In square P13, strata 9B-6A could be ascribed to level 3B. The lower stratum 9B consisted of a floor and associated architectural features. The principal features were rooms 1-2, 21-22 of building I (fig. 2.25), with mud-brick walls built on stone foundations. In addition, a single mud-brick wall (DI) and a pit (DF) were ascribed to stratum 9B. The subsequent stratum 9A consisted of debris accumulated between the stratum 9B features to a height of ca. 20 cm. The debris consisted of compact grey-brown loam laid down in thin layers (each ca. 6 cm thick) within an assumedly rather short period of time. In addition, the fill of pit DF has been ascribed to stratum 9A. Stratum 9A was followed by stratum 8B, which started with the construction of tholos S. Slightly afterwards, tholos N/AE was built. Debris found in and around the tholoi has been designated stratum 8A. Both tholoi were filled with soft grey-brown loam intermingled with mud-brick fragments and charcoal particles. Stratum 7E represents a new period of activities, following the stratum 8A debris accumulation. Five pits (BY, BZ, CA, CC and DC) can be attributed to stratum 7E. The underlying strata 11-8 were heavily disturbed by these pits (cf. fig. 2.30). The fill in these pits represents stratum 7D. Pit DH, which partly cut the stratum 7E pit CA in the north (fig. 2.30), has been ascribed to stratum 7C. The fill of this pit DH represents stratum 7B. The next stratum 7A deposit, ca. 20-60 cm thick, covered the various stratum 7E-7B features as well as the remaining parts of tholoi N/AE and S of stratum 8B. Stratum 7A was a rather compact grey-brown and loamy deposit with charcoal particles. In the western part of square P13, the upper part of the stratum 7A deposit contained a ca. 15 cm thick layer of charred grain. A similar deposit was found further south, above tholos S.

During the 1986 campaign, stratum 6 in square P13 was only partially uncovered. No architectural features could then be ascribed to the stratum; only a rather soft brown loam was reported (Akkermans 1989b:38). However, continued excavations in square P13 in 1993 have made it clear that stratum 6 can be divided into three substrata, i.e. 6C, 6B and 6A. The lower stratum 6C consisted of four pits (CB, CD, DD, DE; no clear floor level could be distinguished). The fill of the various 6C pits has been attributed to stratum 6B. Stratum 6A represented a period of debris accumulation covering the lower stages of occupation. In the north of square P13, stratum 6A was characterised by soft brown loam, slightly sloping towards the south, where it was built of two or three layers of crumbly, reddish-brown soil. Stratum 6A had an average thickness of ca. 40 cm.

In square P14, stratum 6 (excavated in 1986; Akkermans 1989:28-35) was divided into four substrata, viz. 6D to 6A, each of which gave evidence of tholoi (O, AC, S, N/AE, P/K). In addition, six pits have been ascribed to stratum 6 (pit AK to stratum 6D; pits AD, R and T to stratum 6C; pit BE to stratum 6B). Pit AY could not be ascribed to a particular stratum, since its associated floor has disappeared due to slope erosion. Most likely, however, this pit should be related to stratum 6B or 6A.

In trench P15, stratum 1 was characterised by fragments of a tholos floor.

In square Q12, stratum 5B has been ascribed to level 3B. It comprised the construction of the northernmost wall of room 4 of building I. Another mud-brick wall was found while preparing the north section for drawing. Stratum 5A was represented by an accumulation of debris following the use of the level 3B features in square Q12 and will be dealt with in the level 3A discussion (see below).

Stratum 5G in square Q13 and stratum 1C in squares R12-R13 consisted of a rather hard, greenish-grey foundation layer ca. 10 cm thick, which was found below the floor of building I, rooms 3-4, 8, 16-18. The subsequent stratum 5F in square Q13 represented the construction of building I. Strata 5E/5D represented the construction of two succeeding tholoi (N/AE; cf. fig. 2.2), traces of which also appeared in squares Q14, P14 and P13 (strata 5C/5B, 6C/6B and 8B, respectively). Stratum 5C was marked by debris accumulation outside building I and the tholoi. The character of this debris suggests that debris accumulation went along different lines in different areas: in the northeast, the debris consisted of foliated, grey-red loam up to 40 cm in thickness, whereas further south it consisted of hard, red-brown loam including a ca. 15 cm thick layer of burnt grain (also found in square Q14, stratum 4A).

In square Q14, level 3B was represented by strata 6-4A. Stratum 6 consisted of a loam deposit ca. 30 cm thick, containing some pits (AH, AI, AS, AT, BH, BJ, BT) and a basin (BI). The stratum 6 surface gradually sloped towards the southeast but was absent in the south due to slope erosion. In the western part of square Q14, stratum 6 consisted of various thin layers (each ca. 5 cm thick), most of which can be characterised as grey or red-brown, crumbly loam deposits, but in the eastern half of square Q14 stratum 6 was of a more homogeneous nature and was built of compact, grey-brown loam. The subsequent stratum 5A in square Q14 appeared as a succession of thin debris layers in the western part of the square but as a homogeneous grey-brown loam deposit ca. 30 cm thick in the east. The loamy, grey-brown and rather hard layers in the west, each ca. 5 cm thick, were in most cases intermingled with soft grey ashes. Two small, circular pits (AB and AC) have been attributed to stratum 5A. Stratum 4B in square Q14 was represented by a mud-brick wall (M) and a small tholos (I). The subsequent stratum 4A debris accumulation north of wall M (stratum 4A has only been found in the northern half of square Q14 due to slope erosion) started with the deposition of a ca. 15 cm thick layer of burnt grain (cf. fig. 2.6), followed by a homogeneous, loamy layer varying in thickness between 15 and 50 cm. Further west, stratum 4A gave evidence of an accumulation of thin reddish-brown layers, up to ca. 40 cm in thickness. These loamy layers were intermingled with charred grain and charcoal particles. Interestingly, the stratum 4A debris yielded a rather large amount of overfired sherds or wasters, particularly in the northeastern quadrant of square Q14; perhaps a pottery kiln can be found nearby. Finally, at a time when stratum 4A had reached a thickness of about 20 cm and covered wall M and tholos I, a round pit (J) was sunk into it. In addition, two ovens (K and AL) were constructed.

In square Q15, level 3B was represented by the large stratum 1 pit E.

In squares R12, R13 and R14, level 3B was represented by stratum 1B, which marked the construction of the three rectangular buildings I, III and V (fig. 2.25). In square R14, three pits (P, AK and AP) were sunk into the floor related to building V. The next stratum 1A in these squares showed the accumulation of fill in and around the buildings (see the stratum 3A discussion below).

In square S13, stratum 2C yielded some fragments of a stone foundation wall associated with building V, and two pits (B and I) filled with unbaked-clay sling missiles. Strata 2B-2A followed the stratum 2C features and will be presented in the level 3A discussion below (cf. stratum 1A in squares R12, R13 and R14).

In square S12, stratum 2, consisting of various layers of loam and found imme-diately below the topsoil, cannot yet be attributed to a particular level. This deposit partly covered the stratum 3A features (i.e. the burnt level 6 debris) and may there-fore represent terminal level 6 material *or* level 5, 4 or 3 fill (levels 2 and 1 can be safely excluded because these are only present at the top of the mound). At present, stratum 2 is arbitrarily included in the level 3B discussion. Stratum 2 material was only present in the northern half of square S12, heavily disturbed by a very large, Late Bronze Age pit (K). It consisted of three loamy layers, together up to 45 cm in thickness. The lowest of these layers, perhaps representing a floor, was grey-brown in colour and only ca. 10 cm thick. The others were reddish-brown loam depositions with a fine texture, and ca. 15 and 25 cm thick, respectively.

In square R11, stratum 2 cannot be assigned to a specific level with any certainty (it appeared between the level 6 stratum 3 on the one hand and the Late Bronze Age strata 1C-1A on the other hand). Most likely, however, stratum 2 is associated with level 3B. Stratum 2 represented a rather granular, brown-grey loam layer, varying in thickness between 25 and 60 cm. In the west, a soft, black-brown and ashy layer ca. 10 cm thick and intermingled with small pebbles was found on top of the loam. In addition, a pit (B) has been ascribed to stratum 2.

Architecture and related features

In level 3B times, the stone terrace wall was incorporated into the large, rectilinear and multi-roomed building I. Some parts of this building I were constructed on top of the stone wall, whereas other parts were built against it; apparently, the wall was now largely hidden from view (cf. figs. 2.25 and 2.27). Building I was raised immediately upon level 6 remains.

Building I was oriented NWW-SEE. The extensive structure consisted of a large western wing measuring ca. 15.90 × 9.50 m, which was separated by a small court measuring ca. 6.00 × 2.00 m from an elongated eastern wing measuring 16.50 × 3.20 m (figs. 2.25 and 2.27).[17] The building comprised 22 small rooms, varying in size between about 2.60 m^2 (room 14) and 5 m^2 (room 4). The westernmost rooms 1-2, 21-22 may have been added to the building at a slightly later stage, because of (a) the north-south orientation of these rooms, whereas all other rooms were oriented east-west, (b) the shifted east-west walls, leaping northwards with regard to the building's main axis, (c) the separate entrance to room 1, and, finally, (d) the *tannur* in room 2, not found in any of the other rooms.

The area west of rooms 1 and 2 seems to have been a courtyard. Here traces of a NWW-SEE wall (DI, fig. 2.30) were found, which was constructed of mud bricks ca. 30 cm wide and 10 cm thick. This feature was preserved to a height of ca. 40 cm but cannot be related to any structure.

---

[17] In previous publications this building was divided into buildings I and II (Akkermans 1993:57-63; Akkermans and Le Mière 1992; Akkermans in Weiss 1991; Akkermans 1993/94a), but recently it appeared that this structure represents one building: the former level 3 buildings I and II are now termed building I (the term building II has been deleted). Note that also the room numbers of the former building II (now the eastern wing of building I), have been altered; the level 3C/3B building I consists of 22 rooms. Rooms 21 and 22 have been reconstructed on the basis of a stone consolidation wall which has recently been excavated (1993).

With regard to the earlier publications (see above), a number of features have been added to the level 3C/3B plan, in the first instance a stone consolidation wall built against the western, southern and part of the eastern exterior facades of building I. Also added were feature BK in square Q13; features M, AH, AI, AS, AT, BH, BI and BT in square Q14; features BY, BZ, CA, CC, CD, DC, DF, DH in square P13; features R, T, AD, AK, BE and BH in square P14; and features B, D and E and EW in trench P15 and square Q15. Furthermore, the most eastern structure of level 3, which was previously not designated by a number, has now been termed building V. The course of the southern walls of this building, as indicated in the above-mentioned publications, proved incorrect; their proper course can be seen on the present level plan (fig. 2.25).

Figure 2.26. Level 3 building I with part of stone wall (view from the west).

The walls of building I still stood to a considerable height, i.e. between 0.50 and 1.20 m. However, the upper part of some walls was heavily disturbed by the large pit BG sunk from level 2 in square Q13 (cf. fig. 2.2). The walls, each about 50-60 cm thick, were built of pisé, which consisted of two alternating bands of orange-brown and grey-bown loam each ca. 6 cm thick. Remarkably, the walls bounding the two westernmost rooms 1-2 (excavated in 1986; Akkermans 1989b:38-44) consisted of longitudinal rows of mud bricks supplemented by half-sized bricks. Commonly, large and more or less square mud bricks measuring ca. 35/40 × 35 × 10 cm were used as well.

Most walls seem to have been founded simply on the tell surface. Some sort of foundation layer consisting of compact brown loam up to 20 cm in thickness was found only below the northern parts of rooms 1-2. In addition, the walls of the latter rooms, and those of rooms 21-22, were founded on one row of gypsum boulders. Traces of some sort of foundation were also found immediately below the wall dividing rooms 1 and 21. Here fragmentarily preserved, whitish impressions of plaiting were observed over an area of ca. 1.10 × 0.20 m. This plaiting was made of strands each about 1.5 cm wide, which showed a lengthwise, fibrous structure. Perhaps these impressions are the remnants of mats laid below the walls for enforcement.

The buildings' exterior facade was supported by a series of large buttresses each measuring ca. 1.10 × 0.60 m at wall junctions (figs. 2.25 and 2.26). The buttresses actually stood upon a stone foundation which ran along the proper (mud-brick or pisé) facade of the building (cf. fig. 2.2, buttress AL). This foundation wall was built of irregularly hewn gypsum boulders (each measuring ca. 35 × 15 cm), laid down in two rows and one course high. The stones were joined by a loamy mortar and were covered by a mud layer or, perhaps, mud bricks up to 10 cm in thickness. The stones carried a mud plaster ca. 2-3 cm thick, in its turn covered by a thin white coating; apparently, this stone foundation wall was not sunk. A similar plaster was found on both the exterior and interior wall faces of building I.[18] The foundation wall and its buttresses were built along those parts of building I that were vulnerable to slope erosion; they served to consolidate and protect building I. At the same time, they gave the building a monumental, niched appearance. Rooms 21-22 have been reconstructed on the basis of the course of the foundation wall in the south of square P13 (fig. 2.25).

Access to building I was gained in a variety of ways. The main entrance to building I was situated at the end of the small courtyard in the northeast of square Q13. This court could be reached from the south through a passage ca. 1.30 m wide (area 15) between the western and eastern wings. The courtyard was also accessible through a narrow passage from the terrace in the north. The main doorway, ca. 1 m wide, gave a somewhat monumental appearance in that it had a low, thickly white-plastered staircase with two steps. The level 3C stone wall still carried its white coating upon a mud plaster, whereas the opposite clay wall contained a thick and at least twice-renewed white plaster identical to that of the staircase. In addition, the latter wall showed evidence of a large niche, at a later stage (level 3A) divided into two smaller, plastered niches with a shallow basin in front.

So far, it seems that the eastern wing of building I could be entered from the east only, through two doorways situated at the far ends of the building. In the southeast the entrance, ca. 80 cm wide, was marked by two large buttresses. The other, much wider entrance (1.20 m) in the northeast had no buttresses.

Interestingly, some rooms seem to have had separate entrances. Room 1, for example, was accessible only through a ca. 60 cm wide doorway in the western facade of building I. A low, white-plastered bench built of two rows of mud bricks on a stone foundation was found in front of this entrance (actually, this bench resulted from the construction of the stone foundation encircling building I for the larger part). Whether subsequent rooms could be reached from here is doubtful in view of the lack of further doorways. Room 3 in the north of building I seems to have had a separate entrance as well. This room was accessible from the large

---

[18] The white exterior plaster often found upon walls at Sabi Abyad was made of calcite. Plaster in pits or shallow basins was made of pure gypsum or of a combination of gypsum and calcite (Rehhoff et al. 1990).

terrace through a ca. 65 cm wide doorway carrying a door pivot-stone. In view of the considerable height differences between the floor level in room 3 and the neighbouring terrace (ca. 1.15 m), it seems that some kind of ladder must have been used to enter the room.

Circulation through the building itself was enhanced by means of narrow, ca. 40 cm wide doorways, all provided with low, mud-plastered thresholds. The doorway between rooms 11 and 12 was eventually blocked by mud bricks. In some rooms no passages at floor level were found; probably these rooms were accessible from a somewhat higher elevation or even from an upper storey. Akkermans (1993:61) has already made it clear that the main building may have had two storeys (cf. fig. 2.28), because of (1) the considerable thickness of the walls (ca. 50-60 cm), strong enough to support an upper storey (the other structures all lack such thick walls), (2) the presence of stone foundations and large buttresses along the exterior facade, able to withstand the lateral thrust of the building on the sloping tell surface, (3) the absence of doorways at floor level in several rooms, suggesting that these were accessible from above only, (4) the extremely small size of all rooms, which were hardly suitable for living in, and (5) the virtual lack of household structures (only in room 2, a *tannur*-like oven was found; cf. Akkermans 1989b:39).

Generally, most rooms were wholly devoid of finds except for sherds, animal bones, etc., undoubtedly representing secondary fill. However, the floor of the westernmost room yielded a number of small ceramic vessels, a flattened pierced stone and a worked bone fragment, all considered to be in situ (cf. Akkermans 1989b:39, 202 and fig. IV.35, nos. 255-56, fig. IV.46, nos. A-B). Another in-situ find appeared in room 11, where a pile of unbaked clay objects of all sorts was found on the floor, including some very stylised human and animal figurines, miniature vessels, balls, rectangular plaques, discs and cones, most likely representing tokens (see chapter 8). One of these clay objects showed traces of a stamp seal impression (cf. Akkermans 1993:82, fig. 3.23; see also chapter 5, this volume). It is not excluded that room 11 served as some sort of 'archive room', comparable with those found in the level 6 Burnt Village. Finally, fragments of large storage vessels appeared on the floor of room 5, whereas a complete but warped painted bowl was found on the floor in room 4, and a complete painted bowl and a bone awl in room 16. If, indeed, an upper storey was present in building I, this one must have contained the actual areas of living, whereas the lower one may have served mainly for storage.

Building III, situated immediately north of the eastern wing of building I, basically consisted of one room, measuring ca. 3.60 × 2.75 m and divided by a small, free-standing wall (ca. 1.35 m long) into two smaller units. Remarkably, the northern face of the building was wholly open. The walls were built of pisé, which was laid down in two alternating layers of orange-brown bands ca. 6-8 cm thick and grey bands ca. 2 cm thick. Plaster was not observed on the wall faces. Most likely, building III served as a stable or barn. By means of a ca. 1.30 m wide passage this

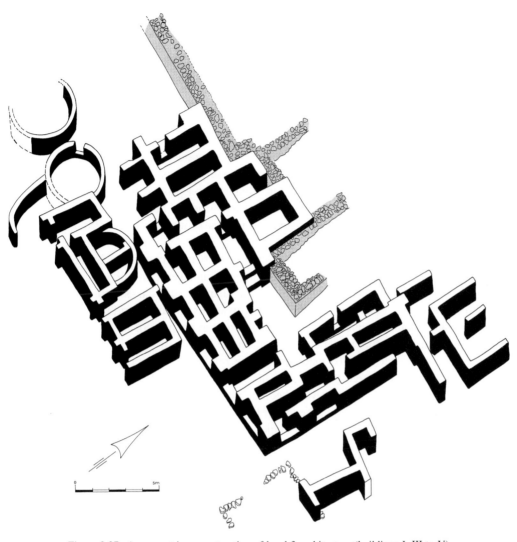

Figure 2.27. Axonometric reconstruction of level 3 architecture (buildings I, III to V).

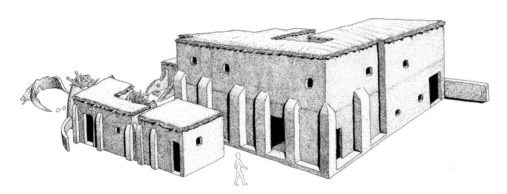

Figure 2.28. Artistic reconstruction of level 3 (buildings I and IV).

building III was separated from building I further south. Originally, this passage seems to have had a doorway, as suggested by the short division-wall in it (fig. 2.25).

Building V was heavily disturbed by erosion; only flimsy traces of its walls were found. Building V mainly consisted of one rectangular room in square R14 measuring at least 4.30 × 3.50 m (fig. 2.25). Its walls were made of pisé and ca. 50 cm thick. Interestingly, these pisé walls were aligned along the exterior facade by a low stone construction consisting of one course of irregularly hewn gypsum boulders (each measuring ca. 15 × 35 cm), joined by a loamy mortar. The stone construction carried a mud plaster, upon which a thin white coating was applied. A similar stone construction was earlier found along the exterior facade of building I. The pisé walls to the north of the main room, perhaps defining two rooms (cf. fig. 2.25), were not founded upon or aligned by stone walls.

The enclosure bounded by white-plastered walls between buildings I and V represented a small courtyard. In this area hundreds of unbaked-clay sling missiles were found, all stored in small pits ca. 20 cm in diameter and ca. 30 cm deep. Sling missiles were also stored in two rather large, oval pits (B and I) north of building V (for a more detailed account, the reader is referred to chapter 8).

In the extreme southwestern corner of square R14, just below the tell surface, remnants of another wall (B) made of gypsum boulders were encountered, one row wide and one course high (fig. 2.25). This wall was most likely part of a building which has virtually completely vanished due to erosion.

The rectangular buildings on the top of the tell were surrounded by a series of circular structures or tholoi along the slopes (fig. 2.25). The tholoi found during the 1986 campaign have already been discussed in detail elsewhere (Akkermans 1989b:28-54, 59-67, 1993:63-64). Here we will limit ourselves to the description of the four circular structures found in 1988 and 1993, viz. tholoi S, I, A and N/AE.[19] Tholos S had an interior diameter of about 2.85 m and stood to a height of ca. 40 cm. It was built of mud bricks each measuring ca. 35 × 30 × 8 cm. The wall exterior was thickly mud-plastered (ca. 2 cm), whereas the interior showed the characteristic burnt mud plaster. The tholos could be entered through a 75 cm wide doorway in the south. Interestingly, two *unburnt* floors of tamped mud were found above various burnt floors.

Immediately below the topsoil in the southeast of square Q14, traces of a highly eroded tholos, I, were discovered (only its northwestern part was preserved). The tholos gave evidence of a mud-brick wall, built of bricks measuring ca. 30 × 25 × 8/10 cm. The wall exterior was simply mud-plastered, whereas the interior was marked by a

---

[19] Actually, fragments of tholos N/AE were first uncovered in square P14 in 1986 (strata 6C-6B; Akkermans 1989b:30-33). During later campaigns, parts of this tholos were also excavated in squares Q14 (strata 5C/5B), square Q13 (strata 5E/5D) and P13 (stratum 8B). The same holds for tholos S: it was first found in square P14 in 1986 (stratum 6C) but its plan was completed in 1993 (excavations in square P13, stratum 8B).

very hard, burnt plaster up to 2 cm thick. The building was ca. 2.60 m in diameter. A door opening may have been present in its southern part.

Like tholos I, tholos A in trench P15 was found immediately below the surface of the mound and, consequently, considerably eroded. It showed parts of a hard, grey-burnt interior (fig. 2.3).

Finally, tholos N/AE, situated immediately south of building I, consisted of two superimposed tholoi (cf. figs. 2.5 and 2.6). Both tholoi had an interior diameter of ca. 3.00 m. The northern half of both features was preserved to a height of ca. 80 cm, whereas the southern half only stood to about 40 cm. The lower tholos was indicated by a ca. 8 cm thick, burnt floor plaster carried up onto the wall remains. When the tholos was rebuilt at a later stage, the lower one was removed almost entirely. This second tholos was built of mud bricks each measuring about 35 × 30 × 8 cm, and joined by a grey mortar ca. 2 cm thick. The exterior facade carried a ca. 5 cm thick mud plaster, in its turn covered by a thin white coating. The floor was similar to that of its immediate predecessor and consisted of a burnt mud plaster ca. 8 cm thick. An identical burnt plaster was found on the wall interior. Akkermans (1989b:64ff) has suggested that this kind of hard-burnt plaster was used to protect the goods stored in the building from vermin. The upper tholos was divided into two units by a short wall oriented north-south. This wall showed no traces of the characteristic burnt plaster, and must have been added to the tholos at a somewhat later stage (actually, the western face of this division wall was covered by whitish-grey mud plaster ca. 1 cm thick). The upper tholos was accessible from the south (the entrance was largely hidden in the baulk between squares P14 and Q14). Ultimately, the tholos was incorporated into building IV (see the level 3A discussion below).

Immediately south of tholos N/AE, the remains of mud-brick wall M were found. This wall seems to end in the baulk between squares Q14 and P14 (cf. figs. 2.5 and 2.25). The north section of square Q14 (fig. 2.6) shows that at the time of construction of wall M, the eastern part of tholos N/AE must still have been visible to a height of at least 25 cm. The western part of the tholos, however, was levelled to enable the construction of the floor related to wall M. The east-west oriented wall M, preserved to a height of ca. 20 cm, was built of two rows of mud bricks of various sizes. The western part of this wall (partially disturbed by the level 1 pit O) was constructed of grey-brown mud bricks measuring ca. 50 × 25 × 8/10 cm, whereas its eastern part consisted of bricks measuring ca. 40 × 30 × 8/10 cm. The wall stood perpendicularly to another wall running north-south and made of compact grey-brown loam (pisé). On both walls, fragments of white plaster ca. 1 cm thick were found. The tholos remains immediately north of wall M make it very unlikely that this wall functioned as part of a roofed building; more likely, it defined a small court.

On the floor related to wall M, a ca. 15 cm thick homogeneous layer of charred grain (*Triticum dicoccum*) was found (see chapter 10). This layer was placed against the remnants of tholos N/AE and building I. Towards the east the deposit rapidly decreased in thickness. Since wall M nor its floor showed any traces of burning, it seems that the grain caught fire elsewhere and was subsequently dumped on the floor near wall M.

Finally, attention is drawn to two *tannur*-like ovens found next to each other in the topmost level 3B debris in the northwestern part of square Q14 (i.e. stratum 4A materials which covered wall M and tholos I). Both ovens were very eroded, and only their hard-burnt bases ca. 2 cm thick were preserved. Both features were ca. 50 cm in diameter.

Pits. Building I was surrounded by a large number of pits. In square P13, eight pits were discovered, viz. (in chronological order) features DF (stratum 9B), BY, BZ, CA, CC and DC (stratum 7E), DH (stratum 7C), CB, CD, DD and DE (stratum 6C), and pit BE (stratum 6B).[20]

Pit DF was a small, circular pit, ca. 60 cm in diameter and about 35 cm deep. Its interior showed a ca. 3 mm thick hard mud plaster. It was filled with soft grey-brown loam. The eastern part of pit DF was cut by another pit (i.e. the stratum 7E pit CC).

The stratum 7E pits BY, BZ, CA and CC shared some characteristics. First, all had an oblong outline, widening towards one of the ends (somewhat resembling the keyhole-shaped kilns; cf. fig. 2.25). Second, their fill was more or less similar. The bases were covered with a soft layer of charcoal and ashes ca. 10 cm thick. Subsequently, a layer of grey-black burnt, heat-cracked stones (each measuring ca. 5-20 cm) appeared. In their turn, these stones were covered with rather soft, brownish loam and mud-brick fragments. Most likely, these pits were used as fireplaces (Akkermans 1989b:69-70), with the stones originally placed upon the fuel (wood and shrubs, as indicated by the charcoal). Pit BY was the smallest of the stratum 7E pits. This feature was oriented east-west, ca. 2.00 m long and maximally 1.10 m wide. It was sunk to a depth of ca. 21 cm. Its interior carried a mud plaster, on its turn covered with a thin white coating (unlike the other stratum 7E pits). Stones, laid on the floor immediately above the ashes and charcoal, were found only in the oblong eastern part of the pit. Originally, this feature may have been a water basin or the like, re-used as a fire pit. The next pit BZ was partly hidden in the western section baulk of square P13, and disturbed by the level 2 kiln AL. In its turn, pit BZ partly disturbed wall DI (cf. fig. 2.25). Pit BZ was at least 2.50 m long and 0.75 cm wide, and oriented north-south. It was sunk to a depth of at least 0.55 m. The heat-cracked stones, on top of ashes and charcoal, were only found in the oblong part of the pit. The fill consisted of soft blackish-grey and ashy soil, including fragments of burnt mud brick. Pit CA was also partly hidden in the western section baulk. It was 2.75 m long, at least 1.00 m wide and sunk to a depth of ca. 90 cm. Burnt stones were present in all parts of the pit (cf. fig. 2.30). Feature CC was a rather large pit, parts

---

[20] Since their outlines were rather unclear, pits CB, DD and DE of stratum 6C and pit BE of stratum 6B are not presented in the level 3C/3B plan (fig. 2.25).

of which were hidden in the southern section baulk. This oblong pit was oriented NNW-SSE, at least 2.00 long, ca. 1.30 m wide (narrowing at the base to 0.85 m) and sunk to a depth of 1.10 m. The heat-cracked stones, which had been laid upon a thin layer of charcoal and ashes, carried a number of mud bricks which rested with their long sides upon the stones. Above the bricks, the pit was filled with dark grey and crumbly loam, mud-brick fragments, charcoal and heat-cracked stones similar to the ones found immediately above the floor. Finally, pit DC was dug in the fill of tholos S. This oblong pit was ca. 75 cm long, 15 cm wide and about 15 cm deep. It was filled with burnt loam, ashes and charcoal.

The stratum 7C pit DH was partly hidden in the western section baulk of square P13. It was at least 80 cm wide and 60 cm deep. The pit was filled with a grey-brown, crumbly and rather loose accumulation of loam and some mud-brick fragments. Finally, this pit was covered with two layers of greyish mud bricks (stratum 7A), perhaps representing the remnants of a wall (fig. 2.30).

Pit CB was circular, ca. 40 cm in diameter and 15 cm deep. Its interior showed a thin white plaster and was filled with soft brown loam. Another stratum 6C feature is the long-drawn, irregularly-shaped pit CD, which was ca. 2 m long, 90 cm wide and 25 cm deep. The base carried a thin layer of charcoal, followed by brown loam. Pit DD was a circular pit 1.45 m in diameter and ca. 20 cm deep. It was filled with orange-brown loam. Pit DE was irregularly shaped in outline and more or less rectangular in cross-section. It was ca. 1.60 m long, 0.75 m wide and 0.30 m deep. The pit contained soft grey and ashy fill, intermingled with a large amount of animal bones.

In square P14, six pits (AY, AK, BE, AD, R and T) have been ascribed to level 3B. Pit AY, largely hidden in the western corner of the south baulk, was ca. 1.70 m long, 0.90 m wide and at least 1.20 m deep (the base has not yet been reached in excavation). It seems to have been gradually filled in with various materials, as suggested by the layers of grey, brown and yellow-brown loam and domestic debris. Pit AK was at least 1.45 m long, 1.40 m wide and 0.90 m deep. Its fill yielded a layer of stones of various sizes approximately halfway. Stones were also found at the base of the pit. Pits AD, R and T have all been ascribed to stratum 6C (Akkermans 1989b:30-31). These features were constructed in the courtyard between the various level 3B tholoi in square P14. Feature AD presented a bell-shaped pit ca. 0.60 m in diameter (at its opening) and 0.90 m deep. The pit was filled with brown loam and mud-brick debris. The two small, white-plastered pits R and T were found in front of tholos S. Pit R was ca. 75 cm in diameter and only about 10 cm deep. Pit T was ca. 50 cm in diameter and 20 cm deep. Pit BE in square P14, partly hidden in the western section baulk, was sunk from stratum 6B (i.e. the floor level belonging to tholoi P and AE; Akkermans 1989b:32-33). This flat-based pit was at least ca. 60 cm long and wide, and ca. 90 cm deep. It was filled with brown loam, upon which some ash lenses had accumulated.

In square Q13, the rounded pit BK was sunk from the top of stratum 5C (representing debris accumulation around building I) into the small courtyard between the western and eastern wings of building I. Pit BK was ca. 1.10 m in diameter and ca. 60 cm deep. Stone cobbles were found on its base. The pit was filled with brown-grey loam.

In square Q14, 19 pits were ascribed to level 3B, although not all pits were simultaneously in use. Seven pits (AH, AI, AS, AT, BH, BJ, BT,) and a basin (BI) have been ascribed to stratum 6.[21] These features were situated in close proximity of each other in the northern half of the square (fig. 2.25). These pits had a circular (AH, AI, BJ and, most likely, BT) or rather irregular outline (AS, AT). One pit (BH) is more or less keyhole-shaped in plan. Pit BT, partly hidden in the northern section baulk (cf. fig. 2.6), was at least 0.95 m wide and 0.75 m deep. Its fill consisted of several alternating layers of very hard, loamy debris and soft, ashy material. Pit AI was ca. 0.95 m long, 0.85 m wide and 0.30 m deep. The next pit AH, located immediately south of pit AI, was rather large, measuring ca. 1.30 × 1.15 × 0.20 m. A rather large amount of sherds and bones was recovered from both pit AI and AH; probably these features served as refuse pits. Pit AH cut pit BH, which in its turn cut pit BJ. Pit BJ was ca. 0.65 m in diameter, and preserved to a depth of 8 cm only. It was mainly filled with soft grey ashes. Pit BH, ca. 0.90 m long, 0.70 m wide and about 0.30 m deep, was also filled with grey ashes but in addition it contained numerous charcoal particles. Pit AS in the northwestern part of square Q14 was ca. 1.75 m long, about 1 m wide and 0.30 m deep. Its interior carried a white plaster ca. 5 mm thick. The pit contained numerous animal bones, as well as a large number of overfired, painted Halafian sherds. These wasters indicate that pottery was locally produced at Tell Sabi Abyad. A true pottery kiln, however, has not yet been attested. Pit AT, found at a short distance east of pit AS, was ca. 2 m long, 1 m wide and 20 cm deep. Its loamy fill contained some animal bones and sherds. In the northeast of square Q14, and partly hidden in the eastern section baulk, a shallow white-plastered basin was encountered: feature BI. The basin was at least 50 cm long, 35 cm wide and 14 cm deep. The interior carried a white plaster ca. 4 cm thick; probably it was repeatedly re-plastered.

Stratum 5A in square Q14 yielded two circular pits (AB and AC), situated near each other. The largest of these, pit AC, was ca. 70 cm in diameter (at its opening; the base diameter was only 45 cm) and ca. 22 cm deep. Immediately southwest of pit AC, the bell-shaped pit AB was found, ca. 25 cm in diameter at its opening and 55 cm in diameter at its base. Pit AB was ca. 40 cm deep.

South of wall M in square Q14, nine very small and shallow, round pits appeared, sunk into a ca. 3 cm thick floor of tamped loam (stratum 4B). The pits were ca. 5 cm deep, with diameters ranging from 8 to 19 cm. Four pits carried a white plaster on the interior (probably gypsum; cf. Rehhoff et al. 1990), which was renewed once in

---

[21] Pit BJ is not indicated on the level 3C/3B plan (fig. 2.25); this pit is largely disturbed by pit BH, situated immediately above it.

the case of the southernmost features. Moreover, one of these replastered pits was lined with sherds. These small, shallow pits have close counterparts in the level 3C (stratum 7) pits in square Q14 (see above). The function of these features remains enigmatic.

Pit J has been ascribed to stratum 4A in square Q14. This pit was ca. 65 cm in diameter and about 24 cm deep. Its interior carried a white plaster ca. 1 cm thick. It was filled with grey-brown loam.

In square Q15, pit E has been ascribed to level 3B. This irregularly shaped, flat-based feature was partly hidden in the northern section baulk. Pit E was at least 1.20 m wide and ca. 1 m deep. It was filled with alternating layers of grey, red-brown or greenish soil and ashes. Small numbers of animal bones and sherds were recovered from this fill.

In square R14, three pits (P, AK and AP) were sunk from the floor south and west of the level 3B building V. Feature P was a small, circular pit ca. 70 cm in diameter and 40 cm deep. It was filled with grey-brown loam and dark ashes; in addition, it yielded a rather large amount of painted Halaf sherds. The bell-shaped pit AK was most likely circular in outline, at least 1.00 m in diameter and 0.50 m deep. The interior wall was covered with a blackish-brown mud plaster ca. 5 mm thick. The pit was filled with rather homogeneous compact, brown loam. Pit AP, largely hidden in the western section baulk, was U-shaped in cross-section, minimally 80 cm wide and 75 cm deep. Near the base, traces of a ca. 1.5 cm thick, reddish-brown mud plaster were found. The pit was filled with a hard, brown loam layer ca. 5 cm thick at the base, followed by a black and ashy deposit ca. 20 cm thick, a soft, grey-brown, loamy deposit ca. 20 cm thick and, finally, another soft but brown-coloured loam layer ca. 30 cm thick.

In square R11, the shallow pit B, ca. 60 cm in diamter and 10 cm deep, has been ascribed to level 3B. The pit was filled with stones of various sizes.

Level 3A

Stratigraphy

Level 3A is mainly represented by the small building IV, which was raised immediately south of building I (figs. 2.28-2.29).[22] The latter structure, and the other level 3B buildings III and V, remained in use in the level 3A period. Parts of building IV were excavated in 1986 (strata 5 and 3 in squares P13 and P14, respectively; Akkermans 1989b:36, 38-44). The remaining parts were uncovered in squares Q13 and Q14 (strata 5B and 3B, respectively) during the 1988 campaign.

---

[22] With regard to the earlier publications (Akkermans 1993:65, fig. 3.15; Akkermans and Le Mière 1992:16, fig. 19), a number of features have been added to the level 3A plan: the earlier mentioned stone consolidation walls around buildings I and V, room 23 in the east of building I, oven AF in room 2 of building I, pit R in square Q13 and hearth I in square R14.

The various level 3A buildings were surrounded by fill layers, some of which were laid down during the use of these structures, others when these features had already been deserted. This fill mainly consisted of grey-brown or red-brown loam, followed by collapsed wall and roof fragments. Large quantities of sherds and animal bones suggest that dumping of waste products contributed to this debris accumulation to a considerable extent. Several pits were sunk into the level 3A fill. These pits were more or less contemporaneous, and all have been ascribed to the topmost stratum in each of the relevant squares.

In squares R12 and R13, stratum 1A consisted of a ca. 20 cm thick, soft deposit of reddish-brown and grey loam, intermingled with some mud-brick fragments (i.e. fill related to the eastern wing of building I and to buildings III and V). Pit AA, in the northwestern part of square R13, has been attributed to stratum 1A.

In the northeast of square R14, stratum 1A consisted of several thin layers of hard or granular loam (fill related to building V). Most layers were between 1.20 and 2.20 long and 10-20 cm thick (however, one is ca. 40 cm thick). In the other parts of square R14, stratum 1A was of a much more homogeneous character and consisted of hard, grey-brown loam varying in thickness between 20 and 80 cm cm. Two features, viz. hearth I and pit C, were found in the topmost part of stratum 1A.

In square Q12, level 3A is represented by stratum 5A, i.e. a ca. 50 cm thick layer of soft, occasionally granular, red-brown loam.

Level 3A in square S13 is represented by strata 2B-2A. Stratum 2B was found only in the southern half of the square, due to slope erosion, and consisted of a series of granular, greyish layers, compact light-brown depositions and granular, red-brown materials, together up to 20 cm thick. Stratum 2A was marked by three pits (J, W and X).

In square Q13, level 3A is represented by strata 5B-5A. Stratum 5B comprised the construction of the northern part of building IV, a new floor in the stratum 5E/5D tholos N/AE, and a basin (R) and its associated floor in the northeast of the square. Stratum 5A was characterised by a ca. 50 cm thick deposit of red-brown wall debris, which accumulated in the various rooms of building I. Outside the building, the red-brown debris was mixed with grey-brown loam. Large numbers of artefacts were recovered from the fill in the various rooms. From the top of stratum 5A, a small and rounded pit (BI) was sunk into the fill of the former room 13 of building I.

In square Q14, level 3A equals stratum 3A, which yielded fill material laid down in the stratum 3B building IV. Grey-brown mud-brick debris and considerable quantities of painted sherds and animal bones accumulated up to a height of 50 cm upon the floors of the various rooms of building IV. Outside building IV, stratum 3A was represented by an accumulation of hard grey-brown loam ca. 20-30 cm thick, occasionally mixed with grey ashes.

Architecture and related features

In the level 3A period a new room (no. 23) was added to the eastern wing of building I (cf. fig. 2.27 and 2.29). The walls of this room 23 abutted the former northwestern facade of the wing. Room 23 was a rather large, oblong room, measuring ca. 4.50 × 1.00 m. A buttress divided the room into two smaller units. These could be entered through a ca. 50 cm wide doorway from the small court between the western and eastern wings of building I. The walls defining this room 23 were in a poor state of preservation, but seem to have been built of mud bricks. The northern wall carried a white plaster ca. 5 mm thick. A more or less north-south oriented, free-standing wall stood north of room 23. Its western facade was white-plastered.

In the courtyard in front of the northeastern entrance of the western wing of building I, traces of a ca. 5-10 cm thick floor of red tamped loam were unearthed. The floor covered the lowest (i.e. level 3B) step of the two-stepped northeastern entrance. The large niche in the mud-brick wall bounding the courtyard towards the south (see the level 3B discussion) was now divided into two smaller, white-plastered niches. A shallow basin (R) ca. 1.10 m in diameter and 15 cm deep had been sunk into the floor in front of these niches. Its fill consisted of four very hard, water-logged layers of yellow-brown, fine-grained loam.

Apart from the modification of building I, the main level 3A architectural feature is building IV (cf. Akkermans 1987a:27, 1989b:36), which consisted of a series of elongated, narrow rooms oriented roughly north-south on the flanks, connected by a similarly small-sized room oriented east-west (fig. 2.29). The structure measured ca. 13.50 × 4.00 m. The rather narrow walls stood to a height of ca. 40 cm and were built of mud bricks each measuring ca. 35 × 30 × 8 cm. The bricks were joined by a red mortar. The walls were simply founded on earth, without any foundation works. None of the walls showed traces of plaster. The floors in the various rooms consisted of a layer of hard-tamped mud ca. 3 cm thick. Access to the tiny rooms was gained from the south through narrow doorways each between 40 and 80 cm wide, marked on both sides by buttresses. In the open area immediately in front of the easternmost rooms, traces were found of a largely eroded pavement of small sherds and whitish fragments of limestone or gypsum (each measuring ca. 5 × 5 cm). In front of the western half of the building, some walls bounded a small, unroofed enclosure.

Building IV consisted of five rooms of various sizes, viz. 2.40 × 1.40 m (room 1), 2.60 × 0.90 m (room 2), 2.70 × 1.00 m (room 4) and 2.60 × 0.75 m (room 5).[23] In the centre of room 5, a large flat stone was found on the floor, which may have served to support a wooden post or, alternatively, as a kind of working surface. Interestingly, rooms 4 and 5 originally seem to have been part of a larger, more or less square room, measuring ca. 2.60 × 2.60 m, which was divided into two smaller units

---

[23] Room 3 measures at least 1.50 × 1.00 m but part of it is hidden in the north baulk, thus preventing a more exact figure.

S12

LATE BRONZE AGE PIT

S13

R13

BUILDING V

C

R12

BUILDING III

20

19

18

17

23

16

15

R14

I

B

Q12

P12

BUILDING I

4

3

2

AF

1

5

6

7

8

9

10

14

13

12

11

22

21

R

THOLOS N/AE

THOLOS N

THOLOS AH

LATE BRONZE AGE PITS

Q14

BUILDING IV

1

2

3

4

5

P14

5m

0

at a certain moment (the floor in rooms 4-5 ran below the the wall separating both rooms, this in contrast with the other walls which each bounded the floor; cf. wall E on fig. 2.6).

Building IV partly cut a tholos (N), which was already out of use but which was still standing to a considerable height (Akkermans 1989b:44 and fig. III.16). West of tholos N, fragments of another tholos (AH) were found. This building had been heavily disturbed by the level 2 kilns AI and AL and pit AJ; only parts of the hard-baked floor and wall were recovered. Tholos AH had more or less the same dimensions as tholos N, i.e. an interior diameter of ca. 3.00 m.

Remarkably, apart from tholos N, building IV cut another level 3B circular structure, viz. tholos N/AE. The southern half of this tholos was levelled to enable the construction of building IV, but its northern half still stood to a considerable height (comparable to tholos N; cf. fig. 2.28). Perhaps the tholoi incorporated in building IV served as animal pens.

Two pits, AA and BI, were sunk into the upper fill in building I. The circular pit AA was ca. 50 cm in diameter and about 10 cm deep. It was filled with grey loamy debris. Pit BI was only about 25 cm in diameter and 11 cm deep. The interior carried traces of a mud plaster. The base was enforced by sherds, all placed with their concave sides downwards. Pit BI was filled with soft, burnt, orange-brown loam, containing some painted sherds.

Traces of an oval hearth (I) were found in the northwestern part of square R14 (fig. 2.29). It was at least 1.90 m long and 1.00 m wide, and partly sunk to a depth of ca. 50 cm. The lower part of the hearth was filled with grey and black ashes and burnt, granular loam. This fill was covered with brown-black loam and some red-burnt loam. A small amount of burnt animal bones and some sherds were recovered from hearth I. Pit C was another feature sunk in stratum 1A in square R14. The circular pit was about 1.00 m in diameter and 0.50 m deep. It cut part of the wall of the level 3B building V (cf. fig. 2.29). The pit was filled with soft brown and hard grey pieces of loam, red-burnt loam, charcoal and ashes.

Pits J, W and X in square S13 were all found immediately below the topsoil, and sunk into the fill of the building V ruins.[24] Pit J, partly hidden in the west baulk, had an irregular outline and measured at least 80 × 75 cm. It was 65 cm deep. The pit was filled with grey-brown loam, containing numerous lime spots. Pit X, located south of pit J and also partly hidden in the section baulk, was at least 65 cm in diameter and ca. 80 cm deep. This pit had a white coating ca. 1 cm thick, indicating its use as a water basin. Finally, pit W, which was only recognised in the south section, was a large, irregularly shaped pit filled with at least seven alternating layers of grey-brown loam. Pit W was ca. 1.80 m wide and 0.50 m deep.

---

[24] Actually, it cannot be excluded that these pits were sunk from a level 2 phase of occupation.

Level 2

Somewhere around 5050 B.C. the level 3 occupation came to an end. The various level 3 buildings went out of use and were largely filled in with fallen mud bricks and occupational debris. However, the buildings must still have stood to some height in a ramshackle state in level 2 times and were reused for various open-air domestic activities. Numerous pits, ovens or kilns, fireplaces and white-plastered basins appeared (fig. 2.31). These features were not all constructed and used at the same time. The area must have had a highly disturbed appearance marked by an uneven and rapidly changing surface. So far, no dwellings have been found; apparently, the residential architecture was moved to another part of the site. The appearance of a tholos (L) in the southwest of square P13 may indicate that houses can be found in the nearby western squares O13 and O14.

Level 2 is part of the Early Halaf or Balikh IIIB period, and is dated at around 5050-5000 B.C.

Stratigraphy

During the 1986 campaign, level 2 features were exposed in squares O14 (stratum 2), P13 (strata 4 to 2) and P14 (stratum 2). These strata have already been treated extensively elsewhere (Akkermans 1989b:36-37, 44-50, 55); below a summary is presented.

Stratum 2 in square O14 represented a ca. 60 cm thick succession of loam layers intermingled with ash lenses and ashy spots.[25]

Stratum 4 in square P13 consisted of a small, circular pit (O), a keyhole-shaped kiln (AK), a circular oven (P) and an oval fireplace (DJ). No dwellings were found. Large parts of the lower level 3 architecture must still have stood to a considerable height. These features may have acted as wind shields or other protective devices for the various level 2 features. Stratum 3 presented a continuous accumulation of ashes, mainly attested in the northern half of square P13. The keyhole-shaped kiln AI and five pits of varying shape and dimension (Q, AJ, AL, AM and AN) have been ascribed to stratum 3 (Akkermans 1989b:48-50). However, the 1993 excavations in square P13 revealed that features AL and AM in fact represent keyhole-shaped kilns instead of pits (see below).

Stratum 2 in square P13 consisted of parts of a tholos (L), associated with a ca. 10-20 cm thick, brown loam accumulation.

The 1988 season of excavations at Tell Sabi Abyad revealed another series of occupation layers which should be ascribed to level 2, viz. strata 4 to 2 in square Q13 and stratum 2 in square Q14. Stratum 4 in square Q13 has been divided into two substrata: 4B and 4A. Stratum 4B comprised three ovens (N, O and BL) and two pits

---

[25] A considerable part of square O14 was disturbed by a large Late Bronze Age pit; originally, architectural features may very well have been present in this area.

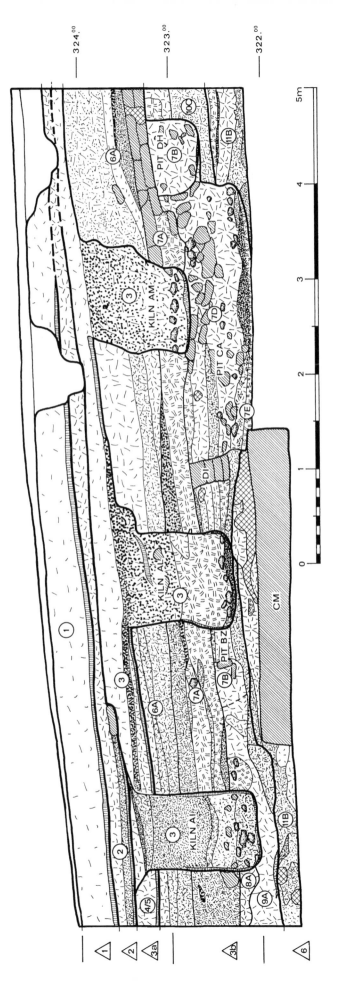

P 13 : WEST SECTION

Figure 2.30. West section of square P13 (legend: see fig. 2.2).

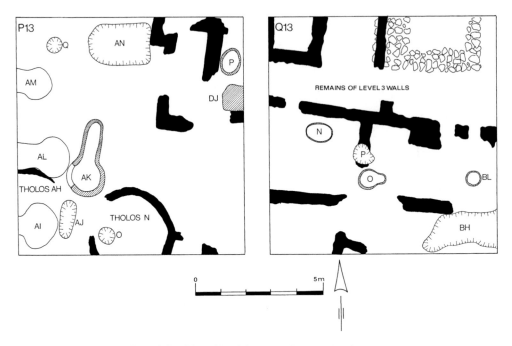

Figure 2.31. Plan of level 2 ovens, pits and other features.

(P and BH). During the period in which the ovens and kilns were used, ashes and other occupational debris accumulated in the area surrounding these features: stratum 4A. This stratum 4A deposit varies in thickness between 10 and 40 cm. Ultimately, stratum 4A covered the stratum 4B features entirely. Stratum 3 in square Q13 was represented by a ca. 30 cm thick deposit of soft grey-brown loam, which accumulated upon the ashy stratum 4A materials. No architectural features could be ascribed to this stratum. The subsequent stratum 2 was represented by a large pit (BG). Unfortunately, pit BG cannot be associated with a floor level due to erosion (pit BG appeared immediately below the topsoil). Stratigraphically, stratum 2 in square Q13, and consequently pit BG, are related to stratum 2 and tholos L in the neighbouring square P13 (Akkermans 1989b:50).

Stratum 2 in square Q14 presented a grey-brown, loamy deposit, ca. 30 cm thick. Due to slope erosion, stratum 2 could only be traced in the northern half of the square. The western wall of room 3 of the level 3A building IV (see below) was levelled in stratum 2 times.

Ovens, kilns and pits

The earliest level 2 features in square P13 (stratum 4) were kiln AK, pit O, oven P and fireplace DJ. These structures were constructed between the ruins of level 3

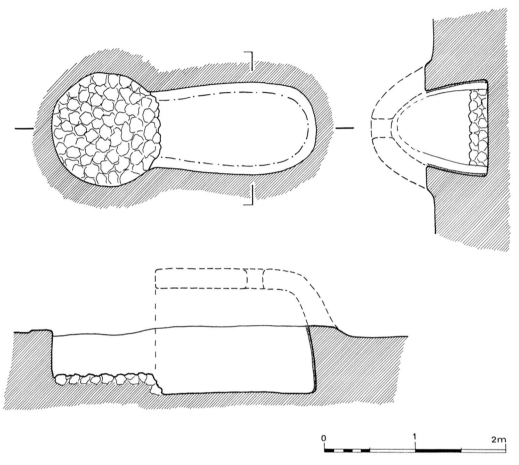

Figure 2.32. Plan and sections of level 2 kiln AK.

building I and tholoi AH and N (cf. fig. 2.31). These features have been dealt with in detail by Akkermans (1989b:44-47), and are therefore only shortly commented upon here. The keyhole-shaped kiln AK was oriented NE-SW. The kiln consisted of an absidal combustion chamber, about 1.60 m long, 75 cm wide and sunk into the ground to a depth of ca. 70 cm, and a circular heating chamber, about 1.20 m in diameter and also ca. 70 cm deep. Most likely, the kiln had a dome-shaped, mud-brick superstructure (cf. fig. 2.32). An oblong opening was probably present at the western side. The kiln interior was mud-plastered. Superficial traces of firing were observed only in the combustion chamber; apparently, the fire in the kiln did not reach very high temperatures. The fill in the combustion chamber largely consisted of dark ashes, containing many animal bones. The circular heating chamber was partly filled up with blackened, heat-cracked stones. This kiln has close counterparts in level 4.

A shallow, white-plastered pit (O) had been sunk south of kiln AK, in the fill of the tholos N remains. The cylindrical, flat-based pit had a diameter of ca. 60 cm and a depth of 20 cm. Oven P was built upon the fill in room 2 of the ruined level 3 building I. Oven P was raised in coils ca. 5 cm thick and preserved to a height of about 60 cm. Its base diameter was ca. 75 cm. The oven wall slightly curved inwards towards the top. Fireplace DJ, located immediately south of oven P, was constructed of both mud bricks and packed mud. Originally, this fireplace seems to have been part of an oven (Akkermans 1989b:47). The fireplace was surrounded by grey ashes and red-burnt mud-brick fragments.

Three keyhole-shaped kilns (AI, AL, AM) were constructed in the west of square P13 (figs. 2.30 and 2.31). These kilns were oriented east-west, with the oval or circular heating chamber situated in the east. The elongated combustion chambers were largely hidden in the west baulk of square P13 (consequently, exact measurements cannot be given as yet). The kilns were sunk to a depth of ca. 1.50 m. No evidence of some sort of superstructure was found. The floors consisted of hard-tamped mud, whereas the sides were covered by a hard and smooth mud plaster. In two cases (i.e. features AI and AL), this mud plaster was covered by a thin white coating. Characteristically, grey-black, heat-cracked stones (each measuring ca. 5-20 cm) were situated upon a thin layer of charcoal and ashes. Interestingly, the level 2 features resemble the firepits BZ, CA and CC ascribed to level 3B to some extent; both the level 2 firepits and level 3B kilns were keyhole-shaped, and all were located in the western half of square P13. All were filled with heat-cracked stones, charcoal and ashes. Apparently, this part of the tell was used for conducting similar (specialised) activities for a considerable period of time.

Kiln AI had an oval heating chamber ca. 1.75 m long and 1.20 m wide. It was sunk to a depth of 1.40 m. The elongated combustion chamber was ca. 70 cm wide, and likewise sunk to a depth of 1.40 m. At a time when kiln AI had lost its original function, it was filled with soft brown loam, mixed with charcoal particles, sherds and bones. The upper part of the antechamber showed a ca. 30 cm thick accumulation of alternating layers of black and grey ash (cf. Akkermans 1989b:47-48).

Kiln AL was situated about one metre north of kiln AI. The oval heating chamber measured ca. 1.60 × 1.25 m, whereas its oblong antechamber was 90 cm wide. The floor was covered with charcoal, grey ashes and stones. Subsequently, the kiln was filled with soft grey-brown loam, containing pieces of reddish-burnt loam, ashes, charcoal and charred grain. In the upper part of the kiln, near its opening, a fragmented crust of white plaster appeared, the meaning of which remains unknown. A few ceramic wasters (greenish, very brittle ceramics) were recovered from the fill of pit AL, but it remains highly doubtful whether these ceramics were actually produced in the kiln.

Kiln AM had a more or less circular heating chamber ca. 1.25/1.00 m in diameter. The oblong antechamber was about 95 cm wide. Both were sunk to a depth of ca. 1.20 m. The kiln was filled with soft grey-brown loam, grey ashes and large quantities of charred grain (cf. kiln AL). However, it is clear by now that these burnt cereals should not be considered as in-situ remains but as secondary pit fill.

Feature AJ, immediately east of kiln AI, presented an oblong and shallow pit, ca. 1.60 m long, 40-70 cm wide and ca. 20 cm deep. Pit AJ was filled with black ashes containing charred twigs of ash (*Fraxinus*); most likely, this pit served as a fireplace.

A large and more or less rectangular pit (AN) was found in the north of square P13. The pit measured ca. 2.60 × 1.50 m and was ca. 1 m deep. It was filled with grey and black ashes.

West of pit AN, the small white-plastered pit Q was found (resembling pit O in the south of square P13). Pit Q was cylindrical and had a flat base. It was ca. 60 cm in diameter and preserved to a depth of ca. 15 cm (the upper part of the pit was eroded; cf. Akkermans 1989b:49).

Oven N in square Q13 was an oval structure, 1.05 m long, 0.65 m wide, and standing to a height of about 15 cm. The ca. 2 cm thick oven wall and floor were hard-burnt.

The small, keyhole-shaped oven O was preserved to a height of ca. 30 cm. The circular part of the oven had a diameter of about 80 cm, whereas the longitudinal part was ca. 35 cm long and 30 cm wide. The oven wall and floor were ca. 2 cm thick and hard-burnt. The oven was filled with grey-black ashes.

About four metres east of oven O, traces of another 2 cm thick, hard-burnt oven floor were found. The wall of this oven (BL) was completely eroded. The circular outline of the oven floor (diameter ca. 60 cm) suggests that oven BL was of the *tannur*-type.

Directly north of oven O, a shallow, circular pit (P) was found, ca. 80 cm in diameter and 11 cm deep. It was filled with soft grey ashes, possibly representing waste materials from oven O.

Pit BH was a rather large, oval pit, ca. 3.75 m long, 1.50 m wide and 20 cm deep.

Finally, pit BG was ca. 5.50 m long, 2.50 m wide and between 15 and 60 cm deep. It formed a basin-like area on the southern slope of the mound (cf. fig. 2.2), and was filled with red-burnt mud-brick debris containing ash pockets and charcoal particles.

Level 1

The topmost level of prehistoric occupation is represented by fragments of three small rectilinear buildings (I-III, fig. 2.33), exposed in squares O14, P14, P13 and Q13. It is not yet clear whether the level 1 settlement was originally much larger than appears from the present plan; it is not excluded that considerable parts have disappeared due to erosion (particularly along the slopes of the mound). Level 1 is part of the Early Halaf or Balikh IIIB period, and is dated at about 5000 B.C.

The level 1 features have already been discussed in detail elsewhere (Akkermans 1989b:50-54, 1993:66-68); the following is largely a summarised account, with some additions and adjustments.

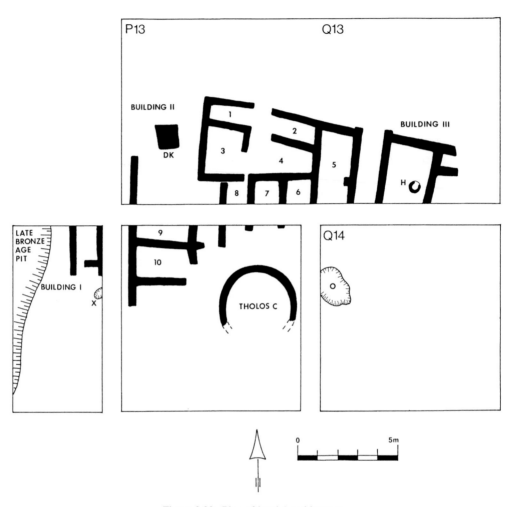

Figure 2.33. Plan of level 1 architecture.

Stratigraphy

The level 1 buildings and associated debris comprise stratum 1 in squares O14, P14, P13 and Q13. Only in the latter square has this stratum been subdivided into strata 1B and 1A, with stratum 1B comprising the construction buildings II and III and stratum 1A consisting of the ca. 40 cm thick accumulation of grey-brown mud-brick fragments and mud-brick debris in and around the structures. This stratum 1A debris has been completely eroded in the northern part of square Q13, but it could be traced along the entire east section of the neighbouring square P13 (Akkermans 1989b:52 and fig. III.21).

A rather large pit in the west of square Q14 has been ascribed to level 1.

Architecture and related features

Buildings I, II and III, separated by narrow alleys, are more or less east-west oriented (fig. 2.33). The various walls, built of crumbly, reddish-brown and rectangular mud bricks and simply founded on earth, appeared immediately below the tell surface; they were heavily eroded and preserved to a height of ca. 25 cm (i.e. one to three bricks) only.

The westernmost building I was largely ruined by a Late Bronze Age pit. The structure was accessible from the south through a narrow, ca. 40 cm wide doorway. In front of the building a shallow pit (X) was found, containing the spine and skull fragments of a bovine. It has been suggested that this pit had been deliberately constructed to bury these animal remains (Akkermans 1989b:55); perhaps its contents have to be regarded as a foundation deposit.

Building II is the largest structure and measured ca. 11 × 10 m. It was composed of at least 10 narrow, oblong rooms, oriented either north-south or east-west. The rooms varied in width between 0.80 and 1.65 m, while the length varied between ca. 2.50 and 3.50 m. Some walls of building II were not bonded; apparently the building was not conceived and constructed at once, but built in stages. Circulation through the building was restricted: the various southern rooms of building II were accesible from the south, whereas the four northern rooms could only be entered from the north. The walls were constructed of rather large, red-brown mud bricks measuring ca. 50 × 35/40 × 8 cm. The wall faces were mud-plastered. In addition, the interior faces occasionally showed traces of a white plaster.

In the northwestern corner of room 5, a small quantity of burnt grain was found, associated with a lightly burnt cattle scapula. Radiocarbon analysis of the grain yielded a date of 5025±30 B.C. (uncalibrated).

The area north and west of building II yielded an uneven surface, which was virtually free of artefacts. Apparently this area represents a courtyard kept meticulously clean. A square mud-brick platform (DK), measuring ca. 1 × 1 m and ca. 20 cm high, stood in this court.[26] In square P14, south of the building II, traces of a very eroded tholos (C) were found. This building was ca. 3.20 m in diameter.[27]

So far, building III is represented by one north-south oriented room, which is at least 2.65 m long and 1.15 m wide. Another room may have been present east of this room, as suggested by two east-west running wall stubs. The walls were built of square or slightly rectangular mud bricks measuring ca. 35/30 × 35/25 × 6 cm. The wall faces carried a mud plaster. The northeastern corner of building III was marked by a rather small buttress, ca. 35 cm wide and 20 cm long. A similar buttress was present at the northwestern corner of building II. Near the eastern wall of building

---

[26] Earlier, a small oven (K) and a wall (AT) in this area were ascribed to level 2 (Akkermans 1989b:51, 53 and fig. III.22) but subsequent excavations have made it clear that these features are part of a late 2nd millennium, Middle-Assyrian phase of occupation (cf. Akkermans and Rossmeisl 1990).

[27] This tholos was earlier incorrectly ascribed to level 2 (Akkermans 1989b:36-37).

III, a low, circular oven with a domed superstructure (H) was sunk sligthly into the floor. The oven was preserved to a height of ca. 20 cm, and was ca. 70 cm in diameter. The oven wall was ca. 3 cm thick and carried a mud plaster, in its turn white-coated. This plaster had been renewed once. Two small pestles (one of basalt, the other of granite), a stone hammer and a broken but restorable painted jar were found on the floor immediately west of the oven. A large basalt mortar was found on the floor level at the northern end of the alley between buildings II and III.

In square Q14, the large, irregularly-shaped pit O, partly hidden in the west baulk, has been ascribed to level 1 (cf. fig. 2.5).[28] Unfortunately, the floor level from which the pit was sunk was eroded. The pit was at least 1.75 m long, 1.50 m wide and 1.50 m deep. Various layers of debris (mainly soft, greyish-brown loam) could be discerned.

Note on the Human Skeletal Remains (Nico Aten)

Burial SAB91-B1

The skeletal remains of a little child were found in oven T of the level 6 building I, room 2. The bone condition is very good. All parts have a brown colour and are much less brittle than those of the other two child burials found at Sabi Abyad (SAB92-B1 and SAB92-B2, see below). Nevertheless, a strong fragmentation has occurred and, in addition, the remains are far from complete. The lower legs, the left humerus, the right arm and all parts of the hands and feet are missing. The remaining bones lack essential parts and, consequently, no measurements could be taken. Sex diagnosis was not performed.

In the case of the dentition, merely fragments of three elements have been recovered: 16, 55 and 84. However, on the basis of these fragments it appears that the age at death must have been 18 months ± 6 months. This coincides well with the size of the femora fragments. The spinal arcs, as far as present, are all closed and show no traces of union with the spinal bodies.

No abnormalities or pathologies of any kind have been observed.

Burial SAB92-B1

This burial yielded the well-preserved remains of a child. The bones were rather brittle and a pale yellowish-brown. Some fragmentation had occurred as a result of mechanic soil pressure as well as of excavation and transport. The skeleton was virtually complete, with only some of the smallest bones missing. The following measurements were taken:

---

[28] This pit O was added to the earlier published level 1 plan (Akkermans 1993:67 and fig. 3.16).

Left humerus, maximum diaphysial length	121.7 mm
Right humerus, maximum diaphysial length	122.0 mm
Right ulna, maximum diaphysial length	104.4 mm
Left ulna, maximum diaphysial length	104.2 mm
Left radius, maximum diaphysial length	93.2 mm
Left femur, maximum diaphysial length	159.0 mm
Right tibia, maximum diaphysial length	130.7 mm
Left tibia, maximum diaphysial length	131.4 mm
Right fibula, maximum diaphysial length	126.3 mm
Left fibula, maximum diaphysial length	127.2 mm

Age determination by means of tooth eruption (cf. Ubelaker 1978) resulted in an age of 3 years ± 12 months, since the crowns of the elements 11, 21, 26, 31 and 46 were virtually complete. Determination on the basis of the union of the spine suggested an age of 2 to 3 years, since all spinal arcs were closed but no traces of union with the spinal bodies are found. The age diagnosis by means of the tooth eruption is certainly the most reliable, although the other two make a slightly younger age likely. The suggested age is 2.5 to 3 years ± 12 months.

The sex of the dead child could not be established because of the young age.

The 63 element showed a rare variation in the form of two clearly developed additional cusps on the lingual side. The 53 element showed the same variation in a much less developed way. No other abnormalities or pathologies were observed.

Burial SAB92-B2

As with the above burial, the preservation of the skeletal remains of burial SAB92-B2 was good and bone conditions were similar. Even some growth plates of the metacarpals were present. The following measurements were taken:

Left humerus, maximum diaphysial length	115.6 mm
Right ulna, maximum diaphysial length	102.4 mm
Left ulna, maximum diaphysial length	102.0 mm
Left radius, maximum diaphysial length	89.9 mm
Right femur, maximum diaphysial length	155.3 mm
Left femur, maximum diaphysial length	155.0 mm
Left tibia, maximum diaphysial length	125.7 mm
Right fibula, maximum diaphysial length	120.8 mm
Left fibula, maximum diaphysial length	120.1 mm

Again, age was diagnosed firstly by means of tooth eruption. The elements 55 and 65 had not yet erupted, though their cusps already peaked over the rim of the mandibula. The elements 75 and 85 had clearly erupted, and so had the elements 53 and 63, although the latter two elements did not yet occlude. This suggests an age of 2 years ± 8 months. On the basis of the union of the spine, an age of about 2 to 3 years is likely. All spinal arches were completely closed, while no trace of union with the spinal bodies was found. Therefore, the result of the diagnosis by means of the tooth eruption seems appropriate, i.e. 2 years ± 8 months.

As with the former burial, the sex of the dead child could not be established because of the young age.

The left calcaneus showed some thickening on its lateral side, probably caused by periostitis or other prolonged periosteal reaction. The 54 element showed some calculus on the labial side. The sutura frontalis still persisted. No other abnormalities or pathologies were observed.

Burial SAB92-B3

In the fill of room 7, high above the floor, of the level 6 building V, the skeletal remains were found of two adults (burials SAB92-B3 and SAB92-B4), with the bones completely crushed and burnt.

The SAB92-B3 remains were all lying in anatomical order on the left side, with the legs tightly flexed and the head facing south. This makes it impossible for the bones to have been deposited after the fire, since at the temperatures concerned (see below) most if not all connection between the various bones would have been lost. In this respect it seems that either the body had already been deposited in the debris before the onset of the fire that devastated building V (which is highly unlikely in view of the stratigraphic and contextual evidence) or that this person fell down from the roof when building V collapsed in the fire. In the latter case, however, the clearly intentionally flexed position of the legs must have been fixed, either by a strong rigor mortis (which only occurs within a short period of time within the first three days after death) or by a bondage. Merely macerated corpses would be likely to have been broken into parts during the collapse of the building.

Burial SAB92-B3 consists of a partially preserved skeleton. Besides the highly fragmented skull, large parts of the left and right scapulae, the right humerus, the right ulna and radius, the left and right femora, the proximal joint of the right tibia and parts of the hands were found in room 7. Remains of the left foot were found in the adjacent room 8 and seem to have been in articulation with the other skeletal parts (rooms 7 and 8 are connected through a doorway). Of the spine only the axis is present and no ribs nor any part of the pelvis have been recovered. All bones are burnt and show a greyish-blue colour spread very regularly throughout the preserved parts. Only the dentition elements have a dark blueish-purple colour with almost black edges. All remains are brittle and light. The colour of the bones as well as that of the teeth indicates that these parts were exposed to a temperature between 500 and 600°C (stage III according to Wahl 1982). However, the extremely regular colouring of all bones suggests a very constant heating over a prolonged period of time, with no direct contact with the flames.

Some morphological features as well as metrical characteristics permit a sex diagnosis. The following scores were obtained using the methods recommended in *Homo*
30 (1979):

Right processus mastoideus	0 / -1
Right crista supramastoidea	-1
Relief of the os occipitale	0 / +1
Protuberantia occipitalis externa	-2
Glabella	-2
Arcus superciliaris	-1 / -2
Left angle of the mandibula	-1 / -2

This results in a total score of -1.058. The vertical diameter of the right caput
humeris measures 37 mm ± 1 mm. The horizontal diameter of the right caput
femoris measures 38.1 mm ± 0.5 mm. The morphological scores as well as the
metrical data, with the latter taking a first stage of shrinkage of about 1% into
account, lead to the conclusion that the skeletal remains are most likely of a woman.

Some indications for age at death can be found in the dentition, although all elements suffered considerably from the heat. The 28 element, being the only intact
one, shows an attrition of 4+ to 5 on the scale of Brothwell (1965). Other elements,
for as far as attrition could be determined, score around 4. Apart from the dentition,
a progressed fusion of the lambdoid suture was observed. Both the dental attrition
and the progressed fusion of at least part of the cranial sutures are indicative of an
age over 30 years.

No pathologies or abnormalities of any kind have been observed.

Burial SAB92-B4

The second skeleton found in room 7 of building V consists of large parts of the
skull, femora, tibiae, fibulae, patellae, humeri, ulnae, feet, hands, pelvis and some
ribs. Most, if not all, of the bones were lying in anatomical order; it was impossible
to determine articulation in the case of the upper half of the body, due to the high
fragmentation and the circumstances of deposition.

The bones are irregularly burnt. Most parts have a greyish-blue colour, indicating
that these parts were exposed to a temperature between 500 and 600°C (stage III
according to Wahl 1982), but some, especially the distal two-thirds of the humeri
and the lower arms, have a bright white colour with a yellowish-brown surface,
indicative of a higher temperature of 600 to 800 °C (Wahl's stage IV). In contrast,
the skull is hardly burnt at all, having a pale brown colour. The atlas shows some
stronger burning on its lateral sides, whereas the axis shows an extreme transition
from hardly burnt on its proximal side to strongly burnt (stage IV) on its distal side.
The sharp divisions between the colours suggests that the chest and parts of the arms
were directly exposed to the flames, whereas the skull and, most likely, most other

parts of the body must have been protected from direct contact with the flames by the surrounding building debris. In view of the above, any form of regular burial in room 7 can be excluded; this person (as B92-B3) must have fallen from the roof of building V when this structure collapsed.

The incompleteness of the skeletal remains makes a sex diagnosis problematic. Only two morphological features could be scored:

Left processus mastoideus	+1 / +2
Right margo supraorbitale	+1

The vertical diameter of the left caput femoris measures 43.7 mm. The gross appearance of the bones is masculine and contrasts strongly to skeleton B92-B3, as illustrated by two other measurements:

	B92-B3	B92-B4
Midshaft medial-lateral diameter of the femur	22.9 mm (left)	27.2 mm (right)
Medial-lateral size of the left trochlea tali	24.9 mm	28.0 mm

Although the evidence is poor, I suggest that skeleton B92-B4 is that of a male.

No elements of the dentition were found. The maxillae are completely absent. The remaining parts of the mandibula show significant, if not total, ante mortem loss of teeth. Loss of the elements 31, 32, 41, 42, 43, 44, 46 and 47 is certain. The elements 33, 34, 45 and 48 are missing, too, but in these cases the alveolars show minor alterations. No alveolars are present of the remaining elements. The alveolar of the 45 element shows a small but clear apical abscess.

The lambdoid and sagittal suture show progressed fusion. This makes an age at death of over 30 years likely.

Miscellaneous

In addition to the above, some isolated human skeletal remains (both belonging to adults and children) appeared as stray finds mainly in open areas. These finds suggest that repeatedly human burials have been disturbed during construction works or other domestic activities.

Between the level 6 ovens CR and CS a right femur measuring 82.7 mm ± 1 mm was found as well as four metacarpals, nine phalanges, a large part of a fibula and two skull fragments, all belonging to a newly-born child. Most likely, this child's grave was largely destroyed when the ovens were constructed.

CHAPTER 3

THE PREHISTORIC POTTERY

Marie Le Mière and Olivier Nieuwenhuyse

Introduction

This chapter intends to give a detailed account of the prehistoric pottery found on the southeastern part of Tell Sabi Abyad during the 1988-1993 seasons of excavation. Beforehand, it is stressed that this study is not the final publication of the Sabi Abyad ceramics but an extensive preliminary report. A vast amount of pottery from various squares and levels awaits further analysis.

This study adds to the report on the ceramics of the 1986 campaign (Akkermans 1989d). However, in comparison to the material available after the first season, we are now dealing with an almost completely new corpus of ceramics: new from a quantitative point of view since over 70,000 pieces of pottery have been found during the 1988 to 1993 campaigns; new from a chronological point of view since pottery is now available from levels not reached before; new also from a contextual point of view since ceramics are now available from both a deep sounding and broad horizontal exposures, including complete house plans.

Originally, the pottery from the first season of excavation was considered to belong to two different periods, viz. the 'Late Neolithic', characterised by 'coarsely made and undecorated ceramics' (ibid.:77), and the 'Early Halaf', characterised by 'the mass appearance of well-made painted pottery' (ibid.). Both periods were thought to be separated by a hiatus in settlement, although there were already some hints towards a continuous development with the Halaf emerging 'out of an earlier locally founded Neolithic tradition' (ibid.:140). However, the quantity of pottery available for analysis at that time was simply too small to confirm this continuity with certainty. The continuous sequence, firmly documented in subsequent seasons of excavation (see chapter 2), has first been emphasised in Akkermans' 1990 thesis (cf. Akkermans 1993). This study, however, mainly dealt with the more general problems of the Halaf and not specifically with ceramics. Moreover, up to the 1988 season of excavation, the emphasis of research at Sabi Abyad was mainly upon the Halaf period (e.g. Akkermans and Le Mière 1992), with only little attention given to the preceding period. More recently, however, research interests have shifted to a considerable extent towards this Pre-Halaf period; the 1991-1993 seasons of excavations have yielded a detailed insight in the earliest levels of occupation at the site and considerably widened our perspective of analysis and interpretation.

The aims of the present report are threefold, viz. (a) to give an account of this new material, (b) to establish the chronological positioning of the ceramics, in both local terms and in a wider, regional and interregional framework, and (c) to contribute to a better understanding of the stratigraphic sequence.[1] The latter presents two major problems: first, the relationship between the lowest levels 11 and 10 in the deep sounding P15 is far from clear; actually, a hiatus in occupation between both levels is not excluded (see chapter 2); second, the question of whether our levels 6 to 4 represent a real transition from a ceramic point of view between the Pre-Halaf levels 11-7 and the Early Halaf levels 3-1. To answer this last question, the so-called Transitional levels 6-4 have been studied from both the Pre-Halaf (by M. Le Mière) and the Halaf point of view (by O. Nieuwenhuyse), i.e. as representing a possible further development of the Pre-Halaf ceramic tradition and as representing a possible first stage or 'announcement' of the Halaf pottery tradition.

Processing of the ceramics

Three steps in the processing of the pottery are distinguished, viz. (1) sorting and counting of the pottery bulk into broad categories, (2) detailed description of the diagnostic ceramics, and (3) physicochemical analysis of a sample of the diagnostic pottery.

Sorting and counting of the pottery bulk. All pottery was sorted and counted into broad categories, in order to come to a basic record of all sherds (the 'undiagnostic' sherds are subsequently discarded; see below) and to receive a quick, first overview of the material in the field. Various categories were established on the basis of easily identifiable criteria (or combinations of them) such as the presence or absence of plant inclusions, painting, burnishing, slip, etc. This ordering proceeded in a somewhat 'opportunistic' way: the various criteria were not all systematically identified and applied from the beginning but some were recognised as such in the course of processing. Consequently, it is stressed that these broad categories are provisional, to be regrouped more precisely at a later stage of the analysis.

All ceramics were sorted into diagnostic sherds (i.e. rims, bases, handles, spouts and decorated body sherds) and undecorated body sherds. Non-descript body sherds that did not fit any of the diagnostic sherds were discarded; both the Standard Ware and the Halaf Fine Ware (which can easily and unambiguously be sorted) were found in such large quantities that the diagnostic sherds alone provided the complete range of variability within these ware categories. In the case of other wares, however, the actual number of sherds was much more restricted and consequently (in order to come to a sample as large as possible) all sherds were included in further analysis. For this reason, the amount of sherds used for the description of, for example,

---

[1]   It is stressed again that the present study is an interim report, not aiming at fullness; further research will include spatial distribution, systematic decoration analysis, specific technical aspects related to the use of the pottery, study of the circulation and production of pottery both in and outside the Balikh valley, etc.

technological aspects may be very different from the one used to describe, for example, shape (see below).[2]

Detailed description of the diagnostic ceramics. All diagnostics were described in detail; no selection has been carried out so far (despite the occasionally extremely large samples). This detailed analysis is far from completed at present (below it will be stated precisely which part of the material has been taken into consideration). Beforehand, it is pointed out that the pottery from the Pre-Halaf levels 11-7 differs in many respects (technological, typological, decorative) from that of the later, Early Halaf strata of occupation 3-1; the Sabi Abyad sequence shows the development of pottery manufacture from a rather new technique, associated with certain technological and typological restrictions, into a very sophisticated and common craft. Although the main questions are the same per period, it is clear that each period introduces specific items and as such requires a different approach and way of description. The intermittent Transitional period (levels 6-4) has basically yielded two ceramic assemblages, one consisting of pottery closely resembling that of the lower levels, the other consisting of ceramics newly introduced and strongly associated with those found in the topmost Halaf strata. For matters of convenience, the former is described according to the system used for the Pre-Halaf pottery, the latter according to the system used for the Halaf ceramics. Every effort has been made to correlate both approaches for comparative purposes.

A physicochemical analysis of a sample of the diagnostic pottery. This research, carried out in the 'Laboratoire de Céramologie de Lyon', mainly comprises an analysis of the chemical composition of the ceramics and the measurement of their firing temperatures and conditions (Le Mière and Picon, in prep.). This third step contributes to the identification of various wares and their origin, either local or foreign. The latter allows an investigation of the intra and extra-regional relationships of Sabi Abyad and the organisation of production, including specialisation and related social structures. In addition, the physicochemical analyses serve many other purposes, notably the study of the choice of clay and of the adaptation of firing to these clays in relationship to the intended use of the pottery. Below some of the results of the analyses (which are still in process) will be presented.

Levels 11 to 7: The Balikh II or Pre-Halaf Period

Introduction

The Balikh II or Pre-Halaf pottery comes from levels 11 to 7, which have each been unearthed over an area of 4.50×2 m in trench P15 exclusively (see chapter 2).[3]

---

[2] An exception is the level 11 pottery which at first sight seems to be wholly different from that found in the other levels and of which some undiagnostic coarse sherds have been included in the description.
[3] Actually, level 7 has been reached over a very limited area also in squares P14, Q15, P12, Q14 and R14; however, these squares have not yielded any homogeneous ceramic assemblage so far.

In total, ca. 13,600 sherds have been retrieved from these levels; no complete vessel has been found. Table 3.1 gives the total amount of sherds and the number of diagnostic sherds used in this study per level (the analysis comprises only ceramics which can be ascribed to a specific level with certainty).[4] Only in the case of level 10, analysis proceeded per stratum (10B and 10A) in order to investigate the precise nature of the stratum 10B sherd pavement, made of re-used sherds of as yet puzzling provenance. Detailed comparison of the various layers of occupation is somewhat hampered by the restricted sample size of stratum 10A of level 10 and level 9 (about 100 sherds each). These small samples also make it difficult to base the analysis of the Pre-Halaf period primarily on rim sherds (see table 3.1; this in contrast with the Halaf period).

	Level 11	Stratum 10B	Stratum 10A	Level 9	Level 8	Level 7	Pre-Halaf period
Total amount of sherds	2440	1762	375	368	3186	1087	9218
Studied sherds	468	281	110	91	759	292	2001
Studied rims	209	118	43	41	315	140	866

Table 3.1. Amount of Pre-Halaf pottery collected and studied per level or stratum.

The Balikh II pottery is mainly characterised by simplicity, irregularity and unevenness; standardisation is hardly perceptible. Moreover, the sample consists of sherds only, without any complete vessels and hardly any reconstructable profiles. In this respect, description often has to proceed at a very elementary level. The system of description used for the pottery of the Pre-Halaf period and for the 'Pre-Halaf' wares of the Transitional levels is given in table 3.2 (cf. Le Mière 1986). The intrinsic traits (Gardin 1979:123) are either physical (condition, fabric, surface), geometric (shape, dimensions) or semiotic (decoration) in nature. The extrinsic characteristics concern the spatial distribution and chronological positioning of the pottery. Regarding the aims of the present study (see above), it is evident that we will have to restrict ourselves; for each trait the modalities, significant either by themselves or in combination with another feature, will be presented and subsequently attention will focus on those criteria which contribute to our goals.

---

[4] Intervals of confidence have been systematically calculated for every percentage and, in the case of dimensions, for every mean in order to check the validity of comparisons; however, the tables do not present these intervals for matters of convenience.

1 – Condition	a – Presence/absence of Damaging		
	b – Cause	* Concretion	
		* "Rolling"	
2 – Paste	a – Inclusions	* Vegetal	• Size (small, large, very large)[1]
			• Quantity (rare, abundant, very abundant)
		* Mineral	• Size (small, medium, large, very large)[2]
			• Quantity (rare, abundant, very abundant)
			• Colour (black, grey, red, white)
	b – Coulour	* Tone (black, grey, brown, buff, red/pink, light cream	
		* Homogeneity	• Only the core
			• The whole thickness
3 – Surface	a – Treatment	* Type	• None
			• Smoothing[3]
			• Burnishing[4]
			• Slip[5]
			• Burnished slip
		* Position	• On the whole vessel
			• Rim
			• Neck
			• Body
			• Base
		* Traces of this treatment	
	b – Colour	* See colour of the paste	
	c – Colour of the slip	* Red	
		* Brown	
		* Light cream	

[1] Small: diameter cannot be messured; very large: diameter > 0.2-0.3 mm.
[2] Small: unvisible; medium: < 0.5 mm; large: 0.5 mm < × < 1 mm; very large: > 1 mm.
[3] Rice, 1987, 138.
[4] Rice, 1987, 138.
[5] Rice, 1987, 149.

Table 3.2a. System of description of the pottery.

	d – Some specific
	   elements
		* Irregularity of
		  the surface
		* Cracks on the
		  surface		

	e – Plaster	* White plaster
		* Black plaster
		  (Bitumen or soot)
		* Black traces
		  (idem)		

4 – Measurements	a – Thickness	* Body * Carination * Base		
	b – Height	* Body * Neck * Rim (when distinct) * Pedestal		
	c – Diameter	* Rim * Maximum * Base		
	d – Angle of opening			
5 – Shape (Fig. ??)	a – Section of the vessel	* Round * Quadrangular * Oval		
	b – Base	* Surface	• Convexe • Flat • Concave	
		* Joining with horizontal	• Rounded (without CP[1]) • Angular (1 CP) • Annular (2 CP)	

		* Lower part of
		  the body
			• Shape	• Undistinct
				  base[2]
				• Distinct
				  base[3]

			• Direction	• Closed • Vertical • Open
	c – Body	* Direction	• Closed • Vertical • Open	

[1] CP: *Corner Point*; IP: *Inflexion Point*; see *characteristic points* in Shepard, 1956, p. 226.
[2] Neither IP[1] nor CP determining the limit between base and lower part of the body.
[3] An IP or a CP determine the limit between base and lower part of the body.

Table 3.2b. System of description of the pottery.

		* Carination	
		* Shape[1]	• Convex
			• Straight
			• Concave
		* Neck • Direction	• Closed
			• Vertical
			• Open
		• Shape	• Convex
			• Straight
			• Open
		* Rim • Sides	• Direct[2]
			• Undistinct[3]
			• Distinct[4]
		• Joining with horizontal	• Rounded (no CP)
			• Sharp (1 CP)
			• Flat (2 CP)
	d – Handles	* Plastic band	
		* Simple handle[5] • Direction	• Vertical
			• Horizontal (Ledge handle)
		• Shape	• Unpierced
			• Pierced
		* Loop handle[6] • Direction	• Vertical
			• Horizontal
	e – Husking-trays	* With grooves	
		* With holes	
6 – Decoration	a – Pattern-burnishing		
	b – Impressions		
	c – Incisions		
	d – Incrustations		
	e – Painting		
	f – *Appliqué*		

[1] Shape of the upper and of the lower part of the body in the case of a carination.
[2] Without any changing of thickness
[3] With a changing of thickness, without an IP or a CP determining this changing.
[4] With changing of thickness, with an IP or a CP determining this changing.
[5] One point of fixing on the vessel.
[6] Two points of fixing on the vessel.

Table 3.2c. System of description of the pottery.

Condition of the pottery

As a whole, the pottery material from the Pre-Halaf levels is in a reasonably good condition (cf. table 3.3). An exception, however, are the ceramics from the lower level 11 and stratum 10B of level 10, which are extremely weathered: almost 90% of the sherds show some sort of damage, largely preventing the identification of features like surface treatment or even rim orientation. Moreover, most sherds are 'rolled', pointing towards secondary deposition. The latter is obvious in the case of the stratum 10B sherd pavement but in the case of level 11, which lacks architectural features, it raises some questions: what is the precise nature of this level? Does level 11 truly represent an occupation level or is it merely a debris accumulation? Is there a hiatus between levels 11 and 10 (see also chapter 2)?

	Level 11	Stratum 10B	Stratum 10A	Level 9	Level 8	Level 7
No damaging	5.1%	6.4%	60.0%	57.1%	58.8%	64.4%
Total of sherds	468	281	110	91	759	292

Table 3.3. Pre-Halaf pottery — condition of the pottery per level or stratum.

Technological characteristics

Before presenting the bulk of the levels 11-7 ceramics, attention is drawn to three wares which differ from this bulk in terms of fabric and surface treatment, viz. Dark-Faced Burnished Ware, Grey-Black Ware and Mineral Coarse Ware. Each of these categories is defined by a specific set of technological traits. However, this set of traits cannot always be used in too strict a manner: some variability is usual.

Dark-Faced Burnished Ware

Dark-Faced Burnished Ware is characterised by the combined occurrence of (1) large (≥ 1 mm and often ≥ 2 mm) and mainly black mineral inclusions (plant temper[5] is wholly absent) in large quantities, and (2) the colour of the vessel surface and the fabric which varies from red to black but which is mainly chocolate brown or dark grey. Actually, Dark-Faced Burnished Ware is not always as dark as its name

---

[5] Generally, the term 'inclusions' is preferred instead of 'temper' since the latter implies both that these inclusions were added to the clay and that this was done to temper the clay. Actually, in the case of mineral inclusions it is often difficult to distinguish between added and natural inclusions; however, in the case of plant inclusions it is obvious that these must have been added deliberately, most likely for tempering purposes.

implies; moreover, it was not darkened on purpose but received its colour as a result of the kind of clay used for manufacture. Actually, the term Dark-Faced Burnished Ware would better fit our group of Grey-Black Ware (see below) but here we will stick to the term for matters of convenience: unquestionably our Dark-Faced Burnished Ware is the same as the Levantine Dark-Faced Burnished Ware first described by Braidwood and Braidwood (1960:49),[6] found in the Amuq and at many sites elsewhere in northern Syria and Cilicia, e.g. Ras Shamra, Mersin and Sakçe Gözü. Dark-Faced Burnished Ware must have been an import product at Sabi Abyad, possibly brought in from these areas in the west (Le Mière 1989a:234;[7] Le Mière and Picon 1987:136; Le Mière and Picon, in prep.).

The Sabi Abyad Dark-Faced Burnished Ware is rather thin-walled (mean thickness= 7.2 mm, standard deviation= 1.6). About one-fourth of the sherds show black traces (soot or bitumen) on the outer or inner surface. Dark-Faced Burnished Ware is represented by 153 sherds in the Pre-Halaf levels (table 3.4). So far, only one Dark-Faced Burnished-Ware sherd has been found in the lowest level 11; it is not excluded that this fragment is intrusive here. The subsequent levels 10 and 9 have each yielded a small percentage of Dark-Faced Burnished Ware but from level 8 onwards it significantly increased in importance (table 3.4).

	Level 11	Stratum 10B	Stratum 10A	Level 9	Level 8	Level 7	Pre-Halaf period
Dark-Faced Burnished Ware	1 (0.2%)	4 (1.4%)	10 (9.1%)	6 (6.6%)	86 (11.3%)	46 (15.8%)	153
Grey-Black Ware	–	2 (0.7%)	6 (5.5%)	–	32 (4.2%)	10 (3.4%)	50
Mineral Coarse Ware	1 (0.2%)	3 (1.1%)	1 (0.9%)	2 (2.2%)	12 (1.6%)	3 (1%)	22
Standard Ware	466 (99.6%)	272 (96.8%)	93 (84.5%)	83 (91.2%)	629 (82.9%)	233 (79.8%)	1776
Total of sherds	468 (100%)	281 (100%)	110 (100%)	91 (100%)	759 (100%)	292 (100%)	2001

Table 3.4. Pre-Halaf pottery — amounts of sherds per level or stratum.

[6] Actually, the description by the Braidwoods does not exactly fit Matson's description on the same page; perhaps one has to reckon with the presence of both Dark-Faced Burnished Ware and Grey-Black Ware in the Amuq. Here the description by the Braidwoods is used for matters of convenience.
[7] In this report, Dark-Faced Burnished Ware was not yet recognised as a separate ware at Sabi Abyad but included in the group of Grey-Black Ware (cf. Akkermans 1989d:117).

Grey-Black Ware

This kind of pottery is defined by the combined occurrence of (1) the grey or (rarely) black surface colour, (2) the burnishing of the vessel surface, (3) the buff or light brown colour of the fabric (when oxidised) and (4) the very fine fabric, with mineral inclusions virtually always smaller than 0.5 mm (95% of all sherds) and plant inclusions smaller than 1 mm in diameter; the plant inclusions, moreover, appear in restricted quantities. About 80% of the Grey-Black Ware has these plant inclusions. In contrast to Dark-Faced Burnished Ware, the characteristic dark colour of Grey-Black Ware is clearly intentionnally produced and not due to the type of clay used in manufacturing (which in this case is highly calcareous; Le Mière and Picon, in prep.).

The wall thickness is rather restricted, with an average of 7.4 mm (std= 2.2). Grey-Black Ware is rare in the Pre-Halaf levels: in total, only 50 sherds were found (table 3.4). None appeared in levels 11 and 9 (their absence in level 9 may be related to the small overall sample size but in the case of level 11 other variables may be at work; see the conclusions below).

Mineral Coarse Ware

This pottery is characterised by (1) large (between 1 and 2 mm) mineral inclusions only, usually occurring in large quantities, sharply angled (due to crushing) and whitish or grey (glimmering) coloured, and (2) the burnishing of the vessel surface. Commonly, ceramics exclusively containing mineral inclusions are considered to represent 'fine ware' (see below) but in this case the average wall thickness is clearly much higher (m= 12.8 mm, std= 3.2) than that of all other wares, hence the name Mineral 'Coarse' Ware. The colour of the pottery widely varies from buff to grey.

About one-third of the sherds showed black traces (soot or bitumen) on their outer and/or inner surfaces. These black traces, in association with the high quantities of mineral inclusions of more or less the same size (very often calcite) and the common occurrence of closed vessel shapes[8] and lugs, may suggest that this kind of pottery served for cooking (Le Mière and Picon 1994; Le Mière and Picon, in prep.).

So far, Mineral Coarse Ware has appeared in minute quantities in the Pre-Halaf levels: only 22 sherds were found (table 3.4). One (extremely small) specimen was found in the lowest level 11 and may be intrusive here. It seems clear that the very restricted sample of Mineral Coarse Ware per level prevents any definite statement about the earliest appearance of this pottery at Sabi Abyad.

---

[8] Actually, the vessel shape is largely inferred from Mineral Coarse Ware ceramics from the Transitional levels; the Pre-Halaf layers yielded only very few Mineral Coarse Ware and, consequently, hardly any information on shape.

Standard Ware

Standard Ware does not represent a homogeneous ware but seems to consist of a variety of ceramic groups which cannot yet be identified with certainty. In this respect, Standard Ware is not a ware in the proper sense of the word. It includes all ceramics except the three wares earlier defined.

General description. The Standard Ware sample consists of 1774 sherds. Over 95% of these ceramics contain plant inclusions (table 3.5). About 30% shows small plant inclusions. Only very few sherds (1.2%) show very large plant inclusions. Visible mineral inclusions (table 3.6) occur in very restricted quantities (ca. 10% of all sherds). The main surface colours (table 3.7) are buff (ca. 60%) and reddish-pink (37%). About half of the ceramics have a grey core, not surprising given the proportion of plant inclusions (plant inclusions are the main cause of limited reoxydation; in the case of ceramics without plant inclusions only one-quarter shows a grey core). Surface treatment (table 3.8) mainly consists of burnishing (42%) and smoothening (38%).[9] Red or (very occasionally) brown-slipping is rather commonly found as well (17%).

In general, the presence or absence of plant inclusions is the first criterium used in the sorting, simply because it is the easiest to recognise and because it is generally the most significant trait. However, in the case of the Balikh II pottery it hardly

	Level 11	Stratum 10B	Stratum 10A	Level 9	Level 8	Level 7	Pre-Halaf period
No plant inclusions	4.9%	3.0%	2.2%	1.2%	3.2%	3.9%	3.6%
Small plant inclusions	22.6%	50.9%	20.4%	38.6%	39.0%	22.3%	33.3%
Large plant inclusions	68.2%	46.1%	77.4%	60.2%	57.7%	73.8%	62.0%
Very large plant inclusions	4.3%	–	–	–	0.2%	–	1.2%
Total of sherds	465	271	93	83	629	233	1774

Table 3.5. Pre-Halaf pottery — amount and size of plant inclusions of Standard Ware per level or stratum.

[9] These percentages are based only on ceramics with recognisable surface treatment.

	Level 11	Stratum 10B	Stratum 10A	Level 9	Level 8	Level 7	Pre-Halaf period
Small	89.8%	96.7%	96.8%	96.3%	89.5%	84.5%	90.7%
Medium	8.7%	2.6%	3.2%	–	7.3%	9.4%	6.7%
Large	1.3%	0.4%	–	3.7%	2.1%	4.3%	1.9%
Very large	0.2%	0.4%	–	–	1.1%	1.7%	0.7%
Total of sherds	460	272	93	82	626	233	1766

Table 3.6. Pre-Halaf pottery — size of mineral inclusions of Standard Ware per level or stratum.

serves as a useful criterium since only 4% of the material does not contain any plant inclusions (table 3.5). Commonly, the presence of plant inclusions is used to separate 'coarse ware' from 'fine ware' but atlhough it must be recognised that it cannot always be used as such. For example, plant-tempered ceramics are indeed part of our Grey-Black Ware, yet the latter is definitely a fine ware. In this respect one may wonder whether the low percentage of ceramics without plant inclusions simply means that 'fine ware' is poorly represented in the earliest levels at Sabi Abyad or that it occurs in another form in these layers.

Beside the mere presence or absence of plant inclusions, the main features used in the sorting of the pottery were (1) the size and quantity of plant inclusions,[10] (2) the size and quantity of mineral inclusions, (3) the surface treatment and (4) the thickness of the fabric (the colour of surfaces and fabric seems to be of no significance at this stage of the analysis). When analysing these traits, either separately or in combination, it appears that none is really a determinant in terms of recognition and definition of specific wares within the Standard Ware.

Significant technological features. The size of the mineral inclusions is associated with the presence or absence of plant inclusions: hardly 10% of the plant-tempered sherds contain visible mineral inclusions as well, whereas about 60% of the pottery without plant material show visible mineral inclusions. Actually, our group of ceramics with both rare and small plant inclusions shows a similar picture. In the case of the pottery without plant temper, the size of the mineral inclusions is rather fine, i.e. less than 1 mm in diameter (hardly 2% of the pottery contains larger inclusions). In contrast, the vast majority (over 90%) of our Dark-Faced Burnished Ware

---

[10] Both size and quantity of plant inclusions have been estimated; their relevance is checked in association with other ceramic traits.

	Level 11	Stratum 10B	Stratum 10A	Level 9	Level 8	Level 7	Pre-Halaf period
Black	–	–	–	–	0.3%	2.1%	0.5%
Grey	1.3%	1.5%	2.2%	1.2%	2.2%	1.7%	1.7%
Brown	1.3%	1.1%	3.2%	4.9%	3%	1.3%	2.1%
Buff	57.3%	55.5%	62.4%	58.5%	60.7%	55.4%	58.3%
Red/pink	40.1%	41.9%	32.3%	35.4%	33.8%	39.5%	37.4%
Total of sherds	466	272	93	82	628	233	1774

Table 3.7. Pre-Halaf pottery — surface colour of Standard Ware per level or stratum.

	Level 11	Stratum 10B	Stratum 10A	Level 9	Level 8	Level 7	Pre-Halaf period
None	1.5%	4.9%	4.7%	6.3%	2.7%	0.9%	2.8%
Smoothing	65.7%	44.0%	28.2%	35%	27.1%	35.4%	38.1%
Burnishing	30.6%	37.7%	57.6%	33.8%	48.2%	43.2%	42.3%
Slipping	2.2%	15.4%	10.6%	25%	22.1%	20.5%	16.8%
Total of sherds	268	182	86	80	602	229	1447

Table 3.8. Pre-Halaf pottery — surface treatment of Standard Ware per level or stratum.

and Mineral Coarse Ware, likewise wares without plant inclusions, contains mineral inclusions larger than 1 mm.

Another link seems to exist between presence/absence of plant inclusions and wall thickness: the mean thickness of sherds without plant inclusions is much lower (m= 8.4 mm, std= 2.4) than that of sherds with plant inclusions (m= 11.7 mm, std= 3.8). The size of the plant inclusions evidently contributes to the thickness of the sherds: the mean thickness of ceramics with small plant inclusions is 9.8 mm (std= 2.6), whereas the mean thickness in the case of large plant inclusions is 12.7 mm (std= 4). Pottery with very large plant inclusions has a mean thickness of 14.4 mm (std= 3.4). The overall density of plant inclusions, however, does not seem to affect the thickness of the pottery.

There seems to be a clear relationship between both the presence and size of plant inclusions and surface treatment. It appears that about 80% of the slipped ceramics contain plant inclusions of small size (however, the other way round it appears that only one-third of the ceramics with small plant inclusions is slipped). Burnished pottery, too, contains a rather high percentage of small-plant inclusions (20%), whereas in the case of smoothened sherds this number is considerably lower (10%). Actually, burnishing is also slightly more common than smoothening in the case of pottery without plant inclusions (11% and 7%, respectively).

Surface treatment is also related to the thickness of the pottery. First, it has been found that the mean thickness of burnished sherds is significantly smaller (m= 11 mm, std= 3.1) than that of smoothened sherds (m= 12.8 mm, std= 4.4). Second, it appears that the mean thickness of slipped sherds is slightly smaller than that of the remaining unslipped sherds with small plant inclusions. Both features seem to be related to aspects of 'fineness' of certain surface treatments.

Evolution of technological features. The proportions of ceramics with or without plant inclusions remain more or less equal throughout the Pre-Halaf period. However, in the case of plant-tempered pottery, the size of the inclusions does show certain trends (table 3.5). Pottery with very large plant inclusions has been found exclusively in the lowest level 11. Interestingly, the stratum 10B (level 10) sherd pavement consisted of a rather high number of sherds with small plant inclusions, i.e. about 50%, whereas in level 11 and stratum 10A it was only about 20%. Apparently, the pottery used for this pavement seems to have been selectively chosen. In the subsequent levels 9 and 8 the amount of ceramics with small plant inclusions increases significantly to about 35-40%, after which it decreases to 20% in level 7.

The overall quantity of plant inclusions, whether rare (ca. 10%) or very abundant (5%), does not show any noticeable change in the course of time.[11]

Analysis of the kinds of surface treatment (table 3.8) is strongly affected by the condition of the sherds, as e.g. clearly shown by the large percentage of ceramics with non-recognisable surface treatment in level 11 and stratum 10B of level 10, each characterised by strongly weathered assemblages. Smoothened ceramics appear in level 11 and stratum 10B in quantities more or less comparable to the other levels, i.e. about 25-35%. Burnished pottery, however, has been found in much smaller quantities in the lower than in the upper layers, perhaps due to the extreme weathering of the pottery in these lowest levels (in addition, small sample sizes may have affected the distribution of burnished pottery as well; cf. table 3.8). Finally, slipped pottery is rarely found in level 11 (1%) but rather common in the subsequent strata 10B-A (10%); apparently, in contrast with burnishing, slipped surfaces can be

---

[11] However, ceramics with very large numbers of plant inclusions seem to be absent from level 7 for reasons not yet clear.

much easier recognised despite the weathering. In this respect, the low percentage of slipped pottery in level 11 seems to be rather significant. In the subsequent levels 9 to 7 it increases to about 20%.

Any trends in sherd thickness throughout the ceramic sequence can hardly be considered significant, since thickness seems to depend largely on the presence/absence of plant inclusions or their size.

Shape

The shape analysis is based on all diagnostic ceramics found in levels 11-7, i.e. those of Standard Ware and those of the three wares earlier distinguished (Dark-Faced Burnished Ware, Grey-Black Ware and Mineral Coarse Ware).

About 1380 sherds, including only ten complete profiles, give some clues about the original vessel shape. Unfortunately, most sherds are rather small and standardisation is largely absent. In this respect, an analysis of shape will only be possible by studying element by element.

General description. A very small number of vessels (n= 16) seems to have had an oval shape but, of course, the generally small size of the sherds may easily prevent us from recognising more sherds as being originally oval in shape.

So far, 340 sherds give some clues as to the direction of the rim (table 3.9): about half is open (fig. 3.2, nos. 13-20), one-third is vertical (fig. 3.2, nos. 6-12) and only 16% is closed (fig. 3.2, nos. 1-5). Rims are extremely monotonous and in most cases indistinct (95%) and simply rounded (97%). Only very few specimens (4.5%) show some sort of elaboration. Rim diameters could be established in 175 cases, and vary between 3 and 35 cm (m= 18.3 cm, std= 6.8). Necks (table 3.10), ranging in diameter between 7 and 30 cm, have been found in rather large numbers (n= 287) but almost half of these merely consist of body fragments (i.e. the very beginning at the junction of neck and shoulder) without any indication of direction or shape. The most common directions are opened or vertical (a few closed necks have been found as well), whereas the most common shapes are concave or straight (in addition, some convex ones have been found). There appears to be no preferential combination of these two characteristics.

The shape of the body is in most cases convex (88%) or, to a much lesser extent, straight (10%) or, very rarely, concave (2%). Only very few sherds (n= 34) gave evidence of some sort of carination (table 3.11).

Bases (n= 298) are generally simple, flat (less than 1% is concave) and rounded (without an angular point; less than 5% is angular). Only a few distinct bases have been found (14%). Convex bases were recognised only twice with certainty. The base diameter, measurable in 21 cases only, varies between 4 and 28 cm (m= 11.2 cm, std= 6.0).

Finally, handles mainly consist of pierced handles and ledge handles (n= 52) but in addition one plastic band and one loop handle has been recorded (table 3.12).

	Level 11	Stratum 10B	Stratum 10A	Level 9	Level 8	Level 7	Pre-Halaf period
Closed	10	1	–	2	23	19	55 (16.2%)
Vertical	11	14	7	8	57	33	130(38.2%)
Opened	20	13	5	7	73	37	155(45.6%)
Total of sherds	41	28	12	17	153	89	340

Table 3.9. Pre-Halaf pottery — direction of body sherds per level or stratum.

	Level 11	Stratum 10B	Stratum 10A	Level 9	Level 8	Level 7	Pre-Halaf period
Necks	19	48	33	20	124	43	287

Table 3.10. Pre-Halaf pottery — number of necks per level or stratum.

	Level 11	Stratum 10B	Stratum 10A	Level 9	Level 8	Level 7	Pre-Halaf period
Carinations	2	1	–	1	13	17	34

Table 3.11. Pre-Halaf pottery — number of carinated sherds per level or stratum.

	Level 11	Stratum 10B	Stratum 10A	Level 9	Level 8	Level 7	Pre-Halaf period
Plastic band	1	–	–	–	–	–	–
Simple handles	47	3	–	–	2	–	–
Loop handle	1	–	–	–	–	–	–

Table 3.12. Pre-Halaf pottery — number of handles per level or stratum.

In conclusion, it appears that the Pre-Halaf shapes are rather simple and for the main part of the assemblage rather monotonous.

Links between shape and technological traits. Distinct bases have mainly been found in association with ceramics containing large plant inclusions and smoothened surfaces. These two groups of ceramics generally have the thickest vessel wall as well. Therefore it seems that this base feature should probably not be considered as a mark of elaboration but should more likely be related to some technological problem in pottery manufacture.

Rim sherds containing small plant inclusions are less often closed and more often vertically oriented than the rest. Smoothened sherds are more closed than burnished or slipped ones.

Necks are often associated with the group of ceramics without plant inclusions, whereas the group with large plant inclusions shows necks to a lesser extent. No connection has been found between necks and some specific surface treatment. Remarkably, our group of Dark-Faced Burnished Ware ceramics has yielded a very large number of necks (30 necks versus only two rims associated with non-collared vessels). Indeed, the overall sample size is restricted but nevertheless this figure seems to be highly significant. The large number of necks, in combination with the usually very shallow curve of the body sherds, suggests that rather large jars with distinct necks are a characteristic feature of Dark-Faced Burnished Ware.

Carinated pottery, found in very small quantities, rarely contains large plant inclusions and is rarely smoothened. Usually, the pottery is rather thin-walled (mean thickness: 9.3 cm). Attention is drawn to the three Dark-Faced Burnished Ware and three Grey-Black Ware sherds found among the very small sample of carinated ceramics.

As for the handles, it appears that the unique plastic band belongs to a smoothened sherd with large plant inclusions. The unique loop handle is plant-tempered as well. Concerning the pierced handles and ledge handles, it has been found that most contain large plant inclusions and occasionally even very large plant inclusions. None of them appeared in association with burnishing or slipping. Two specimens belong to our category of Mineral Coarse Ware.

Special attention is drawn to the so-called husking trays, of which 65 fragments have been found in the Pre-Halaf levels (table 3.13). These vessels are characterised by bases which are either finger-impressed (n= 45) or ridged (n= 7). The interior walls are sometimes ridged as well (n= 13). All husking trays are plant-tempered (the inclusions are generally large in size). The trays are commonly smoothened (n= 24); burnished husking trays were rarely found (n= 2). Very little can be said about the shape of the trays: three specimens have an oval shape, whereas the bases are flat and indistinct. The mean base thickness of husking trays is 26.9 mm (std= 4.2); the trays have much thicker bases than the other ceramics, which have a mean base thickness of 16 mm (std= 6.7).

	Level 11	Stratum 10B	Stratum 10A	Level 9	Level 8	Level 7	Pre-Halaf period
Finger impressed	–	19	2	4	17	3	45
Ridged	–	2	–	–	2	3	7
Ridged rims	1	4	1	1	6	–	13

Table 3.13. Pre-Halaf pottery — number of husking trays per level or stratum.

Finally, it repeatedly appears, particularly in the case of Dark-Faced Burnished Ware, that the upper part or the neck of some collared vessels has been sawn off and removed; the edge has subsequently been smoothened in order to re-use these vessels as closed holemouth pots.

Evolution of shape. The entire repertory of Balikh II vessel shapes is already present in level 11, with the exception of the flat rims which first appear in level 10 and the direct rims which first appear in level 8 (and are very rare anyway). Three variables of shape show some development in the course of time. First, carinated ceramics are found in small quantities already in level 11 but most (50%) occur in level 7. Second, vessels with clear necks are present in small quantities (ca. 5%) in level 11 but increase significantly in importance in level 10 (up to 20%). The amount of collared ceramics remains more or less equal up to level 7. Third, handles are found exclusively in level 11, except for three specimens found in stratum 10B of level 10 and two specimens in level 8.

Decoration

In total, 183 Balikh II sherds are decorated. Almost one-third of these belong to our category of Dark-Faced Burnished Ware (n= 51); when excluding this group from tabulation, it appears that 7.3% of the Standard Ware from levels 11-7 carries some kind of decoration (table 3.14).[12] The techniques of decoration vary widely and include painting, *appliqué*, incision, impression and pattern-burnishing. Painting occurs most often, whereas pattern-burnishing is rarely found. Motives are generally very simple and geometric (interestingly, crosshatching, one of the most common designs in the Transitional and Early Halaf periods, does not yet appear).

---

[12] Actually, this proportion is lower because not all body sherds have been included in the calculation (this in contrast with Dark-Faced Burnished Ware). When including the body sherds, the overall percentage of decorated ceramics is only about 1.5%.

	Standard Ware	Dark-Faced Burnished Ware	Grey-Black Ware
Painting	58	37	–
Appliqué	13	–	–
Incision	24	11	2
Impression	34	1	–
Incision and impression[1]	–	–	1
Pattern burnishing	–	2	–
Total	129	51	3

[1] The other combinations of techniques – plastic decoration/painting, incision/painting, impression/painting – are counted with plastic decoration, incision or impression because in these combinations painting shows rarely motives

Table 3.14. Pre-Halaf pottery — techniques of decoration per ware.

	Level 11	Stratum 10B	Stratum 10A	Level 9	Level 8	Level 7	Pre-Halaf period
Painting	2	2	3	5	52	31	95
Appliqué	5	1	2	–	3	2	13
Incision	–	7	5	–	15	6	37
Impression	–	–	–	–	11	24	35
Incision and Impression	–	–	–	–	1	–	1
Pattern Burnishing	–	–	–	–	1	1	2

Table 3.15. Pre-Halaf pottery — techniques of decoration per level or stratum.

Decoration of Dark-Faced Burnished Ware comprises painting, incision, painting-and-incision, impression and pattern-burnishing (table 3.14). Dark-Faced Burnished Ware is *a priori* hardly suited for painting due to its dark surface colour but this restriction is bypassed by using a rather bright and lustrous red colour. In addition, designs consist of simple patterns, i.e. large vertical, diagonal or horizontal bands (each 15/20 mm wide); very often, these bands are lined with very thin and roughly made incisions, which do not seem to have any decorative meaning but may have been required for technological reasons during the process of painting. Occasionally, the large bands of paint are combined with diagonal incised lines (including one example of 'herringbones'). Necks are often painted.

Only three sherds ascribed to our Grey-Black Ware are decorated by means of incision and incision-and-impression (table 3.14).

Mineral Coarse Ware is never decorated.

In the case of the Standard Ware, decoration consists of painting, *appliqué*, impression (commonly in combination with painting) and incision (likewise sometimes in combination with painting) (table 3.14). The paint is of a red colour. Designs mainly consist of triangles, whether plain, hatched or *en reservé*, and are organised in horizontal zones, sometimes lined by chevrons. *Appliqué* is limited to blobs and horizontally fixed crescents (two specimens); it is not yet certain whether these are truly decorative elements or served as some sort of handles. Incised patterns are hardly recognisable due to small sherd size; we can recognise only parallel lines, mostly obliquely oriented. In a few cases the lines are converging. Generally, the impressions are made with a comb, especially when they occur in association with painting. The comb was mainly used to create dotted lines but sometimes also applied in a 'trailed' manner (to judge by the generally very shallow impressions) to produce vertical or oblique bands of parallel, straight lines or horizontal wavy bands of parallel lines. One sherd seems to have been impressed by means of a shell, whereas some other specimens carry deep impressions made by a smooth rounded point or a sharp (tri)angular point. Finally, in one case the impression resulted from the use of a tool with a hollow stem. Impression in combination with painting mainly occurs in the form of alternating bands of solid paint and impressed designs.

Finally, technological traits and decoration show some trends, although these are far from exclusive. Most ceramics carrying *appliqué*, incisions or impressions contain large plant inclusions, while painted pottery generally contains small plant inclusions or, rarely, no inclusions at all. The incised and, in particular, painted ceramics are burnished in most cases. Ceramics carrying *appliqué* or impressions are usually simply smoothened.

So far, decoration cannot be associated with a specific vessel shape.

Painting and *appliqué* are found from level 11 onwards, whereas incision is present from level 10 onwards and impressions and pattern-burnishing from level 8 onwards (table 3.15). Sample size does not seem to affect the distribution of the various techniques of decoration, for, once present, every technique is consistently found in the subsequent levels as well.

The Balikh II pottery: conclusions and discussion

The Balikh II pottery of Sabi Abyad is characterised by a considerable variability: ceramic traits occur in a wide array of varieties and associations, which are never determinant but only point out trends in the case of the bulk of the pottery. This variability increases through time. For example, Grey-Black Ware and incised pottery are first introduced in level 10, whereas impressed and pattern-burnished ceramics first appear in level 8. Once present, each trait remains in use throughout the sequence, although its relative importance may vary.

So far, no definite ware categories other than Dark-Faced Burnished Ware, Grey-Black Ware and Mineral Coarse Ware can be identified with certainty. Standard Ware cannot be regarded as one homogeneous group; at least some ceramics are 'finer' in various respects than others and perhaps point to the existence of some sort of 'fine ware'. The absence of plant inclusions, which is the usual characteristic of fine-ware pottery, seems really to be an indicator of fineness when further taking into account that pottery without plant inclusions has a low wall thickness and rarely contains very large mineral inclusions. However, fine ware is not necessarily restricted to mineral-tempered pottery only. The size of plant inclusions is another element defining ceramic 'fineness': small plant inclusions are associated with a low wall thickness. When taking into account that pottery with very large plant inclusions is found in level 11 only, whereas ceramics with small plant inclusions increase in the subsequent levels, it seems that there is a tendency towards an increasing fineness. Two techniques of surface treatment also seem to indicate a relative fineness: slipping and, to a lesser extent, burnishing are linked with rather thin-walled ceramics containing small plant inclusions. The rare occurrence of slipped ceramics in level 11 and their considerable increase from level 9 onwards supports the above-noted trend towards finer pottery. Painting, too, seems to be indicative of fineness, this in view of the rather large percentages of (a) painted pottery containing either no or small plant inclusions only and (b) pottery which is both painted and burnished.

Although it is impossible to determine with certainty a distinct 'fine ware' amongst plant-tempered sherds, we can try to come to a rough estimate[13] of the 'finer' part of this group by taking together all sherds which contain small plant inclusions and are slipped or painted as well. All together, these ceramics appear to account for over 12% of the Standard Ware of levels 11-7, or even for 16% when also including the sherds containing no plant inclusions at all. When furthermore considering all ceramics with mineral temper as 'fine ware', it is clear that Grey-Black Ware and Dark-Faced Burnished Ware should be included in this fine-ware group as well. The many indicators of fineness of Grey-Black Ware (see above), the

[13] It is an estimate by necessity, simply because the size of plant inclusions cannot be determined with great accuracy.

considerable number of painted Dark-Faced Burnished pottery and its restricted wall thickness, despite the size and quantity of mineral inclusions, are all in favour of this assignment. In this manner, our group of 'fine' pottery comprises up to 24.7% of the overall Pre-Halaf ceramic assemblage.[14]

Interestingly, it seems that most of the above-mentioned 'fine-ware' ceramics were not locally produced at Sabi Abyad but imported to the site. Dark-Faced Burnished Ware definitely represents an import product at our site but the same might hold for our Grey-Black Ware as well as for a rather large amount of the 'finer' ceramics of the Standard Ware (further research is required; see Le Mière and Picon, in prep.). A similar picture was earlier obtained at Bouqras in eastern Syria and at some other 6th millennium sites (Le Mière and Picon 1987; Bader et al. 1994).

In terms of stratigraphy, it appears that the Pre-Halaf ceramic sequence at Sabi Abyad presents a continuum without any major breaks; only between the lowest levels 11 and 10 a hiatus may exist (this in accordance with the overall stratigraphy; see chapter 2). Indeed, the pottery from level 10 and later layers of occupation resembles the ceramics found in level 11 to a considerable extent but some important differences occur as well: some features seem to be restricted to level 11 only, such as the pottery with very large plant inclusions or the abundance of pierced handles, whereas other traits are found only in the strata postdating level 11, such as Grey-Black Ware or ceramics with incised decoration (in addition, Mineral Coarse Ware may have been a later feature as well). At present, the assumed hiatus can neither be confirmed nor denied with certainty; however, we are inclined towards the former option, although it may have been a gap of very short duration.

The assumption that the stratum 10B (level 10) sherd pavement (cf. chapter 2) was built of sherds from an earlier period, i.e. level 11, should probably be rejected, this in view of the considerable differences between the pottery from level 11 and stratum 10B. The pavement has yielded an increasing number of collared vessels and, in addition, Grey-Black Ware and incised ceramics not found before, whereas characteristic level 11 features (such as handles and pottery with very large plant inclusions) are either absent or very rare. In general, the stratum 10B pottery is closely comparable to that of the later Pre-Halaf levels. The material used for this pavement must belong to a stratum, or perhaps even level, pre-dating the stratum

---

[14] As said before, this percentage refers only to the selected sample used for the present study, i.e. the various categories are not all equally represented. For comparative purposes it seems most accurate to base calculations on rim sherds only. However, it is questionable whether rim sherds are always truly representative. For example, the number of Dark-Faced Burnished Ware rim sherds is very low, perhaps due to the fact that this ware mainly consists of large vessels with narrow necks which, when broken, yield only very few rim sherds. Grey-Black Ware, on the other hand, consists of much smaller and more opened vessels, yielding many more rim sherds. When basing calculations upon *all* sherds (i.e. upon the general count, before discarding of the non-diagnostic sherds) other problems arise: the estimate of the size of the plant inclusions did not yet take place at this initial stage of processing. As a consequence, it seems hardly possible to come to a more precise percentage of the group of 'fine' ceramics, which is, moreover, mainly of use for intra-site comparison.

10B occupation; however, this stratum or level closely adheres to the subsequent layers of occupation. Some differences, e.g. the large amount of small-plant tempered sherds found in this stratum, are perhaps related to a specific selection of sherds for this pavement.

When relating our Pre-Halaf ceramic sequence to Akkermans' chronological framework for the Balikh valley as a whole (Akkermans 1993:111ff), it appears that two phases can be recognised, viz. (late) Balikh IIA, comprising our level 11, and Balikh IIC, comprising our levels 10-7. Akkermans' intermittent phase IIB has not yet been attested in excavation but may comprise the assumed hiatus between levels 11 and 10. With the beginning of level 8 some changes in the pottery assemblage occur which might suggest a further subdivision of phase IIC but limited sample sizes in the case of levels 10 and 9 hamper any definite conclusions.

Surveys in the Balikh region have yielded many sites with early ceramics (cf. Copeland 1979; Akkermans 1993). Two of these sites have been sounded, viz. Tell Assouad (Cauvin 1972; Le Mière 1979, 1986) and Tell Damishliyya (Akkermans 1988a). Interestingly, our level 11 ceramic assemblage, with its plant inclusions of very large size and abundant occurrence of handles, resembles to some extent the ones found at Tell Assouad VIII-VII and Tell Damishliyya 3-7. However, considerable differences appear as well: Sabi Abyad level 11 features like red-slipping, collared and carinated vessels, painting or *appliqué* are all absent from Assouad and Damishliyya. These differences do not seem to be merely due to local variability in material culture but most likely point towards a chronological distinction, with the Sabi Abyad ceramics being of a somewhat younger date than those of Assouad and Damishliyya[15] (see below).

Whereas sites with Assouad/Damishliyya-like pottery (Balikh IIA) are widely distributed in the Balikh valley (Akkermans 1993:170-172), the opposite holds for sites with ceramics comparable to those found in our levels 10-7 (Balikh IIC): only four sites (apart from Sabi Abyad) have yielded more or less similar materials on their surfaces (ibid.:172-175).

Earlier it was suggested that the Sabi Abyad Pre-Halaf pottery has little to do with the ceramic assemblages found in the northern Mesopotamian area east of the Khabur, including Bouqras (Akkermans and Le Mière 1992; this contra Le Mière 1989a).[16] At present, we can be much more certain in this respect: the Sabi Abyad Pre-Halaf pottery differs completely from that found further east. Characteristic

---

[15] It is not excluded that a slight chronological distinction is also perceptible in the case of Tells Assouad and Damishliyya. The latter site has yielded collared vessels which were not found at Assouad; in this respect, Damishliyya may be chronologically somewhat closer to Sabi Abyad level 11, where ceramics with distinct necks were commonly attested (for a detailed account on the chronology of both Assouad and Damishliyya, see Akkermans 1991; Nishiaki 1992).

[16] The various sites either excavated (Tell Kashkashok, Tell Khazna; cf. Matsutani ed. 1991; Munchaev et al. 1993) or surveyed (Lyonnet, in prep.; Le Mière, in prep.) in this area have all revealed Proto-Hassuna pottery.

Mesopotamian shapes (like carinated vessels, concave bodies or the 'double-ogee') or decorative features (like plastic decorations) are either rarely found or wholly absent from our site. The other way round, Sabi Abyad features like collared vessels or the commonly found incisions and impressions are very rare in the east. Initially, we suggested that husking trays are the only true 'Mesopotamian' element within the Sabi Abyad Pre-Halaf ceramic assemblage but this suggestion holds little significance: husking trays have recently been reported in Pre-Halaf levels at sites as far west as Tell Aray 2 (Nishino et al. 1991) and Ras Shamra (Contenson 1992) in Syria and as far north as Çayönü in southeastern Anatolia (Özdoğan and Özdoğan 1993). Most recently, husking trays have also been found at the site of Dja'de along the Syrian Euphrates (Coqueugniot, in press). The virtual absence of Mesopotamian traits in the Pre-Halaf pottery of Sabi Abyad (and other sites in the Balikh basin) suggests some sort of borderline, at least in ceramic terms, between the Balikh and the Khabur. It is, however, stressed that relationships between northern Syria-Cilicia and Mesopotamia are not wholly absent but are largely restricted to the circulation of western Dark-Faced Burnished Ware, which has been found at the Proto-Hassunan sites in the Sinjar (Bader et al. 1994), at Bouqras on the Syrian Euphrates (Le Mière and Picon 1987) and at sites in the upper Khabur valley (Le Mière, in prep.).

Northwestern Syria and Cilicia share many features in terms of ceramics, as shown by sites like Tell Judaidah and Tell Dhahab in the Amuq (Braidwood and Braidwood 1960), Ras Shamra (Contenson 1992), Tabbat el-Hammam (Hole 1959), Tell Kerkh 2 (Iwasaki et al. 1993), Tell Aray 2 (Nishino et al. 1991), Mersin[17] (Garstang 1953) and the river Qoueiq sites (Mellaart 1981). However, only the northernmost of these sites, viz. Mersin and the sites in the Amuq and the Qoueiq, are truly useful for comparative purposes with Sabi Abyad. There is a general resemblance concerning the main characteristics of shape (rather varying shapes, convex or straight bodies, necks of various shapes and sizes, very few carinations) and decoration (impression, incision and also painting). On the other hand, differences have been found as well. Most noteworthy is the relative small proportion of Dark-Faced Burnished Ware but large amount of plant-tempered, light-coloured wares at Sabi Abyad, while the reverse holds for the sites in the west: the reason for this is that the geological environment of the latter sites is very different from that of the Balikh valley, where the clays used to make Dark-Faced Burnished Ware are not available.

Chronological variables must be taken into account as well: the Pre-Halaf pottery of Sabi Abyad gives evidence of a variety of techniques, wares and decorations,

---

[17] The site of Sakçe Gözü (Garstang 1908, 1937; du Plat Taylor et al. 1950) is situated in the same area (even much closer to Sabi Abyad) but seems to antedate levels 11-7 at Sabi Abyad: painted pottery very similar to our Transitional 'Standard Fine Ware' (see below) has been found already in period I at Sakçe Gözü.

which are not yet found in the Amuq A period or at Mersin XXXII-XXVII but which develop in the subsequent Amuq B phase or Mersin XXVI-XXV or XXIV. Within this period the closest comparisons between Sabi Abyad and the sites in northwestern Syria and Cilicia are found: slipping, painting, incision on coarse ware, combination of painting and impression or incision now appear at these sites. Techniques of decoration are, of course, related to the type of clay used in manufacture: the dark clays commonly found in early layers of the sites in the west contributed to the development of the techniques of impression and incision and not to that of painting. However, simple painting has been found on Dark-Faced Burnished Ware already in the Amuq A period (the Washed Impressed Ware). Light-coloured wares with more elaborately painted designs occur later in the Amuq (phase B) or at Mersin (levels XXVI-XXV). At Sabi Abyad, however, painting appeared earlier than impression, probably due to the light clays available. The painted designs found at Sabi Abyad are all very simple; more complicated motifs, like hatched triangles or lines of triangles, are not associated with painting but with incision. Specific Amuq B or Mersin XXVI-XXV motives, like vertical wavy lines, are absent from Sabi Abyad. It seems clear that, despite some obvious parallels, the ceramic assemblages of Pre-Halaf Sabi Abyad and the sites in the northwest are not identical. The Balikh region has its own characteristics and seems to occupy a specific place in the ceramic traditions of northwestern Syria and Cilicia. However, recent research has made it clear that this area has to be extended up to the east bank of the Euphrates. Excavations at Dja'de (Coqueugniot, in press) and Kosak Shamali (Matsutani and Nishiaki, in press) have yielded ceramics which comprise nearly all elements of the Sabi Abyad Pre-Halaf assemblage. However, the site of Halula on the west bank of the river (Molist, in press) has yielded Pre-Halaf material more comparable to the pottery found further west, like that of the Qoueiq region (Faura Vendrell, in press). In this respect, the Euphrates may have acted as a true borderline in ceramic terms. Regional variability seems to be mainly based on the distribution of light and dark wares with their associated decorative traits.

So far, the discussion has focussed on the Pre-Halaf period as a whole. However, in the case of the Balikh IIA pottery true comparisons are hard to find but the main features of this pottery are generally comparable to those of the sites of northwestern Syria and Cilicia mentioned above. In addition, attention is drawn to two sites with early pottery in the Euphrates valley north of modern Urfa, viz. Kumartepe (Roodenberg et al. 1984) and Sürük Mevkii (Stein 1992).[18] Their pottery is very similar to the Balikh IIA ceramics (closed shapes, abundant occurrence of handles, no decoration and light-coloured, plant-tempered fabric). In this respect, it seems that, from the early 6th millennium onwards, the pottery traditions of the western Jezirah extend further northwards.

---

[18] The pottery from Çayönü (Özdoğan and Özdoğan 1993) is not similar to the Sabi Abyad ceramics but nevertheless displays some resemblances which require a more careful comparison as soon as more data are available.

In the light of the above, it seems that the Sabi Abyad Pre-Halaf ceramic assemblage was distributed over a rather limited area, i.e. the western Jezirah bounded by the Euphrates in the west, the Taurus in the north and the Balikh in the east (cf. Akkermans 1993:294-297). It remains unknown whether or not the region between the Balikh and Khabur should be included as well.

Some radiocarbon samples from Damishliyya suggest a date at around 5800/5700 B.C. for the final occupation level at this site (Akkermans 1991:124, 1993:113ff); if so, our level 11 at Sabi Abyad may date somewhat later, perhaps around 5700/5600 B.C. Unfortunately, the present set of radiocarbon dates from Sabi Abyad (ibid.; see also Foreword) does not present any definite clues in this respect. Little can be said with certainty on the duration of the assumed gap between levels 11 and 10. So far, only two dates are available for the Pre-Halaf period at Sabi Abyad, both from level 8 and yielding a date of 7080±80 BP (UtC-1009) and 7145±30 BP (GrN-16805; ibid.), respectively. More recently, two dates were obtained from in-situ level 6 deposits (Transitional period), yielding a date around 7075±25 BP (GrN-19367) and 7100±60 BP (GrN-19368). Both the level 8 and level 6 samples are in agreement with the stratigraphic sequence and as such seem to be highly reliable. The chronological distinction between both levels is apparently minimal, suggesting a rapid replacement of settlement (actually, the latter holds for the Transitional and Early Halaf periods as well; cf. Akkermans 1993:115ff; Akkermans and Verhoeven 1995). (M.L.M.)

Levels 6-4: The Balikh IIIA or Transitional Period

Introduction

The Balikh IIIA or Transitional period comprises levels 6 to 4 at Sabi Abyad. The lower level 6 has been exposed over a very large area (ca. 800 m²). The subsequent levels 5 and 4 have been unearthed over a much more restricted area (less than 300 m²; cf. chapter 2). Level 6 ceramics have been found in vast quantities (ca. 17,400 sherds and about 50 complete vessels). The unique find circumstances (cf. chapter 2) and the overall richness of the level 6 material will allow extensive studies concerning shape reconstruction, spatial distribution, etc.

The Balikh IIIA or Transitional period can be distinguished from the lower Balikh II or Pre-Halaf period by the appearance of three new wares, two of which continue and develop further in the Halaf era (see below). All wares existing in the Pre-Halaf period are still found in the Transitional levels (table 3.17) but occasionally show some evolution. Below, the latter pottery will be discussed first and subsequently the new wares will be presented, to conclude with a comparison between the 'old' and 'new' ceramics.

A. The 'Pre-Halaf' wares

The sample

At the moment, only a very restricted sample out of the total bulk of level 6-4 pottery has been studied in detail, viz. all ceramics from the deep sounding (trench P15) and those of building II, room 6. In addition, ca. 300 selected ceramics from various other contexts have been taken into account, either because of their good state of preservation or because they presented shapes or kinds of decoration not known before. These 300 specimens enlarged our repertory but cannot be used in the comparative quantitative analysis (they are a selection taken from much larger but as yet unstudied pottery samples). Occasionally, material from mixed contexts (i.e. belonging to either levels 4 or 5, 4 or 6, or 5 or 6) has been included to enlarge the sample, but only for countings considering the Transition period as a whole (table 3.16).

	Level 6	Level 5	Level 4	Mixed lots (6/5, 6/4, 5/4)	Transition period
Total amount of sherds	17 428	3 085	6 184	4 098	30,795
Amount of sherds of studied lots	3 848	701	5 782	2 218	12,549
Studied sherds	689	157	531	355	1732
Studied rims	322	68	254	176	810

Table 3.16. Transitional pottery — amount of pottery collected and studied per level.

	Level 6	Level 5	Level 4	Mixed lots (6/5, 6/4, 5/4)	Transition period
Dark-Faced Burnished Ware	82 (11.9%)	24 (15.3%)	77 (14.5%)	35	218
Grey-Black Ware	13 (1.9%)	9 (5.7%)	22 (4.1%)	16	60
Mineral Coarse Ware	9 (1.3%)	8 (5.1%)	44 (8.3%)	28	89
Standard Ware	585 (84.9%)	116 (73.9%)	388 (73.1%)	336	1425
Total of sherd	689 (100%)	157 (100%)	531 (100%)	415	1792

Table 3.17. Transitional pottery — amount of sherds per ware per level.

In the case of levels 6 and 4 the present sample comprises over 1000 sherds each, but in the case of the intermittent level 5 hardly 200 sherds are available for analysis. The analysis will proceed in a way similar to that of the earlier Balikh II pottery, i.e. level by level; it is felt that the main ceramic elements illustrating the transition between the lower, Pre-Halaf period (levels 11-7) and the upper, Early Halaf period (levels 3-1) can be identified, despite the fact that some details of this transition through levels 6 to 4 will be missed due to the rather poorly documented level 5 ceramic assemblage.

Condition of the pottery

Generally, the pottery from level 6 is in a better condition than that from levels 5 and 4 (table 3.18), due to different circumstances of deposition and preservation (the level 6 material stems from burnt in-situ contexts, whereas the ceramics from levels 5 and 4 mainly come from refuse deposits; cf. chapter 2). However, the burning of the level 6 settlement affected the pottery to some extent: some ceramics burst into pieces or show very deep cracks due to this secondary overfiring, others are completely blackened (neither original surface colours nor painted decoration can be determined anymore). Some Grey-Black Ware sherds, originally grey-coloured, have been refired in an oxydising atmosphere during the burning of the level 6 village and turned into buff-brown. In general, it appears that the percentage of weathered or damaged sherds from the Transitional period is more or less comparable to that of the Pre-Halaf levels 10-7 (with the exclusion of stratum 10B).

	Level 6	Level 5	Level 4
No damaging	58.6%	51.6%	54.2%
Total of sherds	689	157	531

Table 3.18. Transitional pottery — condition of the pottery per level.

Technological characteristics

Dark-Faced Burnished Ware

This group of pottery does not show any important changes in the Transitional period, except in terms of wall thickness which is somewhat higher (8.4 mm) than in the Pre-Halaf period (7.2 mm). The proportion of Dark-Faced Burnished Ware, which increased in level 8, remains more or less equal in the various Transitional levels (table 3.17).

Grey-Black Ware

The Transitional Grey-Black Ware, too, is largely identical to that found in the lower levels. The main difference is an increasing percentage of sherds containing no plant inclusions, particularly in level 4. However, the amount of medium or large mineral inclusions within the pottery does not change; this feature must be related to the fineness of this ware. Level 6 Grey-Black Ware shows more ceramics with buff or brown surfaces than that from the other levels, most likely due the secondary firing during destruction of the settlement. The proportion of Grey-Black Ware does not change significantly throughout the Sabi Abyad sequence (table 3.17).

Mineral Coarse Ware

This ware seems to be identical to that of the earlier levels and shows no change, apart from its slight increase in importance in level 5 and, more significantly, level 4 (table 3.17).

Standard Ware

General description. The levels 6-4 Standard Ware consists of 1425 sherds, the vast majority of which is plant-tempered (ca. 93%; table 3.19). Less than 20% of these show plant inclusions of small size, whereas only two sherds (0.1%) contain inclusions of very large size. About 87% of the pottery does not show any visible mineral inclusions (table 3.20). About 5% of the pottery, however, contains very large mineral inclusions (>1 mm). Surface colours (table 3.21) are mainly buff (55%) and pinkish-red (33%). New is the appearance of cream and orange-red colours, albeit in very small quantities (each ca. 1%). The fabric has a predominantly grey core. In terms of surface treatment (table 3.22), it appears that still almost one-third of the sherds is burnished but that smoothening is by far the most common (58.3%). Slipped pottery, mostly red-coloured and burnished, is found in small quantities (7.6%). Nearly 5% of the Standard Ware seems to be deliberately untreated.[19]

As in the case of the Pre-Halaf Standard Ware, it is clear that also within the Transitional Standard Ware no ceramic trait, or combination of traits, is determinant to define specific categories. However, some features are useful to delineate the Transitional character of the levels 6-4 pottery.

Significant technological features. Hardly any traits are new in the Transitional period; only the orange-reddish and cream surface colours are now found for the first time; the latter is perhaps related to new techniques of firing (however, this finds little support when taking into account that the proportion of ceramics with grey cores hardly decreases).

---

[19] These percentages are based only on ceramics with *recognisable* surface treatment (severely weathered or damaged sherds, comprising 5.2% of the bulk, have not been taken into account).

	Level 6	Level 5	Level 4	Transition period (including mixed lots)
No plant inclusions	6.3%	4.3%	11.9%	7.4%
Small plant inclusions	15.2%	19.8%	20.4%	16.8%
Large plant inclusions	78.3%	75%	67.7%	75.6%
Very large plant inclusions	0.2%	0.9%	–	0.1%
Total of sherds	585	116	387	1424

Table 3.19. Transitional pottery — amount and size of plant inclusions of Standard Ware per level.

	Level 6	Level 5	Level 4	Transition period including mixed lots
Small	87.4%	90.5%	87.1%	87.4%
Medium	6.2%	5.2%	5.7%	5.8%
Large	1.2%	1.7%	2.3%	1.8%
Very large	5.2%	2.6%	4.9%	5.1%
Total of sherds	579	116	387	1417

Table 3.20. Transitional pottery — size of mineral inclusions of Standard Ware per level.

As in the Pre-Halaf period, the size of mineral inclusions largely depends upon the presence or absence of plant inclusions: hardly 8% of the plant-tempered sherds contain visible mineral inclusions as well, whereas about 70% of the pottery without plant inclusions show a visible mineral temper. Mineral inclusions of very large size are found in much larger quantities within the group of ceramics without plant temper (about 60%) than within the group with plant temper (30%).

As before, there seems to be a link between the occurrence of small plant inclusions and the presence of a slip: over 70% of the slipped ceramics contain vegetal inclusions of small size. Likewise, the link between wall thickness and both the presence and the size of plant inclusions is still very strong. The mean wall thickness

	Level 6	Level 5	Level 4	Transition period including mixed lots
Black	0.7%	–	1.3%	0.6%
Grey	5.2%	3.4%	3.6%	3.9%
Brown	10.7%	4.3%	1.3%	5.8%
Buff	60.1%	46.6%	55.4%	54.9%
Red/pink	23.4%	44.8%	32.5%	33%
Cream	–	0.9%	1%	0.5%
Orange	–	–	4.9%	1.3%
Total of sherds	582	116	388	1422

Table 3.21. Transitional pottery — surface colour of Standard Ware per level.

	Level 6	Level 5	Level 4	Transition period including mixed lots
None	3.8%	4.7%	5.3%	4.3%
Smoothing	57.8%	50%	63.4%	58.3%
Burnishing	31.7%	38.7%	21.5%	29.9%
Slipping	6.7%	6.6%	9.8%	7.6%
Total of sherds	555	106	358	1340

Table 3.22. Transitional pottery — surface treatment of Standard Ware per level.

is 9 mm (std= 2.9) in the case of sherds with no plant inclusions and 13.7 mm (std= 4.5) in the case of sherds with plant inclusions. The difference between the groups of ceramics with small or very large plant inclusions remains the same as in the Pre-Halaf period (m= 10.2, std= 2.9, and m= 14.6, std= 4.4, respectively).

The link between wall thickness and surface treatment is recognisable once more in the mean thickness of burnished sherds (m= 12.2 mm, std= 3.9), which is significantly lower than that of smoothened ones (m= 14.4 mm, std= 4.8).

Evolution of technological features. The proportion of sherds without plant inclusions doubles in the Transitional era when compared with the Pre-Halaf period (table 3.19). The main increase takes place in level 4 (the amount of pottery without plant inclusions in level 6 is only slightly different from that of level 7).

The Transitional period as a whole shows a strong increase of ceramics with large plant inclusions when compared with the earlier Pre-Halaf phase. However, within the Transitional period there is a significant decrease from levels 6 to 4. The increase of pottery with large plant inclusions, and the decrease of ceramics containing small plant inclusions in vast numbers, starts already in level 7 and continues in level 6. In the subsequent levels 5 and 4 these ceramics are found in more or less equal proportions. Pottery containing small plant inclusions in minute quantities does not show any change when comparing the Pre-Halaf and Transitional periods; only a slight increase in level 4 is perceptible, associated with the increase of the group without plant inclusions and the decrease of the group with large plant inclusions in vast quantities.

The amount of ceramics with very large mineral inclusions increases in the Transitional period when compared with the former period; however, within the Transitional levels no trend is recognisable in this respect (table 3.20).

In terms of surface treatment, the pottery from the Transitional period as a whole differs in various ways from that of the Pre-Halaf period (cf. tables 3.8 and 3.22): (1) the amount of ceramics without any deliberate treatment increases slightly (from 2.8% to 4.3%), (2) the number of smoothened pottery increases strongly (from 38.1% to 58.3%), (3) burnished ceramics decrease in importance (from 32.3% to 29.9%), and (4) the amount of slipped pottery is more than halved (from 16.8% to 7.6%). This decrease of slipped pottery is a clear characteristic of the Transitional period and it affects all groups, in particular the group with abundant small plant inclusions. However, when restricting ourselves to the Transitional levels only (table 3.22), it appears that (1) the amount of pottery without surface treatment is more or less equal per level, (2) smoothened ceramics (which actually started to increase in level 7) rapidly increase in number in level 6, subsequently decreasing in level 5 but increasing again in level 4, (3) parallel to the rise in importance of smoothened pottery, a marked fall in the number of burnished ceramics is perceptible in level 6 and, once again, in level 4, (4) the amount of slipped pottery remains more or less equal in each of the Transitional levels.

The wall thickness of the Transitional ceramics is considerably higher than that of the Pre-Halaf pottery. Wall thickness increases from levels 6 to 4,[20] particularly in the case of ceramics with plant inclusions (whatever their size) and burnished pottery.

When comparing the Standard Wares of both the Pre-Halaf and the Transitional periods, the latter definitely shows less technological variability and allows a more precise definition of 'coarse' and 'fine' ceramics. Interestingly, it seems that the pottery assemblage as a whole becomes coarser in many respects: a considerable

---

[20] It is recalled that wall thickness did not show any particular trend during the Pre-Halaf period.

increase is perceptible of (1) the number of ceramics with large plant inclusions (at the expense of pottery with small plant inclusions), (2) the amount of sherds without any deliberate surface treatment or smoothening only (at the expense of burnished and slipped pottery), and (3) the wall thickness of the ceramics (particularly in the case of plant-tempered pottery). Most of these changes occur already in level 6 but become stronger in the final Transitional level 4.

Shape

The shape analysis is based on 1259 ceramics, including 29 complete profiles (these figures include both the Standard Ware and the three wares earlier defined). In order to enlarge the shape repertory, a selection of 236 ceramics, including 35 complete profiles, taken from the vast corpus of as yet not further studied pottery, will be presented as well (however, they will not be used for counting).

General description. So far, 48 ceramics with an oval shape have been recognised in the Transitional material. In the case of the Pre-Halaf pottery, it was earlier suggested that the small size of many sherds may prevent the recognition of oval shapes but one may wonder whether this is truly correct when taking into account the rather large number of oval shapes in levels 5 and 4, despite the overall small size of the sherds in these levels. However, it may also be the case that oval shapes increase in importance through time.

The direction of the rim is known in the case of 372 sherds (table 3.23): about half is open, one-third is vertical and 19.1% is closed (it is recalled that the small size of many sherds may cause some distortion). Rims are predominantly indistinct (96%) and rounded (97%); they hardly show any elaboration. The rim diameters could be measured in 355 cases and varied between 6 and 40 cm (m= 19.9 cm, std= 7.6). So far, 378 jar necks have been recognised (table 3.24) but almost two-thirds of these do not give any clues of wall direction, and about one-third presents no evidence on any specific shape. The necks are predominantly vertical or open. Their shape is mainly concave, whereas another third of the necks is both open and concave (however, numerous different combinations of direction and shape have been found). The necks vary in diameter between 6 and 39 cm. Special attention is drawn to the vessel shoulders which are in some cases highly pronounced, with some being nearly horizontal (fig. 3.10, no. 4, fig. 3.11, nos. 1-2, 4-5, and fig. 3.13, nos. 1-2), and to the junction between neck and shoulder which is often angular. The shape of the body is mostly convex or, to a much lesser extent, straight (ca. 10%) or concave (2%). Only very few sherds (n= 18) gave evidence of some sort of carination (table 3.25). Handles are rare in the Transitional levels (table 3.26): so far, only three loop handles and twelve pierced handles and ledge handles have been recognised. Finally, the height of the vessels widely varies between 2 and 60 cm.

	Level 6	Level 5	Level 4	Transition period including mixed lots
Closed	34	9	16	71 (19.1%)
Vertical	59	10	23	122 (32.8%)
Opened	81	11	47	179 (48.1%)
Total of sherds	174	30	86	372

Table 3.23. Transitional pottery — direction of body sherds per level.

	Level 6	Level 5	Level 4	Transition period including mixed lots
Necks	163	24	163	378

Table 3.24. Transitional pottery — number of necks per level.

	Level 6	Level 5	Level 4	Transition period including mixed lots
Carinations	15	–	1	18

Table 3.25. Transitional pottery — number of carinated sherds per level.

	Level 6	Level 5	Level 4	Transition period including mixed lots
Simple handles	3	2	4	12
Loop handles	1	2	–	3

Table 3.26. Transitional pottery — number of handles per level.

Bases (n= 283) are in most cases simply flat (over 90%). Convex or concave bases account for about 4% each, whereas pedestal bases are extremely rare (0.7%). Over three-quarters of the bases are rounded; only 10% are distinct from the body. The base diameters, measurable in 120 cases, vary between 2 and 38 cm (m= 11.7 cm, std= 5.3).

In the light of the above, the general impression concerning the Transitional pottery is, as in the Pre-Halaf period, one of monotony, with half of the sample composed of collared jars, hardly any carinations, very few handles and very simple bases or rims. Only the necks point towards some variety in size and shape (fig. 3.10-3.14), particularly in regard of the relative dimensions of neck and body (fig. 3.10, nos. 1 and 3, fig. 3.11, nos. 1 and 5). Even within the same shape category a considerable variability in size is perceptible, as clearly shown by the complete level 6 profiles (figs. 3.6-3.8).

Links between shape and technological traits. It appears that distinct bases, as in the lower levels, with only one exception all contain large plant inclusions and show either no deliberate surface treatment or smoothening only (except three specimens, which are either burnished or slipped). Apparently, distinct bases are not so much an elaborative feature but seem to have had a technological reason instead (see above).

Mineral Coarse Ware seems to be characterised by closed vessels (10 out of the 14 rims). A relatively large amount of these ceramics carried ledge handles (n= 4; in contrast, the much larger Standard Ware sample yielded only 15 handles). The Dark-Faced Burnished Ware sample has yielded hardly any rim sherds but necks are very common (23 necks versus only 3 rim sherds of uncollared vessels), suggesting that collared vessels are a main feature of this kind of pottery. Collared vessels also seem to be rather abundant within our category of Grey-Black Ware, comprising two-thirds (n= 14) of the rim-sherd sample (n= 21). In the case of the Standard Ware of the Transitional pottery, jars have been found in much smaller relative quantities and cannot be associated with any specific technological trait. They vary widely in shape and size. As in the Pre-Halaf period, re-used vessels commonly occur, particularly in the case of Dark-Faced Burnished Ware: jars with apparently damaged necks have been transformed into hole-mouth pots by entirely removing the neck and subsequently grinding the break.

Husking trays comprise ca. 3.2% (n= 47) of the Transitional pottery (table 3.27). The husking trays, often oval in shape (n= 13), have mainly ridged (n= 38) or, to a much lesser extent, finger-impressed bases (n= 9). These bases are flat, rounded (except for two angular ones) and indistinct (except one). The mean base thickness

	Level 6	Level 5	Level 4	Transition period including mixed lots
Finger impressed	3	–	4	8
Ridged	6	5	18	38
Ridged rims	1	–	–	1

Table 3.27. Transitional pottery — number of husking trays per level.

is 23.8 mm (std= 4.4); husking-tray bases are apparently much thicker than those of the other ceramics which have a mean thickness of 17 mm (std= 6.3). All trays are plant-tempered; only one contained small plant inclusions, whereas the remainder yielded large inclusions. Most husking trays are smoothened (n= 22), whereas two specimens are burnished.

The earlier mentioned variability of neck shapes, proportion between neck and body and dimensions seems to concern all groups and wares to some extent; however, most of the very large vessels are plant-tempered.

Evolution of shape. All ceramic traits defining the Pre-Halaf pottery are still found in the Transitional period and none is disappearing. When compared with the earlier levels, some main trends in the Transitional period seem to be (1) an increase in oval vessels, (2) a somewhat larger and more elaborate variety of bases, (3) an increasing number of collared vessels, (4) a decreasing number of handles (which was expected since they are characteristic of level 11), (5) an inversed proportion of the two types of husking trays, and (6) an increase in vessel diameters (consequently, it was expected that ceramics would also increase in height but the limited sample has not provided any definite clues in this respect).

At present, little can be said on the evolution of shape per level. Carinated vessels, which are very rare anyway, nearly all come from level 6 (n= 15), whereas two stem from either a level 6 or level 5 context, and only one from level 4. In addition, it appears that vessels with clear necks are mainly found in level 6 (their number seems to decrease slightly in level 4).

Decoration

The present sample has yielded 187 decorated ceramics in total, 45 of which belong to our category of Dark-Faced Burnished Ware, 8 to our Grey-Black Ware and the remainder to the Standard Ware (Mineral Coarse Ware is never decorated). Clearly, Dark-Faced Burnished Ware is much more often decorated than the other kinds of ceramics: 25% of the Dark-Faced Burnished Ware carries some kind of decoration, whereas only 7% of the Standard Ware[21] is decorated. Below, a selection of 67 decorated sherds, taken from the vast corpus of as yet unstudied ceramics, will be taken into account as well, in order to enlarge the repertory of motifs and to investigate the relationship between decoration and technique or shape.

The techniques of decoration are: painting, *appliqué*, incision (white-filled in one case), impression and pattern-burnishing (cf. table 3.28). Occasionally, some of these techniques have been combined on one and the same vessel. Painting occurs most often, whereas pattern-burnishing is very rare. The designs are mainly geometric but one or two naturalistic patterns have appeared as well. Some vessels show more than one motif, now and again organised in zones occasionally enclosed by lines.

---

[21] When taking all body sherds into account, about 1% of the bulk is decorated.

Dark-Faced Burnished Ware is decorated in a variety of ways: painting, incision, painting-and-incision, pattern-burnishing and *appliqué* (table 3.28). Painted decoration, usually carried out in a rather bright red colour, always consists of broad horizontal and/or oblique bands generally 15-20 mm wide but bands up to 50 mm wide have been found as well (see above). In the case of collared vessels, it appears that the necks have often been painted. As in the Pre-Halaf levels, the bands of paint are often lined by thin and very shallow, roughly incised lines. Occasionally, the bands are combined with vertical parallel or converging incised lines. Incised designs further consist of crosshatching and oblique parallel lines in groups of two. Designs of pattern-burnishing consist of zones of hatching with various orientations, crosshatched triangles and chevrons. Plastic decoration is limited to one or more horizontal bands in *appliqué* encircling the vessel; perhaps these bands served as grips as well (however, some are extremely thin and appear, sometimes in groups, low on the body, and as such are hardly suitable as handles). Occasionally, the applied bands have been found in combination with painted patterns.

	Standard Ware	Dark-Faced Burnished Ware	Grey-Black Ware
Painting	66	31	1
Appliqué	12	3	–
Incision	14	10	5
Impression	41	–	–
Pattern burnishing	1	1	2
Total	134	45	8

Table 3.28. Transitional pottery — techniques of decoration per ware.

	Level 6	Level 5	Level 4	Transition period including mixed lots
Painting	39	5	31	97
Appliqué	10	1	–	15
Incision	10	2	4	30
Impression	28	5	5	41
Pattern burnishing	–	1	3	4

Table 3.29. Transitional pottery — techniques of decoration per level.

Grey-Black Ware is decorated by means of comb-impression, incision or pattern-burnishing (table 3.28). Incised motifs mainly consist of horizontal bands of chevrons or crosshatching (often framed by incised lines) and triangles hatched with converging lines (fig. 3.18, no. 5 and fig. 3.19, nos. 1-5).

In the case of the Standard Ware, decoration consists of painting, impression, incision, pattern-burnishing and *appliqué* (table 3.28). Impression is often found in combination with painting. The paint is mainly red and burnished but can occasionally be black as well (the raw material for the black paint has not yet been identified but it remains doubtful whether it is ochre). In addition, one example of white paint has been found. Designs mainly consist of plain or crosshatched triangles, parallel lines (either vertical, horizontal or oblique), chevrons and herringbones. Some more complex patterns have been found as well, like crosshatched lozenges or triangles included in crosshatched bands. In the case of jars, necks sometimes carry one of the above-mentioned designs but often decoration is restricted to a band of paint at the junction of neck and shoulder. Interestingly, the black paint has usually been applied in a very rough manner and is, moreover, associated with some specific designs, like the rather wide but short vertical lines pendent from the rim or from the base of the neck (fig. 3.17, nos. 1 and 4), or a large cross on the interior base of a vessel (fig. 3.17, no. 3). Impressed decoration is largely identical to that found in the lower, Pre-Halaf levels: the impressions have been made with a comb or, occasionally, with a smooth or (tri)angular sharp point, or with an implement with a hollow stem. The combs, consisting of four to twelve teeth, have been used to produce dotted lines or, when used in a 'trailed' manner, straight or wavy bands of parallel, shallow lines. Incisions are occasionally extremely coarse but some very thin incised patterns (made with a very sharp blade or point) have been found as well. Motifs mainly consist of chevrons, zigzags, parallel or diverging lines, crosshatched triangles and groups of short linear incisions in zones (fig. 3.18, nos. 1-4). Plastic decoration is restricted to blobs and horizontal crescents, as in the Pre-Halaf period; as pointed out before, it is not excluded that these plastic elements had a functional rather than a decorative meaning (they may have served as grips). Only one or two specimens seem to be entirely decorative, like the five small blobs oriented in a vertical line on a vessel's neck and shoulder (fig. 3.16, no. 8).

Technological and decorative features are related to each other to some extent, although these relationships are very rarely exclusive. First, decoration is clearly associated with temper: 35% of the ceramics with no plant inclusions carry some kind of decoration, whereas less than 10% of the plant-tempered pottery is decorated. The size of the plant inclusions is equally of importance: pottery with small plant inclusions is much more often decorated (16.7%) than ceramics with large plant inclusions (5.3%). Second, although the various techniques of decoration are generally not restricted to a particular group of ceramics, it appears that over half of the painted pottery belongs to the group without plant inclusions (which comprises only 7.5% of the Standard Ware). However, painting in black and *appliqué* are exclusively found in association with ceramics with large plant inclusions. Third, surface treatment and decoration show only very few relationships: slipped ceramics are very rarely decorated and most of the sherds with *appliqué* are smoothened.

Decoration can hardly be associated with any particular vessel shape; only in the case of the painted-and-impressed sherds it appears that most of these belong to jars.

The various techniques of decoration found in the lower, Pre-Halaf levels of occupation are still in use in the Transitional levels (cf. table 3.29). However, *appliqué* is largely restricted to level 6; only one specimen has been found in level 5 and none in level 4. The use of black paint in a coarse manner seems to be limited to level 6 as well; no example has been found in one of the other Transitional layers (except one in an unclear, either level 6 or 5, context). In terms of design, the Transitional period gives evidence of the introduction of crosshatching, a more elaborate organisation of designs in zones and a wider variety of (combinations of) motives and techniques. As a matter of fact, most of the complex designs come from level 6 but this may be due to the restricted size of the levels 5-4 pottery samples. Painted-and-impressed ceramics, first found in level 8, are rather abundant in levels 7 and 6 but seem to decrease in importance (together with simple impressions) towards the end of the Transitional period, i.e. level 4. On the other hand, painted pottery increases somewhat in level 4, mainly within the group of ceramics without plant inclusions.

The 'Pre-Halaf' wares: some concluding remarks

It will be clear from the above that the pottery from the Transitional levels 6-4 is less varied than that of the lower levels 11-7. The distinction between 'coarse' and 'fine' in ceramic terms becomes clearer. Vessel shape gives virtually no clues in this respect but decoration does: when compared with the Pre-Halaf material, the proportion of decorated ceramics without plant temper has strongly increased. However, the proportion of decorated pottery remains more or less the same in the group of plant-tempered ceramics. Painting occurs more often in the group without plant inclusions than in the preceding period. When defining the 'fine' ceramics of the Transitional Standard Ware on the basis of the same criteria as used earlier for the Pre-Halaf pottery, it appears that this category counts less than 6% of the Standard Ware, i.e. twice less than in the Pre-Halaf period. At the same time it appears that the 'coarse' component of the Standard Ware becomes even coarser in the Transitional levels, particularly in level 4. The group without plant inclusions represents 7.4% of the Standard Ware; together with the Dark-Faced Burnished Ware and the Grey-Black Ware, the group of fine wares can be estimated at 26% of the overall Transitional 'Pre-Halaf' pottery (cf. notes 14-15). This figure closely compares to that earlier given for the Balikh II material. However, any interpretation or comparison needs the inclusion of the new, mainly mineral-tempered wares in the discussion.

Actually, the pottery presented so far can hardly be termed Transitional in its true sense; virtually all ceramic traits found in the Transitional levels were already present in the lower, Pre-Halaf strata of occupation and several trends characterising the Transitional period already start in level 7. In this respect, there is no reason to assume a break in the ceramic sequence between levels 7 and 6. However, it is the appearance of the three new wares which marks the beginning of the new era. The question is now whether these new wares have their origins in the Pre-Halaf pottery or whether they represent foreign traits incorporated in the local assemblage.

B. **The new wares**

Introduction

The present analysis is based on 1680 diagnostic sherds and some complete vessels. This includes all available Transitional fine ware[22] from the 1988 and 1992 seasons of excavation, as well as a very small selection of the pottery excavated in 1991. The pottery recovered during the 1993 campaign awaits further study in its entirety. Most of the material comes from level 4, while level 5 is least represented. For reasons earlier discussed, the description differs to some extent from that of the 'Pre-Halaf' wares; it adheres much more closely to the procedures earlier followed by Akkermans (1989d).

The introduction of three new wares in level 6 represents a true innovation in local pottery production. These ceramics were found in small quantities in level 6 for the first time,[23] comprising about 10% of the overall rim-sherd sample, but rapidly increased in importance in the subsequent levels to about 60% of all rim sherds in level 4. The new pottery strongly distinguishes itself from the other Transitional ceramics by its generally well-controlled firing under oxidising circumstances. Over three-quarters of the pottery show an even, light-coloured section and seem to have been fired either at high temperatures or during rather long periods of time (cf. Rice 1987:80-86). The emphasis on better control during firing is perhaps related to the development of new firing techniques and more advanced kilns. Overfired sherds, having a brittle texture and greenish surface colour, and some true wasters (fig. 3.32, no. 1) comprise ca. 6% of the overall sample of diagnostic ceramics and prove that this kind of pottery was locally produced at Sabi Abyad.

Almost 86% of the pottery (based on the rim-sherd sample) are decorated. Decoration mainly consists of painting but small numbers of painted-and-impressed

---

[22] Below, the use of the term 'fine ware' refers only to the three wares newly introduced in the Transitional period; the 'finer' component of the earlier presented 'Pre-Halaf' wares is excluded.
[23] Actually, three Fine Ware sherds, including a painted-and-impressed specimen (fig. 3.36, no. 5), had already been found in the upper erosion fill of level 7; however, in view of their context, these ceramics should most probably be considered as intrusive in level 7.

vessels have been found as well (exclusively impressed or incised vessels are not attested). The painted decoration is always monochrome, although a polytone effect is often produced by small variations in paint thickness or firing circumstances.[24]

Decoration of the Transitional ceramics was not carried out in a 'random' or wholly idiosyncratic manner, but followed certain principles in a hierarchical order (cf. Hardin 1970:333; Hole 1984; see also Akkermans 1989d:124). The emphasis is on horizontal banding, delimiting decoration zones. Vertical bands (metopes) have been attested in a few cases only. Usually, a horizontal band of paint is found at the rim and at the vessel's carination near the base; in the case of jars, an additional band is present at the junction of the neck and the body and, sometimes, on the shoulder. The resulting spatial zones suitable for decoration have been filled in by a particular motif or set of motifs. However, often more ('optional') horizontal bands have been added, thus increasing the number of basic decoration zones. The actual number of horizontal bands and the use of multiple decoration zones steadily increases from levels 6 to 4. For example, the level 6 vessels show maximally four decoration zones, whereas in level 4 five or six zones occur frequently (one jar even shows eight areas of decoration). As a rule, the motifs are attached to the horizontal bands; unbounded, 'free-floating' designs have rarely been found and seem to represent mainly naturalistic scenes.

A wide variety of mainly geometric motifs has been used to fill the various zones. Generally, the motifs are not restricted to a particular level, although some designs are more common in one level than in the other. For example, parallel zigzags, vertically oriented undulating lines and chevrons are most often found in level 6, whereas solidly filled triangles and conical bars become much more common in levels 5 and 4. A variety of stepped patterns is found in all Transitional levels but increases in importance in level 4, where, in addition, they are presented in a more simple manner than in the lower levels (compare e.g. fig. 3.24, no. 4 and no. 6). A very characteristic level 4 design is the so-called 'dotted-line' motif, consisting of multiple horizontal lines carrying rounded dots at intervals (e.g. fig. 3.25, no. 6). Crosshatching, either on its own or as part of other more complex designs, is most often found at Sabi Abyad. A change in the use of crosshatching can be demonstrated: whereas in level 6 simple diagonal crosshatching predominates, the so-called 'horizontal' crosshatching (cf. Akkermans 1989d:113) has become a very common design in level 4. Significantly, the use of horizontal crosshatching increases in importance even more in the Early Halaf levels (see below).

Naturalistic representations, always 'free-floating', have been found in minute quantities at Sabi Abyad. One sherd possibly shows a tree or other plant on its interior (fig. 3.32, no. 6). Two other sherds seem to carry capricorn representations (fig. 3.32, nos. 3 and 5). Unique is the painted-and-impressed jar which shows a

---

[24] Bichrome painted pottery has been found at several later Neolithic sites, although in very small numbers, e.g. at Yarim Tepe I (Merpert and Munchaev 1973:105), Tell Hassuna (Lloyd and Safar 1945:281), Tell as-Sawwan (Ippolitoni 1970:127) and, perhaps, Baghouz (Braidwood et al. 1944:52).

somewhat irregular row of male animals with twisted horns, clearly depicted ears and tongues hanging from their mouths. Shallow impressions cut through a second row of possible animals on the vessel's shoulder (fig. 3.32, no. 7a-b).

Interior decoration is always very simply executed when compared with the exterior painting. Generally, interior decoration is restricted to a single band of paint along the rim or, less commonly, pendent lines or zigzags (e.g. fig. 3.22, nos. 4 and 12). Undulating lines or short waves (e.g. fig. 3.22, nos. 2 and 7) increase in importance after level 6. The so-called 'dancing ladies' are found in all three Transitional levels in small numbers. These 'dancing ladies' consist either of lines (e.g. fig. 3.26, no. 17) or, restricted to level 4, of lines with solidly painted triangles (e.g. fig. 3.21, nos. 16 and 18).

Count col. pct	Level 6	Level 5	Level 4	mixed lots	row total
Standard Fine ware	48 57.8	93 93.9	278 95.5	90 84.1	509 87.8
Orange Fine ware	23 27.7	5 5.1	8 2.7	13 12.1	49 8.4
Fine Painted ware	12 14.5	1 1.0	5 1.7	4 3.7	22 3.8
Column total	83 14.3	99 17.1	291 50.2	107 18.4	580 100.0

Table 3.30. Transitional pottery — distribution of fine wares per level.

At present, three kinds of fine ware can be distinguished, viz. (1) Standard Fine Ware, (2) Orange Fine Ware, and (3) Fine Painted Ware. The latter two wares are mainly found in level 6, where together they comprise about 40% of all fine-ware rim sherds (table 3.30). In the subsequent levels, the amount of Orange Fine Ware and Fine Painted Ware rapidly decreases to less than 5% in level 4 (however, small numbers of Orange Fine Ware have still been found in the Early Halaf level 3). Generally, Orange Fine Ware and Fine Painted Ware are each distinguished on the basis of temper, firing, surface treatment and decoration; most likely, these wares represent different pottery workshops, or perhaps they are even the products of different pottery-producing regions (in other words: they may have come to the site as trade or exchange products). However, our group of Standard Fine Ware, comprising the bulk of the true fine ware from levels 6 to 4, is less homogeneous both from the technological and the stylistical point of view; it is not excluded that this Standard Fine Ware comprises a variety of 'sub-wares', or consists of both locally produced ceramics and imported pottery. For example, many of our Transitional sherds closely resemble

Samarran pottery from north-central Iraq in shape and decoration (cf. Akkermans 1993:126; Akkermans and Le Mière 1992:10). At several Neolithic sites 'imported' Samarran pottery seems to occur in association with a 'local' assemblage, e.g. at Shimshara (Mortensen 1970), Hassuna (Lloyd and Safar 1945) and Yarim Tepe I (Merpert and Munchaev 1973). In the case of Sabi Abyad, a preliminary analysis (Le Mière 1989a) did not show a distinction between the Samarra-like pottery and the Halaf ceramics; it was assumed that both were locally produced. However, new analyses in progress do suggest that the Samarran pottery and probably also part of the Halaf material are of a foreign origin (Le Mière and Picon, in prep.).

Standard Fine Ware

Standard Fine Ware (figs. 3.21-33) has been found in levels 6-4 only. It is made of finely textured clay and is mainly mineral-tempered or shows no inclusions at all.

Count col. pct	Level 6	Level 5	Level 4	mixed lots	row total
No visible inclusions	70 35.7	86 37.2	277 39.4	123 42.0	556 39.0
Lime exclusively	49 25.0	124 53.7	403 56.9	133 45.4	709 49.6
Lime and other mineral	12 6.1	6 2.6	9 1.3	7 2.4	34 2.4
Coarse grit	3 1.5	–	1 .1	1 .3	5 .4
Small grit	36 18.4	10 4.3	16 2.3	21 7.2	83 5.8
Vegetal	12 6.1	3 1.3	1 .1	5 1.7	21 1.5
Vegetal and lime	10 5.1	1 .4	–	2 .7	13 .9
Vegetal and grit	4 2.0	1 .4	1 .1	1 .3	7 .5
Column total	196 13.7	231 16.2	708 49.6	293 20.5	1428 100.0

Table 3.31. Transitional pottery — Standard Fine Ware temper materials (all sherds).

Some changes in the use of temper are perceptible in the course of time. Whereas in level 6 about 13% of the overall Standard Fine-Ware sample shows plant inclusions and another 20% shows sand or other grit, these kinds of inclusions rapidly decrease in importance in the subsequent levels 5 and 4 in favour of exclusively lime-tempered pottery or ceramics with no visible inclusions at all (cf. table 3.31). Only a quarter of the Standard Fine-Ware pottery found in the lower level 6 is exclusively lime-tempered, whereas almost 57% of the pottery in the final Transitional level 4 shows lime inclusions (thus foreshadowing the importance of lime as a tempering material in the subsequent Early Halaf levels 3 to 1).

The pottery is well-fired and usually completely oxidised (over 80%). About 11% of all sherds show a slightly reduced, 'sandwich' effect, whereas dark grey or black, incompletely oxidised cores are rare (less than 1%; this feature is associated with the occurrence of plant inclusions). Surface colours are buff (55%) or cream (24%), or, to a much lesser extent, greenish (6%), grey (5%) or red, brown or orange (together 10%). About a quarter of the Standard Fine Ware shows a wash or selfslip. The surface is usually carefully smoothed (ca. 89%). Up to 11% of the Standard Fine Ware ceramics found in level 6 shows evidence of an overall burnish. In the subsequent levels the importance of burnishing rapidly decreases to hardly 1% in level 4.

Count col. pct	Level 6	Level 5	Level 4	mixed lots	row total
Not decorated	3 6.3	12 13.8	38 14.4	7 8.0	60 12.3
Painted	43 89.6	75 86.2	226 85.6	81 92.0	425 87.3
Painted & impressed	–	–	2 4.2	–	2 .4
Column total	48 9.9	87 17.9	264 54.2	88 18.1	487 100.0

Table 3.32. Transitional pottery — decoration of Standard Fine Ware per level (only rim sherds).

The vast majority (ca. 87%) of the pottery was painted, but painting in combination with impression has been found in small numbers as well (cf. table 3.32). Impressions have only been found on the shoulder[25] of collared vessels (e.g. fig. 3.33, nos. 1-12. 16). The paint was mainly of a matt black or brown colour. Most common

[25] In this respect, the number of impressed vessels may be underrepresented in table 3.32, which is based on rim sherds. So far, eleven painted-and-impressed sherds come from level 6, one from level 5 and six from level 4. Four painted-and-impressed sherds cannot be attributed to a particular level with certainty.

in all three levels is a matt, black (54%) or brown (35%) paint. Ceramics carrying a lustrous paint have been found in small quantities, increasing from ca. 9% in level 6 to about 13% in level 4. Some paint colours seem to be largely restricted to a particular level. For example, varieties of a red paint are very common in level 6 but almost disappear thereafter, whereas a thick, purplish paint occurs mainly in level 4. A volatile greenish paint occurs sporadically in all three levels (ca. 1% of all painted sherds).

Interestingly, the Standard Fine Ware vessels often show traces of repair and re-use; apparently, these ceramics were highly valued. Three jars were reshaped into pots after the breakage of the neck. Jar necks were repeatedly re-used as pot stands (for example, a series of necks stood on the floor along the wall of room 6 in the level 6 building IV). Five sherds show small conical holes, occasionally in associa-tion with bitumen, which facilitated the repair of breaks (fig. 3.22, no. 14, and fig. 3.24, no. 4).[26] Eight other vessels are thickly plastered with bitumen or gypsum (or both), most likely in order to reduce the permeability of the vessel wall (fig. 3.30, nos. 1-3). One jar has a very irregular rim with bitumen on an indention, which may have served as a spout (fig. 3.25, no. 11).

Generally, it seems that jars are more common than bowls, except in level 6 where bowls and jars appear in more or less equal numbers (table 3.33). Pots are rare; only two examples have been found. Most vessels have plain rims. Flat rims (n= 5) or pinched rims (n= 5) occur in small proportions in the Transitional levels, including about 2% of all rims. Occasionally, some handles were found (n= 6; cf. fig. 3.23, no. 18).

Count col. pct		Level 6	Level 5	Level 4	mixed lots	row total
Bowls		27 57.4	27 29.3	74 30.5	28 35.4	156 33.8
Pots		1 2.1	–	–	1 1.3	2 .4
Jars		18 38.3	39 42.4	117 48.1	33 41.8	207 44.9
Everted rims		1 2.1	26 28.3	52 21.4	17 21.5	96 20.8
	Column total	47 10.2	92 20.0	243 52.7	17 17.1	461 100.0

Table 3.33. Transitional pottery — Standard Fine Ware vessel shapes per level (only rim sherds).

[26] Occasionally, such holes appear without any evidence of cracks or bitumen; in these cases, the per-forations most likely served to attach lids.

Simple, *rounded bowls* (fig. 3.21) are the most common type of bowl, including about 25% of all Standard Fine Ware bowls (table 3.34). The orientation of the wall grades from flaring to vertical and closed. The wholly hemispherical bowls with vertical walls have been found most often (n= 22; e.g. fig. 3.21, nos. 4, 12-15). Rounded, flaring bowls are much less common (n= 8; fig. 3.21, nos. 5-6), as are rounded bowls with an inward-turned, closed profile (n= 4; fig. 3.21, nos. 10-11; these vessels were found only in level 4). Most rounded bowls seem to have had a flattened or sagging base. Most bowls vary in diameter between 11 and 22 cm, with an average diameter of 16 cm. A few larger specimens have been found, varying in diameter between 26 and 34 cm (fig. 3.21, nos. 1-3). The average wall thickness is 0.8 cm. Most rounded bowls were painted, with only a few vessels left undecorated (n= 7). Designs mainly consist of simple patterns like crosshatching, diagonal lines and herringbones. Level 4 has yielded a small group of tall and attractively decorated bowls showing solid triangles, crosshatched lozenges and stepped patterns, arranged in various zones (fig. 3.21, nos. 16-18). Often the same motif is repeated once or twice or two patterns appear in an alternating way. The interiors show a row of 'dancing ladies' along the rim.

Low, carinated bowls (fig. 3.22, nos. 1-26, and fig. 3.23, nos. 1-8) are very common in the Transitional levels (particularly in level 4), comprising 30% of all Standard Fine Ware bowls (table 3.34). These vessels are characterised by a carinated but flaring, straight or slightly concave wall. The base is slightly rounded or flat. The diameter ranges from 10 to 26 cm, with an average of 16 cm. One bowl was 31 cm in diameter. The average wall thickness is 0.7 cm. The decoration is restricted to a single motif in the lower levels 6 and 5, but it often shows a repetitive pattern of, occasionally alternating, designs in narrow zones in level 4. Motifs like horizontal crosshatching and herringbones (e.g. fig. 3.22, nos. 3-5 and fig. 3.22, no. 20, 23) are commonly found, as well as a variety of stepped patterns (fig. 3.22, nos. 6, 13). One bowl showed evidence of repair in antiquity: a conically perforated hole in the wall and bitumen on the crack (fig. 3.22, no. 14).

Figure 3.23, nos. 9-15, shows a number of bowls which are similar in size and kind of decoration to the low, carinated bowls. Even the shape is largely the same, apart from the vertical orientation of the vessel wall. Most likely these *carinated, vertical bowls* constitute a variety of our group of low, carinated bowls. They have been found most often in level 6, after which they tend to become less common (table 3.34).

The *carinated, closed bowls* (fig. 3.23, nos. 16-21) have so far only been found in levels 6 and level 5 (table 3.34). These vessels seem to constitute an intermediate type between the low, carinated bowls on the one hand and the S-shaped bowls on the other hand. All specimens are painted with the same motifs as found on the low, carinated bowls. One vessel shows a handle (fig. 3.23, no. 18). The bowls vary in diameter between 7 and 36 cm.

Count	Level 6	Level 5	Level 4	mixed lots	row total
Rounded bowls	4	4	17	9	34 21.8
Flat-based straight-sided bowls	–	–	2	–	2 1,3
Low, carinated bowls	5	7	26	8	46 29.5
Carinated vertical bowls	5	1	2	1	9 5.8
Carinated closed bowls	4	1	–	1	6 3.8
S-shaped bowls	9	11	15	7	42 26.9
Short-collared bowls	–	3	9	2	14 9.0
(Small) cream bowls	–	–	3	–	3 1.9
Column total	27 17.3	27 17.3	74 47.4	28 17.9	156 100.0

Table 3.34. Transitional pottery — Standard Fine Ware bowl shapes per level (only rim sherds).

S-shaped bowls (fig. 3.24, nos. 2-14, and fig. 3.33, nos. 13-20) are a very charac-teristic type of the Transitional levels, and comprise over 25% of all Standard Fine-Ware bowls. They seem to be somewhat more common in the lower levels 6-5 than in level 4 (table 3.34). These bowls are characterised by a rounded, S-shaped profile and a low rim curving inwards or outwards. All seem to have rounded bases. The diameter varies between 8 and 26 cm, with an average diameter of 16 cm. The average wall thickness is 0.8 cm. All S-shaped bowls except two are painted or, in one case, painted-and-incised (fig. 3.33, no. 16). The decoration on these vessels seems more varied than on other bowls, and commonly includes both diagonal and horizontal crosshatching, herringbones and simple, linear motifs. Some vessels show various kinds of stepped patterns or alternating bands of crosshatched triangles. Our S-shaped bowls resemble the vessels with rounded profiles and everted lips commonly found in Samarran pottery assemblages, e.g. at Baghouz (Du Mesnil du

Buisson 1948, Pl. 21; Braidwood et al. 1944, Pls. 1-2) or Tell as-Sawwan (Ippolitoni 1970-71, Fig. T-V).

Typical for level 5 and, particularly, level 4 are the *short-collared bowls* (table 3.34). These vessels have short, everted collars maximally 3 cm high (fig. 3.24, nos. 15-17, and fig. 3.25, nos. 1-8). Their diameters vary widely between 9 and 32 cm, with an average diameter of 18.6 cm. One complete vessel with a flat base appears to have been mended in antiquity by means of bitumen (fig. 3.25, no. 5). Apart from their distinctive shape, the short-collared bowls distinguish themselves from the other types of bowl in terms of decoration. Commonly, the rims are painted with conical bars (fig. 3.25, nos. 1-3, 6-7), a motif not found on any other type of bowl, but which does occasionally occur on jar necks. The bodies are decorated by means of horizontal bands, crosshatching or various stepped patterns. The so-called 'dotted-line' pattern is characteristic for level 4: a series of horizontal lines with elongated dots at intervals (fig. 3.25, nos. 3, 6-7).

The *flat-based, straight-sided bowls* appear in very small numbers in the Transitional levels; only two rim fragments and one base fragment have been found, all in level 4 (fig. 3.24, no. 1, and fig. 3.33, no. 21). These vessels have flat bases and a straight, flaring wall, which is rather thick (1.3 cm). The vessels are 17 and 18 cm in diameter, respectively (they seem to be much smaller than their Early Halaf counterparts; see below). Both bowls were painted. One vessel shows a rare pattern of crosshatching and chevrons in pannels (fig. 3.24, no. 1); this design was found earlier in association with two pattern-burnished Grey-Black Ware bowls found at Sabi Abyad (cf. Akkermans 1989d:118 and fig. IV.19, no. 138). The other is heavily worn, not allowing identification of its design.

Finally, three fragments of *small cream bowls* have been found in the topmost Transitional level 4. They are virtually identical to the cream bowls found in the Early Halaf levels. Actually, it is not excluded that these few vessels belong to level 3 and are intrusive in the present stratum of occupation. All have a low, everted neck, with a diameter over 14 cm. The decoration mainly consists of horizontal crosshatching.

Pots are extremely rare among the Standard Fine Ware: only two *holemouth* vessels have been found. One is 22 cm in diameter and decorated by means of vertical lines and a discontinous band of chevrons, the other is 13 cm in diameter and decorated with simple horizontal lines (fig. 3.25, no. 9).

The larger part of the Standard Fine Ware consists of *angle-necked jars* of various sizes and shapes, distinguished by a sharp junction between neck and shoulder (ca. 45%; table 3.33). These vessels often have straight but flaring necks (ca. 58% of angle-necked jars, cf. table 3.35; e.g. fig. 3.26, nos. 22-25; see also Akkermans 1989d:123). Less common (ca. 23% of all angle-necked jars) are the jars with vertical necks or necks curving inwards, which give these vessels a closed appearance (e.g. fig. 3.25, nos. 13, 18; ibid.:124). Finally, the angle-necked vessels with concave

Count	Level 6	Level 5	Level 4	mixed lots	row total
Flaring, straight	6	26	67	21	120 58.0
Vertical, straight	6	7	28	7	48 23.2
Concave	6	6	22	5	39 18.8
Col. total	18 8.7	39 18.8	117 56.5	33 15.9	207 100.0

Table 3.35. Transitional pottery — Standard Fine Ware angle-necked jar shapes per level (only rim sherds).

necks (fig. 3.25, no. 15) comprise less than 20% of all jars. Virtually all jars have simple, plain rims, although occasionally some flat rims have been found (n= 3; fig. 3.26, no. 18). The jars have globular or oval bodies, sometimes with a distinct carination. They vary in rim diameter between 6 and 32 cm, with an average diameter of 14.3 cm. The average wall thickness is 0.8 cm.

The jars show a wide variety of decorative patterns, with a clear difference between the neck and the body. Generally, the necks are decorated in a simpler manner than the bodies and show crosshatching, zigzags, herringbones and parallel lines. Horizontal crosshatching is much more common in the upper Transitional strata of occupation than in the lower level 6. A characteristic level 4 design is constituted by the conical bars, found only on the neck of jars (fig. 3.27, nos. 1-6). The bodies of the jars show all of the above patterns but, in addition, carry rather intricate designs like various kinds of steps, crosshatched lozenges and solid triangles. The interior decoration is restricted to the rim. A row of short waves or undulating lines is found most often. Pendent lines and so-called 'dancing ladies' occur in small numbers.

The decoration of jars is not restricted to painting. Impressions occur in small numbers in all three Transitional levels but always in combination with painting (table 3.32). The impressions are always placed on the shoulder of the vessel in a technique different from the one used on other kinds of ware: the Fine-Ware impressions are always stabbed, with usually short strokes or dots in rows (fig. 3.32, no. 7, and fig. 3.33, nos. 1-12, 16).

Finally, a series of bases (fig. 3.33, nos. 21-24) has been recovered from the Transitional levels (n= 67), the vast majority of which are flat (n= 54). Their diameter varies widely from 3 to 19 cm (average diameter is 9.7 cm). The average thickness of these flat bases is 0.8 cm. At present, it seems that flat bases can be associated with all types of vessels except with the S-shaped bowls. Round bases occur in small numbers (n= 13). They are 0.6 cm thick on average.

Orange Fine Ware

This kind of pottery, with its pinkish-orange surface colour and usually orange-red paint, is mainly found in level 6, where it comprises over 27% of the overall fine-ware sample (table 3.30). The amount of Orange Fine Ware decreases considerably in the subsequent levels; it comprises only 3% of all fine ware in the last Transitional level 4 and is virtually non-existent in the Early Halaf strata of occupation (see below).

Orange Fine Ware is predominantly grit-tempered, including a mixture of black or orange-red grit with or without white limestone (72% and 18%, respectively). A smaller amount shows exclusively limestone inclusions (5%) or no visible inclusions (5%). Generally, the inclusions are large (i.e. up to 0.5 mm in diameter) and occur in considerable densities. Most ceramics were fired under completely oxidising conditions (85%), with only a small portion showing grey to dark grey cross-sections (13%). The latter pottery shows a sharp contrast between the dark section and the bright surface colour. Only a few ceramics seem to have been overfired (2%) but no true wasters have been found. As the name indicates, Orange Fine Ware is characterised by a bright, pinkish-orange (52%) or orange-red (17%) surface colour. Less common are buff or brown surfaces. Generally, about 50% of the Orange Fine Ware sample are slipped, while a thin wash was noted on about 7% of all Orange Fine Ware. The slip or wash is always pinkish-orange or orange-red. The ceramics are carefully smoothed (56%) or burnished (40%). Traces of scraping have occasionally been found on sherds belonging to large jars (4%).

About two-thirds of the Orange Fine Ware vessels were painted; no incised or impressed ceramics have been found. Characteristically, the paint is of a bright orange-red to dark-red colour (over 80% of all decorated sherds). Brown or black paint is found in restricted cases (each comprising ca. 9% of the decorated sherds). The paint is predominantly matt (72%). Generally, the decoration of Orange Fine Ware vessels seems to have been carried out in a somewhat simpler and less varied manner than that of other fine-ware ceramics. Crosshatching is commonly found. Restricted to Orange Fine Ware are the chevrons arranged in metopes, which occur mainly in association with our group of flat-based, straight-sided bowls.

So far, Orange Fine Ware has been represented only by bowls (56% of the rim-sherd sample) and jars (44%); no pots have been found. The most common type of bowl is the *rounded* vessel (fig. 3.34, nos. 1-7) with an everted (n= 4) or vertical (n= 5) wall. Closed specimens hardly occur (n= 1). Most rounded bowls are of medium size, with a diameter varying between 7 and 18 cm (average diameter is 16 cm). The vessel wall is 0.9 cm thick on average. Interestingly, one rounded bowl has a loop handle (fig. 3.34, no. 1). Handles are a rare feature on fine-ware vessels. Only four out of the ten rounded bowls were painted. The decoration is rather simple, and consists of irregular, vertical waves or alternating zones of crosshatched triangles. Interior decoration has been recognised only once, and consists of a narrow band along the rim.

Low, carinated bowls (n= 6; fig. 3.34, nos. 8-11) all have flaring walls except for one specimen which has a straight, vertical wall (fig. 3.34, no. 12). The vessels vary in diameter between 12 and 22 cm (average diameter is 19 cm). The vessel wall is 0.8 cm thick on average. All bowls except one were painted. The motifs consist of crosshatched triangles in a zigzag pattern, horizontal crosshatching or herringbones. Interior decoration is found on two bowls only and consists of vertical strokes and 'dancing ladies' (fig. 3.34, nos. 10-11).

Three fragments of *S-shaped bowls* have been found in level 6 (fig. 3.34, nos. 13-15). These vessels are small, with diameters varying between 12 and 13 cm, and hardly 10 cm high. The bowls are painted in various zones, and show conical bars along the rim, crosshatching, chevrons and crosshatched triangles. In one case the interior shows part of a naturalistic, plant design.

Finally, a small number (n= 5) of *flat-based, straight-sided bowls* has been found in levels 6 and 4 (fig. 3.34, nos. 16-21). This vessel shape is rare in the Transitional levels. The bowls are rather large, with a diameter varying between 14 and 27 cm. The average wall thickness is 1 cm, and exceeds that of the other Orange Fine Ware bowls. The flat bases are large as well, i.e. up to 20 cm in diameter. Interestingly, all bowls are painted with chevrons arranged in metopes and various zones. The interior decoration consists of a band of solidly painted, pendent triangles, crosshatched lines with solidly filled triangles or a naturalistic, plant representation.

The flaring, *angle-necked jar* (fig. 3.35, nos. 5, 8) is the most common type of jar (n= 9), but angle-necked jars with straight, vertical necks (n= 4; fig. 3.35, nos. 1, 9) or concave necks (n= 3; fig. 3.35, no. 6) have appeared as well. The jars vary in rim diameter between 7 and 26 cm (average diameter is 13 cm). One specimen was unusually large, measuring 29 cm in diameter (fig. 3.36, no. 1). It shows a deep ridge at the shoulder. The fragments of this large neck were found scattered widely in the burnt ruins of the level 6 building V. All jars except three were painted. The decoration of the neck is rather simple and consists mainly of parallel diagonal lines or crosshatching. Unique is the jar with a spiral decoration, later used as a potstand (fig. 3.35, no. 4). Interestingly, only a quarter of all vessels shows interior decoration. One jar shows a possible naturalistic representation, perhaps a bucranium, on the inside (fig. 3.35, no. 3).

The small number of Orange Fine Ware bases mainly belong to our type of flat-based, straight-sided bowls (n= 5). Mean diameter is 16 cm, mean thickness is 1.3 cm. In addition three round bases have been found, with an average thickness of 0.9 cm.

Fine Painted Ware

Fine Painted Ware appears in minute quantities in the Transitional levels. It has mainly been found in level 6, where it comprises ca. 15% of the fine-ware rim-sherd sample. The other Transitional levels each yielded only a handful of Fine Painted Ware (cf. table 3.30). The vessels are made of a fine fabric, with almost half of the sherds (48%) showing no visible temper. The remainder shows small lime particles (24%) or sand (28%). The inclusions are small in size (less than 0.5 mm in diameter) and sparsely distributed. Fine Painted Ware was fired under oxidising circumstances, showing in most cases an even, brown coloured section (95%). A greyish section occurs rarely. Most ceramics have a buff (61%) or brown surface (35%). One jar was red-slipped (fig. 3.36, no. 4). About 80% of all Fine Painted Ware sherds are burnished, while the remainder is carefully smoothed. This gives Fine Painted Ware vessels a typically smooth, glossy appearance.

Typical is also the very distinctive and carefully executed decoration in red to dark-red paint (some sherds were painted an orange-red or reddish-brown). This paint is in most cases matt (ca. 70%). Designs are often painted in very thin lines hardly found on other wares. Occasionally painting occurs in combination with impressions (n= 5, or 12% of all Fine Painted Ware sherds). At least one impressed sherd gave evidence of a white filling (fig. 3.36, no. 5). Impressed designs include rows of small round stabs or short jabs, placed diagonally or horizontally on the shoulders of jars.

So far, the restricted rim-sherd sample (n= 22) has allowed recognition of a few shapes only. Five *S-shaped bowls* have been found, varying in diameter between 5 and 17 cm (fig. 3.36, nos. 22-26). However, small, thin-walled *angle-necked jars* with flaring necks are predominant (n= 17; fig. 3.36, nos. 9-17, 19-21). These jars vary in diameter between 5 and 18 cm, with an average diameter of 11.4 cm. The height of the neck never exceeds 6 cm, with an average height of 3.9 cm. The vessel wall is 0.6 cm thick on average. Some sherds suggest that these jars had a rounded, globular body. Two rounded bases have been found as well.

The necks and bodies of these small jars have been decorated in a different manner. The neck is commonly decorated by means of parallel or crosshatched zigzags (fig. 3.36, nos. 10-13, 17). Other motifs include simple vertical or diagonal lines and crosshatching. The body commonly shows one or two undulating lines, crosshatching or zigzag patterns. Solidly painted triangles, filling triangular open spaces, are found only in association with Fine Painted Ware (fig. 3.36, nos. 6, 12-13, 21). Finally, about half of the jars showed evidence of an interior decoration, i.e. a single horizontal band along the interior rim (n= 8) or, rarely, a row of short waves (n= 1) or 'dancing ladies' (n= 2).

The Balikh IIIA pottery: conclusions and discussion

It will be clear from the above that the new wares differ very strongly, both from a technological and decorative point of view, from the so-called 'Pre-Halaf' wares in the Transitional layers. For example, decoration of 'old' and 'new' wares can hardly be compared. Indeed, the decoration of the former pottery is somewhat more elaborate in the Transitional levels than in the Pre-Halaf period but the decoration of the new wares is much more complex and sophisticated. It appears that in the case of the 'Pre-Halaf' wares the framing of motifs is associated with impression and incision (particularly on Grey-Black Ware), whereas in the case of the 'new' wares this holds for painting. The colour of the paint of the Transitional 'pre-Halaf' wares is mainly red; the sudden appearance of the peculiar coarse black paint in level 6 is an isolated phenomenon which does not persist in later levels. In the case of the new Standard Fine Ware, paint colour is mainly black or brown from level 6 onwards. However, some resemblances have been found as well. Technologically, Fine Painted Ware is only slightly different from the group of 'Pre-Halaf' ceramics without plant inclusions, the main difference being the fineness of the paint. In addition, it appears that within our Standard Fine Ware the use of plant inclusions for tempering purposes steadily decreases in the Transitional levels, a trend which is also perceptible within the 'Pre-Halaf' wares. Other resemblances concern the appearance of new colours of fabric and surface (cream and orange) in both the 'old' and 'new' wares, particularly in level 4. However, it remains puzzling for the moment whether these new colours in the case of the 'Pre-Halaf' wares should be associated with changing techniques of firing (grey cores are still found in numbers more or less equal to the ones found in the early levels, despite the decrease of plant-tempered sherds in level 4). Finally, the generally simple shapes and kinds of decoration found among the 'Pre-Halaf' wares are also recognisable in the new wares but it seems that these resemblances are of a rather superficial nature. The number of jars (necks) among both the 'old' and 'new' wares is more or less equal in level 6 but the subsequent levels 5-4 show an increase of jars among our Standard Fine Ware, associated with a slight decrase among the 'Pre-Halaf' wares. The 'Pre-Halaf' wares show hardly any carinated ceramics,[27] this in contrast with the new wares which contain low, carinated bowls in considerable quantities (this holds for level 4 in particular). Angle-necked jars and S-shaped bowls, too, are much more common among the new wares than in the 'Pre-Halaf' assemblage.

The rather few links between the 'old' and 'new' wares at Transitional Sabi Abyad suggest that both groups largely developed along independent lines in some sort of parallel evolution. In this respect one may wonder whether these ceramics were all locally manufactured or whether some perhaps represent import products. Actually, analyses carried out so far strongly suggest that at least part of both the 'old' and 'new' fine wares at Sabi Abyad are of foreign origin (Le Mière and Picon, in prep.; this contra Le Mière 1989a).

When considering the Transitional pottery as a whole (both the 'old' and 'new' wares), it seems that 50% of the assemblage consist of fine (or 'finer') wares. However, there is a clear trend towards an increasingly fine pottery: whereas in level

---

[27] Only six carinated jars have been found: two belong to our Dark-Faced Burnished Ware, two to Grey-Black Ware and two to the bulk.

6 fine ware comprises 26.4% (more or less the same as in the preceeding levels), in level 4 this kind of pottery increases up to 68.2% of the sample. Apart from the 'Pre-Halaf' wares, Standard Fine Ware becomes finer in the course of time as well. The new wares obviously contribute to a better definition of coarse and fine ware.

So far, only few parallels have been found for the Transitional pottery of Tell Sabi Abyad. Our new wares are best compared in fabric and decoration with the pottery of the Samarran sites in central Iraq and eastern Syria, such as Sawwan, Baghouz and Samarra itself (cf. Akkermans 1989d:94-95, 129-130, 1991:123, 1993:125-28). The basic Transitional vessel shapes from Tell Sabi Abyad all have their correlates at these sites. For example, our low, carinated bowls correspond to the *Schüssel* found at Samarra (Herzfeld 1930), whereas our rounded bowls compare with the *Näpfe* (ibid.). The same holds for our S-shaped bowls and the angle-necked jars, which resemble Herzfeld's *flache und tiefe Töpfe* and *Flaschen mit kurzem und hohem Hals*, respectively (ibid.). These shapes have also been found at Tell es-Sawwan levels III to V: low, carinated bowls with concave sides (Ippolitoni 1970-71:128 and Figs. L-O), S-shaped bowls (ibid.:133 and Figs. T-U), and 'deep beaker-like bowls' (ibid.:134 and Fig. V). Design patterns found on these vessels are often either identical or closely comparable to those found at Sabi Abyad. Impressed or incised decoration in combination with painting is found in small quantities at the Samarran sites (with the incisions usually restricted to jar shoulders only; ibid., Figs. I-K). In fact, some vessels from Sabi Abyad show such strong similarities to ceramics from Samarran sites that one would expect them to represent import products (see above; compare e.g. our figs. 3.33, no. 12 and 3.24, no. 11, with Herzfeld 1930, Pl. XL:271 and Pl. XXXII:212, respectively).

However, the differences between Sabi Abyad and the sites further east cannot be ignored. The *Fussschalen* of Samarra (Herzfeld 1930) or the overall incised fine-ware vessels of Tell as-Sawwan (Ippolitoni 1970-71:142, Table II and Figs. F-H) are virtually absent from Sabi Abyad. Likewise, the intricate interior decoration found on many bowls at Samarra and Sawwan and the potter marks commonly occurring at these sites (Herzfeld 1930:95-99; Ippolitoni 1970-71:136 and Fig. Y, no. 2) are lacking at Sabi Abyad (perhaps one Orange Fine Ware jar at Sabi Abyad carries a potter's mark; cf. fig. 3.35, no. 3). It also appears that, despite the sharing of numerous designs, some of the most common motifs are not found at Sabi Abyad and *vica versa*. For example, the characteristic Sabi Abyad horizontal crosshatching has not been found in the east, with the exception of Baghouz on the east-Syrian Euphrates (cf. Du Mesnil du Buisson 1948, Pl. XXI, no. R, and Pl. XXXIV). Baghouz has also yielded a vessel closely comparable to the short-collared bowls of Sabi Abyad level 4 (cf. Braidwood et al. 1944, Pl. II, no. 2) and may stand somewhat closer to our site than the other Samarran settlements (not surprising in view of its closer geographical location). Generally, however, Baghouz distinguishes itself from Sabi Abyad in the same way as the Samarran sites in Iraq.

Interestingly, a survey by Bertille Lyonnet in the upper Khabur region of north-eastern Syria has yielded some Orange Fine Ware sherds, very similar to those found at Sabi Abyad (Nieuwenhuyse, in press). Some ceramics from Khirbet Garsour in the Iraqi Sinjar look very similar to some of the Fine Painted Ware vessels from Sabi Abyad (cf. Campbell 1992a, Fig. 3.6, no. 3 and Fig. 3.8, no. 5). Campbell regards the phase in which this pottery has been found as an outgrowth of the Hassunan ('Hassuna III'). Both the Orange Fine Ware and the Fine Painted Ware of Sabi Abyad meet the Archaic Painted Ware found at Tell Hassuna and other Hassunan sites to some extent (Lloyd and Safar 1945:262, 265, 278; Merpert and Munchaev 1993:87-89). This pottery is characterised by a lustrous red paint on a burnished surface, and shares some motifs with the Transitional wares found at Sabi Abyad (particularly those of the levels 6 and 5). However, it seems that these resemblances are largely superficial and hold little validity for a comparative analysis. For example, the exclusively incised fine-ware vessels commonly found at Hassunan sites are completely absent from our site, whereas the Hassunan painted-and-incised ceramics look very different from their counterparts at Sabi Abyad (cf. Lloyd and Safar 1945, Figs. 13-14). In fact, it is mainly the Samarra-like vessels found at the Hassunan sites (often considered to represent imports; see e.g. Merpert and Munchaev 1973:104) and at Sabi Abyad that are comparable.

In short, it appears that the main bulk of the new fine wares from the Transitional levels at Sabi Abyad shows the closest similarities with the Samarran ceramic assemblages. The spread of Samarran traits over a large part of the Fertile Crescent seems to have taken place during the Classical Samarra period, dated about 5300-5000 B.C. on the basis of some radiocarbon dates from Tell as-Sawwan (see e.g. Mellaart 1975:154; Copeland and Hours 1987:407). The present series of radiocarbon dates from Sabi Abyad has yielded a more precise date for this wide distribution; the Transitional levels 6-4 are dated at ca. 5200/5150-5100 B.C. (uncalibrated; Akkermans 1991, 1993:113-16; see also Foreword). It seems too far-fetched to regard Sabi Abyad as the westernmost, true Samarran site but it cannot be denied that a massive adoption of Samarran traits replaced an earlier, localised cultural tradition to a considerable extent. Perhaps our Standard Fine Ware represents a local, western variety of the Mesopotamian Samarra style (cf. Akkermans 1989d:129, 1993:73, 125-128). It seems evident that the process of adoption and assimilation of Samarran traits did not only affect the Balikh valley but took place simultaneously over a much larger part of Greater Mesopotamia. Samarran ceramics have occasionally been found in the upper Khabur region in Syria, e.g. at Chagar Bazar (Mallowan 1936:13), Tell Brak (D. Oates 1982:64; J. Oates, pers. comm.) and, most recently, at some sites found during a survey lead by Bertille Lyonnet (Lyonnet 1992; Nieuwenhuyse, in press). Further west, the excavations in the Amuq have yielded some ceramics closely comparable to the Sabi Abyad Standard Fine Ware, but unfortunately these come from the 'First Mixed Range' (compare e.g. our figs. 3.24, no. 1 and 3.25, nos. 1-3, with Braidwood and Braidwood 1960:111, 116 and Figs. 81:1 and 89:2, respectively). Samarra-related pottery has also been reported from Sakçe Gözü, situated north of the Amuq (Garstang et al. 1937; du Plat Taylor et al. 1949:87 and Fig. 13, no. 1). While it may be too early to place these, admittedly small, samples of Samarra-like ceramics in their proper context, it seems that at least some of them adhere more closely to the Transitional wares from Sabi Abyad than to the Classical Samarran sites, thus emphasising localised trends in ceramic manufacture.

The Standard Fine Ware at Sabi Abyad rapidly changed in the course of time. The level 4 ceramics differ from those of the lower level 6 in fabric, shape and decoration to a considerable extent: the fabric becomes finer, there is a growing emphasis upon painting in lustrous colours, new shapes appear, and new patterns of decoration are introduced. Actually, many of the level 4 ceramics would not be out of place in the subsequent Early Halaf levels 3-1. The earlier Samarra-related pottery is more and more replaced by ceramics made in a new stylistic tradition, ultimately resulting in the Early Halaf. On the basis of the stratigraphic sequence and the available radiocarbon dates from Sabi Abyad, it appears that this fundamental change must have taken place in a short period of time, i.e. less than a few generations (cf. Akkermans and Verhoeven 1995). Tell Sabi Abyad clearly shows that the Early Halaf in the Balikh valley represents a local development directly derived from an earlier Neolithic cultural tradition in the area, without any break in occupation (cf. Akkermans 1993; Akkermans and Le Mière 1992:21). Campbell (1992a) argues for a similar gradual transition in the Iraqi Jezirah, with the Early Halaf arising from a local, Hassunan tradition. Above, the importance of Samarran 'influences' in this process of cultural change was already emphasised. Apparently, there was a widespread sharing of cultural traits and a considerable degree of interregional communication and interaction, prior to the full onset of the Halaf around 5100/5000 B.C.

Comparisons for the 'Pre-Halaf' wares in the Transitional levels at Sabi Abyad are rather hard to find; comparative sites were either excavated a long time ago (in these cases often only a part of the pottery was taken into account in subsequent publication) or are known from surveys only (their surface assemblages cannot always be easily identified). At Sakçe Gözü, 'Samarra-related' pottery was found in association with Grey-Black Ware, Dark-Faced Burnished Ware and red-slipped pottery in period II; however, little is reported on the period II coarse ware (which is said to be very common in the preceding period I; du Plat Taylor et al. 1950). A clear correspondence between the Sabi Abyad sequence and Sakçe Gözü cannot be established for the moment, but it seems clear that some links do exist (e.g. the incised or impressed Grey-Black Ware displays a considerable similarity at both sites). Before, it has been pointed out that the Samarran pottery found at Baghouz shows close resemblances to Sabi Abyad; the Coarse Ware (Braidwood et al. 1944:50-51) and the occasionally pattern-burnished, dark-coloured pottery (Dark-Faced Burnished Ware or Grey-Black Ware; Mesnil du Buisson 1948:19, 21), unfortunately only briefly mentioned in the report, may strengthen this relationship. Attention is also drawn to the site of Dja'de on the Euphrates, which yielded a single sherd decorated with the same peculiar black paint found in level 6 at Sabi Abyad (Le Mière, in prep.).[28] Finally, the earlier-mentioned Khabur survey sites have also yielded red-slipped pottery, some Dark-Faced Burnished Ware and coarse pottery, in addition to the Sabi Abyad-like Transitional fine wares, indicating that our Transitional assemblage as a whole was widely distributed (however, it has to be taken into account that the Khabur material is unstratified and restricted in shape).

To conclude, it appears that the 'new' wares have little to do with the 'old' wares. In this respect, the role of the local tradition in the rise of the Early Halaf may have been rather restricted. The other way round, the new wares also seem to have had a very limited influence on the local tradition. It now appears to be of ultimate importance to determine the local or non-local nature of ceramic production for each ware per level. As said before, it may be the case that at least a part of both the Transitional 'Pre-Halaf' and 'new' fine wares at Sabi Abyad are foreign in origin (Le Mière and Picon, in prep.).

The important role of Samarran 'influences' mentioned before is supported by the rather loose links between the 'Pre-Halaf' and the 'new' wares. Actually, the same picture is obtained from northeastern Iraq, where pottery similar to both our Transitional and Early Halaf ceramics has been found (cf. Campbell 1992a). Apparently, two completely different local pottery traditions, with the Sabi Abyad-like tradition on the one hand and the Proto-Hassuna on the other hand, lead to the same outcome, i.e. Early Halaf, which emphasises the role of Samarran 'influences' in this process of cultural change. (M.L.M./O.N.)

Levels 3 to 1: The Balikh IIIB or Early Halaf Period

Introduction

The transition between the final Transitional level 4 and the earliest Halaf level 3 was most gradual in nature; many level 3 wares, shapes and designs were already present in the lower level 4. Nevertheless, the Early Halaf pottery constitutes a very distinct assemblage. The vast majority of the pottery consists of Halaf Fine Ware, increasing in importance from ca. 72% in level 3 to over 80% in the topmost level 1 (table 3.36). This apparent increase is related to a decrease of Vegetal Coarse Ware (the latter decreases from about 19% in level 3 to less than 10% in level 1). Orange Fine Ware and Red-Slipped and Burnished Ware, too, are found in ever-decreasing numbers until they finally disappear. Many Early Halaf vessel shapes are already

---

[28] However, in chronological terms, the Dja'de pottery assemblage (including the black-painted sherd) has so far been considered to fit our Balikh II or Pre-Halaf period (see above); the precise relationship between Dja'de and Sabi Abyad is still puzzling.

Count col. pct	Level 3	Level 2	Level 1	mixed lots	row total
Halaf Fine ware	699 72.4	47 73.4	60 81.1	123 80.4	929 73.9
Orange Fine ware	6 .6	–	1 1.4	1 .7	8 .6
Vegetal Coarse ware	180 18.6	11 17.2	5 6.8	16 10.5	212 16.9
Red-Slipped Burnished ware	14 1.4	1 1.6	–	1 .7	16 1.5
Mineral Coarse ware	28 2.9	4 6.3	2 2.7	6 3.9	40 3.2
Grey-Black ware	27 2.8	1 1.6	5 6.8	3 2.0	36 2.9
Dark-Faced Burnished	9 .9	–	1 1.4	3 2.0	13 1.0
Column total	966 76.8	64 5.1	74 5.9	153 12.2	1257 100.0

Table 3.36. Halaf pottery — ceramic wares per level (only rim sherds).

found in the final Transitional strata of occupation (level 4 in particular). However, some shapes, like the S-shaped bowls and the carinated bowls with vertical
walls, dissappear in the Halaf levels, while others are newly introduced, e.g. the
cream bowls, or are now found in massive numbers, such as the flat-based,
straight-sided bowls. Most vessels have plain rims or, to a much lesser extent,
flattened rims or inward-bevelled rims (the latter are mainly found in association
with Mineral Coarse-Ware holemouth pots). Some vessel shapes seem to be
restricted to a particular ware. For example, virtually all holemouth pots (fig.
3.59, nos. 1-7) have been found within the Mineral Coarse Ware assemblage,
while the low, oval bowls (fig. 3.57, nos. 1-6) are restricted to the Vegetal Coarse
Ware assemblage.

   Important changes also took place in the decoration of the pottery. About 70% of
all Early Halaf rim sherds is decorated. In contrast with the earlier levels, decoration
is largely restricted to our category of Halaf Fine Ware (table 3.37) and consists

almost exclusively of painting. Some eroded traces of simple painted decoration were noted on a few Vegetal Coarse Ware sherds. The disappearance of other decorative techniques, like pattern burnishing or comb impression, and the disappearance of combinations of various decorative techniques on the same vessel constitutes a clear break with the Transitional levels. Numerous new decoration motifs are found, mainly applied in broad zones covering the larger part of the vessels; particularly in the case of bowls, the earlier emphasis on two or more alternating designs in narrow bands is largely abandoned. Earlier designs are commonly used in a coarser, simplified version or disappear completely. Some of the most common Transitional motifs are no longer found in the Halaf strata, such as the chevrons, herringbones and a wide variety of intricate stepped patterns. However, other early designs, in particular horizontal crosshatching, are now found in massive numbers and become almost a *Leitfossil* of the Early Halaf period. New is also the strong association between some vessel shapes and their patterns of decoration. The most noteworthy examples in this respect are the small cream bowls and the low, carinated bowls, both always decorated by means of horizontal crosshatching, and the flat-based, straight-sided bowls, which are mainly associated with lozenges. Finally, burnishing and slipping, commonly found in the Transitional levels, appear much less often in the Early Halaf levels.

So far, seven wares have been recognised (table 3.36), viz. (1) Halaf Fine Ware, (2) Orange Fine Ware, (3) Vegetal Coarse Ware, (4) Red-Slipped and Burnished Ware, (5) Mineral Coarse Ware, (6) Grey-Black Ware, and (7) Dark-Faced Burnished Ware.

Count col. pct	HFW	OFW	VCW	RSB	MCW	GBW	DFB	Row Tot.
No decoration	91 10.1	8	204 98.6	16	40	35	13	404 33.1
Painted	810 89.8	–	2 .9	–	–	–	–	814 66.7
Incised	–	–	1 .5	–	–	–	–	1 .1
Painted & incised	1 .1	–	–	–	–	–	–	1 .1
Column Total	902 73.9	8 0.7	207 17.0	16 1.3	40 3.3	35 2.9	13 1.1	1221 100

Table 3.37. Halaf pottery — decoration of wares per level (only rim sherds).

Halaf Fine Ware

About three-quarters of the levels 3 to 1 ceramic assemblages consist of Halaf Fine Ware, characterised by a fine and relatively soft, calcareous fabric. The Halaf Fine-Ware ceramics show either no visible temper or white limestone inclusions exclusively; only a very small amount (ca. 1% of the rim-sherd sample) shows dark-coloured sand in combination with lime. These inclusions are usually small (≤ 0.5 mm) and sparsely distributed. Vegetal inclusions are completely absent.

Most Halaf Fine-Ware sherds have a lightly coloured, buff or cream surface (89% of the overall sample). Most sherds (83%) also have an even, light-coloured section, indicating firing under oxidising conditions. About 12% of the pottery shows a grey core; however, this 'sandwich' effect is usually not strong (really black cores are virtually absent). Overfired ceramics with a greenish surface colour and an often crumbly, brittle texture have been found in small numbers (ca. 5% of the sample). Some deformed vessels or true wasters have appeared as well, pointing towards local pottery production (e.g. fig. 3.40, no. 15). The surfaces are virtually always carefully smoothened (98%). This treatment effectively erases most traces of prior activities like coiling or scraping. It gives a vessel a very even surface, which sometimes almost looks like a burnish. Real burnishing, however, is rare in the case of fine-ware pottery (less than 1%). Some Halaf Fine Ware vessels carry a light-coloured, cream or buff 'self-slip', most likely as a result of the smoothing of the vessel's surface, causing the finer particles to come to the surface ((Noll 1991:252; Rice 1987:151). A true (cream-coloured) slip has been noted in a few cases only (less than 2% of the rim-sherd sample).

The vast majority (ca. 90%) of the Halaf Fine Ware is decorated. Decoration consists nearly exclusively of painting. So far, only two incised bodysherds (fig. 3.55, nos. 2-3) have been found among thousands of painted fragments.[29] One Halaf Fine Ware sherd showed evidence of simple linear incisions in combination with painting (fig. 3.55, no. 1; actually, the virtual absence of incised pottery is characteristic for the Halaf period as a whole). Generally, the paint was thinly applied (often the limestone particles used for tempering are visible through the paint) and seems to erode rather easily (on many sherds the decoration is only preserved in negative). Painting is always monochrome. However, a bitone effect is commonly produced by differences in paint thickness or firing conditions. The paint usually has a black (70%) or brown (23%) colour, with dark-red, reddish-brown or orange-red each occurring rarely. In most cases the paint is non-lustrous (ca. 64%).

Interestingly, when compared with the fine ware from the Transitional levels, Halaf Fine Ware rarely shows traces of repair. So far, only two sherds had holes

---

[29] A painted-and-impressed jar fragment found in 1986 (Akkermans 1989d, fig. IV.32, no. 231) may be attributed to the Transitional levels. The fragment was found in a stratum without any architectural features but already showing a glimpse of the underlying burnt level 6 settlement (ibid.:38).

Count col. pct	Level 3	Level 2	Level 1	mixed lots	row total
Bowls	170 26.0	9 20.5	10 18.2	31 –	220 25.5
Pots	8 1.2	–	–	–	8 .9
Jars	206 32.0	19 43.2	13 23.6	30 26.3	268 31.1
Everted rims	264 40.7	16 36.4	32 58.2	54 47.4	366 42.5
Column total	648 75.2	44 5.1	55 6.4	115 13.3	862 100.0

Table 3.38. Halaf pottery — Halaf Fine Ware vessel shape per level (only rim sherds).

pierced through their walls, whereas another two sherds showed evidence of bitumen to mend broken edges.

About 26% of the Halaf Fine Ware consists of bowls (table 3.38). The so-called *cream bowls* (figs. 3.37, nos. 1-13, 3.38, nos. 1-16 and 3.39, nos. 1-9) are the most common type of bowl by far, comprising ca. 38% of all reconstructed bowls (table 3.39). These vessels are characterised by a carinated lower body with a second angular break at the shoulder. At present, two groups can be distinguished, viz. small and large cream bowls, this on the basis of rim diameter, height of the neck, and decoration.[30]

Small cream bowls are the most frequent bowl shape (n= 74, or 34% of all bowls). They have an everted, flaring neck, a flattened, gently rounded base and an often rather sharp carination (fig. 3.37, nos. 7-13, 3.38, nos. 1-16 and 3.39, nos. 1-9). The bowls vary in diameter between 9 and 24 cm (the average diameter is ca. 17 cm). The vessel wall can be extremely thin; the average thickness is 0.6 cm but often it is not more than 0.2 or 0.3 cm thick. The bowls are always painted. A marked contrast exists between the exterior and the interior decoration: the exterior decoration is highly standardised, while the interior shows a large variety of different motifs. The exterior body is decorated almost exclusively with so-called horizontal crosshatching, occasionally in association with one or more horizontal lines. Solidly painted

[30] Akkermans (1989d: 120-21) distinguished three types, viz. (1) the 'small-collared bowl', which is our small cream bowl, (2) the 'large, tall-collared bowl' which corresponds to our large cream bowl, and (3) the intermediate 'medium-sized bowls with a sharp carination' found only once. The latter type has not been found in the present assemblage.

Count	Level 3	Level 2	Level 1	mixed lots	row total
Rounded bowls	18	1	–	4	23
Flat-based straight-sided bowls	42	2	4	10	58
Miniature flat-based, straight-sided bowl	1	–	–	1	2
Straight-sided, everted bowl	7	–	–	–	7
Straight-sided, closed bowl	2	–	–	–	2
Low, carinated bowl	29	1	3	3	36
Carinated, concave-sided bowl	13	–	–	–	13
Small cream bowl	57	4	2	11	74
Large cream bowl	2	1	1	3	7
Col. Total row. pct	168 76.5	9 4.2	10 4.7	31 14.2	220 100.0

Table 3.39. Halaf pottery — Halaf Fine Ware bowl shapes per level (only rim sherds).

vessels or vessels exclusively carrying a simple pattern of horizontal lines are rare (both occurring only twice). In contrast, the interior, always painted along the rim, commonly carries pendent lines, interrupted by either crossed or V-shaped lines (fig. 3.37, nos. 7-9, 3.38, nos. 1-2), or, to a much lesser extent, wavy lines (fig. 3.37, no. 10) and so-called 'dancing ladies' (fig. 3.39, no. 3). The 'dancing-ladies' motif seems to be restricted to small cream bowls and, in addition, to our low, flaring bowls. Three rim fragments were decorated by means of a single horizontal band only. Two other bowls showed a rather complex interior design consisting of a combination of vertical and horizontal lines or waves (fig. 3.38, nos. 3, 10). Interestingly, the small cream bowls seem to have been the only type of bowl occasionally carrying a painted decoration on its interior base, consisting of simple concentric lines, crosshatching or naturalistic representations (plants, trees and birds; fig. 3.39, nos. 1-9).

Large cream bowls (fig. 3.37, nos. 1-6) have been found in rather restricted numbers (n= 7, or 3% of all bowls; cf. table 3.39). They are characterised by everted, flaring necks and a rounded body, which is less sharply carinated when compared with the small cream bowls. So far, no wholly reconstructable vessels have been found, but it seems clear that these bowls are among the largest Halaf Fine Ware shapes found at the site. The rim diameter varies between 19 and 34 cm, whereas the wall thickness is 1 cm on average. Like their smaller counterparts, large cream bowls are always painted but the decoration is more varied. Horizontal crosshatching is predominant but chequerboards appear as well (fig. 3.37, nos. 2, 6). Three fragments from level 1 show a design not found on any other bowl shape, viz. parallel rows of horizontal, undulating lines on the lower body (fig. 3.37, nos. 1, 3, 5). The interior rim always shows a horizontal band, commonly in association with horizontal waves or pendent oblique lines.

Another very common type at Sabi Abyad is the *flat-based, straight-sided bowl* (n= 57, or 26% of all bowls). These vessels show a straight and flaring, or occasionally slightly concave, wall and have a clear, flat base (fig. 3.42, nos. 3-13, and fig. 3.43, nos. 1-6). They belong among the largest Halaf Fine Ware vessels, varying in diameter between 16 and 30 cm (the average diameter is 22.7 cm) and are between 12 and 15 cm high (average height is 13.6 cm). The base diameters range from 11 to 29 cm, with an average of 16.2 cm. Interestingly, the range of designs used for the decoration of these bowls is very restricted; motifs used on flat-based straight-sided bowls are rarely found on other bowls and *vice versa* (cf. Akkermans 1989d:119; however, the designs do occur on jars). Crosshatched lozenges arranged in one or more continuous bands or vertical panels are predominant by far (83% of these bowls carry this kind of decoration). Interior decoration consists of one or more horizontal bands near the rim or, to a much lesser extent, short waves and pendent lines. The interior base seems never to have been decorated but is always carefully smoothed, which in some cases even resulted in a slight burnishing.

In addition, two miniature flat-based, straight-sided bowls have been found, one in level 1, the other in a stratum attributed to either level 1 or level 3 (fig. 3.43, nos. 7-8). The vessels are 9 and 10 cm in diameter, and 3.5 and 5 cm high, respectively. Both were painted, by means of either diagonal or horizontal crosshatching.

The *low, carinated bowls* (figs. 3.39, nos. 10-11, 3.40, nos. 1-15, 3.41, nos. 1-2) are another type of vessel that is very common in the Early Halaf levels (n= 36, 17% of all bowls). They resemble the small cream bowls in shape, size and decoration. The bowls are characterised by an often rather sharply carinated body and a flaring rim. The base is flattened or slightly rounded. The vessels display more or less the same diameter range as the small cream bowls, with an average diameter of 15.7 cm. All bowls except one were painted in a simple manner, and almost exclusively by means of horizontal crosshatching covering the whole body. The base usually carries one or more bands. Some bases were painted solidly. The interior often shows one or more horizontal bands just along the rim or, to a lesser extent, undulating lines, short waves, pendent lines and 'dancing ladies'.

The *carinated, concave-sided bowls* (fig. 3.41, nos. 3-11) have been found in restricted numbers in level 3 only (n= 13, or 6% of all bowl shapes; table 3.39).

These vessels differ from the group of low, carinated bowls in the orientation of the vessel wall (which is often slightly closed) and kind of decoration; in size both types are virtually identical (cf. Akkermans 1989d:120). The carinated, concave-sided bowls vary in diameter between 10 and 22 cm (the average diameter is 15.5 cm). All vessels were painted, mainly by means of horizontal crosshatching. In addition, simple diagonal crosshatching and a chequerboard pattern occurred (fig. 3.41, nos. 3-5).

The *straight-sided, everted bowls* (fig. 3.41, nos. 12-16) represent another type found in limited quantities in level 3 only (n= 7, 3% of all bowls). These vessels have a slight carination near the base and straight but flaring walls. Bases are flattened or slightly rounded. The bowls are rather large, varying in diameter between 14 and 28 cm. The vessel wall is ca. 1 cm thick on average. Interestingly, two vessels had loop handles (fig. 3.41, no. 14). Handles are rare on Early Halaf pottery, and are found only in association with these straight-sided, everted bowls and their closed counterparts (see below). All vessels are painted, showing broad bands, crosshatching or obliquely crossed lines.

The *carinated, closed bowls* (fig. 3.42, nos. 1-2) are represented only twice in level 3 (1% of all bowls) and are characterised by a carinated profile with a restricted upper body straight but turning inwards. One vessel has a loop handle. Both bowls are 23 cm in diameter. One bowl carries a decorative pattern of diagonal parallel lines with crossing ends, while the other has a design more commonly found on jars, viz. diagonal bands filled with horizontal crosshatching. The handle shows a vertical herring-bone pattern. Both vessels carry a simple horizontal band along the interior rim. These vessels closely resemble the carinated, closed bowls found in the Transitional levels.

The *rounded bowls*, comprising 11% of all bowls (n= 23; table 3.39), are more or less hemispherical with an either vertically oriented wall (n= 15) or, less commonly, everted (n= 4) or slightly closed (n= 4) wall (figs. 3.43, nos. 9-14, 3.44, nos. 1-10). These bowls vary widely in size, with the diameter ranging from 6 to 38 cm (average diameter being 19 cm). All bowls except five were painted (the number of non-decorated vessels is rather large when compared with the other types of bowls). The designs consist of various varieties of crosshatching, simple parallel lines, crossed diagonal lines or, in one instance, crosshatched triangles (this last design has not been found on any other bowl but commonly occurs on jars). The interior usually has only one or two horizontal bands at the rim. Two vessels have no interior decoration at all. The rims are plain, except one which is flat (fig. 3.44, no. 4). Flat rims are extremely rare at Sabi Abyad but seem to be characteristic of the later stages of the Halaf period (see e.g. Davidson 1977:120; Akkermans 1989d:122).

Pots are extremely rare in the Halaf Fine Ware assemblage of Tell Sabi Abyad, comprising less than 1% of all rim fragments, all of which have been found in level 3 (table 3.39). Only one type is represented, viz. the *holemouth pot* with a plain or, occasionally, inward-bevelled rim (fig. 3.44, nos. 11-16; actually, in one case the bevelled rim was produced by sowing the neck of a collared vessel; see also Akkermans 1989d:123 and fig. IV.19, nos. 135-137). The rim diameters display a wide range between ca. 11 and 28 cm, with an average of 16.9 cm. The average wall thickness is 0.9 cm. Only half of the pots is decorated, by means of simple diagonal lines, horizontal crosshatching or a single horizontal band near the lip. Interior decoration consists only of a band along the rim.

Jars comprise over 31% of the Halaf Fine Ware assemblage (table 3.38). This category consists almost exclusively of *angle-necked jars* (n= 264, or 98.5% of all jars), displaying a large variation in shape, size and decoration (cf. Akkermans 1989d:123-24). Most angle-necked jars (n= 249, or about 93% of all jars) vary in diameter between 4 and 33 cm, with an average of 13 cm. The jar necks are between 1 and 12 cm high, with an average height of 5.2 cm. The wall thickness is 0.8 cm on average. These vessels have flaring (66%) or, occasionally, straight (26%) or concave (hardly 8%) necks. The medium-sized jars display a wide variety of designs, although over three-quarters of all decoration are made up of barely ten different motifs. Generally, the vessels carry two main areas suited for decoration, viz. the neck and the upper body. The former is decorated in a rather simple manner in most cases by means of (mainly horizontal) crosshatching, horizontal or zigzag lines or, rarely, solidly painted surfaces. The upper body carries these simple motifs as well, but in addition we find a much wider variety of designs here such as crosshatched lozenges and triangles, undulating lines, solidly painted triangles and diagonal ladders. Naturalistic designs are rarely found (less than 2% of all jars). Plants are represented by vertical or diagonal 'trees' with branches and, sometimes, hanging leaves (fig. 3.53, nos. 6, 13-14). Animal representations consist of birds, occasionally surrounded by small dots (fig. 3.53, nos. 9-10, 12). One sherd showed a combination of animals and trees: a horned animal surrounded by birds standing next to a tree (fig. 3.53, no. 11). Again the animals are surrounded by dots (dots occur only in association with naturalistic figures at Sabi Abyad; see also Akkermans 1989d, fig.IV.43, nos. 346-348, 350). Finally, a fragment of a large jar shows two standing human figures and the legs of a third person in front of them. Most likely, the figures hold a bow in their hands and carry a quiver on their backs (fig. 3.53, no. 7). Archers are known from other Halafian sites such as Arpachiyah (Hijara 1978, Pl. XLVIIIA; see also Ippolitoni-Strika 1990; Breniquet 1992) and, possibly, Sakce Gözü (Garstang et al. 1937, Pl. XXV.15). Another human person is shown by figure 3.53, no. 8. The interior decoration of the jars is rather uniform. Usually it consists of one or more horizontal bands (54%), sometimes found in association with short waves (28%), pendent lines (10%) and undulating lines (5%). Other motifs occur only sporadically.

Special attention is drawn to the small group of exceptionally large angle-necked jars (fig. 3.54, nos. 3-6), which comprise ca. 3% of all jars (n= 9) and which have mainly been found in level 3 (in addition, three specimens could not be attributed to a particular level). These vessels have diameters varying between 16 and 40 cm (average diameter is 22.2 cm) and tall, straight or, occasionally, slightly concave necks. The average height of the neck is 16.8 cm but it can easily reach 20 cm. The average wall thickness is 1.2 cm. Less than half of these vessels was decorated, always in a very simple manner by horizontal bands (n= 4). Only one rim fragment showed evidence of interior decoration (a single horizontal band along the rim). The large size of these jars as well as their sparse and simple decoration suggest that they were used in a different context than the other jars, e.g. storage (cf. Akkermans 1989d:123).

Some angle-necked jars (n= 6, or 2% of all jars) show extremely tall but narrow necks (fig. 3.54, no. 7). Most have been found in level 3 but an example from level 1 suggests that they are present throughout the Early Halaf phase at Sabi Abyad. These vessels have small diameters varying between 10 and 13 cm, whereas the height of the neck is in all cases over 20 cm. They are all undecorated. A complete specimen found earlier in a level 2 context shows an unpainted, globular body (Akkermans 1989d:182 and Fig. IV.15., no. 113).

The *low-collared jars* (n= 4, or 2% of all jars) are found in small quantities in the lower Halaf level 3 (fig. 3.54, nos. 1-2). They are characterised by a low, vertical collar (less than one centimetre high) evolving from the body without the sharp carination found on all other kinds of jars. The diameters vary between 14 and 25 cm. The jars are all painted, showing simple linear designs. The interior decoration is restricted to the rim and consists of a single horizontal band or short waves. In one case, the interior carried a pattern of crossed lines in combination with horizontal, undulating lines (fig. 3.54, no. 1).

So far, 197 Halaf Fine Ware bases (fig. 3.55, nos 4-25) have been found, over half of which (n= 108) are flat. Generally, the transition from base to body is rather sharp. Flat bases vary in diameter between 3 and 26 cm. They are 0.7 cm thick on average. Round bases are found in large numbers as well (n= 87, or 44% of all bases; the actual number may be larger, since this kind of base is often hard to distinguish from unpainted body sherds). Round bases are 0.8 cm thick on average. It seems that rounded bases are mainly associated with jars, whereas flat bases may be more characteristic for bowls. Finally, two pedestal bases have been found, both in level 3. One is painted, showing part of a bird (fig. 3.55, no. 25), the other is flat-footed and undecorated (fig. 3.55, no. 24).

Vegetal Coarse Ware

Pottery with vegetal inclusions has been found in limited quantities in the Early Halaf levels. On the whole, about 17% of the Early Halaf ceramic assemblage consists of Vegetal Coarse Ware, but it decreases in importance from about 19% in level 3 to less than 10% in the topmost level 1 (table 3.36; note, however, that the limited sample size in levels 2 and 1 may give a distorted picture). Generally, the rather large (≥ 1 mm) plant inclusions occur in dense quantities. Very few sherds

were both plant-and-mineral (mainly limestone) tempered. The vast majority of the
Vegetal Coarse Ware sherds (up to 80%) show a distinct grey to black section, indicating incomplete oxidation during firing. The surfaces mainly have a brown or
dark-brown colour. Orange or buff surfaces are less frequently found. Some ceramics show traces of blackish soot on the exterior surface, suggesting that the vessels
were used on or over a fire (cf. Rice 1987:235; actually, similar traces can be found
on Mineral Coarse Ware). Vegetal Coarse Ware is rather coarsely finished and often
shows traces of scraping, without further surface treatment (up to 16% of the overall
sample). Burnishing commonly occurs (ca. 10%). Decoration is virtually absent:
only two painted rim fragments and seven incised or impressed sherds have been
found (fig. 3.56, no. 13, and fig. 3.58, no. 10, 21-23).

Count col. pct	Level 3	Level 2	Level 1	mixed lots	row total
Bowl	80 53.4	4	–	3	87 49.4
Pot	4 2.6	–	1	–	5 2.8
Jar	39 26.0	5	3	7	54 30.7
Everted rims	27 18.0	1	–	2	30 17.1
Column total	150 85.2	10 5.7	4 2.3	12 6.8	176 100.0

Table 3.40. Halaf pottery — Vegetal Coarse Ware vessel shape per level (only rim sherds).

About half of the Vegetal Coarse Ware sample consists of bowls (table 3.40). Jars
comprise about 30% of the ceramic assemblage, whereas pots are rare, comprising
barely 2.8% (about 17% of the rim-sherd sample cannot be attributed to a particular
shape with certainty). Rounded bowls with plain, simple rims (fig. 3.56, nos. 1-15,
and fig. 3.57, no. 1) are predominant by far (n= 78, or 91% of all bowls). Most of
these vessels seem to be hemispherical. Bowls with wide, flaring or, in contrast,
inward-turning rims occur in small numbers. Diameters range widely between 7 and
40 cm (however, most vessels are between 15 and 25 cm in diameter). The bowls are
rather thick-walled, with an average thickness of 1.4 cm. One hemispherical bowl
carries a red-painted band on a burnished surface (fig. 3.56, no. 13). Six rounded-
bowl fragments are oval in shape (fig. 3.57, no. 1; actually, it is not excluded that

these are husking-tray fragments). In addition to the rounded bowls some rare bowl shapes occur, such as the two flat-based, straight-sided vessels found in level 3 (fig. 3.57, no 7). These bowls have close counterparts in the fine-ware assemblage but are larger (33 and 36 cm in diameter, respectively). Level 3 has also yielded a fragment of a rounded bowl with a short collar, ca. 20 cm in diameter (fig. 3.57, no. 8).

Low trays are often oval in shape. So far, only one circular specimen 26 cm in diameter has been found (fig. 3.57, no. 9), as well as a flat-based fragment belonging to a rectangular tray with straight, slightly everted walls (fig. 3.58, no. 20). The remaining six trays are so-called husking trays (fig. 3.57, nos. 2-6), which have been found in small but consistent numbers in the Early Halaf levels (cf. Akkermans 1989d:115). The Halafian husking trays all have an interior base with broad, parallel grooves, up to 1 cm deep and 2 cm wide. One vessel shows grooves at right angles (fig. 3.57, no. 3). Husking trays with finger-impressed bases, which commonly occur in the lower levels, are no longer found in the Early Halaf strata. Husking trays have either slightly everted or vertical walls, with plain or flattened rims. The trays have solid, flat bases varying in thickness between 2 and 3.5 cm, standing in a sharp angle to the wall. Two trays show low but heavy disc bases.

Pots occur in very small numbers only (table 3.40). Their diameter could be established in one instance only: 11 cm. All vessels have simple, rounded rims (fig. 3.57, no. 10). In contrast with the Mineral Coarse Ware pots, the Vegetal Coarse Ware specimens are not burnished.

Jars comprise ca. 30% of the Vegetal Coarse Ware shapes (table 3.40). They vary in diameter between 5 and 36 cm, with an average diameter of 19.1 cm. Angle-necked jars with straight necks (n= 39, or 72% of the jar sample) occur most often (fig. 3.58, nos. 1-3). Flaring angle-necked jars (fig. 3.58, no. 4) and jars with rounded collars (fig. 3.58, no. 5) have each been found in restricted numbers (13% and 9% of the jar sample, respectively). Finally, a few holemouth jars have appeared (6% of all jars), which are characterised by a wide, low collar gradually evolving from the body (fig. 3.57, nos. 12-14). One of these holemouth vessels seems to have a spout (fig. 3.57, no. 12).

Bases (n= 37) appear in three varieties. Flat bases are most common (n= 26, or ca. 70% of the base sample). They show a rounded or, less commonly, sharply carinated transition to the body. Flat bases have an average thickness of 1.6 cm and an average diameter of 12 cm. Round bases are much less common, including 16.2% of the base sample (n= 6), whereas disc bases include another 13.5% of all Vegetal Coarse Ware bases (n= 5). Disc bases may be related to large vessels with rather steep lower bodies (cf. fig. 3.58, no. 19). The average thickness of disc bases is 2 cm, and their average diameter is 20.3 cm.

Red-Slipped and Burnished Ware

Red-Slipped and Burnished ceramics have been found in very small and decreasing quantities in the Early Halaf levels (1.3% of the rim-sherd sample; table 3.36), until they finally disappear in the topmost level 1. Red-Slipped and Burnished Ware is, like the Vegetal Coarse ware, characterised by a plant temper. The fabric, however, is much finer and often shows very small vegetal inclusions ($\leq$ 0.5 mm). Moreover, Red-slipped and Burnished sherds are more often completely oxidised during firing than the (unslipped) Vegetal Coarse Ware; about 40% show an even, light-coloured section.

The small number of Red-Slipped and Burnished sherds hardly show evidence of decoration. Usually the red-coloured slip and the burnish cover the whole exterior surface. On the interior the slip is often restricted to the upper part of the vessel, just below the rim. One rim sherd was painted in dark-red.

This ware is mainly represented by bowls (n= 11). In addition, a few jar fragments have been found (n= 4). Rims are plain or, rarely, beaded. Simple, rounded bowls are predominant (n= 9; fig. 3.69, nos. 6-9). Most are hemispherical, but others are flaring or slightly inverted. The diameter varies between 9 and 30 cm (average diameter is 19 cm). The average wall thickness is 0.9 cm. In addition to the rounded bowls, one fragment of a straight-sided, everted bowl has been found, ca. 28 cm in diameter (fig. 3.60, no. 5).

Jars mainly have everted, concave necks or, in one instance, a flaring, straight neck, varying in diameter between 9 and 12 cm (fig. 3.60, nos. 1-4). The average wall thickness is 0.8 cm.

Mineral Coarse Ware

This thick-walled coarse ware has been found in all three Halaf levels and comprises ca. 3.2% of the rim-sherd sample (table 3.36). The Halafian Mineral Coarse Ware closely resembles that of the lower levels (see above). The pottery is characterised by a dense mineral temper. The inclusions are usually large (up to 5 mm). The dense grit temper may have served to make the vessels more resistant to thermal stress when used for cooking (cf. Rye 1981:27; Rice 1987:229). The pottery has black or dark-grey cores and dark-coloured, brown to black surfaces. Most vessels (87%) are burnished, which may have reduced permeability during cooking of liquid substances (cf. Rice 1987:231). Decoration is wholly absent.

The ceramics show a very restricted range of vessel shapes. Generally, the vessels have rounded shapes without distinct carinations (fig. 3.59, nos. 1-16). About two-thirds of the rims are plain, whereas the remainder is inward-bevelled. Characteristic are the lug handles (fig. 3.59, nos. 8-9; actually, lug handles are found only in association with this kind of ware), which were made separately and inserted in holes in the vessel wall. Subsequently the edges were smoothed and the vessel was burnished. Spouts were attached to the vessels in the same way.

Shapes are mainly represented by holemouth pots (n= 35; fig. 3.59, nos. 1-7, 10), the vast majority of which (n= 24) was found in level 3. Levels 2 and 1 have yielded only four and one specimens, respectively. Diameters vary between 9 and 31 cm, with an average diameter of 18.2 cm. Rims are simply rounded or, to a lesser extent, inward-bevelled. About a quarter of the pots gave evidence of lug handles. Lugs also appeared as isolated stray finds.

In addition to the holemouth pots, a few bowl fragments were found (n= 3). One large bowl from level 1 is 32 cm in diameter and has an inward-bevelled rim and a spout (fig. 3.59, no. 12). Two other rim fragments from level 3 have smaller diameters (13 cm and 17 cm, respectively) and plain rims (fig. 3.59, no. 11). Finally, a small number of bases has been found, either rounded or flat and varying in diameter between 9 and 12 cm.

Grey-Black Ware

Small quantities of Grey-Black Ware have consistently been found in levels 3 to 1 (2.9% of the rim-sherd sample; table 3.36). This pottery hardly differs from that found in the lower levels, except for the fact that decoration (pattern-burnishing or incision) is now wholly absent.

The small Grey-Black Ware sample mainly consists of bowls and small jars. Rounded bowls with everted walls are most common (fig. 3.60, nos. 10-14). Some of these vessels are extremely low and wide, and perhaps represent plates (fig. 3.60, nos. 10-11). The rims are plain or, rarely, flattened. Rounded bowls have diameters between 9 and 39 cm, with an average diameter of 21.1 cm. The average wall thickness is 0.8 cm. Other kinds of bowls each occur in small numbers. One bowl has a worked rim with traces of sowing and smoothening; probably this vessel was originally a jar, which after breakage of the neck was re-used as a bowl. Some fragments of straight-sided, everted bowls (fig. 3.60, no. 17) have been found, varying in diameter between 15 and 24 cm and with an average wall thickness of 0.9 cm. Level 3 has yielded a body fragment of a small cream bowl (fig. 3.60, no. 18). Apparently, Grey-Black Ware and Halaf Fine Ware are related in shape and, perhaps, function.

Grey-Black Ware jars mainly have straight, vertical necks all 8 cm in diameter (fig. 3.60, nos. 19-20). In addition, some jar fragments with flaring, straight or concave necks have appeared, varying between 7 and 11 cm in diameter (fig. 3.60, nos. 15-16). The average wall thickness of Grey-Black jars is 0.7 cm.

Dark-Faced Burnished Ware

Levantine Dark-Faced Burnished Ware (fig. 3.60, nos. 23-27), virtually identical to that found in the lower strata, appears in minute quantities in the Halaf levels (1% of rim-sherd sample; cf. table 3.36). These imported ceramics seem to form a genuine part of the Early-Halaf ceramic assemblage (although it cannot be excluded that some sherds stem from earlier occupation levels and are intrusive in the Halaf strata). Dark-Faced Burnished Ware has been found in close association with Halafian pottery at Tell Kurdu in the Amuq (phase C; Braidwood and Braidwood

1960:141-3) but hardly occurs at (later) Halafian sites further inland. For example, at Tell Aqab a single Dark-Faced Burnished Ware fragment was recorded among a sample of over 9000 Halaf sherds (Davidson 1981:76). At later Halaf Girikihacyan, some of the 'alien' red-painted and incised sherds are very similar to the Dark-Faced Burnished Ware (cf. Watson and LeBlanc 1990:79-80).

The vessel-shape repertoire is very restricted, partly due to the small number of reconstructable fragments, partly perhaps to the specific nature of these imported ceramics. A few rounded, hemispherical bowls (fig. 3.60, no. 23) have been found, as well as some jars with straight, vertical or everted necks (fig. 3.60, nos. 24-26). These vessels vary in diameter between 11.0 and 21.0 cm. In addition, a flat base ca. 16 cm in diameter has appeared.

Orange Fine Ware

A small number of Orange Fine-Ware sherds have been found in the Early Halaf levels (0.6% of the Early Halaf pottery sample; table 3.36). Orange Fine Ware is common in the Transitional levels, and the small size and eroded state of many fragments suggest that at least some of these sherds are intrusive in the Halaf levels. Some ceramics carry a reddish-orange slip. Others are burnished or painted. Painted decoration mainly consists of crosshatching and simple parallel or diagonal lines (fig. 3.60, no. 28).

Recognisable shapes include a rounded, hemispherical bowl from level 3, ca. 8 cm in diameter and burnished, and two straight, vertical jars, one found in level 3, the other in level 1. Both jars have burnished necks, and are 10.0 and 20.0 cm in diameter, respectively. In addition, a pedestal base (diameter 8.5 cm; fig. 3.60, no. 29) and two flat-base fragments (diameters 7.0 and 14.0 cm) have been found.

The Balikh IIIB pottery: some chronological remarks

An account of the chronology of the Early Halaf ceramic assemblage of Tell Sabi Abyad has already been presented in detail elsewhere (e.g. Akkermans 1989d, 1993) and until now our views have undergone little change. Apart from Sabi Abyad, there are at present only a few sites that have yielded Early Halaf material in a stratified context, viz. Arpachiyah in northern Iraq and Tell Aqab in northern Syria. Akkermans (1989d:130-36, 1993:123-132) has pointed out that the Early Halaf uncovered at these sites is not the same as the Sabi Abyad Early Halaf; the latter undoubtedly precedes, at least partially, that of Arpachiyah and Aqab. These chronological differences have led Campbell (1992a) to distinguish more formally between a Halaf 1a and 1b: the Sabi Abyad Early Halaf represents his Halaf 1a, while the earliest levels uncovered at Arpachiyah and Aqab represent his Halaf 1b. Interestingly, recent surveys in the upper Jezirah north of the Jebel Sinjar in Iraq (Wilkinson 1990a, 1990b, in press) have yielded numerous sites fitting Campbell's Halaf 1a phase

(Campbell 1992a). In particular site NJP 72 has yielded a representative collection of Sabi Abyad-like ceramics. Characteristic shapes include small cream bowls, carinated bowls and everted jars (Campbell 1992a, fig. 4.2). Horizontal crosshatching seems to be one of the most common designs used at NJP 72 (ibid., table B.46). Similar ceramics have recently been collected from the surface of some mounds in the Khabur area north of Hassake in northeastern Syria (Lyonnet 1992; Nieuwenhuyse, in press). Further south along the Khabur, the site of Tell Rachman South has yielded Sabi Abyad-like ceramics (H. Kühne, pers. comm.; S. Kulemann, pers. comm.). So far, no other sites with Sabi Abyad Early Halaf pottery are known along the Khabur or the Euphrates. While undoubtedly this picture is partly due to the present state of research, it is tempting to see the distribution of the Early Halaf (Campbell's Halaf 1a) as bounded between the Balikh in the west and the Tigris in the east. (O.N.)

Catalogue

Order of presentation: ware, level, type of inclusion, core, surface colour, surface treatment, decoration, diameter (when appropriate).

Fig. 3.1
1. Base. Joining with horizontal surface: rounded (1a); angular (1b); annular (1c).
2. Base. Shape of the lower part of the body: indistinct base (2a); distinct base (2b).
3. Rim. Sides: direct (3a); indistinct (3b); distinct (3c).
4. Rim. Joining with horizontal surface: rounded (4a); sharp (4b); flat (4c).

Fig. 3.2
1. Standard Ware. Level 8. Large plant. Grey core. Buff. Smoothened.
2. Standard Ware. Level 10, stratum 10A. Large plant. Reddish-pink core. Buff. Burnished.
3. Standard Ware. Level 9. Large plant. Reddish-pink core. Reddish-pink. Burnished.
4. Standard Ware. Level 10, stratum 10B. Large plant. Reddish-pink core. Reddish-pink. Smoothened.
5. Standard Ware. Level 11. Small plant. Grey core. Red-slipped. Burnished.
6. Standard Ware. Level 10, stratum 10B. Small plant. Reddish-pink core. Red-slipped. Burnished.
7. Standard Ware. Level 8. Large plant. Grey core. Buff. Smoothened.
8. Standard Ware. Level 8. Large plant. Grey core. Buff. Smoothened.
9. Standard Ware. Level 9. Large plant. Grey core. Reddish-pink. Smoothened.
10. Standard Ware. Level 10, stratum 10B. Large plant. Grey core. Reddish-pink. Smoothened.
11. Standard Ware. Level 8. Small plant. Buff core. Red-slipped. Burnished
12. Standard Ware. Level 8. Large plant. Grey core. Buff. Burnished.
13. Standard Ware. Level 8. Large plant. Grey core. Buff. Burnished.
14. Standard Ware. Level 10, stratum 10B. Large plant. Reddish-pink core. Reddish-pink. No treatment.
15. Standard Ware. Level 8. Small plant. Grey core. Reddish-pink. Burnished.
16. Standard Ware. Level 11. Large plant. Buff core. Red-slipped. Burnished.

17. Standard Ware. Level 11. Small mineral. Buff core. Buff. Smoothened.
18. Standard Ware. Level 8. Large plant. Grey core. Buff. Smoothened.
19. Standard Ware. Level 8. Large plant. Reddish-pink core. Buff. Burnished.
20. Standard Ware. Level 8. Small plant. Grey core. Reddish-pink. Burnished.

Fig. 3.3

1. Grey-Black Ware. Level 10, stratum 10A. Small plant. Grey core. Grey. Burnished.
2. Standard Ware. Level 10, stratum 10A. Large plant. Buff core. Buff. Burnished.
3. Standard Ware. Level 9. Large plant. Reddish-pink core. Buff. Smoothened.
4. Standard Ware. Level 10, stratum 10B. Large plant. Buff core. Reddish-pink. Smoothened.
5. Standard Ware. Level 9. Small plant. Buff core. Red-slipped. Burnished.
6. Standard Ware. Level 8. Small plant. Buff core. Red-slipped. Burnished.
7. Standard Ware. Level 9. Large plant. Buff core. Buff. Smoothened.
8. Standard Ware. Level 10, stratum 10B. Small plant. Grey core. Buff. Burnished.
9. Standard Ware. Level 9. Small plant. Red-slipped. Burnished.
10. Standard Ware. Level 10, stratum 10B. Large plant. Grey core. Reddish-pink. Smoothened.
11. Standard Ware. Level 11. Large plant. Grey core. Buff. Smoothened.
12. Standard Ware. Level 8. Small plant. Grey core. Buff. Burnished.
13. Standard Ware. Level 8. Large plant. Grey core. Buff. Burnished.
14. Grey-Black Ware. Level 8. Small plant. Grey core. Grey. Burnished.
15. Standard Ware. Level 10, stratum 10B. Small plant. Reddish-pink core. Reddish-pink. Smoothened.
16. Standard Ware. Level 8. Large plant. Grey core. Buff. Burnished.
17. Standard Ware. Level 8. Large plant. Grey core. Reddish-pink. Smoothened
18. Standard Ware. Level 8. Large plant. Grey core. Reddish-pink. Burnished.
19. Standard Ware. Level 8. Large plant. Grey core. Buff. Smoothened
20. Standard Ware. Level 8. Small plant. Grey core. Red-slipped. Burnished.
21. Standard Ware. Level 10, stratum 10B. Small plant. Brown core. Buff. Smoothened.
22. Standard Ware. Level 11. Small plant. Grey core. Buff. Smoothened.
23. Standard Ware. Level 8. Small plant. Grey core. Buff. Burnished.
24. Standard Ware. Level 8. Large plant. Grey core. Reddish-pink. Burnished.
25. Standard Ware. Level 8. Large plant. Grey core. Grey. Burnished.
26. Standard Ware. Level 8. Large plant. Grey core. Buff. Burnished.
27. Grey-Black Ware. Level 10, stratum 10A. Small plant. Brown core. Grey. Burnished.
28. Standard Ware. Level 11. Large plant. Buff core. Buff. Smoothened.

Fig. 3.4

1. Standard Ware. Level 11. Large plant. Grey core. Buff. Smoothened.
2. Standard Ware. Level 11. Large plant. Grey core. Buff. Smoothened.
3. Standard Ware. Stratum 10B. Large plant. Grey core. Reddish-pink. No surface treatment.
4. Standard Ware. Level 11. Large plant. Buff core. Buff. Unknown surface treatment.
5. Standard Ware. Level 11. Large plant. Grey core. Reddish-pink. Smoothened.
6. Standard Ware. Level 11. Large plant. Grey core. Reddish-pink. No surface treatment.
7. Standard Ware. Level 11. Large plant. Brown core. Reddish-pink. Smoothened.
8. Standard Ware. Level 11. Large plant. Grey core. Buff. Unknown surface treatment.
9. Standard Ware. Level 11. Large plant. Reddish-pink core. Reddish-pink. Unknown surface treatment.
10. Standard Ware. Level 11. Large plant. Buff core. Buff. Smoothened.
11. Standard Ware. Level 11. Large plant. Grey core. Reddish-pink. Smoothened.

12. Standard Ware. Level 11. Small plant. Grey core. Buff. Smoothened.
13. Standard Ware. Level 11. Large plant. Buff core. Buff. Smoothened.
14. Standard Ware. Level 8. Large plant. Grey core. Buff. Burnished. Red paint.
15. Standard Ware. Level 7. Small plant. Grey core. Reddish-pink. Burnished. Red paint.
16. Standard Ware. Level 7. Small plant. Grey core. Reddish-pink. Burnished. Red paint.
17. Standard Ware. Level 7. Small plant. Buff core. Buff. Burnished. Red paint.
18. Standard Ware. Level 8. Small plant. Grey core. Reddish-pink. Burnished. Red paint.

Fig. 3.5
 1. Standard Ware. Level 8. Large plant. Grey core. Buff. Burnished. Red paint.
 2. Standard Ware. Level 10, stratum 10B. Small plant. Buff core. Reddish-pink. Burnished. Red paint.
 3. Standard Ware. Level 8. Small plant. Grey core. Buff. Burnished. Red paint.
 4. Dark-Faced Burnished Ware. Level 8. Very large mineral. Grey. Burnished. Red paint.
 5. Standard Ware. Level 8. Large plant. Grey core. Buff. Smoothened. Red paint.
 6. Standard Ware. Level 8. Small plant. Reddish-pink core. Reddish-pink. Burnished. Red paint.
 7. Standard Ware. Level 10, stratum 10A. Small plant. Grey core. Reddish-pink. Burnished. Red paint.
 8. Standard Ware. Level 9. Large plant. Grey core. Buff. Burnished.
 9. Standard Ware. Level 10, stratum 10B. Large plant. Grey core. Buff. Burnished.
10. Standard Ware. Level 10, stratum 10A. Large plant. Grey core. Buff. Burnished.
11. Dark-Faced Burnished Ware. Level 10, stratum 10A. Very large mineral. Brown core. Reddish-pink. Burnished.
12. Standard Ware. Level 7. Small plant. Buff core. Buff. Smoothened. Red paint.
13. Standard Ware. Level 7. Small plant. Grey core. Buff. Smoothened. Red paint.
14. Standard Ware. Level 8. Large plant. Grey core. Buff. Smoothened. Red paint.
15. Standard Ware. Level 8. Small plant. Grey core. Buff. Smoothened.
16. Standard Ware. Level 9. Large plant. Grey core. Buff. Smoothened.
17. Standard Ware. Level 10, stratum 10B. Large plant. Buff core. Buff. Smoothened.

Fig. 3.6
 1. Standard Ware. Level 6. Large plant. Grey core. Buff. Smoothened.
 2. Standard Ware. Level 6. Large plant. Grey core. Reddish-pink. Smoothened.
 3. Standard Ware. Level 4. Large plant. Buff core. Buff. Smoothened.
 4. Mineral Coarse Ware. Level 5. Very large mineral. Buff core. Buff. Burnished.
 5. Standard Ware. Level 6. Large plant. Grey core. Brown. Burnished.
 6. Standard Ware. Level 4. Large plant. Grey core. Reddish-pink. Smoothened.

Fig. 3.7
 1. Standard Ware. Level 5/4. Large plant. Buff core. Buff. Smoothened.
 2. Standard Ware. Level 6. Small plant. Buff core. Buff. Smoothened.
 3. Standard Ware. Level 6. Large plant. Buff core. Buff. Smoothened.
 4. Standard Ware. Level 6. Large plant. Brown core. Buff. Smoothened.
 5. Standard Ware. Level 6/5. Large plant. Reddish-pink core. Buff. Smoothened.
 6. Standard Ware. Level 6. Large plant. Grey core. Buff. Burnished.
 7. Standard Ware. Level 6. Large plant. Buff core. Buff. Smoothened.
 8. Standard Ware. Level 6. Large plant. Grey core. Brown. Burnished.
 9. Standard Ware. Level 6. Large plant. Buff core. Buff. Burnished.

Fig. 3.8
1. Standard Ware. Level 6. Large plant. Buff core. Buff. Smoothened.
2. Standard Ware. Level 6. Large plant. Grey core. Buff. Smoothened.
3. Standard Ware. Level 6. Large plant. Grey core. Reddish-pink. Burnished.
4. Standard Ware. Level 6. Large plant. Brown core. Reddish-pink. Smoothened.
5. Standard Ware. Level 6. Large plant. Buff core. Buff. Smoothened.
6. Standard Ware. Level 6. Large plant. Grey core. Buff. Smoothened.
7. Standard Ware. Level 6. Small plant. Grey core. Reddish-pink. Smoothened.
8. Standard Ware. Level 6. Large plant. Grey core. Reddish-pink. Smoothened.
9. Standard Ware. Level 6. Small plant. Reddish-pink core. Reddish-pink. Burnished.
10. Standard Ware. Level 6. Large plant. Buff core. Buff. Smoothened.
11. Standard Ware. Level 5/4. Large plant. Grey core. Buff. Burnished.

Fig. 3.9
1. Standard Ware. Level 6. Large plant. Grey core. Reddish-pink. Burnished.
2. Standard Ware. Level 6. Large plant. Grey core. Reddish-pink. Burnished.
3. Standard Ware. Level 6. Large plant. Grey core. Reddish-pink. Smoothened.
4. Standard Ware. Level 6. Large plant. Brown core. Reddish-pink. Burnished.
5. Standard Ware. Level 6. Large plant. Buff core. Buff. Burnished.
6. Standard Ware. Level 6. Large plant. Grey core. Reddish-pink. Burnished.
7. Standard Ware. Level 6. Large plant. Reddish-pink core. Buff. Smoothened. Red paint.

Fig. 3.10
1. Standard Ware. Level 6. Large plant. Grey core. Buff. Burnished.
2. Standard Ware. Level 6. Large plant. Buff core. Buff. Smoothened.
3. Standard Ware. Level 6. Large plant. Reddish-pink core. Reddish-pink. Smoothened.
4. Standard Ware. Level 6. Large plant. Buff core. Buff. Burnished.
5. Standard Ware. Level 6. Large plant. Grey core. Buff. Smoothened.

Fig. 3.11
1. Standard Ware. Level 6. Large plant. Grey core. Buff. Smoothened.
2. Standard Ware. Level 6. Large plant. Grey core. Buff. Smoothened.
3. Standard Ware. Level 6. Small plant. Reddish-pink core. Reddish-pink. Burnished.
4. Standard Ware. Level 6. Large plant. Grey core. Buff. Smoothened.
5. Standard Ware. Level 6/5. Large plant. Grey core. Buff. Smoothened.

Fig. 3.12
1. Standard Ware. Level 6. Large plant. Grey core. Reddish-pink. Burnished. *Appliqué*.
2. Standard Ware. Level 6. Large plant. Grey core. Reddish-pink. Smoothened.
3. Standard Ware. Level 6. Large plant. Grey core. Reddish-pink. Smoothened.
4. Standard Ware. Level 5. Large plant. Grey core. Reddish-pink. Burnished.
5. Standard Ware. Level 6. Small plant. Grey core. Buff. Burnished. Reddish paint and impressions.

Fig. 3.13
1. Standard Ware. Level 6. Large plant. Buff core. Buff. Smoothened.
2. Standard Ware. Level 6. Large plant. Brown core. Buff. Smoothened.
3. Standard Ware. Level 6. Large plant. Grey core. Reddish-pink. Burnished.
4. Standard Ware. Level 6. Large plant. Grey core. Reddish-pink. Smoothened.

5. Standard Ware. Level 6. Large plant. Brown core. Brown. Smoothened.
6. Standard Ware. Level 6. Large plant. Grey core. Reddish-pink. Smoothened.
7. Standard Ware. Level 4. Large plant. Grey core. Reddish-pink. Smoothened.
8. Standard Ware. Level 6. Large plant. Buff core. Reddish-pink. Smoothened.

Fig. 3.14
1. Standard Ware. Level 6. Large plant. Grey core. Reddish-pink. Smoothened.
2. Dark-Faced Burnished Ware. Level 6. Very large mineral. Reddish core. Red-slipped. Burnished.
3. Dark-Faced Burnished Ware. Level 6. Very large mineral. Grey core. Red-slipped. Burnished.
4. Dark-Faced Burnished Ware. Level 6. Very large mineral. Grey core. Red paint.
5. Dark-Faced Burnished Ware. Level 6. Very large mineral. Grey core. Red paint.
6. Dark-Faced Burnished Ware. Level 6. Very large mineral. Brown core. Red paint.
7. Dark-Faced Burnished Ware. Level 6. Very large mineral. Black core. Red-slipped. Burnished.
8. Dark-Faced Burnished Ware. Level 6. Very large mineral. Grey core. Buff. Burnished.
9. Dark-Faced Burnished Ware. Level 6. Very large mineral. Grey core. Grey. Burnished.

Fig. 3.15
1. Standard Ware. Level 6. Small plant. Grey core. Buff. Burnished.
2. Standard Ware. Level 5/4. Large plant. Grey core. Buff. Smoothened.
3. Standard Ware. Level 6/5. Large plant. Buff core. Buff. Burnished.
4. Standard Ware. Level 6. Large plant. Brown core. Buff. Burnished.
5. Standard Ware. Level 6. Large plant. Grey core. Buff. Smoothened.
6. Standard Ware. Level 5/4. Large plant. Grey core. Buff. Smoothened.
7. Standard Ware. Level 6. Large plant. Grey core. Buff. Smoothened.
8. Standard Ware. Level 4. Large plant. Grey core. Buff. Burnished.
9. Standard Ware. Level 6. Large plant. Grey core.
10. Standard Ware. Level 6. Large plant. Grey core. Brown. Burnished.
11. Standard Ware. Level 6. Large plant. Grey core. Buff. Burnished.
12. Standard Ware. Level 4. Large plant. Grey core. Buff. Smoothened.
13. Standard Ware. Level 6. Small plant. Grey core. Buff. Burnished.
14. Standard Ware. Level 6. Large plant. Grey core.
15. Standard Ware. Level 6. Large plant. Buff core. Buff. Burnished.
16. Standard Ware. Level 6. Large plant. Brown core. Grey. Burnished.
17. Standard Ware. Level 6. Large plant. Grey core. Buff. Smoothened.
18. Standard Ware. Level 6. Large plant. Buff core. Buff. Burnished.
19. Standard Ware. Level 6. Large plant. Buff core. Buff. Smoothened.

Fig. 3.16
1. Standard Ware. Level 6. Large plant. Grey core. Brown. Smoothened. Ridged interior base.
2. Standard Ware. Level 6. Large plant. Grey core. Buff. Burnished. Ridged interior base.
3. Standard Ware. Level 5. Small plant. Grey core. Reddish-pink. Burnished.
4. Dark-Faced Burnished Ware. Level 6. Very large mineral. Grey core. Red-slipped. Burnished.
5. Dark-Faced Burnished Ware. Level 6/3A. Very large mineral. Grey core. Brown. Burnished.

6. Standard Ware. Level 6. Large plant. Grey core. Buff. Smoothened. *Appliqué.*
7. Standard Ware. Level 6. Large plant. Grey core. Buff. Smoothened. *Appliqué.*
8. Standard Ware. Level 6. Large plant. Buff core. Buff. Smoothened. *Appliqué.*
9. Standard Ware. Level 6. Large plant. Grey core. Buff. Smoothened. *Appliqué.*

Fig. 3.17
1. Standard Ware. Level 6. Large plant. Reddish-pink core. Light cream. Burnished. Black paint.
2. Standard Ware. Level 6. Large plant. Buff core. Buff. Smoothened. Black paint.
3. Standard Ware. Level 6. Large plant. Reddish-pink core. Reddish-pink. Burnished. Black paint.
4. Standard Ware. Level 5/4. Large plant. Buff core. Buff. Burnished. Black paint.
5. Standard Ware. Level 6. Large plant. Grey core. Reddish-pink. Smoothened. Red paint.
6. Standard Ware. Level 6. Medium mineral. Buff core. Buff. Smoothened. Red paint.
7. Standard Ware. Level 5. Large plant. Buff core. Buff. Smoothened. Red paint.
8. Standard Ware. Level 6. Small mineral. Buff core. Buff. Smoothened. Red paint.
9. Dark-Faced Burnished Ware. Level 6. Very large mineral. Brown core. Brown. Burnished. Red paint.

Fig. 3.18
1. Standard Ware. Level 6. Large plant. Grey core. Buff. Smoothened. Incised.
2. Standard Ware. Level 6. Large plant. Grey core. Brown. Smoothened. Incised.
3. Standard Ware. Level 6/5. Large plant. Grey core. Reddish-pink. Burnished. Incised.
4. Standard Ware. Level 6. Large plant. Grey core. Brown. Smoothened. Incised.
5. Grey-Black Ware. Level unknown. Small plant. Grey core. Buff. Burnished. Incised.

Fig. 3.19
1. Grey-Black Ware. Level 6. Small plant. Brown core. Buff. Burnished. Incised.
2. Grey-Black Ware. Level 6. Small plant. Grey core. Grey. Burnished. Incised.
3. Grey-Black Ware. Level 6. Small plant. Brown core. Brown. Burnished. Incised/impressed.
4. Grey-Black Ware. Level 6/3B/3A. Small plant. Grey core. Brown. Burnished. Incised.
5. Grey-Black Ware. Level 6. Small plant. Grey core. Grey. Burnished. Incised.
6. Standard Ware. Level 6. Small plant. Buff core. Brown. No treatment. Impressed.
7. Standard Ware. Level 6. Small plant. Buff core. Buff. Burnished. Red paint. Impressed.

Fig. 3.20
1. Standard Ware. Level 6. Small plant. Grey core. Buff. Smoothened. Red paint. Impressed.
2. Standard Ware. Level 5. Large plant. Grey core. Buff. Smoothened. Red paint. Impressed. Found in grave SAB92-B2.
3. Grey-Black Ware. Level 6. Large plant. Grey core. Red-slipped. Burnished. Impressed.
4. Standard Ware. Level 6. Small plant. Grey core. Buff. Burnished. Incised.

Fig. 3.21
1. Standard Fine Ware. Level 4. Lime. Oxidised. Buff. Smoothened. Brown matt paint. D:34 cm.
2. Standard Fine Ware. Level 6. Lime and glitters. Oxidised. Buff. Smoothened. Brown matt paint. D:26 cm.
3. Standard Fine Ware. Level 6. Small plant and (black) mineral. Incompletely oxidised (grey core). Brown. Smoothened. Orange-red matt paint. D:27 cm.

4. Standard Fine Ware. Level 6. Sand. Oxidised. Cream. Burnished. Orange-red matt paint. D:21 cm.
5. Standard Fine Ware. Level 5. Lime and glitters. Oxidised. Buff. Smoothened. Brown matt paint. D:23 cm.
6. Standard Fine Ware. Level 6. Small plant and lime. Oxidised. Brown Smoothened. Orange-red matt paint. D:18 cm.
7. Standard Fine Ware. Level 4. No visible inclusions. Oxidised. Buff. Smoothened. Brown matt paint. D:22 cm.
8. Standard Fine Ware. Level 4. Lime. Oxidised. Buff. Smoothened. Black lustrous paint. D:21 cm.
9. Standard Fine Ware. Level 4. No visible inclusions. Oxidised. Cream. Slipped. Brown matt paint. D:19 cm.
10. Standard Fine Ware. Level 4/5. Lime. Oxidised. Buff. Smoothened. Brown matt paint. D:14 cm.
11. Standard Fine Ware. Level 5/6. Lime. Oxidised. Buff. Smoothened. Black matt paint. D:19 cm.
12. Standard Fine Ware. Level 4/5. Lime. Oxidised. Buff. Smoothened. Black matt paint. D:15 cm.
13. Standard Fine Ware. Level 4. Lime. Oxidised. Cream. Smoothened. Black lustrous paint. D:13 cm.
14. Standard Fine Ware. Level 5. No visible inclusions. Oxidised. Cream. Smoothened. Brown matt paint. D:17 cm.
15. Standard Fine Ware. Level 5/6. Lime. Overfired (?). Green. Smoothened. Black matt paint. D:12 cm.
16. Standard Fine Ware. Level 4. No visible inclusions. Incompletely oxidised (grey core). Cream. Slipped. Brown lustrous paint. D:14 cm.
17. Standard Fine Ware. Level 4. Lime. Overfired. Green. Smoothened. Black matt paint.
18. Standard Fine Ware. Level 4. Lime. Overfired. Green. Smoothened. Purplish matt paint. D:15 cm.

Fig. 3.22
1. Standard Fine Ware. Level 6. Lime. Oxidised. Cream. Smoothened. Black matt paint. D:31 cm.
2. Standard Fine Ware. Level 4. Lime. Oxidised. Cream. Smoothened. Brown matt paint. D:20 cm.
3. Standard Fine Ware. Level 4. No visible inclusions. Oxidised. Cream. Smoothened. Black matt paint. D:20 cm.
4. Standard Fine Ware. Level 6. Small (black) mineral. Oxidised. Cream. Smoothened. Brown lustrous paint. D:19 cm.
5. Standard Fine Ware. Level 4. Lime. Oxidised. Buff. Smoothened. Black matt paint. D:17 cm.
6. Standard Fine Ware. Level 4. No visible inclusions. Overfired. Green. Smoothened. Brown matt paint. D:16 cm.
7. Standard Fine Ware. Level 4/5. No visible inclusions. Oxidised. Buff. Smoothened. Black matt paint. D:15 cm.
8. Standard Fine Ware. Level 4. Lime. Oxidised. Cream. Smoothened. Black matt paint. D:12 cm.
9. Standard Fine Ware. Level 4. Lime. Incompletely oxidised (grey core). Buff. Smoothened. Black matt paint. D:13 cm.

10. Standard Fine Ware. Level 5. No visible inclusions. Overfired. Green. Smoothened. Greenish matt paint. D:18 cm.
11. Standard Fine Ware. Level 4. Lime. Incompletely oxidised (grey core). Buff. Slipped. Black matt paint. D:16 cm.
12. Standard Fine Ware. Level 5. Lime. Oxidised. Buff. Smoothened. Black matt paint. Found in grave SAB92-B2. D:13 cm.
13. Standard Fine Ware. Level 4. No visible inclusions. Oxidised. Buff. Smoothened. Black matt paint. D:13 cm.
14. Standard Fine Ware. Level 4. Lime. Oxidised. Buff. Smoothened. Black matt paint. Small repair holes and bitumen. D:14 cm.
15. Standard Fine Ware. Level 5/6. Lime. Oxidised. Buff. Smoothened. Wash. Black matt paint. D:15 cm.
16. Standard Fine Ware. Level 6. Lime. Oxidised. Buff. Smoothened. Black matt paint. D:13 cm.
17. Standard Fine Ware. Level 4/5. Lime. Oxidised. Cream. Smoothened. Black matt paint. D:14 cm.
18. Standard Fine Ware. Level 4. No visible inclusions. Oxidised. Cream. Smoothened. Black matt paint. D:12 cm.
19. Standard Fine Ware. Level 4. Lime. Overfired. Green. Smoothened. Black matt paint. D:10 cm.
20. Standard Fine Ware. Level 4. Lime. Oxidised. Buff. Smoothened. Black matt paint. D:19 cm.
21. Standard Fine Ware. Level 4. No visible inclusions. Oxidised. Cream. Smoothened. Wash. Black matt paint. D:18 cm.
22. Standard Fine Ware. Level 4. Lime. Incompletely oxidised (grey core). Buff. Smoothened. Brown matt paint. D:14 cm.
23. Standard Fine Ware. Level 5. Lime. Oxidised. Buff. Smoothened. Orange-red matt paint. D:14 cm.
24. Standard Fine Ware. Level 4/5/6. Lime. Incompletely oxidised (grey core). Cream. Smoothened. Brown matt paint. D:15 cm.
25. Standard Fine Ware. Level 5. Lime. Oxidised. Buff. Smoothened. Black matt paint. D:14 cm.
26. Standard Fine Ware. Level 4. Lime. Oxidised. Buff. Smoothened. Black matt paint. D:12 cm.

Fig. 3.23
1. Standard Fine Ware. Level 5. Lime. Oxidised. Buff. Smoothened. Orange-red matt paint. D:22,6 cm.
2. Standard Fine Ware. Level 4/5. Lime. Oxidised. Buff. Smoothened. Orange-red matt paint. D:25 cm.
3. Standard Fine Ware. Level 4. Lime. Oxidised. Buff. Smoothened. Brown matt paint. D:23 cm.
4. Standard Fine Ware. Level 4. Lime. Oxidised. Buff. Smoothened. Black matt paint. D:20 cm.
5. Standard Fine Ware. Level 4. Lime. Incompletely oxidised (grey core). Cream. Smoothened. Wash. Black matt paint. D:22 cm.
6. Standard Fine Ware. Level 4. No visible inclusions. Oxidised. Buff. Smoothened. Wash. Brown matt paint. D:22 cm.
7. Standard Fine Ware. Level 4/5. Lime. Oxidised. Buff. Smoothened. Black matt paint. D:12 cm.

8. Standard Fine Ware. Level 6. Small (black) mineral. Oxidised. Buff. Smoothened. Black matt paint. D:12 cm.
9. Standard Fine Ware. Level 4/5/6. Sand. Oxidised. Buff. Smoothened. Black matt paint. D:10 cm.
10. Standard Fine Ware. Level 6. Lime. Overfired. Grey. Smoothened. Black matt paint. D:13 cm.
11. Standard Fine Ware. Level 6. Medium-sized plant and lime. Oxidised. Orange. Smoothened. Black matt paint. D:13 cm.
12. Standard Fine Ware. Level 6. Small mineral. Oxidised. Buff. Smoothened. Black matt paint. D:17 cm.
13. Standard Fine Ware. Level 5. Lime. Oxidised. Buff. Smoothened. Brown matt paint. D:21 cm.
14. Standard Fine Ware. Level 6. Medium-sized plant. Oxidised. Cream. Burnished. Orange-red matt paint. D:17 cm.
15. Standard Fine Ware. Level 6. Lime and black mineral. Oxidised. Buff. Smoothened. Wash. Black matt paint. D:17 cm.
16. Standard Fine Ware. Level 6. Lime. Oxidised. Orange. Smoothened. Orange-red matt paint. D:36 cm.
17. Standard Fine Ware. Level 5/6. No visible inclusions. Oxidised. Buff. Smoothened. Red matt paint. D:22 cm.
18. Standard Fine Ware. Level 5. No visible inclusions. Oxidised. Buff. Smoothened. Brown matt paint. D:17 cm.
19. Standard Fine Ware. Level 6. No visible inclusions. Oxidised. Cream. Smoothened. Black matt paint. D:15 cm.
20. Standard Fine Ware. Level 6. Lime. Oxidised. Cream. Smoothened. Wash. Brown matt paint. D:10 cm.
21. Standard Fine Ware. Level 6. Lime. Oxidised. Orange. Smoothened. Orange-red matt paint. D:10 cm.

Fig. 3.24
1. Standard Fine Ware. Level 4. Lime. Oxidised. Cream. Smoothened. Black matt paint. D:17 cm.
2. Standard Fine Ware. Level 4/5. Lime. Oxidised. Cream. Smoothened. Wash. Brown matt paint. D:14 cm.
3. Standard Fine Ware. Level 6. Large plant. Oxidised. Buff. Burnished. Brown matt paint. D:17 cm.
4. Standard Fine Ware. Level 6. Medium-sized plant. Oxidised. Buff. Burnished. Black matt paint. D:15 cm.
5. Standard Fine Ware. Level 4. Lime. Oxidised. Buff. Smoothened. Black matt paint. D:16 cm.
6. Standard Fine Ware. Level 4. Lime. Oxidised. Buff. Smoothened. Black matt paint. D:18 cm.
7. Standard Fine Ware. Level 6. Lime. Oxidised. Brown. Smoothened. Orange-red matt paint. D:16 cm.
8. Standard Fine Ware. Level 6. Lime and sand. Oxidised. Buff. Smoothened. Black matt paint. D:11 cm.
9. Standard Fine Ware. Level 5. Lime. Incompletely oxidised (grey core). Buff. Smoothened. Orange-red matt paint. D:15 cm.
10. Standard Fine Ware. Level 4. Lime. Oxidised. Buff. Smoothened. Brown matt paint. D:17 cm.

11. Standard Fine Ware. Level 4. Small (black) mineral. Oxidised. Buff. Smoothened. Wash. Thick purplish matt paint. D:16 cm.

12. Standard Fine Ware. Level 6. Medium-sized plant. Oxidised. Buff. Smoothened. Brown matt paint. D:13 cm.

13. Standard Fine Ware. Level 4/5. No visible inclusions. Oxidised. Buff. Smoothened. Black matt paint. D:12 cm.

14. Standard Fine Ware. Level 4. Lime and glitters. Oxidised. Buff. Smoothened. Black matt paint. D:16 cm.

15. Standard Fine Ware. Level 5. Lime. Oxidised. Buff. Smoothened. Brown matt paint. D:32 cm.

16. Standard Fine Ware. Level 5. Lime. Oxidised. Buff. Smoothened. Black matt paint. D:24 cm.

17. Standard Fine Ware. Level 5. No visible inclusions. Oxidised. Buff. Smoothened. Brown matt paint. D:14 cm.

Fig. 3.25

1. Standard Fine Ware. Level 4/5. No visible inclusions. Oxidised. Buff. Smoothened. Black matt paint. D:24 cm.

2. Standard Fine Ware. Level 4. No visible inclusions. Oxidised. Buff. Smoothened. Black matt paint. D:20 cm.

3. Standard Fine Ware. Level 4/5. No visible inclusions. Oxidised. Cream. Burnished. Black matt paint. D:22 cm.

4. Standard Fine Ware. Level 4. Lime. Oxidised. Buff. Smoothened. Wash. Brown matt paint. D:20 cm.

5. Standard Fine Ware. Level 4. Lime. Oxidised. Buff. Smoothened. Black matt paint. Repaired with bitumen. D:14.5 cm.

6. Standard Fine Ware. Level 4. No visible inclusions. Oxidised. Buff. Smoothened. Black lustrous paint. D:13 cm.

7. Standard Fine Ware. Level 4. No visible inclusions. Oxidised. Buff. Smoothened. Black matt paint. D:14 cm.

8. Standard Fine Ware. Level 4. Lime. Incompletely oxidised (grey core). Buff. Smoothened. Black matt paint. D:9 cm.

9. Standard Fine Ware. Level 5/6. No visible inclusions. Oxidised. Buff. Smoothened. Brown matt paint. D:13 cm.

10. Standard Fine Ware. Level 6. Small mineral. Oxidised. Buff. Smoothened. Black matt paint. D:10 cm.

11. Standard Fine Ware. Level 5. Lime. Overfired. Green. Smoothened. Black matt paint. Irregular rim with indention (spout?) covered with bitumen. Found in grave SAB92-B2. D:9.5 cm.

12. Standard Fine Ware. Level 4/5. Lime. Oxidised. Buff. Smoothened. Black matt paint. D:10 cm.

13. Standard Fine Ware. Level 6. Lime/small plant. Oxidised. Buff. Burnished. Brown matt paint. D:9 cm.

14. Standard Fine Ware. Level 6. No visible inclusions. Oxidised. Buff. Smoothened. Red lustrous paint. D:8 cm.

15. Standard Fine Ware. Level 6. Sand. Oxidised. Buff. Smoothened. Brown matt paint. D:12 cm.

16. Standard Fine Ware. Level 6. Lime. Oxidised. Cream. Smoothened. Brown matt paint. D:9 cm.

17. Standard Fine Ware. Level 6. No visible inclusions. Oxidised. Cream. Smoothened. Brown matt paint. Probably re-used as potstand. D:11 cm.
18. Standard Fine Ware. Level 4/5/6. Lime. Oxidised. Buff. Smoothened. Black matt paint. Repaired with bitumen. D:12 cm.
19. Standard Fine Ware. Level 6. Sand. Oxidised. Buff. Smoothened. Black matt paint. D:11 cm.
20. Standard Fine Ware. Level 6. Lime. Oxidised. Cream. Smoothened. Black matt paint. D:15 cm.
21. Standard Fine Ware. Level 6. Lime/large plant. Oxidised. Cream. Smoothened. Black matt paint. D:10 cm.

Fig. 3.26
1. Standard Fine Ware. Level 5/6. Large plant. Oxidised. Brown. Smoothened. Black matt paint. D:23 cm.
2. Standard Fine Ware. Level 6. No visible inclusions. Oxidised. Buff. Smoothened. Orange-red matt paint. D:20 cm.
3. Standard Fine Ware. Level 5/6. No visible inclusions. Oxidised. Buff. Smoothened. Black matt paint. D:16 cm.
4. Standard Fine Ware. Level 5/6. Large plant. Oxidised. Cream. Smoothened. Black matt paint. D:13 cm.
5. Standard Fine Ware. Level 5/6. No visible inclusions. Oxidised. Cream. Smoothened. Black matt paint. D:12 cm.
6. Standard Fine Ware. Level 6. No visible inclusions. Reduced (black core). Grey. Smoothened. Black matt paint. D:10 cm.
7. Standard Fine Ware. Level 6. Lime. Oxidised. Cream. Smoothened. Black matt paint. D:11 cm.
8. Standard Fine Ware. Level 6. Lime and sand. Oxidised. Cream. Smoothened. Brown matt paint. D:6 cm.
9. Standard Fine Ware. Level 5/6. No visible inclusions. Oxidised. Orange. Smoothened. Brown lustrous paint. D:5 cm.
10. Standard Fine Ware. Level 5. No visible inclusions. Oxidised. Buff. Smoothened. Brown matt paint. D:22 cm.
11. Standard Fine Ware. Level 5/6. Lime. Oxidised. Brown. Smoothened. Brown matt paint. D:21 cm.
12. Standard Fine Ware. Level 5. Lime. Oxidised. Brown. Smoothened. Brown matt paint. D:15 cm.
13. Standard Fine Ware. Level 5. Lime. Oxidised. Cream. Smoothened. Black matt paint. D:15 cm.
14. Standard Fine Ware. Level 5. No visible inclusions. Oxidused. Cream. Smoothened. Brown matt paint. D:17 cm.
15. Standard Fine Ware. Level 5. Lime and sand. Oxidised. Cream. Smoothened. Black matt paint. D:15 cm.
16. Standard Fine Ware. Level 5. Lime. Oxidised. Buff. Smoothened. Brown matt paint. D:13 cm.
17. Standard Fine Ware. Level 5. No visible inclusions. Overfired. Green. Smoothened. Black matt paint. D:16 cm.
18. Standard Fine Ware. Level 5. No visible inclusions. Reduced (black core). Grey. Smoothened. Black matt paint. D:16 cm.
19. Standard Fine Ware. Level 5. Lime. Incompletely oxidised (grey core). Buff. Smoothened. Black matt paint. D:14 cm.

20. Standard Fine Ware. Level 5. No visible inclusions. Oxidised. Cream. Smoothened. Black matt paint. D:12 cm.
21. Standard Fine Ware. Level 5. No visible inclusions. Oxidised. Buff. Smoothened. Black matt paint. D:11 cm.
22. Standard Fine Ware. Level 5. Sand. Oxidised. Buff. Smoothened. Brown matt paint. D:11 cm.
23. Standard Fine Ware. Level 5/6. Lime. Incompletely oxidised (grey core). Cream. Smoothened. Brown matt paint. D:11 cm.
24. Standard Fine Ware. Level 5. No visible inclusions. Incompletely oxidised (grey core). Buff. Smoothened. Black matt paint. D:9 cm.
25. Standard Fine Ware. Level 5. Lime. Oxidised. Cream. Smoothened. Brown matt paint. Sawn (repaired?) and re-used.

Fig. 3.27
1. Standard Fine Ware. Level 4. Lime. Oxidised. Cream. Slipped. Brown matt paint. D:17 cm.
2. Standard Fine Ware. Level 4. Lime. Oxidised. Cream. Smoothened. Black matt paint. D:18 cm.
3. Standard Fine Ware. Level 4. Lime. Oxidised. Cream. slipped Brown matt paint. D:16 cm.
4. Standard Fine Ware. Level 4/5. Lime. Oxidised. Cream. Smoothened. Brown matt paint. D:14 cm.
5. Standard Fine Ware. Level 4. Lime. Oxidised. Buff. Smoothened. Brown matt paint. D:11 cm.
6. Standard Fine Ware. Level 4. Lime. Oxidised. Buff. Burnished. Black lustrous paint. D:10 cm.
7. Standard Fine Ware. Level 4. Lime. Oxidised. Buff. Smoothened. Brown matt paint. D:17 cm.
8. Standard Fine Ware. Level 4. Lime. Oxidised. Buff. Smoothened. Wash. Black matt paint. D:12 cm.
9. Standard Fine Ware. Level 4/5. Lime. Oxidised. Cream. Smoothened. Black matt paint. D:15 cm.
10. Standard Fine Ware. Level 4. Lime. Oxidised. Cream. Smoothened. Black matt paint. D:12 cm.
11. Standard Fine Ware. Level 4/5. No visible inclusions. Oxidised. Cream. Smoothened. Black matt paint. D:12 cm.
12. Standard Fine Ware. Level 4. Lime. Oxidised. Buff. Smoothened. Wash. Black matt paint. D:13 cm.
13. Standard Fine Ware. Level 4. No visible inclusions. Overfired. Grey. Smoothened. Black lustrous paint. D:15 cm.
14. Standard Fine Ware. Level 4. No visible inclusions. Overfired. Buff. Smoothened. Black matt paint. D:9 cm.
15. Standard Fine Ware. Level 4. Lime. Overfired. Green. Smoothened. Black matt paint. D:12 cm.
16. Standard Fine Ware. Level 4. Lime. Oxidised. Buff. Smoothened. Brown matt paint. D:21 cm.
17. Standard Fine Ware. Level 4. No visible inclusions. Oxidised. Cream. Smoothened. Brown matt paint. D:21 cm.
18. Standard Fine Ware. Level 4. Lime. Oxidised. Buff. Smoothened. Black matt paint. D:15 cm.
19. Standard Fine Ware. Level 4. Lime. Oxidised. Buff. Smoothened. Brown matt paint. D:14 cm.

20. Standard Fine Ware. Level 4/5. Sand. Oxidised. Cream. Smoothened. Black matt paint. D:13 cm.
21. Standard Fine Ware. Level 4. Small mineral. Overfired. Green. Smoothened. Green matt paint. D:9 cm.
22. Standard Fine Ware. Level 4. Lime. Oxidised. Buff. Smoothened. Black matt paint. D:13 cm.
23. Standard Fine Ware. Level 4. Lime. Incompletely oxidised (grey core). Buff. Smoothened. Wash. Brown matt paint. D:12 cm.
24. Standard Fine Ware. Level 4. No visible inclusions. Overfired. Green. Smoothened. Black matt paint. D:12 cm.

Fig. 3.28
1. Standard Fine Ware. Level 4. No visible inclusions. Oxidised. Buff. Smoothened. Black matt paint. D:14 cm.
2. Standard Fine Ware. Level 4. No visible inclusions. Oxidised. Buff. Smoothened. Black matt paint. D:18 cm.
3. Standard Fine Ware. Level 4. Lime. Oxidised. Buff. Smoothened. Brown matt paint. D:16 cm.
4. Standard Fine Ware. Level 4. Lime. Oxidised. Buff. Smoothened. Black matt paint. D:14 cm.
5. Standard Fine Ware. Level 4. No visible inclusions. Reduced (grey core). Grey. Smoothened. Black matt paint. D:13 cm.
6. Standard Fine Ware. Level 4/5. Lime. Overfired. Green. Smoothened. Green matt paint. D:11 cm.
7. Standard Fine Ware. Level 4. Lime. Incompletely oxidised (grey core). Cream. Smoothened. Wash. Brown matt paint. Repaired with bitumen. D:12 cm.
8. Standard Fine Ware. Level 4. No visible inclusions. Oxidised. Buff. Smoothened. Brown matt paint. D:12 cm.
9. Standard Fine Ware. Level 4. Sand. Oxidised. Buff. Smoothened. Brown matt paint.
10. Standard Fine Ware. Level 4. Lime and sand. Oxidised. Cream. Slipped. Black lustrous paint. D:16 cm.
11. Standard Fine Ware. Level 4. Lime. Overfired. Green. Smoothened. Black matt paint. D:13 cm.
12. Standard Fine Ware. Level 4. Lime. Incompletely oxisised (grey core). Buff. Smoothened. Brown matt paint. D:12 cm.
13. Standard Fine Ware. Level 4. No visible inclusions. Oxidised. Buff. Smoothened. Black lustrous paint. D:7 cm.
14. Standard Fine Ware. Level 6. No visible inclusions. Incompletely oxidised (grey core). Buff. Smoothened. D:15 cm.
15. Standard Fine Ware. Level 5. No visible inclusions. Oxidised. Cream. Smoothened. D:14 cm.
16. Standard Fine Ware. Level 4. No visible inclusions. Incompletely oxidised (grey core). Brown. Burnished. D:7 cm.
17. Standard Fine Ware. Level 6. Sand. Oxidised. Cream. Smoothened. Black matt paint.
18. Standard Fine Ware. Level 5/6. Large plant. Overfired. Green. Smoothened. Black matt paint.
19. Standard Fine Ware. Level 6. No visible inclusions. Oxidised. Buff. Smoothened. Black matt paint.
20. Standard Fine Ware. Level 6. No visible inclusions. Oxidised. Buff. Smoothened. Black matt paint.

21. Standard Fine Ware. Level 6. Lime and small plant. Incompletely oxidised (black core). Buff. Burnished. Brown matt paint.
22. Standard Fine Ware. Level 6. Large plant. Overfired. Green. Burnished. Black matt paint.

Fig. 3.29
1. Standard Fine Ware. Level 6. Lime. Overfired. Grey. Smoothened. Black matt paint.
2. Standard Fine Ware. Level 6. Lime. Oxidised. Buff. Smoothened. Brown matt paint.
3. Standard Fine Ware. Level 6. Lime. Oxidised. Brown. Smoothened. Brown matt paint.
4. Standard Fine Ware. Level 6. Small plant and mineral. Oxidised. Cream. Smoothened. Brown matt paint.
5. Standard Fine Ware. Level 6. Lime and small (black) mineral. Oxidised. Cream. Smoothened. Black matt paint.
6. Standard Fine Ware. Level 6. No visible inclusions. Oxidised. Buff. Smoothened. Black matt paint.
7. Standard Fine Ware. Level 5/6. Lime. Oxidised. Buff. Smoothened. Brown matt paint.
8. Standard Fine Ware. Level 5/6. Large plant. Overfired. Grey. Smoothened. Black matt paint. Edges chipped; perhaps re-used as disc (loamer?).
9. Standard Fine Ware. Level 5/6. Lime. Oxidised. Buff. Smoothened. Black matt paint.
10. Standard Fine Ware. Level 5/6. Lime. Overfired. Green. Smoothened. Black matt paint.
11. Standard Fine Ware. Level 5/6. Lime. Oxidised. Cream. Smoothened. Black matt paint.
12. Standard Fine Ware. Level 5/6. No visible inclusions. Reduced (grey core). Grey. Smoothened. Black matt paint.
13. Standard Fine Ware. Level 5. Lime. Oxidised. Cream. Smoothened. Brown matt paint.
14. Standard Fine Ware. Level 5. Lime. Oxidised. Buff. Smoothened. Brown matt paint.
15. Standard Fine Ware. Level 5. Lime. Oxidised. Buff. Smoothened. Black matt paint.
16. Standard Fine Ware. Level 5. Lime. Overfired. Green. Smoothened. Black matt paint.
17. Standard Fine Ware. Level 5. Sand. Incompletely oxidised (grey core). Buff. Slipped. Brown matt paint.
18. Standard Fine Ware. Level 5. Lime. Oxidised. Buff. Smoothened. Brown matt paint.
19. Standard Fine Ware. Level 5. Lime. Oxidised. Buff. Smoothened. Brown matt paint.
20. Standard Fine Ware. Level 5. Sand. Oxidised. Buff. Smoothened. Black matt paint.
21. Standard Fine Ware. Level 5. No visible inclusions. Oxidised. Buff. Smoothened. Black matt paint.
22. Standard Fine Ware. Level 5. No visible inclusions. Oxidised. Cream. Smoothened. Thick purplish matt paint.
23. Standard Fine Ware. Level 5. Lime. Oxidised. Buff. Smoothened. Brown matt paint.
24. Standard Fine Ware. Level 5. Lime. Overfired. Green. Smoothened. Black matt paint.
25. Standard Fine Ware. Level 5. Sand. Overfired. Green. Smoothened. Black matt paint.

Fig. 3.30
1. Standard Fine Ware. Level 5. Lime. Oxidised. Buff. Smoothened. Brown matt paint. Exterior covered by thick layer of (white) gypsum. on its turn covered by a thin layer of (black) bitumen.
2. Standard Fine Ware. Level 5. Lime. Oxidised. Buff. Smoothened. Black matt paint. Traces of bitumen.
3. Standard Fine Ware. Level 5. No visible inclusions. Oxidised. Buff. Smoothened. Brown matt paint. Traces of (black) bitumen on (white) gypsum.
4. Standard Fine Ware. Level 4/5. Lime. Oxidised. Cream. Smoothened. Black matt paint.
5. Standard Fine Ware. Level 4/5. Lime. Oxidised. Buff. Smoothened. Black matt paint.

6. Standard Fine Ware. Level 4/5. No visible inclusions. Oxidised. Buff. Smoothened. Brown matt paint.
7. Standard Fine Ware. Level 4/5. Sand. Oxidised. Cream. Smoothened.surface. wash. Black matt paint.
8. Standard Fine Ware. Level 4/5. No visible inclusions. Oxidised. Buff. Smoothened. Purple matt paint.
9. Standard Fine Ware. Level 4/5. Sand. Reduced (grey core). Grey. Smoothened. Black matt paint.
10. Standard Fine Ware. Level 4/5. Lime. Reduced (grey core). Grey. Smoothened. Black matt paint.
11. Standard Fine Ware. Level 4. Lime and glitters. Oxidised. Buff. Smoothened. Black matt paint.
12. Standard Fine Ware. Level 4. Lime. Oxidised. Buff. Smoothened. Wash. Black matt paint.
13. Standard Fine Ware. Level 4. Lime. Oxidised. Cream. Smoothened. Black matt paint.
14. Standard Fine Ware. Level 4. Lime. Oxidised. Buff. Smoothened. Brown matt paint.
15. Standard Fine Ware. Level 4. Lime. Oxidised. Orange. Smoothened. Red to dark-red lustrous paint.
16. Standard Fine Ware. Level 4. No visible inclusions. Oxidised. Buff. Smoothened. Wash. Black matt paint.
17. Standard Fine Ware. Level 4. Lime. Oxidised. Buff. Smoothened. Brown matt paint.

Fig. 3.31
1. Standard Fine Ware. Level 4. No visible inclusions. Incompletely oxidised (grey core). Cream. Smoothened. Brown matt paint.
2. Standard Fine Ware. Level 4. Lime. Oxidised. Brown. Smoothened. Brown matt paint.
3. Standard Fine Ware. Level 4. Lime. Oxidised. Buff. Smoothened. Wash. Brown matt paint.
4. Standard Fine Ware. Level 4. Lime. Incompletely oxidised (grey core). Cream. Smoothened. Black matt paint.
5. Standard Fine Ware. Level 4. Lime. Oxidised. Buff. Smoothened. Brown matt paint.
6. Standard Fine Ware. Level 4. No visible inclusions. Overfired. Green. Smoothened. Black matt paint.
7. Standard Fine Ware. Level 4. Lime. Oxidised. Buff. Smoothened. Black matt paint.
8. Standard Fine Ware. Level 4. Lime. Oxidised. Buff. Smoothened. Black matt paint.
9. Standard Fine Ware. Level 4. Lime. Reduced (grey core). Grey. Smoothened. Black matt paint.
10. Standard Fine Ware. Level 4. No visible inclusions. Oxidised. Cream. Smoothened. Black matt paint.
11. Standard Fine Ware. Level 4. Small (black) mineral. Oxidised. Buff. Smoothened. Brown matt paint.
12. Standard Fine Ware. Level 4. Sand. Oxidised. Buff. Smoothened. Brown matt paint.
13. Standard Fine Ware. Level 4. Lime. Incompletely oxidised (grey core). Buff. Smoothened. Black matt paint.
14. Standard Fine Ware. Level 4. Lime. Overfired. Green. Smoothened. Black matt paint.
15. Standard Fine Ware. Level 4. No visible inclusions. Oxidised. Buff. Smoothened. Brown matt paint.
16. Standard Fine Ware. Level 4. Small (black) mineral. Oxidised. Buff. Smoothened. Brown matt paint.

17. Standard Fine Ware. Level 4. No visible inclusions. Overfired. Green. Smoothened. Black lustrous paint.
18. Standard Fine Ware. Level 4. No visible inclusions. Oxidised. Cream. Smoothened. Purplish matt paint.
19. Standard Fine Ware. Level 4. No visible inclusions. Incompletely oxidised (grey core). Buff. Smoothened. Black matt paint.
20. Standard Fine Ware. Level 4. Lime and small (black) mineral. Oxidised. Cream. Slipped. Thick purplish matt paint.
21. Standard Fine Ware. Level 4. No visible inclusions. Oxidised. Buff. Smoothened. Black matt paint.
22. Standard Fine Ware. Level 4. Lime. Oxidised. Buff. Slipped. Black lustrous paint.
23. Standard Fine Ware. Level 4. Lime. Oxidised. Brown. Smoothened. Black matt paint.
24. Standard Fine Ware. Level 4. Lime. Oxidised. Buff. Smoothened. Black matt paint.
25. Standard Fine Ware. Level 4. No visible inclusions. Oxidised. Cream. Smoothened. Black matt paint.
26. Standard Fine Ware. Level 4. Small (black) mineral. Incompletely oxidised (grey core). Buff. Smoothened. Wash. Brown matt paint.
27. Standard Fine Ware. Level 4. No visible inclusions. Oxidised. Cream. Smoothened. Black lustrous paint.

Fig. 3.32
1. Standard Fine Ware. Level 4. Lime. Overfired. Green surface. warped shape. No decoration visible. A: interior; B: exterior.
2. Standard Fine Ware. Level 6. Lime. Oxidised. Cream. Slipped. Matt paint. bichrome (?): exterior pinkish dots and stripes; interior white curling line.
3. Standard Fine Ware. Level 4/5. Lime. Oxidised. Cream. Smoothened. Wash. Brown matt paint.
4. Standard Fine Ware. Level 4. Lime. Oxidised. Cream. Smoothened. Wash. Black matt paint.
5. Standard Fine Ware. Level 4. Lime. Incompletely oxidised (grey core). Cream. Slipped. Brown matt paint.
6. Standard Fine Ware. Level 4. No visible inclusions. Incompletely oxidised (black core). Cream. Smoothened. Wash. Black matt paint.
7. Standard Fine Ware. Level 6. Small plant and lime. Oxidised. Buff. Slipped. Burnished. Dark-red to reddish brown lustrous paint and impressions. 7a: reconstructed vessel shape; 7b: additional fragment.

Fig. 3.33:
1. Standard Fine Ware. Level 6. Sand. Oxidised. Buff. Smoothened. Brown matt paint and incision.
2. Standard Fine Ware. Level 6. Small (black) mineral. Oxidised. Buff. Smoothened. Black matt paint and impressions. D:10 cm.
3. Standard Fine Ware. Level 6. Large plant. Oxidised. Buff. Burnished. Black matt paint and impressions.
4. Standard Fine Ware. Level 4/5. Lime and small (black) mineral. Oxidised. Buff. Smoothened. Black matt paint and impressions. D:11 cm.
5. Standard Fine Ware. Level 4/5. Lime and small (black) mineral. Oxidised. Buff. Smoothened. Black matt paint and impressions. D:10 cm.
6. Standard Fine Ware. Level 4/5. Lime and small (black) mineral. Oxidised. Buff. Smoothened. Red to dark-red matt paint and impressions. D:9 cm.

7. Standard Fine Ware. Level 4. Small mineral. Oxidised. Cream. Smoothened. Brown matt paint. impressions.
8. Standard Fine Ware. Level 4. No visible inclusions. Oxidised. Brown. Smoothened. Black matt paint. impressions.
9. Standard Fine Ware. Level 4/5. Small (black) mineral. Overfired. Green. Smoothened. Black matt paint and impressions.
10. Standard Fine Ware. Level 5. Lime and small plant. Incompletely oxidised (grey core). Buff. Smoothened. Brown matt paint and incisions.
11. Standard Fine Ware. Level 4. No visible inclusions. Oxidised. Cream. Smoothened. Brown matt paint and incisions.
12. Standard Fine Ware. Level 6. Sand. Oxidised. Buff. Smoothened. Black matt paint and impressions.
13. Standard Fine Ware. Level 4. No visible inclusions. Oxidised. Buff. Smoothened. Black matt paint. D:14 cm.
14. Standard Fine Ware. Level 4/5. Small mineral. Oxidised. Cream. Smoothened. Wash. Brown matt paint. D:11 cm.
15. Standard Fine Ware. Level 5/6. Sand. Oxidised. Buff. Smoothened. Wash. Red to dark-red matt paint. D:9 cm.
16. Standard Fine Ware. Level 6. Lime and small (black) mineral. Oxidised. Cream. Smoothened. Black lustrous paint and impressions. D:8 cm.
17. Standard Fine Ware. Level 5. No visible inclusions. Oxidised. Orange. Smoothened. Red matt paint. D:22 cm.
18. Standard Fine Ware. Level 4. Lime. Oxidised. Cream. Smoothened. Black matt paint. D:20 cm.
19. Standard Fine Ware. Level 4. Lime. Oxidised. Cream. Smoothened. Brown matt paint. D:14 cm.
20. Standard Fine Ware. Level 4. Lime. Incompletely oxidised (grey core). Cream. Slipped. Black lustrous paint. D:14 cm.
21. Standard Fine Ware. Level 4. Lime. Oxidised. Buff. Smoothened. Black matt paint. Base D:14 cm.
22. Standard Fine Ware. Level 4. Lime. Incompletely oxidised (grey core). Buff. Smoothened.
23. Standard Fine Ware. Level 4. No visible inclusions. Oxidised. Buff. Smoothened. Brown matt paint.
24. Standard Fine Ware. Level 5/6. No visible inclusions. Oxidised. Cream. Smoothened. Black matt paint.

Fig. 3.34
1. Orange Fine Ware. Level 6. Lime and medium-sized mineral. Oxidised. Red-slipped. Burnished. D:18 cm.
2. Orange Fine Ware. Level 5. Lime and orange mineral. Oxidised. Red-slipped. Burnished. D:18 cm.
3. Orange Fine Ware. Level 6. Lime and black mineral. Oxidised. Red-slipped. Burnished. D:18 cm.
4. Orange Fine Ware. Level 6. Lime and large (black and orange) mineral. Oxidised. Red-slipped. Burnished. D:16 cm.
5. Orange Fine Ware. Level 6. Lime and small (black) mineral. Oxidised. Orange. Slipped. Burnished. Red matt paint. D:15 cm.
6. Orange Fine Ware. Level 6. Lime, small mineral. Oxidised. Buff. Burnished. Red to dark-red matt paint. D:12 cm.

7. Orange Fine Ware. Level 6. Lime, orange mineral. Oxidised. Buff. Smoothened. Black matt paint. D:7 cm.
8. Orange Fine Ware. Level 4. Lime, black mineral. Oxidised. Buff. Smoothened. Red lustrous paint. D:22 cm.
9. Orange Fine Ware. Level 4. Lime, black mineral. Oxidised. Orange. Slipped. Red lustrous paint. D:20 cm.
10. Orange Fine Ware. Level 4. Lime and large (black) mineral. Incompletely oxidised (grey core). Orange. Smoothened. Red to dark-red lustrous paint. D:18 cm.
11. Orange Fine Ware. Level 4/5. Lime, black and orange mineral. Oxidised. Orange. Smoothened. Red to dark-red matt paint. D:16 cm.
12. Orange Fine Ware. Level 6. Lime, black mineral. Incompletely oxidised (grey core). Brown. Smoothened. Black matt paint. D:12 cm.
13. Orange Fine Ware. Level 6. Lime, black mineral. Oxidised. Orange. Slipped. Red matt paint. D:12 cm.
14. Orange Fine Ware. Level 6. Lime, black mineral. Oxidised. Orange. Slipped. burnished. Red matt paint. D:13 cm.
15. Orange Fine Ware. Level 6. Lime, black and orange mineral. Incompletely oxidised (grey core;). Orange. Burnished. Red to dark-red matt paint. D:14 cm.
16. Orange Fine Ware. Level 5/6. Lime, black and orange mineral. Oxidised. Orange. Smoothened. Red matt paint. D:27 cm.
17. Orange Fine Ware. Level 4. Lime, black mineral. Oxidised. Buff. Smoothened. Dark-red to redddish-brown matt paint. D:14 cm.
18. Orange Fine Ware. Level 6. Black mineral. Oxidised. Orange. Smoothened. Red lustrous paint. D:24 cm.
19. Orange Fine Ware. Level 5/6. Lime, black mineral. Oxidised. Orange. Smoothened. Red matt paint. D:15 cm.
20. Orange Fine Ware. Level 5. Lime, orange mineral. Oxidised. Orange. Smoothened. Red matt paint. D:13 cm.
21. Orange Fine Ware. Level 6. Lime, black mineral. Incompletely oxidised (black core). Orange. Slipped. Red matt paint. D:16 cm.

Fig. 3.35

1. Orange Fine Ware. Level 4/5. Lime, black and orange mineral. Oxidised. Orange. Smoothened. Red lustrous paint. D:29 cm.
2. Orange Fine Ware. Level 4/5. Lime, black and orange mineral. Oxidised. Buff. Smoothened. Red matt paint. D:16 cm.
3. Orange Fine Ware. Level 5. Lime, black mineral. Oxidised. Red-slipped. Red to dark-red matt paint. D:9 cm.
4. Orange Fine Ware. Level 6. Lime and large (orange) mineral. Oxidised. Orange. Burnished. Red lustrous paint. Probably re-used as potstand. D:11 cm.
5. Orange Fine Ware. Level 4. Lime, black mineral. Oxidised. Brown. Smoothened. Brown matt paint. D:14 cm.
6. Orange Fine Ware. Level 6. Black mineral. Oxidised. Brown. Burnished. Brown matt paint. D:14 cm.
7. Orange Fine Ware. Level 5/6. Lime, black and orange mineral. Oxidised. Orange. Smoothened. Red matt paint. D:8 cm.
8. Orange Fine Ware. Level 6. Black mineral. Oxidised. Red-slipped. Burnished. D:10 cm.
9. Orange Fine Ware. Level 6. Lime and small mineral. Oxidised. Orange-slipped. D:7 cm.
10. Orange Fine Ware. Level 6. Black mineral. Oxidised. Brown. Smoothened. Red lustrous paint. D:11 cm.

11. Orange Fine Ware. Level 5. Lime, black mineral. Oxidised. Buff. Smoothened. Black matt paint.
12. Orange Fine Ware. Level 4. Black mineral. Oxidised. Orange-slipped. Red matt paint.
13. Orange Fine Ware. Level 5/6. Lime and small mineral. Oxidised. Buff. Smoothened. Brown matt paint.
14. Orange Fine Ware. Level 4. Lime, small mineral. Oxidised. Buff. Smoothened. Dark-red to reddish-brown matt paint.
15. Orange Fine Ware. Level 4/5. Lime, black mineral. Incompletely oxidised (grey core). Brown. Smoothened. Dark-red to reddish-brown matt paint.
16. Orange Fine Ware. Level 5. Lime, black mineral. Incompletely oxidised (grey core). Orange. Smoothened. Red matt paint.
17. Orange Fine Ware. Level 5/6. Lime, black and orange mineral. Oxidised. Orange. Smoothened. Red matt paint.
18. Orange Fine Ware. Level 5. Lime, black and orange mineral. Oxidised. Orange. Smoothened. Red matt paint.
19. Orange Fine Ware. Level 4/5. Lime, black and orange mineral. Oxidised. Orange. Smoothened. Wash. Red matt paint.

Fig. 3.36
1. Orange Fine Ware. Level 6. Lime, black mineral. Oxidised. Red-slipped. Burnished. D:29 cm.
2. Fine Painted Ware. Level 6. No visible inclusions. Oxidised. Buff. Burnished. Black matt paint and impressions.
3. Fine Painted Ware. Level 6. Lime. Oxidised. Buff. Smoothened. Black matt paint and impressions.
4. Fine Painted Ware. Level 5/6. No visible inclusions. Oxidised. Red-slipped. Burnished.
5. Fine Painted Ware. Level 7. Sand. Oxidised. Buff. Burnished. Red lustrous paint and white-filled impressions.
6. Fine Painted Ware. Level 6. No visible inclusions. Oxidised. Brown. Burnished. Red lustrous paint. Edges smoothened; probably re-used sherd.
7. Fine Painted Ware. Level 5/6. Lime. Oxidised. Buff. Burnished. Brown matt paint and impressions.
8. Fine Painted Ware. Level 6. No visible inclusions. Oxidised. Buff. Burnished. Red to dark-red lustrous paint.
9. Fine Painted Ware. Level 6. No visible inclusions. Oxidised. Brown. Slipped. Burnished. Black matt paint. D:17 cm.
10. Fine Painted Ware. Level 6. No visible inclusions. Oxidised. Buff. Burnished. Brown matt paint. D:12 cm.
11. Fine Painted Ware. Level 4. Sand. Oxidised. Buff. Burnished. Black matt paint. D:13 cm.
12. Fine Painted Ware. Level 5. No visible inclusions. Oxidised. Buff. Smoothened. Black matt paint. D:10 cm.
13. Fine Painted Ware. Level 4. No visible inclusions. Oxidised. Brown. Burnished. Black matt paint. D:8 cm.
14. Fine Painted Ware. Level 5/6. No visible inclusions. Oxidised. Buff. Burnished. Black matt paint. D:9 cm.
15. Fine Painted Ware. Level 6. No visible inclusions. Oxidised. Buff. Smoothened. Brown matt paint. D:8 cm.
16. Fine Painted Ware. Level 5/6. Lime. Oxidised. Buff. Burnished. Brown matt paint.
17. Fine Painted Ware. Level 6. Sand. Incompletely oxidised (grey core). Brown. Burnished. Brown matt paint. D:12.5 cm.

18. Fine Painted Ware. Level 6. Lime. Oxidised. Brown. Burnished. Red lustrous paint and impressions.
19. Fine Painted Ware. Level 5/6. Lime. Oxidised. Buff. Burnished. Red matt paint. D:9 cm.
20. Fine Painted Ware. Level 4. Sand. Oxidised. Buff. Slipped. Burnished. Orange-red lustrous paint. D:10 cm.
21. Fine Painted Ware. Level 6. Sand. Oxidised. Brown. Burnished. Red paint and impressions. D:9 cm.
22. Fine Painted Ware. Level 6. No visible inclusions. Oxidised. Buff. Burnished. Red lustrous paint. D:12 cm.
23. Fine Painted Ware. Level 5/6. Lime. Oxidised. Buff. Burnished. Red lustrous paint. D:10 cm.
24. Fine Painted Ware. Level 6. No visible inclusions. Oxidised. Buff. Burnished. Red matt paint. D:17 cm.
25. Fine Painted Ware. Level 4. Sand. Oxidised. Brown. Burnished. Black matt paint.
26. Fine Painted Ware. Level 6. No visible inclusions. Oxidised. Cream. Burnished. Brown lustrous paint. D:5 cm.

Fig. 3.37
1. Halaf Fine Ware. Level 1. No visible inclusions. Oxidised. Cream. smoothened. Wash. Brown lustrous paint. D:34 cm.
2. Halaf Fine Ware. Level 1/2/3. No visible inclusions. Overfired. Green. Smoothened. Black matt paint. D:34 cm.
3. Halaf Fine Ware. Level 1. No visible inclusions. Oxidised. Cream. Smoothened. Wash. Brown lustrous paint.
4. Halaf Fine Ware. Level 1. No visible inclusions. Oxidised. Buff. Smoothened. Black matt paint.
5. Halaf Fine Ware. Level 1. Lime. Incompletely oxidised (grey core). Buff. Smoothened. Orange-red matt paint.
6. Halaf Fine Ware. Level 2. No visible inclusions. Oxidised. Buff. Smoothened. Red matt paint. D:23 cm.
7. Halaf Fine Ware. Level 3. Lime incluions. Oxidised. Buff. Smoothened. Black matt paint. D:18 cm.
8. Halaf Fine Ware. Level 173. Lime. Oxidised. Buff. Smoothened. Brown lustrous paint. D:19 cm.
9. Halaf Fine Ware. Level 3. No visible inclusions. Oxidised. Buff. Smoothened. Black matt paint. D:16 cm.
10. Halaf Fine Ware. Level 3. No visible inclusions. Incompletely oxidised (grey core). Cream. Smoothened. Brown matt paint. D:20 cm.
11. Halaf Fine Ware. Level 3. No visible inclusions. Oxidised. Buff. Smoothened. Brown matt paint. D:18 cm.
12. Halaf Fine Ware. Level 3. Lime. Oxidised. Cream. Smoothened. Black lustrous paint. D:20 cm.
13. Halaf Fine Ware. Level 3. No visible inclusions. Oxidised. Buff. Smoothened. Black matt paint. D:18 cm.

Fig. 3.38
1. Halaf Fine Ware. Level 3. No visible inclusions. Incompletely oxidised (grey core). Buff. Smoothened. Brown lustrous paint. D:21 cm.
2. Halaf Fine Ware. Level 1/2/3. No visible inclusions. Oxidised. Buff. Smoothened. Black lustrous paint. D:24 cm.

3. Halaf Fine Ware. Level 3. Lime. Oxidised. Buff. Smoothened. Black matt paint. D:23 cm.
4. Halaf Fine Ware. Level 3. No visible inclusions. Oxidised. Buff. Smoothened. Black lustrous paint. D:23 cm.
5. Halaf Fine Ware. Level 3. No visible inclusions. Oxidised. Buff. Smoothened. Black matt paint. D:20 cm.
6. Halaf Fine Ware. Level 3. Lime. Oxidised. Buff. Smoothened. Black lustrous paint. D:17 cm.
7. Halaf Fine Ware. Level 3. No visible inclusions. Incompletely oxidised (grey core). Buff. Smoothened. Red matt paint. D:17 cm.
8. Halaf Fine Ware. Level 2. Lime. Oxidised. Buff. Smoothened. Black lustrous paint. D:24 cm.
9. Halaf Fine Ware. Level 2. No visible inclusions. Incompletely oxidised (grey core). Buff. Smoothened. Black matt paint. D:21 cm.
10. Halaf Fine Ware. Level 1/3. Lime. Oxidised. Buff. Smoothened. Black matt paint. D:19 cm.
11. Halaf Fine Ware. Level 3. No visible inclusions. Oxidised. Buff. Smoothened. Orange-red matt paint. D:17 cm.
12. Halaf Fine Ware. Level 3. No visible inclusions. Oxidised. Buff. Smoothened. Black lustrous paint. D:16 cm.
13. Halaf Fine Ware. Level 2. No visible inclusions. Oxidised. Buff. Smoothened. Black lustrous paint. D:14 cm.
14. Halaf Fine Ware. Level 3. Lime. Oxidised. Cream. Smoothened. Black lustrous paint. D:14 cm.
15. Halaf Fine Ware. Level 3. No visible inclusions. Oxidised. Buff. Smoothened. Brown lustrous paint. D:13 cm.
16. Halaf Fine Ware. Level 3. Lime. Oxidised. Buff. Smoothened. Black lustrous paint. D:9 cm.

Fig. 3.39
1. Halaf Fine Ware. Level 2/3. Lime. Oxidised. Buff. Smoothened. Black lustrous paint. D:23 cm.
2. Halaf Fine Ware. Level 3. No visible inclusions. Oxidised. Buff. Smoothened. Black matt paint. D:18 cm.
3. Halaf Fine Ware. Level 3. No visible inclusions. Oxidised. Grey-buff. Smoothened. Black matt paint. D:18 cm.
4. Halaf Fine Ware. Level 1/2. No visible inclusions. Oxidised. Buff. Smoothened. Black lustrous paint. D:13 cm.
5. Halaf Fine Ware. Level 1. No visible inclusions. Oxidised. Buff. Smoothened. Black lustrous paint. D:17 cm.
6. Halaf Fine Ware. Level 3. Lime. Oxidised. Buff. Smoothened. Black lustrous paint and incisions (?).
7. Halaf Fine Ware. Level 1/2/3. Lime. Oxidised. Buff. Smoothened. Black matt paint.
8. Halaf Fine Ware. Level 3. Lime. Oxidised. Buff. Smoothened. Brown matt paint.
9. Halaf Fine Ware. Level 1/2/3. No visible inclusions. Oxidised. Buff. Smoothened. Black lustrous paint. D:19 cm.
10. Halaf Fine Ware. Level 3. No visible inclusions. Oxidised. Buff. Smoothened. Black lustrous paint. D:15 cm.
11. Halaf Fine Ware. Level 3. Lime. Oxidised. Buff. Smoothened. Black lustrous paint. D:15 cm.

Fig. 3.40

1. Halaf Fine Ware. Level 3. Lime. Oxidised. Buff. Smoothened. Black matt paint. D:20 cm.
2. Halaf Fine Ware. Level 3. No visible inclusions. Incompletely oxidised (grey core). Buff. Smoothened. Black lustrous paint. D:19 cm.
3. Halaf Fine Ware. Level 3. Lime. Oxidised. Buff. Smoothened. Dark reddish-brown matt paint. D:16 cm.
4. Halaf Fine Ware. Level 3. No visible inclusions. Overfired (?). Grey core. Grey. Smoothened. Black matt paint. D:16 cm.
5. Halaf Fine Ware. Level 3. Lime. Incompletely oxidised (grey core). Buff. Smoothened. Wash. Brown matt paint. D:16 cm.
6. Halaf Fine Ware. Level 3. Lime. Oxidised. Buff. Smoothened. Black lustrous paint. D:17 cm.
7. Halaf Fine Ware. Level 1. Lime. Oxidised. Buff. Smoothened. Black matt paint. Conical hole in unbroken vessel wall. D:14 cm.
8. Halaf Fine Ware. Level 3. No visible inclusions. Oxidised. Buff. Smoothened. Black lustrous paint. D:13 cm.
9. Halaf Fine Ware. Level 3. No visible inclusions. Oxidised. Buff. Smoothened. Black lustrous paint. D:20 cm.
10. Halaf Fine Ware. Level 3. Lime. Overfired. Green. Smoothened. Black paint. D:20 cm.
11. Halaf Fine Ware. Level 2. No visible inclusions. Oxidised. Cream. Smoothened. Black matt paint. D:16 cm.
12. Halaf Fine Ware. Level 3. Lime. Overfired. Grey. Smoothened. Black paint. D:15 cm.
13. Halaf Fine Ware. Level 3. No visible inclusions. Incompletely oxidised (grey core). Buff. Smoothened. Brown lustrous paint. D:18 cm.
14. Halaf Fine Ware. Level 3. Lime. Oxidised. Buff. Smoothened. Black matt paint. D:15 cm.
15. Halaf Fine Ware. Level 3. No visible inclusions. Overfired. Green. Smoothened. Black matt paint. Warped shape.

Fig. 3.41

1. Halaf Fine Ware. Level 3. Lime. Oxidised. Buff. Smoothened. Wash. Black matt paint. D:18 cm.
2. Halaf Fine Ware. Level 3. Lime. Oxidised. Buff. Smoothened. Brown matt paint. D:16 cm.
3. Halaf Fine Ware. Level 3. Lime. Oxidised. Buff. Smoothened. Wash. Brown lustrous paint. D:16 cm.
4. Halaf Fine Ware. Level 3. No visible inclusions. Oxidised. Buff. Smoothened. Brown matt paint. D:10 cm.
5. Halaf Fine Ware. Level 1/2/3. Lime. Oxidised. Buff. Slipped Black matt paint. D:9 cm.
6. Halaf Fine Ware. Level 1/3. No visible inclusions. Oxidised. Cream. Slipped Brown matt paint.
7. Halaf Fine Ware. Level 3. Lime. Oxidised. Buff. Smoothened. Black matt paint. D:17 cm.
8. Halaf Fine Ware. Level 3. Lime. Oxidised. Buff. Smoothened. Black matt paint. D:22 cm.
9. Halaf Fine Ware. Level 1/3. Lime. Oxidised. Buff. Smoothened. Black matt paint. D:21 cm.
10. Halaf Fine Ware. Level 3. Lime. Oxidised. Buff. Smoothened. Black matt paint. D:12 cm.
11. Halaf Fine Ware. Level 3. No visible inclusions. Oxidised. Buff. Smoothened. Wash. Brown lustrous paint. D:10 cm.
12. Halaf Fine Ware. Level 3. No visible inclusions. Oxidised. Cream. Slipped and Burnished. Black matt paint. D:14 cm.
13. Halaf Fine Ware. Level 1. Lime. Oxidised. Cream. Smoothened. Black lustrous paint.
14. Halaf Fine Ware. Level 3. Lime. Oxidised. nuff Smoothened. Brown matt paint. D:19 cm.

15. Halaf Fine Ware. Level 3. Lime. Oxidised. Buff. Smoothened. Black matt paint.
16. Halaf Fine Ware. Level 3. Lime. Oxidised. Buff. Smoothened. Wash. Black matt paint.
    D:15 cm.

Fig.3.42
  1. Halaf Fine Ware. Level 3. Lime. Oxidised. Buff. Smoothened. Black matt paint. D:23 cm.
  2. Halaf Fine Ware. Level 3. Lime. Oxidised. Buff. Smoothened. Black matt paint. D:23 cm.
  3. Halaf Fine Ware. Level 3. No visible inclusions. Oxidised. Buff. Slipped Black lustrous
     paint. D:29 cm.
  4. Halaf Fine Ware. Level 3. Lime. Oxidised. Buff. Smoothened. Wash. Black matt paint.
     D:22 cm.
  5. Halaf Fine Ware. Level 1/3. Lime. Oxidised. Buff. Smoothened. Black matt paint. D:18 cm.
  6. Halaf Fine Ware. Level 3. No visible inclusions. Oxidised. Buff. Smoothened. Brown
     matt paint. D:23 cm.
  7. Halaf Fine Ware. Level 1/2/3. Lime. Oxidised. Buff. Smoothened. Dark-red to reddish-
     brown lustrous paint. D:22 cm.
  8. Halaf Fine Ware. Level 1/3. Lime. Oxidised. Buff. Slipped Brown matt paint. D:22 cm.
  9. Halaf Fine Ware. Level 3. No visible inclusions. Oxidised. Buff. Smoothened. Black
     matt paint. D:25 cm.
 10. Halaf Fine Ware. Level 3. Lime. Oxidised. Buff. Smoothened. Wash. Brown matt paint.
     D:22 cm.
 11. Halaf Fine Ware. Level 1. Lime. Oxidised. Buff. Smoothened. Brown lustrous paint.
     D:19 cm.
 12. Halaf Fine Ware. Level 2. No visible inclusions. Oxidised. Buff. Smoothened. Dark-red
     to reddish-brown lustrous paint. D:27 cm.
 13. Halaf Fine Ware. Level 1. No visible inclusions. Oxidised. Buff. Smoothened. Brown
     matt paint. D:26 cm.

Fig. 3.43
  1. Halaf Fine Ware. Level 2. Lime. Oxidised. Buff. Smoothened. Black matt paint. D:20 cm.
  2. Halaf Fine Ware. Level 3. Lime. Oxidised. Buff. Slipped Orange-red lustrous paint.
     D:22 cm.
  3. Halaf Fine Ware. Level 3. Lime. Incompletely oxidised (grey core). Buff. Smoothened.
     D:23 cm.
  4. Halaf Fine Ware. Level 3. Lime. Oxidised. Buff. Smoothened. Black matt paint. D:21 cm.
  5. Halaf Fine Ware. Level 3. Lime. Oxidised. Buff. Smoothened. Brown matt paint. D:24 cm.
  6. Halaf Fine Ware. Level 1/3. Lime. Oxidised. Buff. Smoothened. Brown lustrous paint.
     D:19 cm.
  7. Halaf Fine Ware. Level 3. Lime. Oxidised. Buff. Slipped Black lustrous paint. D:9 cm.
  8. Halaf Fine Ware. Level 1/3. No visible inclusions. Incompletely oxidised (grey core).
     Orange. Smoothened. Brown matt paint. D:10 cm.
  9. Halaf Fine Ware. Level 3. Lime. Oxidised. Buff. Smoothened. Brown matt paint. Traces
     of bitumen. D:34 cm.
 10. Halaf Fine Ware. Level 1/3. No visible inclusions. Oxidised. Buff. Smoothened. Black
     matt paint. D:29 cm.
 11. Halaf Fine Ware. Level 3. Lime. Oxidised. Buff. Smoothened. Black matt paint. D:19 cm.
 12. Halaf Fine Ware. Level 3. Lime. Oxidised. Buff. Slipped Brown lustrous paint. D:18 cm.
 13. Halaf Fine Ware. Level 3. No visible inclusions. Oxidised. Buff. Smoothened. Black
     paint. D:18 cm.
 14. Halaf Fine Ware. Level 3. Lime. Oxidised. Buff. Smoothened. Black matt paint. D:17 cm.

Fig. 3.44
1. Halaf Fine Ware. Level 3. No visible inclusions. Oxidised. Buff. Smoothened. D:38 cm.
2. Halaf Fine Ware. Level 1/2/3. No visible inclusions. Oxidised. Cream. Smoothened. D:21 cm.
3. Halaf Fine Ware. Level 3. No visible inclusions. Oxidised. Buff. Smoothened. Red lustrous paint. D:21 cm.
4. Halaf Fine Ware. Level 3. No visible inclusions. Oxidised. Buff. Smoothened. Black paint. flattened rim. D:23 cm.
5. Halaf Fine Ware. Level 1/3. No visible inclusions. Oxidised. Buff. Smoothened. Orangered matt paint. D:6 cm.
6. Halaf Fine Ware. Level 3. No visible inclusions. Oxidised. Cream. Smoothened. Brown matt paint. D:8 cm.
7. Halaf Fine Ware. Level 3. No visible inclusions. Oxidised. Buff. Smoothened. Black paint.
8. Halaf Fine Ware. Level 3. Lime. Oxidised. Buff. Smoothened. Brown matt paint. D:12 cm.
9. Halaf Fine Ware. Level 3. Lime. Oxidised. Buff. Smoothened. D:16 cm.
10. Halaf Fine Ware. Level 3. Lime. Oxidised. Buff. Smoothened. Black matt paint. D:14 cm.
11. Halaf Fine Ware. Level 3. Lime. Oxidised. Buff. Smoothened. Black matt paint. D:28 cm.
12. Halaf Fine Ware. Level 3. Lime. Incompletely oxidised (grey core). Buff. Smoothened. Brown matt paint. D:14 cm.
13. Halaf Fine Ware. Level 3. No visible inclusions. Oxidised. Buff. Smoothened. D:13 cm.
14. Halaf Fine Ware. Level 3. Lime. Oxidised. Buff. Smoothened. Black paint. D:12 cm. Rim sawn.
15. Halaf Fine Ware. Level 3. Lime. Oxidised. Buff. Smoothened. D:14 cm.
16. Halaf Fine Ware. Level 3. No visible inclusions. Oxidised. Buff. Smoothened. Brown matt paint. D:11 cm.

Fig. 3.45
1. Halaf Fine Ware. Level 3. Lime. Oxidised. Buff. Smoothened. Brown lustrous paint. D:10.5 cm.
2. Halaf Fine Ware. Level 3. No visible inclusions. Oxidised. Buff. Smoothened. Black matt paint. D:9 cm.
3. Halaf Fine Ware. Level 3. No visible inclusions. Oxidised. Buff. Smoothened. Black lustrous paint. D:14 cm.
4. Halaf Fine Ware. Level 1. Lime. Oxidised. Buff. Smoothened. Brown matt paint. D:10 cm.
5. Halaf Fine Ware. Level 1. No visible inclusions. Oxidised. Cream. Smoothened. Brown lustrous paint. D:8 cm.
6. Halaf Fine Ware. Level 3. Lime. Oxidised. Buff. Smoothened. Black paint. D:6 cm.
7. Halaf Fine Ware. Level 1/3. Lime. Oxidised. Buff. Smoothened. Black matt paint. D:7.5 cm.
8. Halaf Fine Ware. Level 1. Lime. Incompletely oxidised (grey core). Buff. Smoothened. Brown matt paint. D:13 cm.
9. Halaf Fine Ware. Level 2/3. Lime. Oxidised. Buff. Smoothened. Wash. Black matt paint. D:12 cm.
10. Halaf Fine Ware. Level 3. No visible inclusions. Oxidised. Buff. Slipped Brown matt paint. D:22 cm.
11. Halaf Fine Ware. Level 1/2/3. No visible inclusions. Oxidised. Buff. Smoothened. Black matt paint. D:8 cm.
12. Halaf Fine Ware. Level 3. Lime. Oxidised. Buff. Smoothened. Black matt paint. D:8 cm.

Fig. 3.46

1. Halaf Fine Ware. Level 3. Lime. Oxidised. Buff. Smoothened. Black matt paint. D:18 cm.
2. Halaf Fine Ware. Level 3. Lime. Oxidised. Buff. Smoothened. Black matt paint. D:19 cm.
3. Halaf Fine Ware. Level 3. No visible inclusions. Incompletely oxidised (grey core). Buff. Smoothened. Black matt paint. D:18 cm.
4. Halaf Fine Ware. Level 3. Lime. Oxidised. Buff. Smoothened. Black matt paint. Originally lug present. D:17 cm.
5. Halaf Fine Ware. Level 3. Lime. Oxidised. Buff. Smoothened. Black lustrous paint. D:17 cm.
6. Halaf Fine Ware. Level 1/3. No visible inclusions. Oxidised. Cream. Smoothened. No decoration but a single spot of paint. D:8 cm (rim not preserved).
7. Halaf Fine Ware. Level 1. No visible inclusions. Oxidised. Buff. Smoothened. Black matt paint. D:23 cm.
8. Halaf Fine Ware. Level 3. Lime. Oxidised. Cream. Slipped Black matt paint. D:14 cm.
9. Halaf Fine Ware. Level 3. Lime. Oxidised. Buff. Smoothened. Black matt paint. D:16 cm.
10. Halaf Fine Ware. Level 3. No visible inclusions. Oxidised. Buff. Smoothened. Dark-red to reddish-brown lustrous paint. D:14 cm.
11. Halaf Fine Ware. Level 3. Lime. Oxidised. Buff. Smoothened. Wash. Black matt paint. D:14 cm.
12. Halaf Fine Ware. Level 3. Lime. Oxidised. Cream. Smoothened. Black matt paint. Repaired with bitumen. D:18 cm.

Fig. 3.47

1. Halaf Fine Ware. Level 3. Lime. Oxidised. Buff. Smoothened. Black matt paint. D:24 cm.
2. Halaf Fine Ware. Level 3. Lime. Oxidised. Cream. Smoothened. Black matt paint. D:30 cm.
3. Halaf Fine Ware. Level 1. Lime. Oxidised. Buff. Smoothened. Brown lustrous paint. D:7 cm.
4. Halaf Fine Ware. Level 3. No visible inclusions. Oxidised. Buff. Smoothened. Black matt paint. D:7 cm.
5. Halaf Fine Ware. Level 3. Lime. Oxidised. Cream. Smoothened. Black matt paint. D:9 cm.
6. Halaf Fine Ware. Level 3. No visible inclusions. Oxidised. Buff. Smoothened. Black matt paint. D:12 cm.
7. Halaf Fine Ware. Level 2. No visible inclusions. Oxidised. Buff. Smoothened. Black matt paint. D:10 cm.
8. Halaf Fine Ware. Level 3. No visible inclusions. Oxidised. Buff. Smoothened. Black matt paint. D:9 cm.
9. Halaf Fine Ware. Level 3. No visible inclusions. Incompletely oxidised (grey core). Buff. Smoothened. Black lustrous paint. D:10 cm.
10. Halaf Fine Ware. Level 3. Lime. Oxidised. Buff. Smoothened. Black lustrous paint. D:12 cm.
11. Halaf Fine Ware. Level 1/3. No visible inclusions. Oxidised. Buff. Smoothened. Black lustrous paint. D:10 cm.
12. Halaf Fine Ware. Level 3. Lime. Oxidised. Buff. Smoothened. Black matt paint. D:13 cm.
13. Halaf Fine Ware. Level 3. Lime. Oxidised. Buff. Smoothened. Black lustrous paint. D:10 cm.
14. Halaf Fine Ware. Level 3. No visible inclusions. Oxidised. Buff. Smoothened. Black lustrous paint. D:11 cm.
15. Halaf Fine Ware. Level 3. Lime. Oxidised. Buff. Smoothened. Red lustrous paint. D:10 cm.
16. Halaf Fine Ware. Level 3. Lime. Incompletely oxidised (grey core). Buff. Smoothened. Red lustrous paint. D:17 cm.

17. Halaf Fine Ware. Level 3. No visible inclusions. Oxidised. Cream. Smoothened. Black matt paint. D:16 cm.
18. Halaf Fine Ware. Level 2. No visible inclusions. Oxidised. Orange. Smoothened. Black lustrous paint. D:16 cm.
19. Halaf Fine Ware. Level 3. Lime. Oxidised. Buff. Smoothened. Black matt paint. D:19 cm.
20. Halaf Fine Ware. Level 1. No visible inclusions. Oxidised. Buff. Smoothened. Brown matt paint. D:17 cm.
21. Halaf Fine Ware. Level 3. Lime. Oxidised. Cream. Slipped. Black matt paint. D:9 cm.

Fig. 3.48

1. Halaf Fine Ware. Level 3. No visible inclusions. Cream. Smoothened. Black matt paint. D:10 cm.
2. Halaf Fine Ware. Level 2. No visible inclusions. Oxidised. Buff. Smoothened. Black paint. D:10 cm.
3. Halaf Fine Ware. Level 3. No visible inclusions. Oxidised. Buff. Smoothened. Brown matt paint. D:8 cm.
4. Halaf Fine Ware. Level 3. No visible inclusions. Oxidised. Buff. Smoothened. Brown matt paint. D:12 cm.
5. Halaf Fine Ware. Level 3. Lime. Oxidised. Buff. Smoothened. Brown matt paint. D:11 cm.
6. Halaf Fine Ware. Level 2. No visible inclusions. Oxidised. Buff. Smoothened. Black matt paint. D:10 cm.
7. Halaf Fine Ware. Level 3. Lime. Oxidised. Buff. Smoothened. Brown matt paint. D:13 cm.
8. Halaf Fine Ware. Level 3. No visible inclusions. Oxidised. Buff. Smoothened. Black lustrous paint. D:13 cm.
9. Halaf Fine Ware. Level 3. Lime. Oxidised. Buff. Smoothened. Black matt paint. D:16 cm.
10. Halaf Fine Ware. Level 3. No visible inclusions. Oxidised. Cream. Smoothened. Black lustrous paint. D:15 cm.
11. Halaf Fine Ware. Level 3. Lime. Oxidised. Buff. Smoothened. Brown paint. D:17 cm.
12. Halaf Fine Ware. Level 3. Lime. Oxidised. Buff. Smoothened. Black matt paint. D:10 cm.
13. Halaf Fine Ware. Level 3. Lime. Oxidised. Buff. Smoothened. Black matt paint. D:10 cm.
14. Halaf Fine Ware. Level 3. Lime. Oxidised. Buff. Smoothened. Red to dark-red lustrous paint. D:8 cm.
15. Halaf Fine Ware. Level 3. No visible inclusions. Oxidised. Buff. Smoothened. Black matt paint. D:9 cm.
16. Halaf Fine Ware. Level 3. Lime. Oxidised. Buff. Smoothened. Brown matt paint. D:8 cm.
17. Halaf Fine Ware. Level 3. Lime. Oxidised. Cream. Smoothened. Black matt paint. D:16 cm.
18. Halaf Fine Ware. Level 1/3. Lime. Oxidised. Cream. Smoothened. D:18 cm.
19. Halaf Fine Ware. Level 3. Sand inclusions. Oxidised. Buff. Smoothened. D:12 cm.
20. Halaf Fine Ware. Level 3. No visible inclusions. Oxidised. Buff. Smoothened. D:4 cm.
21. Halaf Fine Ware. Level 3. No visible inclusions. Oxidised. Buff. Smoothened. Black matt paint. D:20 cm.
22. Halaf Fine Ware. Level 3. No visible inclusions. Incompletely oxidised (grey core). Buff. Smoothened. Black matt paint. D:12 cm.
23. Halaf Fine Ware. Level 3. No visible inclusions. Oxidised. Buff. Smoothened. Black matt paint. D:17 cm.
24. Halaf Fine Ware. Level 3. Lime. Oxidised. Cream. Smoothened. Brown lustrous paint. D:10 cm.
25. Halaf Fine Ware. Level 3. No visible inclusions. Oxidised. Buff. Smoothened. Black lustrous paint. D:8 cm.

26. Halaf Fine Ware. Level 2/3. No visible inclusions. Oxidised. Buff. Smoothened. Brown lustrous paint. D:12 cm.

Fig. 3.49
   1. Halaf Fine Ware. Level 3. Lime. Oxidised. Buff. Slipped Brown matt paint.
   2. Halaf Fine Ware. Level 3. No visible inclusions. Incompletely oxidised (grey core). Buff. Smoothened. Black matt paint.
   3. Halaf Fine Ware. Level 1/3. No visible inclusions. Oxidised. Buff. Smoothened. Black lustrous paint.
   4. Halaf Fine Ware. Level 3. Lime. Incompletely oxidised (grey core). Cream. Smoothened. Black matt paint.
   5. Halaf Fine Ware. Level 3. Lime. Oxidised. Buff. Smoothened. Black lustrous paint.
   6. Halaf Fine Ware. Level 3. Lime. Oxidised. Cream. Smoothened. Black matt paint.
   7. Halaf Fine Ware. Level 1. Lime. Oxidised. Buff. Smoothened. Black matt paint.
   8. Halaf Fine Ware. Level 3. Lime. Oxidised. Cream. Smoothened. Brown lustrous paint.
   9. Halaf Fine Ware. Level 3. Lime. Oxidised. Buff. Smoothened. Brown matt paint.
  10. Halaf Fine Ware. Level 3. Lime. Oxidised. Buff. Smoothened. Black matt paint.
  11. Halaf Fine Ware. Level 3. Lime. Incompletely oxidised (grey core). Buff. Smoothened. Dark-red to reddish-brown matt paint.
  12. Halaf Fine Ware. Level 3. Lime. Oxidised. Buff. Smoothened. Black matt paint.
  13. Halaf Fine Ware. Level 3. No visible inclusions. Oxidised. Cream. Smoothened. Dark-red to reddish-brown matt paint.

Fig. 3.50
   1. Halaf Fine Ware. Level 3. No visible inclusions. Incompletely oxidised (grey core). Buff. Smoothened. Black lustrous paint.
   2. Halaf Fine Ware. Level 3. No visible inclusions. Oxidised. Buff. Smoothened. Brown matt paint.
   3. Halaf Fine Ware. Level 3. No visible inclusions. Oxidised. Buff. Slipped Brown matt paint.
   4. Halaf Fine Ware. Level 3. No visible inclusions. Oxidised. Buff. Smoothened. Black matt paint.
   5. Halaf Fine Ware. Level 1. No visible inclusions. Oxidised. Buff. Smoothened. Black matt paint.
   6. Halaf Fine Ware. Level 3. No visible inclusions. Oxidised. Cream. Smoothened. Black matt paint.
   7. Halaf Fine Ware. Level 3. No visible inclusions. Oxidised. Buff. Smoothened. Brown matt paint.
   8. Halaf Fine Ware. Level 3. Lime. Oxidised. Buff. Smoothened. Black matt paint.
   9. Halaf Fine Ware. Level 3. Lime. Oxidised. Buff. Smoothened. Wash. Black matt paint.
  10. Halaf Fine Ware. Level 3. Lime. Oxidised. Buff. Smoothened. Black lustrous paint.
  11. Halaf Fine Ware. Level 1. Lime. Oxidised. Buff. Smoothened. Black lustrous paint.
  12. Halaf Fine Ware. Level 2. Lime. Oxidised. Buff. Smoothened. Brown lustrous paint.
  13. Halaf Fine Ware. Level 3. No visible inclusions. Incompletely oxidised (grey core). Buff. Smoothened. Black matt paint.
  14. Halaf Fine Ware. Level 1/2/3. No visible inclusions. Oxidised. Buff. Smoothened. Black matt paint.
  15. Halaf Fine Ware. Level 1. Lime. Oxidised. Cream. Slipped Black lustrous paint.
  16. Halaf Fine Ware. Level 3. Lime. Oxidised. Cream. Smoothened. Black matt paint.

17. Halaf Fine Ware. Level 3. Lime. Oxidised. Buff. Smoothened. Wash. Black matt paint.
18. Halaf Fine Ware. Level1/2/3. Lime. Oxidised. Cream. Smoothened. Brown matt paint.
19. Halaf Fine Ware. Level 3. Lime. Oxidised. Buff. Smoothened. Black matt paint.
20. Halaf Fine Ware. Level 3. Lime. Incompletely oxidised. Buff. Smoothened. Black lustrous paint.
21. Halaf Fine Ware. Level 3. Lime. Oxidised. Cream. Smoothened. Brown lustrous paint.
22. Halaf Fine Ware. Level 3. Lime. Oxidised. Buff. Smoothened. Black matt paint.

Fig. 3.51

1. Halaf Fine Ware. Level 3. Lime. Oxidised. Buff. Smoothened. Black matt paint.
2. Halaf Fine Ware. Level 1/3. No visible inclusions. Incompletely oxidised. Buff. Smoothened. Brown matt paint.
3. Halaf Fine Ware. Level 3. Lime. Oxidised. Buff. Smoothened. Wash. Black matt paint.
4. Halaf Fine Ware. Level 3. Lime. Oxidised. Buff. Smoothened. Black lustrous paint.
5. Halaf Fine Ware. Level 3. No visible inclusions. Incompletely oxidised. Buff. Smoothened. Red lustrous paint.
6. Halaf Fine Ware. Level 3. Lime. Oxidised. Buff. Smoothened. Black matt paint.
7. Halaf Fine Ware. Level 3. No visible inclusions. Oxidised. Cream. Wash. Brown lustrous paint.
8. Halaf Fine Ware. Level 1/2/3. Lime. Oxidised. Buff. Smoothened. Black matt paint.
9. Halaf Fine Ware. Level 3. No visible inclusions. Oxidised. Buff. Smoothened. Black lustrous paint.
10. Halaf Fine Ware. Level 3. Lime. Oxidised. Black matt paint.
11. Halaf Fine Ware. Level 3. Lime. Oxidised. Buff. Smoothened. Orange-red matt paint.
12. Halaf Fine Ware. Level 3. No visible inclusions. Incompletely oxidised. Buff. Smoothened. Orange-red matt paint.
13. Halaf Fine Ware. Level 1/2/3. Lime. Oxidised. Buff. Smoothened. Black matt paint.
14. Halaf Fine Ware. Level 3. Lime. Oxidised. Cream. Smoothened. Brown matt paint.
15. Halaf Fine Ware. Level 1/2/3. Lime. Oxidised. Buff. Smoothened. Orange-red matt paint.
16. Halaf Fine Ware. Level 3. No visible inclusions. Oxidised. Buff. Smoothened. Black matt paint.
17. Halaf Fine Ware. Level 3. No visible inclusions. Oxidised. Buff. Smoothened. Brown matt paint.
18. Halaf Fine Ware. Level 1/3. No visible inclusions. Oxidised. Buff. Smoothened. Black matt paint.
19. Halaf Fine Ware. Level 1. No visible inclusions. Incompletely oxidised. Buff. Smoothened. Black matt paint.
20. Halaf Fine Ware. Level 1. No visible inclusions. Oxidised. Cream. Smoothened. Black lustrous paint.
21. Halaf Fine Ware. Level 3. No visible inclusions. Oxidised. Grey. smoothened. Dark-red to reddish-brown lustrous paint.
22. Halaf Fine Ware. Level 3. No visible inclusions. Oxidised. Cream. Smoothened. Brown matt paint.

Fig. 3.52

1. Halaf Fine Ware. Level 3. No visible inclusions. Oxidised. Cream. Smoothened. Black matt paint.
2. Halaf Fine Ware. Level 3. No visible inclusions. Oxidised. Buff. Smoothened. Black matt paint.

3. Halaf Fine Ware. Level 1/3. No visible inclusions. Oxidised. Buff. Smoothened. Brown matt paint.
4. Halaf Fine Ware. Level 3. No visible inclusions. Oxidised. Buff. Smoothened. Black matt paint.
5. Halaf Fine Ware. Level 1. No visible inclusions. Oxidised. Buff. Smoothened. Brown lustrous paint.
6. Halaf Fine Ware. Level 3. No visible inclusions. Oxidised. Buff. Smoothened. Brown lustrous paint.
7. Halaf Fine Ware. Level 1/3. Lime. Oxidised. Buff. Slipped Black matt paint.
8. Halaf Fine Ware. Level 3. Lime. Oxidised. Cream. Smoothened. Black matt paint.
9. Halaf Fine Ware. Level 3. No visible inclusions. Oxidised. Buff. Smoothened. Brown lustrous paint.
10. Halaf Fine Ware. Level 3. Lime. Incompletely oxidised (grey core). Buff. Smoothened. Black matt paint.
11. Halaf Fine Ware. Level 3. No visible inclusions. Oxidised. Buff. Smoothened. Brown matt paint.
12. Halaf Fine Ware. Level 3. No visible inclusions. Oxidised. Buff. Smoothened. Brown lustrous paint.
13. Halaf Fine Ware. Level 3. No visible inclusions. Oxidised. Buff. Smoothened. Black matt paint.
14. Halaf Fine Ware. Level 3. Lime. Incompletely oxidised (grey core). Cream. Smoothened. Black matt paint.
15. Halaf Fine Ware. Level 3. No visible inclusions. Oxidised. Buff. Smoothened. Black matt paint.
16. Halaf Fine Ware. Level 3. Lime. Oxidised. Buff. Smoothened. Black matt paint.
17. Halaf Fine Ware. Level 3. Lime. Oxidised. Buff. Smoothened. Black matt paint.
18. Halaf Fine Ware. Level 3. Lime. Oxidised. Buff. Smoothened. Black lustrous paint.
19. Halaf Fine Ware. Level 3. Lime. Oxidised. Cream. Smoothened. Black matt paint.
20. Halaf Fine Ware. Level 3. No visible inclusions. Oxidised. Buff. Smoothened. Black matt paint.
21. Halaf Fine Ware. Level 1. No visible inclusions. Oxidised. Buff. Smoothened. Dark-red to reddish-brown lustrous paint.
22. Halaf Fine Ware. Level 3. Lime. Incompletely oxidised (grey core). Cream. Smoothened. Black matt paint.
23. Halaf Fine Ware. Level 3. No visible inclusions. Oxidised. Buff. Smoothened. Black matt paint.
24. Halaf Fine Ware. Level 3. No visible inclusions. Oxidised. Buff. Smoothened. Brown lustrous paint.

Fig. 3.53
1. Halaf Fine Ware. Level 3. Lime. Incompletely oxidised (grey core). Buff. Slipped. Brown lustrous paint.
2. Halaf Fine Ware. Level 1. No visible inclusions. Incompletely oxidised. Buff. Smoothened. Black matt paint.
3. Halaf Fine Ware. Level 1/2/3. Lime. Oxidised. Buff. Smoothened. Dark-red to reddish-brown matt paint.
4. Halaf Fine Ware. Level 3. No visible inclusions. Oxidised. Cream. Smoothened. Black lustrous paint.
5. Halaf Fine Ware. Level 3. No visible inclusions. Oxidised. Buff. Smoothened. Black lustrous paint.

6. Halaf Fine Ware. Level 1. Lime. Overfired. Grey. Smoothened. Black matt paint. D:25 cm.
7. Halaf Fine Ware. Level 3. Lime. Oxidised. Buff. Smoothened. Wash. Red to dark-red matt paint.
8. Halaf Fine Ware. Level 3. Lime. Oxidised. Buff. Smoothened. Brown lustrous paint.
9. Halaf Fine Ware. Level 3. No visible inclusions. Oxidised. Buff. Slipped Brown lustrous paint.
10. Halaf Fine Ware. Level 3. Lime. Oxidised. Buff. Smoothened. Black matt paint.
11. Halaf Fine Ware. Level 3. Lime. Oxidised. Buff. Smoothened. Black matt paint.
12. Halaf Fine Ware. Level 3. Lime. Oxidised. Buff. Smoothened. Black matt paint.
13. Halaf Fine Ware. Level 3. No visible inclusions. Oxidised. Buff. Smoothened. Brown lustrous paint.
14. Halaf Fine Ware. Level 3. Lime. Incompletely oxidised (grey core). Buff. Smoothened. Black matt paint.

Fig. 3.54
1. Halaf Fine Ware. Level 3. Lime. Oxidised. Buff. Smoothened. Black matt paint. D:25 cm.
2. Halaf Fine Ware. Level 3. No visible inclusions. Oxidised. Buff. Smoothened. Black lustrous paint. D:17 cm.
3. Halaf Fine Ware. Level. Level 1/2/3. Lime. Oxidised. Cream. Smoothened. Black matt paint. D:40 cm.
4. Halaf Fine Ware. Level 3. Lime. Oxidised. Buff. Smoothened. Black matt paint. D:22 cm.
5. Halaf Fine Ware. Level 3. No visible inclusions. Oxidised. Buff. Smoothened. D:20 cm.
6. Halaf Fine Ware. Level 3. No visible inclusions. Oxidised. Buff. Smoothened. D:26 cm.
7. Halaf Fine Ware. Level 3. Lime. Oxidised. Cream. Smoothened. D:12.5 cm.

Fig. 3.55
1. Halaf Fine Ware. Level 1. Lime. Oxidised. Buff. Smoothened. Incisions through brown lustrous paint.
2. Halaf Fine Ware. Level 2. No visible inclusions. Oxidised. Cream. Smoothened. Incised.
3. Halaf Fine Ware. Level 3. No visible inclusions. Oxidised. Orange. Smoothened. Incised.
4. Halaf Fine Ware. Level 1/3. No visible inclusions. Oxidised. Brown. Smoothened. Brown lustrous paint. D:17 cm.
5. Halaf Fine Ware. Level 1/3. Lime. Oxidised. Buff. Smoothened. Black lustrous paint. D:14 cm.
6. Halaf Fine Ware. Level 1. No visible inclusions. Oxidised. Buff. Smoothened. Brown lustrous paint. D:15 cm.
7. Halaf Fine Ware. Level 3. No visible inclusions. Oxidised. Buff. Smoothened. Black lustrous paint. D:15 cm.
8. Halaf Fine Ware. Level 1/3. Lime. Oxidised. Cream. Smoothened. Black matt paint. D:12 cm.
9. Halaf Fine Ware. Level 3. Lime. Overfired. Green. Smoothened. Black lustrous paint. D:4 cm.
10. Halaf Fine Ware. Level 3. No visible inclusions. Oxidised. Buff. Smoothened. Black matt paint. D:6 cm.
11. Halaf Fine Ware. Level 3. Lime. Oxidised. Cream. Smoothened. Brown matt paint. D:16 cm.
12. Halaf Fine Ware. Level 1/3. Lime. Oxidised. Buff. Smoothened. Black matt paint. D:16 cm.
13. Halaf Fine Ware. Level 1/2/3. No visible inclusions. Oxidised. Cream. Slipped. Red to dark-red paint. D:12 cm.

14. Halaf Fine Ware. Level 3. No visible inclusions. Oxidised. Brown. Smoothened. D:8 cm.
15. Halaf Fine Ware. Level 3. Lime. Oxidised. Buff. Smoothened. Brown matt paint. D:4 cm.
16. Halaf Fine Ware. Level 3. Lime. Oxidised. Buff. Smoothened. Orange-red matt paint. D:6 cm.
17. Halaf Fine Ware. Level 3. No visible inclusions. Overfired. Green. Smoothened. Black matt paint. D:11 cm.
18. Halaf Fine Ware. Level 2. No visible inclusions. Oxidised. Buff. Smoothened. Orange-red lustrous paint. D:10 cm.
19. Halaf Fine Ware. Level 2. Lime. Oxidised. Buff. Smoothened. Black matt paint.
20. Halaf Fine Ware. Level 3. No visible inclusions. Oxidised. Cream. Smoothened. Black matt paint.
21. Halaf Fine Ware. Level 3. No visible inclusions. Oxidised. Cream. Smoothened. Black matt paint.
22. Halaf Fine Ware. Level 3. Lime. Oxidised. Buff. Smoothened.
23. Halaf Fine Ware. Level 2/3. No visible inclusions. Oxidised. Grey. Smoothened.
24. Halaf Fine Ware. Level 3. No visible inclusions. Incompletely oxidised. Buff. Smoothened. Wash. D:10 cm.
25. Halaf Fine Ware. Level 3. Lime. Oxidised. Buff. Smoothened. Wash. Black matt paint.

Fig. 3.56
1. Vegetal Coarse Ware. Level 3. Large plant. Incompletely oxidised (black core). Brown. Smoothened. D:35 cm.
2. Vegetal Coarse Ware. Level 3. Small plant. Incompletely oxidised (black core). Brown. Smoothened. D:37 cm.
3. Vegetal Coarse Ware. Level 3. Large plant. Incompletely oxidised (black core). Brown. Smoothened. D:38 cm.
4. Vegetal Coarse Ware. Level 3. Large plant. Incompletely oxidised (black core). Brown. Smoothened. D:32 cm.
5. Vegetal Coarse Ware. Level 3. Large plant. Incompletely oxidised (black core). Brown. Smoothened. D:30 cm.
6. Vegetal Coarse Ware. Level 3. Large plant. Incompletely oxidised (grey core). Brown. Smoothened. D:28 cm.
7. Vegetal Coarse Ware. Level 3. Large plant. Incompletely oxidised (black core). Brown. Scraped. D:16 cm.
8. Vegetal Coarse Ware. Level 3. Large plant. Incompletely oxidised (black core). Brown. Smoothened. D:18 cm.
9. Vegetal Coarse Ware. Level 3. Large plant. Incompletely oxidised (black core). Brown. Smoothened. D:18 cm.
10. Vegetal Coarse Ware. Level 3. Large plant. Incompletely oxidised (grey core). Brown. Smoothened. D:18 cm.
11. Vegetal Coarse Ware. Level 3. Large plant. Incompletely oxidised (black core). Brown. Smoothened. D:15 cm.
12. Vegetal Coarse Ware. Level 3. Large plant. Incompletely oxidised (black core). Brown. Smoothened. D:15 cm.
13. Vegetal Coarse Ware. Level 3. Large plant. Incompletely oxidised (black core). Brown. Burnished. Brown lustrous paint. D:24 cm.
14. Vegetal Coarse Ware. Level 3. Large plant. Incompletely oxidised (black core). Brown. Smoothened. D:7 cm.
15. Vegetal Coarse Ware. Level 3. Large plant. Incompletely oxidised (black core). Brown. Smoothened. D:12 cm.

Fig. 3.57
1. Vegetal Coarse Ware. Level 3. Large plant. Incompletely oxidised (black core). Brown. Smoothened. Oval shape.
2. Vegetal Coarse Ware. Level 3. Large plant. Incompletely oxidised (black core). Brown. Smoothened. Oval shape.
3. Vegetal Coarse Ware. Level 3. Large plant. Incompletely oxidised (black core). Brown. Smoothened. Oval shape.
4. Vegetal Coarse Ware. Level 3. Large plant. Incompletely oxidised (black core). Brown. Smoothened. Oval shape.
5. Vegetal Coarse Ware. Level 3. Large plant. Incompletely oxidised (black core). Brown. Scraped.
6. Vegetal Coarse Ware. Level 3. Large plant. Incompletely oxidised (black core). Brown. Scraped.
7. Vegetal Coarse Ware. Level 3. Large plant. Incompletely oxidised (black core). Brown. Scraped. D:33 cm.
8. Vegetal Coarse Ware. Level 3. Large plant and mineral. Incompletely oxidised (black core). Brown. Scraped. D:20 cm.
9. Vegetal Coarse Ware. Level 1/2/3. Large plant. Incompletely oxidised (black core). Brown. Smoothened. D:25 cm.
10. Vegetal Coarse Ware. Level 3. Large plant. Incompletely oxidised (black core). Brown. Smoothened. D:11 cm.
11. Vegetal Coarse Ware. Level 1. Large plant. Incompletely oxidised (black core). Brown. Smoothened.
12. Vegetal Coarse Ware. Level 3. Small plant and lime. Incompletely oxidised (grey core). Brown. Smoothened. Rim indented (spout?) D:12 cm.
13. Vegetal Coarse Ware. Level 3. Large plant. Incompletely oxidised (black core). Brown. Smoothened. D:20 cm.
14. Vegetal Coarse Ware. Level 2. Large plant. Incompletely oxidised (black core). Brown. Smoothened. D:18 cm.

Fig. 3.58
1. Vegetal Coarse Ware. Level 3. Large plant. Incompletely oxidised (black core). Brown. Smoothened. D:28 cm.
2. Vegetal Coarse Ware. Level 3. Large plant. Incompletely oxidised (grey core). Orange. Smoothened. D:20 cm.
3. Vegetal Coarse Ware. Level 3. Large plant and lime. Incompletely oxidised (black core). Brown. Smoothened. D:18 cm.
4. Vegetal Coarse Ware. Level 3. Large plant. Incompletely oxidised (black core). Brown. Smoothened. D:22 cm.
5. Vegetal Coarse Ware. Level 3. Large plant. Incompletely oxidised (grey core). Buff. Smoothened. D:19 cm.
6. Vegetal Coarse Ware. Level 3. Large plant. Incompletely oxidised (black core). Brown. Burnished. D:14 cm.
7. Vegetal Coarse Ware. Level 3. Large plant. Incompletely oxidised (black core). Brown. Burnished. D:17 cm.
8. Vegetal Coarse Ware. Level 3. Large plant. Incompletely oxidised (black core). Brown. Smoothened. D:16 cm.
9. Vegetal Coarse Ware. Level 1. Large plant and mineral. Incompletely oxidised (black core). Brown. Smoothened. D:11 cm.
10. Vegetal Coarse Ware. Level 3. Large plant. Incompletely oxidised (black core). Brown. Smoothened. Irregular incisions. D:10 cm.

11. Vegetal Coarse Ware. Level 1/2/3. Large plant. Incompletely oxidised (black core). Brown. Smoothened. D:11 cm.
12. Vegetal Coarse Ware. Level 1/3. Large plant. Incompletely oxidised (black core). Brown. Smoothened. D:8 cm.
13. Vegetal Coarse Ware. Level 3. Large plant. Incompletely oxidised (black core). Brown. Smoothened. D:5 cm.
14. Vegetal Coarse Ware. Level 3. Large plant. Incompletely oxidised (black core). Brown. Smoothened. D:14 cm.
15. Vegetal Coarse Ware. Level 3. Medium-sized plant and lime. Incompletely oxidised (grey core). Brown. Smoothened. D:5 cm.
16. Vegetal Coarse Ware. Level 1. Large plant. Incompletely oxidised (black core). Brown. Scraped. D:8 cm.
17. Vegetal Coarse Ware. Level 1/3. Large plant. Incompletely oxidised (black core). Orange. Smoothened. D:3 cm.
18. Vegetal Coarse Ware. Level 3. Large plant. Incompletely oxidised (black core). Brown. Burnished. D:8 cm.
19. Vegetal Coarse Ware. Level 3. Large plant and mineral. Incompletely oxidised (black core). Buff. Smoothened. D:9 cm.
20. Vegetal Coarse Ware. Level 1. Large plant and mineral. Incompletely oxidised (grey core). Brown. Burnished.
21. Vegetal Coarse Ware. Level 2. Large plant and lime. Incompletely oxidised (black core). Brown. Smoothened. Incisions.
22. Vegetal Coarse Ware. Level 3. Large plant. Incompletely oxidised (black core). Brown. Smoothened. Incisions.
23. Vegetal Coarse Ware. Level 3. Large plant. Incompletely oxidised (grey core). Brown. Smoothened. Impressions.

Fig. 3.59
1. Mineral Coarse Ware. Level 3. Large mineral. Reduced (black core). Black. Burnished. D:23 cm.
2. Mineral Coarse Ware. Level 3. Large mineral. Oxidised (brown core). Brown. Burnished. D:22 cm.
3. Mineral Coarse Ware. Level 3. Large mineral. Incompletely oxidised (black core). Brown. Burnished. D:27 cm.
4. Mineral Coarse Ware. Level 3. Large mineral. Oxidised (brown core). Brown. Burnished. D:17 cm.
5. Mineral Coarse Ware. Level 3. Medium-sized mineral. Incompletely oxidised (black core). Brown. Burnished. D:22 cm.
6. Mineral Coarse Ware. Level 3. Large mineral. Oxidised (brown core). Brown. Burnished. D:14 cm.
7. Mineral Coarse Ware. Level 1/2/3. Large mineral. Reduced (black core). Black. Burnished. D:11 cm.
8. Mineral Coarse Ware. Level 3. Large mineral. Incompletely oxidised (black core). Brown. Burnished.
9. Mineral Coarse Ware. Level 3. Large mineral. Incompletely oxidised (black core). Brown. Burnished.
10. Mineral Coarse Ware. Level 1/2. Large mineral. Incompletely oxidised (black core). Brown. Smoothened. D:13 cm.
11. Mineral Coarse Ware. Level 3. Large mineral. Oxidised (brown core). Black. Burnished. D:13 cm.

12. Mineral Coarse Ware. Level 1. Large mineral. Incompletely oxidised (black core). Brown. Burnished. D:32 cm.
13. Mineral Coarse Ware. Level 3. Medium-sized mineral. Reduced (black core). Black. Burnished. D:12 cm.
14. Mineral Coarse Ware. Level 1/3. Large mineral. Incompletely oxidised (black core). Brown. Smoothened. D:12 cm.
15. Mineral Coarse Ware. Level 1. Large mineral. Oxidised (brown core). Black. Burnished. D:9 cm.
16. Mineral Coarse Ware. Level 3. Large mineral. Incompletely oxidised (black core). Brown. Burnished.

Fig. 3.60
1. Red-Slipped and Burnished Ware. Level 3. Medium-sized plant. Oxidised (brown core). Red-slipped. Burnished. D:17 cm.
2. Red-Slipped and Burnished Ware. Level 3. Medium-sized plant. Oxidised (brown core). Red-slipped. Burnished. D:12 cm.
3. Red-Slipped and Burnished Ware. Level 3. Small plant. Incompletely oxidised (black core). Red-slipped. Burnished. D:9 cm.
4. Red-Slipped and Burnished Ware. Level 3. Small plant. Oxidised (brown core). Red-slipped. Burnished. D:9 cm.
5. Red-Slipped and Burnished Ware. Level 3. Small plant. Oxidised (brown core). Red-slipped. Burnished. D:28 cm.
6. Red-Slipped and Burnished Ware. Level 3. Small plant and small lime. Oxidised (brown core). Red-slipped. Burnished. Beaded rim. D:23 cm.
7. Red-Slipped and Burnished Ware. Level 3. Small plant. Incompletely oxidised (black core). Red-slipped. Burnished. D:19 cm.
8. Red-Slipped and Burnished Ware. Level 3. Small plant. Oxidised (brown core). Red-slipped. Burnished. D:15 cm.
9. Red-Slipped and Burnished Ware. Level 3. Small plant. Oxidised (brown core). Red-slipped. Burnished. D:9 cm.
10. Grey-Black Ware. Level 3. No visible inclusions. Reduced (grey-brown core). Black. Burnished. D:39 cm.
11. Grey-Black Ware. Level 3. No visible inclusions. Reduced (black core). Black. Burnished. D:33 cm.
12. Grey-Black Ware. Level 3. No visible inclusions. Reduced (brown core). Black. Burnished. D:14 cm.
13. Grey-Black Ware. Level 3. Small plant. Reduced (grey core). Grey. Burnished. D:9 cm.
14. Grey-Black Ware. Level 3. No visible inclusions. Reduced (brown core). Black. Burnished. D:9 cm.
15. Grey-Black Ware. Level 1. No visible inclusions. Reduced (black core). Black. Burnished. D:11 cm.
16. Grey-Black Ware. Level 1/2/3. Small mineral. Reduced (brown core). Brown. Burnished. D:7 cm.
17. Grey-Black Ware. Level 3. No visible inclusions. Reduced (black core). Black. Burnished. D:15 cm.
18. Grey-Black Ware. Level 3. No visible inclusions. Reduced (brown core). Black. Burnished.
19. Grey-Black Ware. Level 3. Small mineral. Reduced (black core). Black. Burnished. D:8 cm.
20. Grey-Black Ware. Level 3. Small mineral. Reduced (grey core). Grey. Burnished. D:8 cm.

21. Grey-Black Ware. Level 3. No visible inclusions. Reduced (brown core). Black. Burnished. D:24 cm.
22. Grey-Black Ware. Level 1/3. No visible inclusions. Reduced (brown core). Black. Burnished. D:22,5 cm.
23. Dark-Faced Burnished Ware. Level 3. Medium-sized mineral. Oxidised (brown core). Red-slipped. Burnished. D:15 cm.
24. Dark-Faced Burnished Ware. Level 3. Large mineral. Reduced (black core). Brown. Burnished. D:11 cm.
25. Dark-Faced Burnished Ware. Level 3. Large mineral. Oxidised (brown core). Red-slipped. Burnished. D:14 cm.
26. Dark-Faced Burnished Ware. Level 3. Medium-sized mineral. Oxidised (brown core). Brown. Burnished. D:13 cm.
27. Dark-Faced Burnished Ware. Level 3. Large mineral. Oxidised (brown core). Brown. Burnished. Red lustrous paint.
28. Orange Fine Ware. Level 3. Lime and large (black) mineral. Oxidised. Orange. Slipped. Red lustrous paint.
29. Orange Fine Ware. Level 1/3. Lime and small (black) mineral. Incompletely oxidised (grey core). Orange. Burnished.

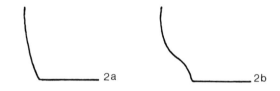

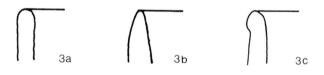

Figure 3.1. Rim and base terminology.

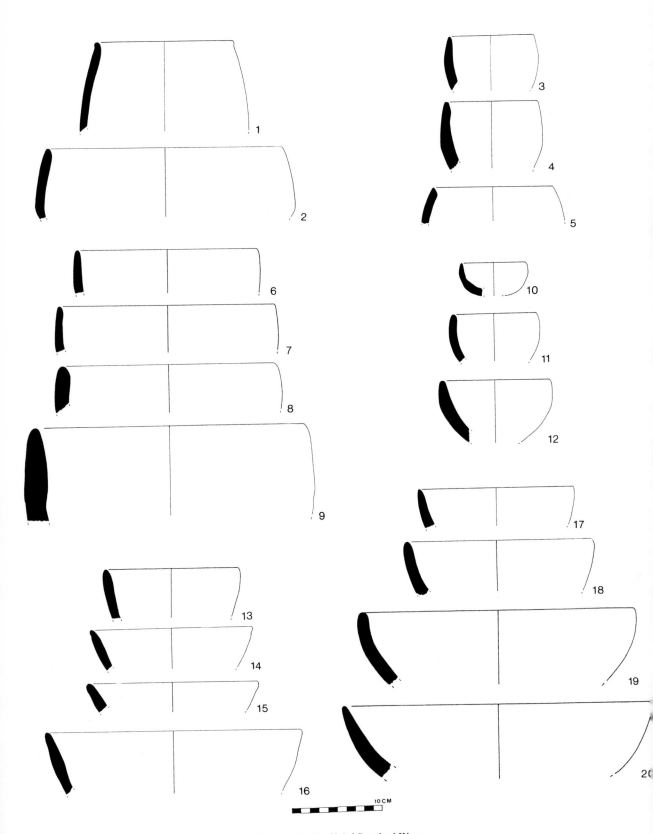

Figure 3.2. Pre-Halaf Standard Ware.

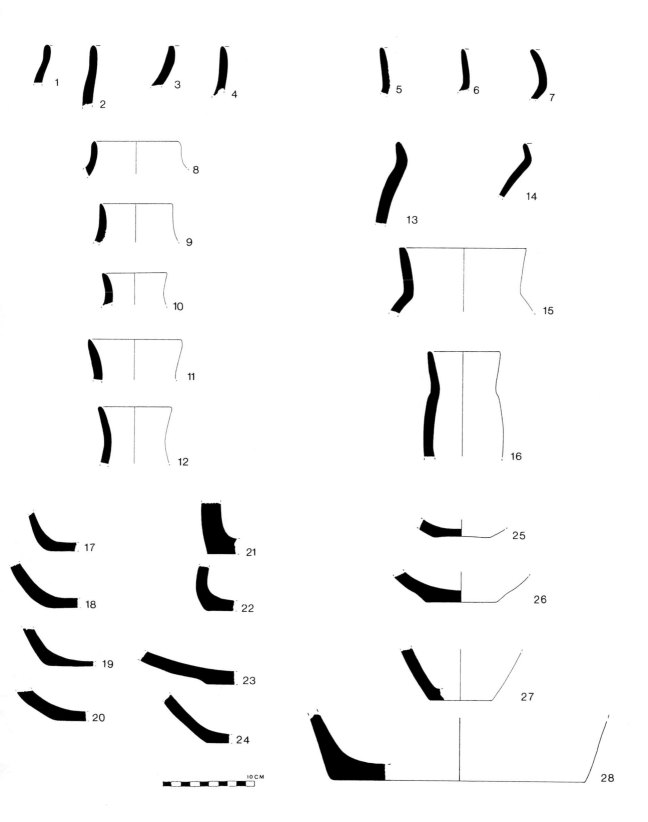

Figure 3.3. Pre-Halaf Standard Ware and Grey-Black Ware (nos. 1, 14, 27).

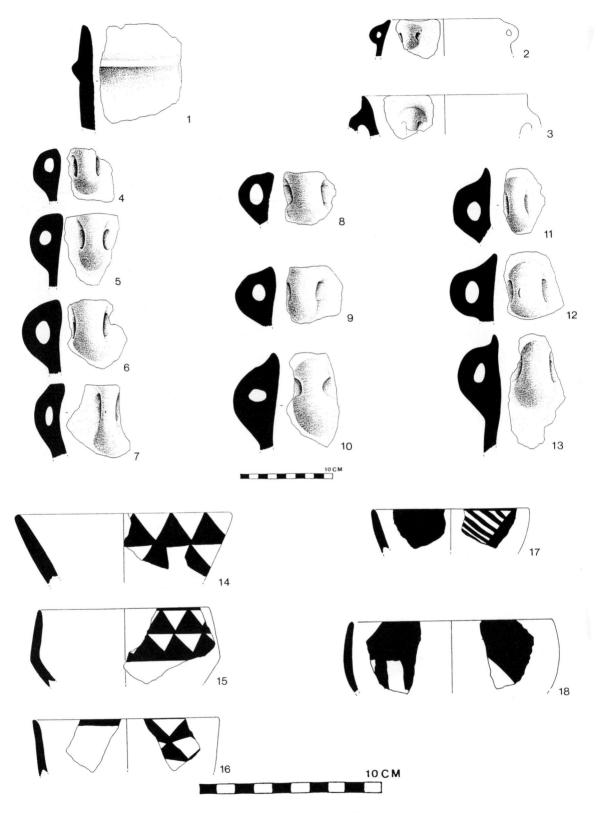

Figure 3.4. Pre-Halaf Standard Ware.

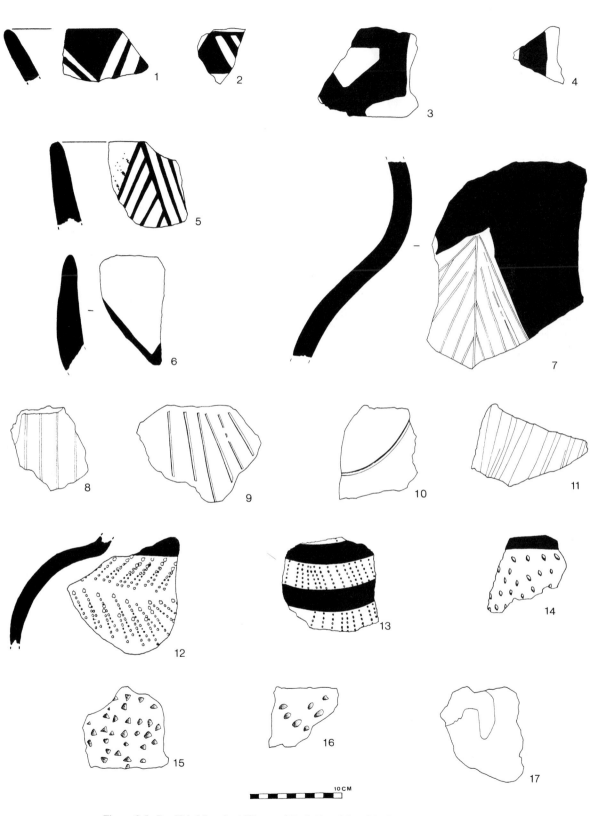

Figure 3.5. Pre-Halaf Standard Ware and Dark-Faced Burnished Ware (nos. 4, 11).

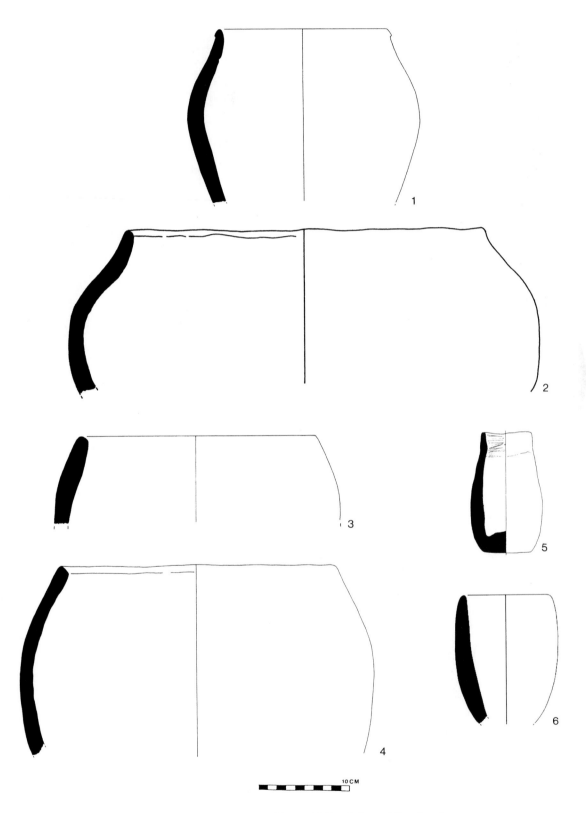

Figure 3.6. Transitional Standard Ware and Mineral Coarse Ware (no. 4).

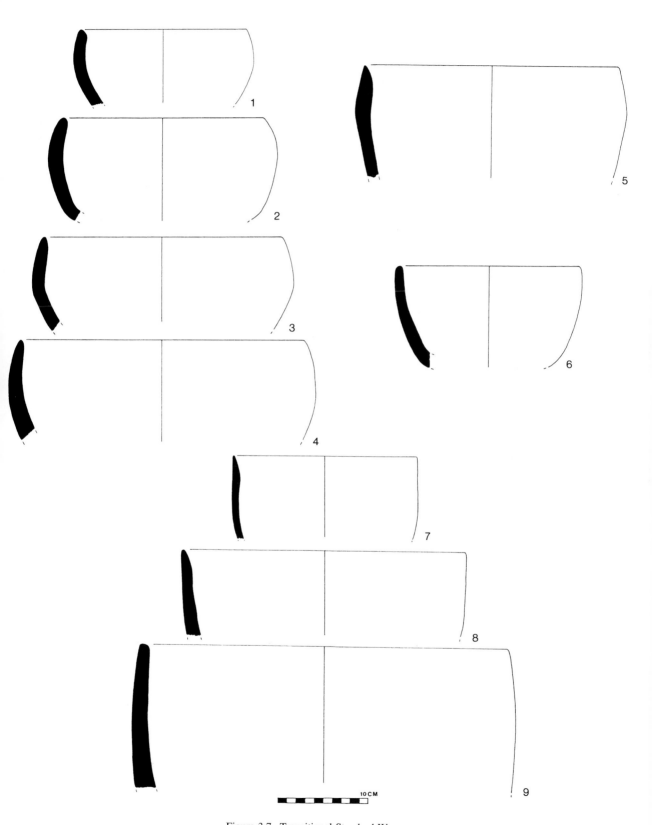

Figure 3.7. Transitional Standard Ware.

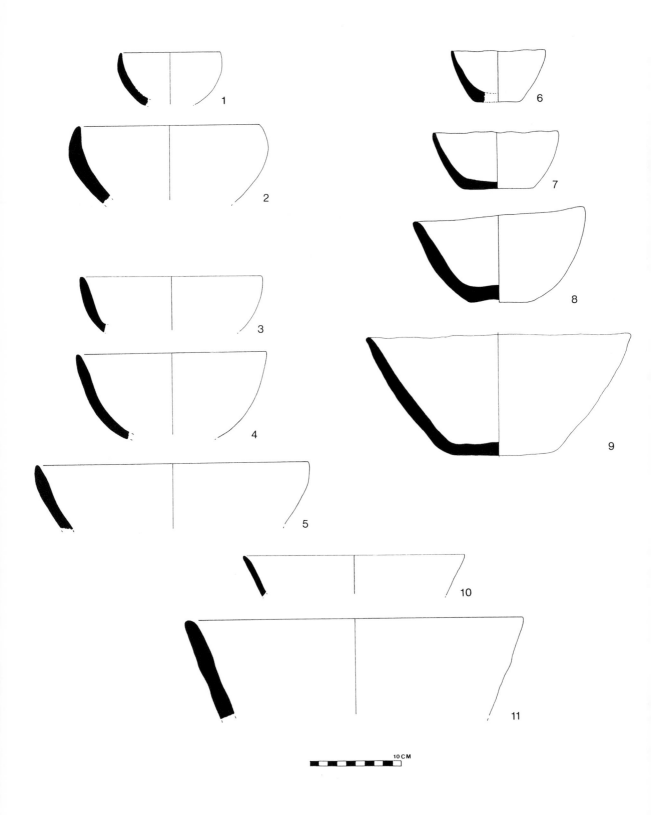

Figure 3.8. Transitional Standard Ware.

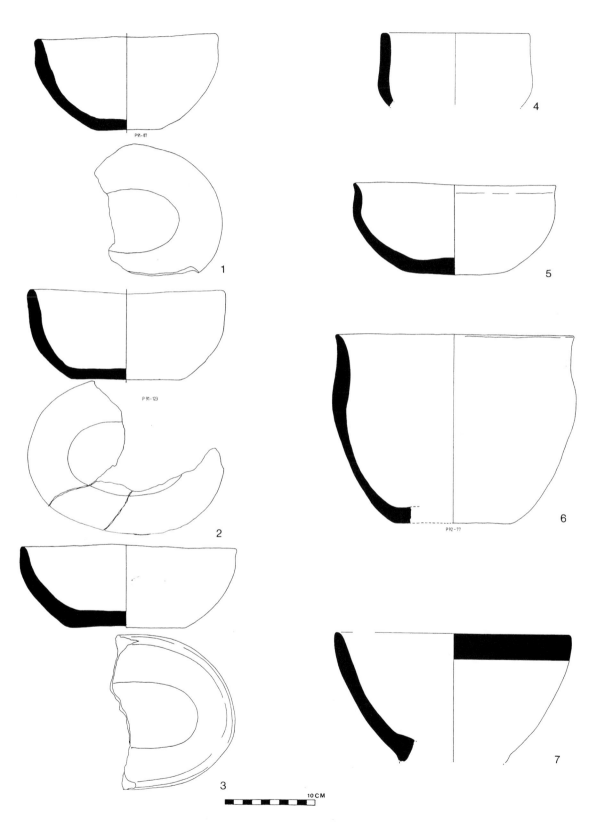

Figure 3.9. Transitional Standard Ware.

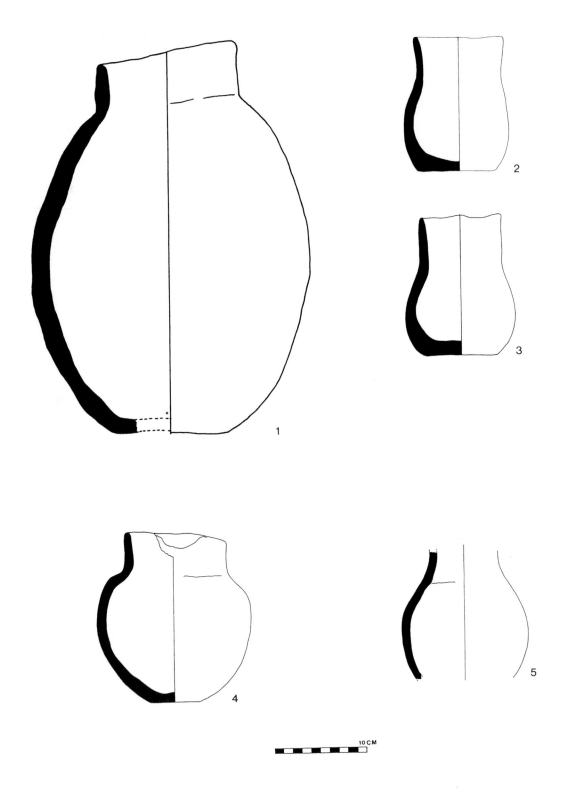

Figure 3.10. Transitional Standard Ware.

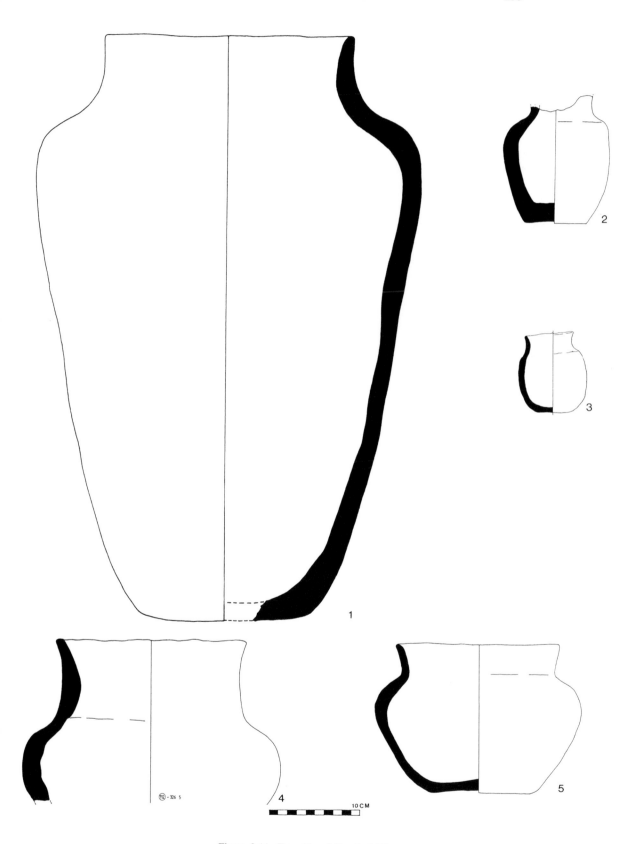

Figure 3.11. Transitional Standard Ware.

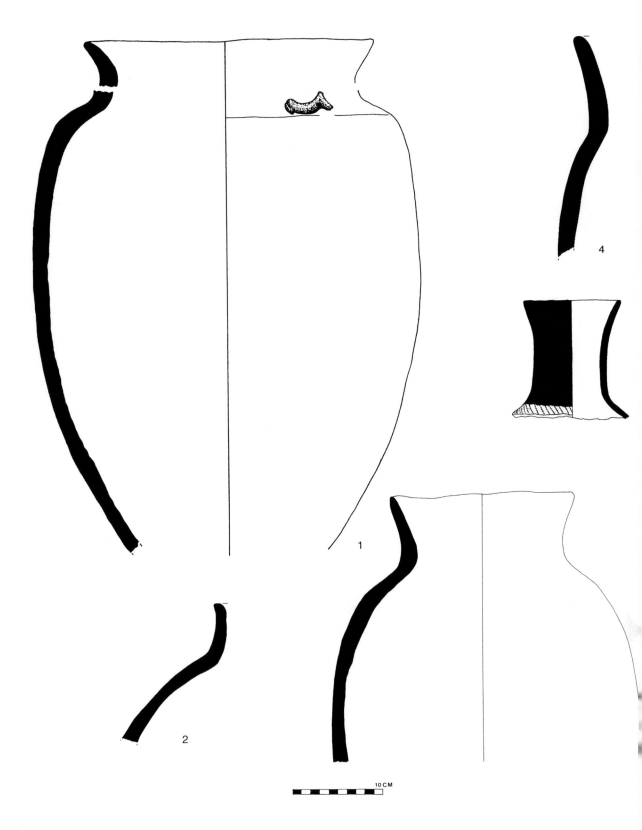

Figure 3.12. Transitional Standard Ware.

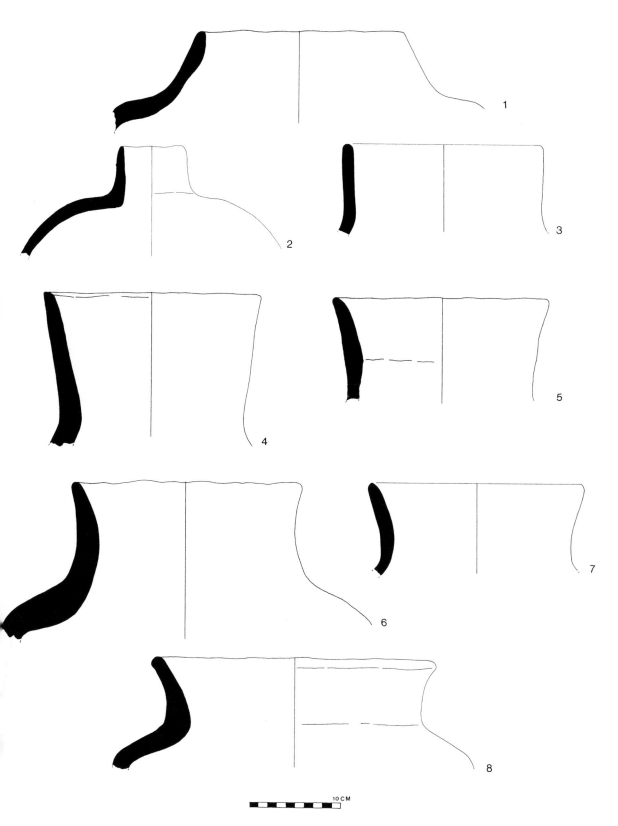

Figure 3.13. Transitional Standard Ware.

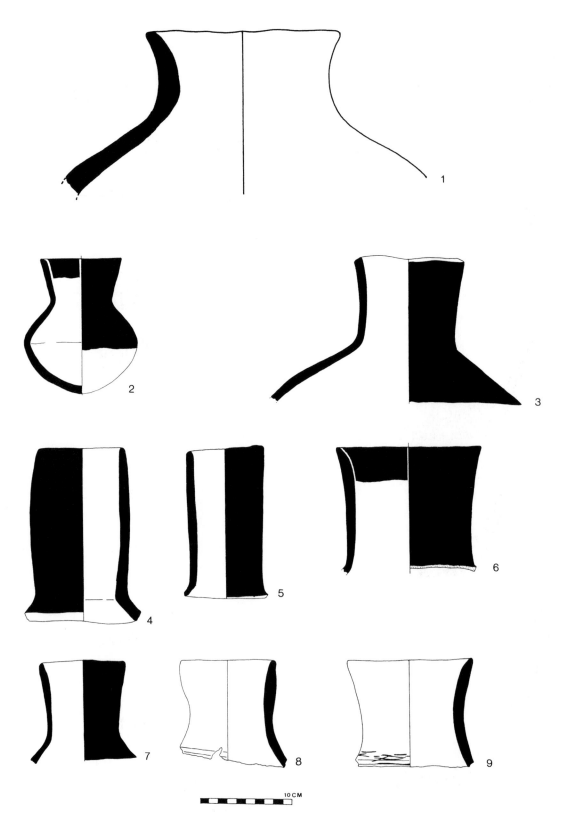

Figure 3.14. Transitional Standard Ware (no. 1) and Dark-Faced Burnished Ware.

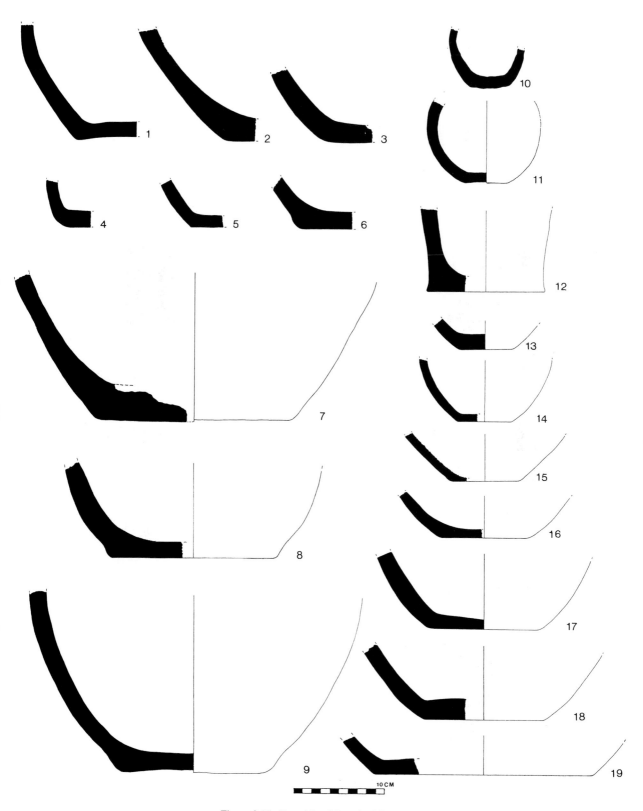

Figure 3.15. Transitional Standard Ware.

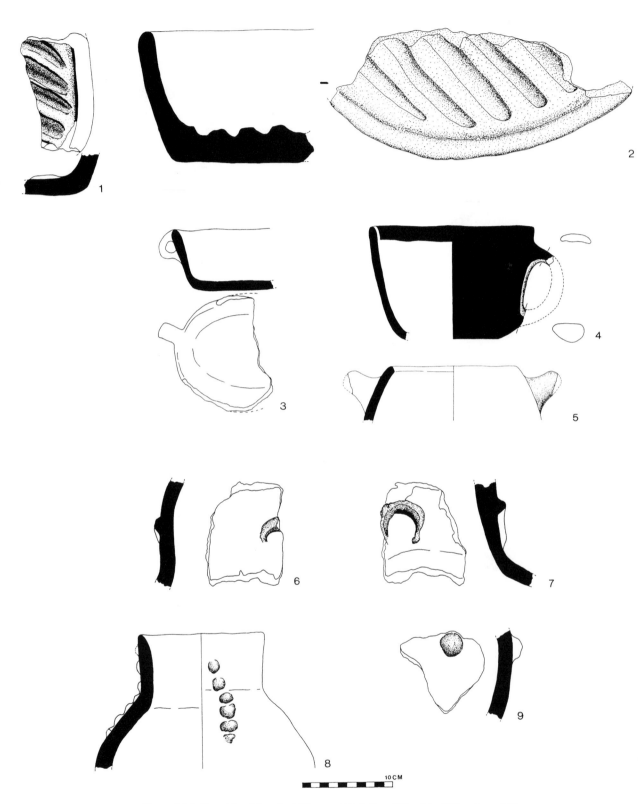

10 CM

Figure 3.16. Transitional Standard Ware and Dark-Faced Burnished Ware (nos. 4-5).

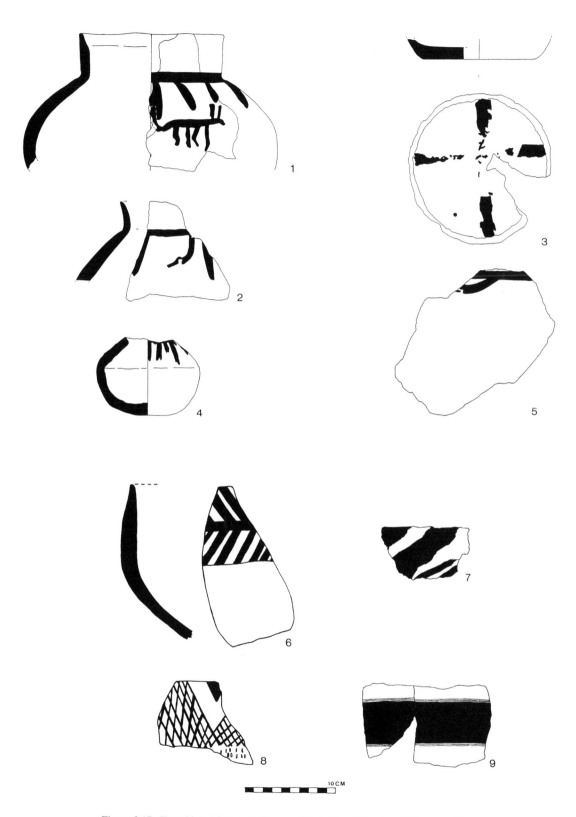

Figure 3.17. Transitional Standard Ware and Dark-Faced Burnished Ware (no. 9).

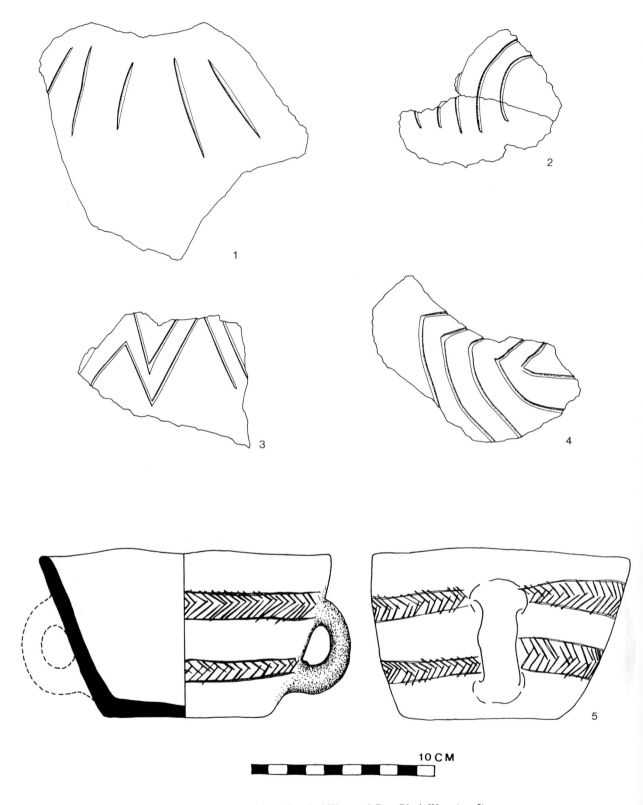

Figure 3.18. Transitional Standard Ware and Grey-Black Ware (no. 5).

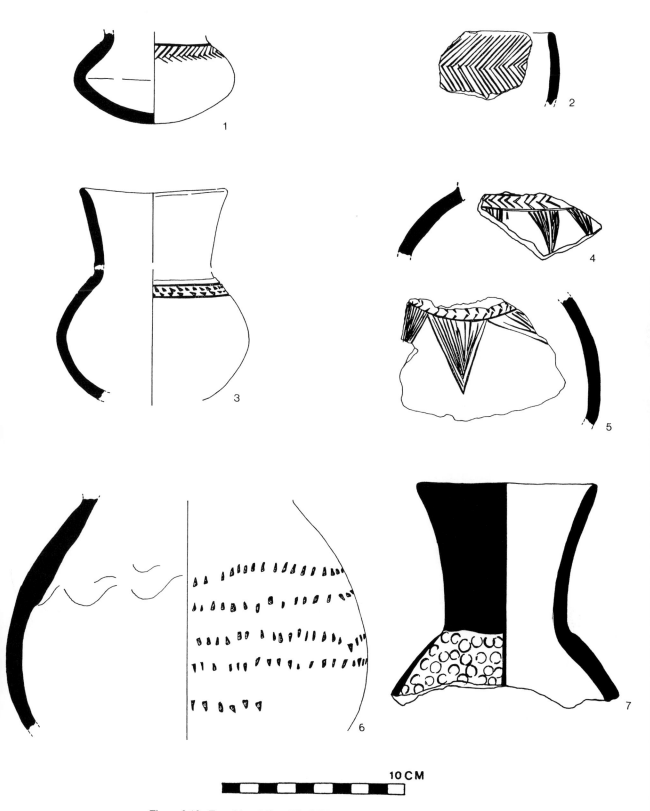

Figure 3.19. Transitional Grey-Black Ware and Standard Ware (nos. 6-7).

Figure 3.20. Transitional Standard Ware and Grey-Black Ware (no. 3).

Figure 3.21. Transitional Standard Fine Ware.

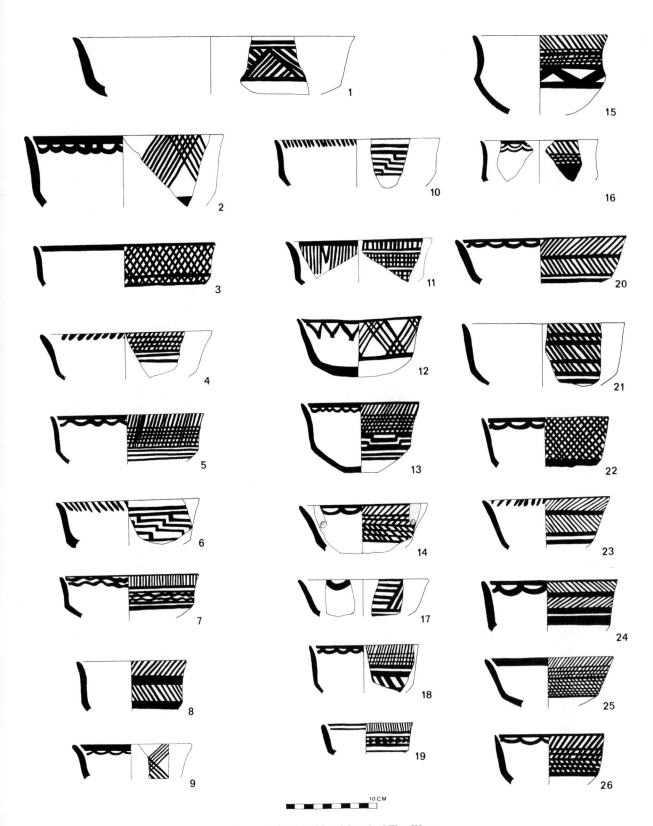

Figure 3.22. Transitional Standard Fine Ware.

Figure 3.23. Transitional Standard Fine Ware.

Figure 3.24. Transitional Standard Fine Ware.

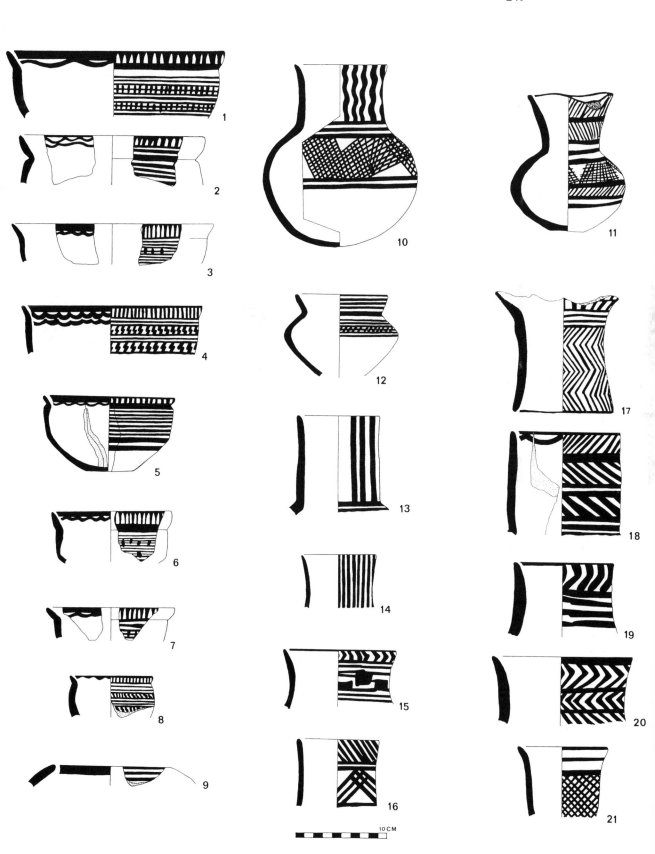

Figure 3.25. Transitional Standard Fine Ware.

Figure 3.26. Transitional Standard Fine Ware.

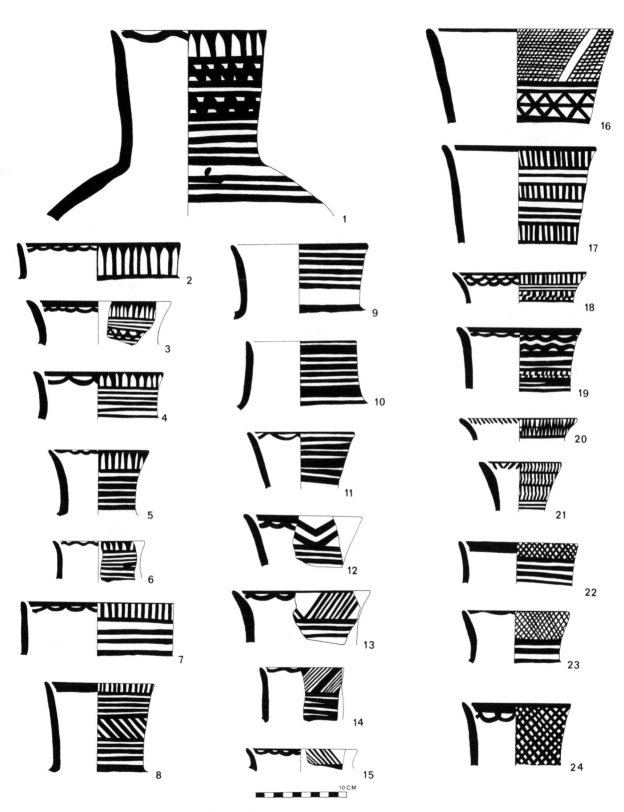

Figure 3.27. Transitional Standard Fine Ware.

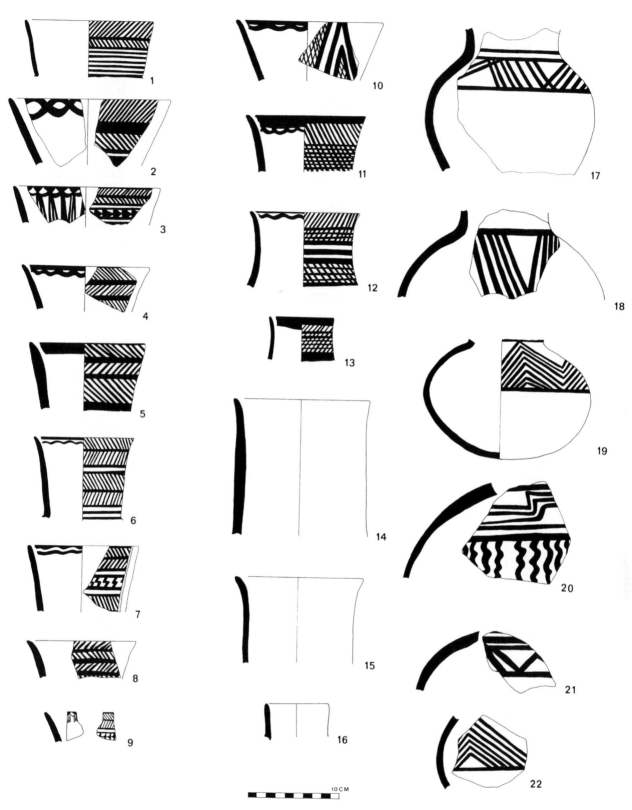

Figure 3.28. Transitional Standard Fine Ware.

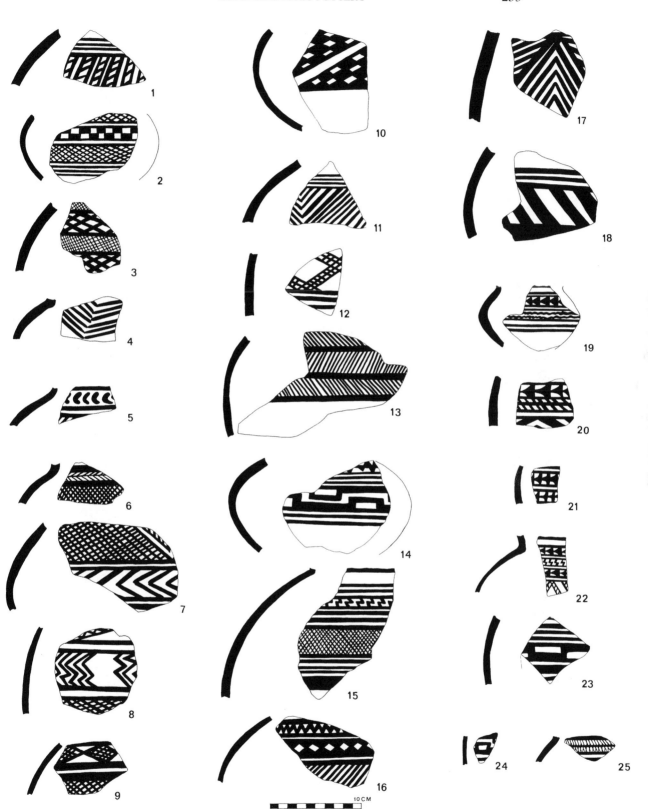

Figure 3.29. Transitional Standard Fine Ware.

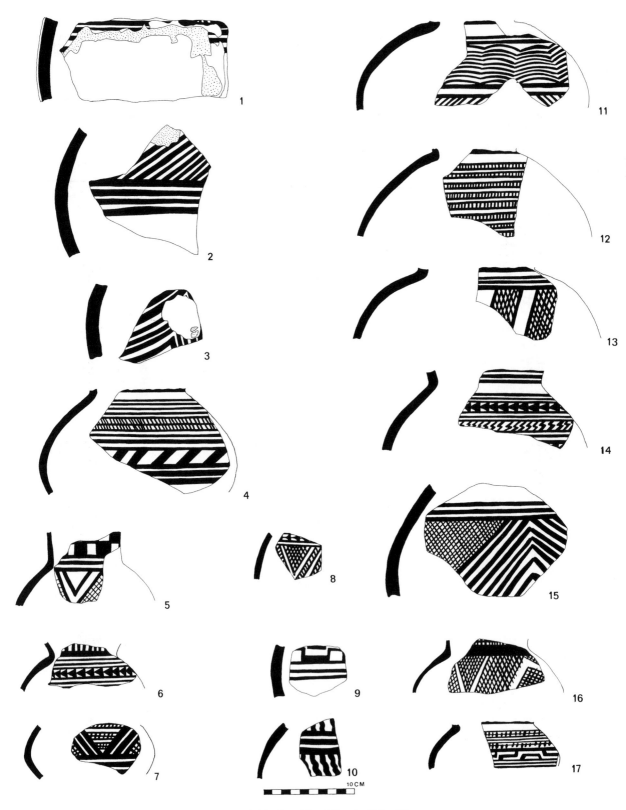

Figure 3.30. Transitional Standard Fine Ware.

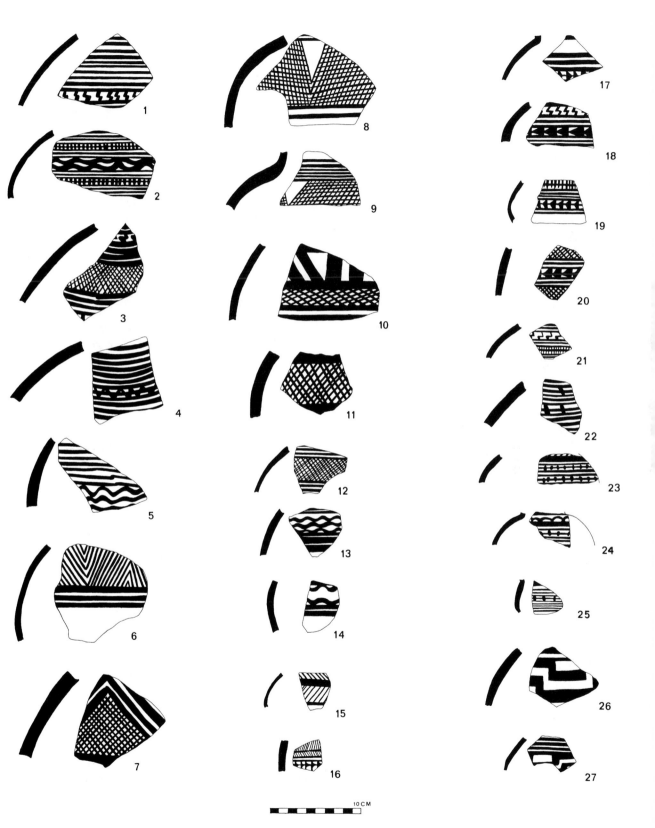

Figure 3.31. Transitional Standard Fine Ware.

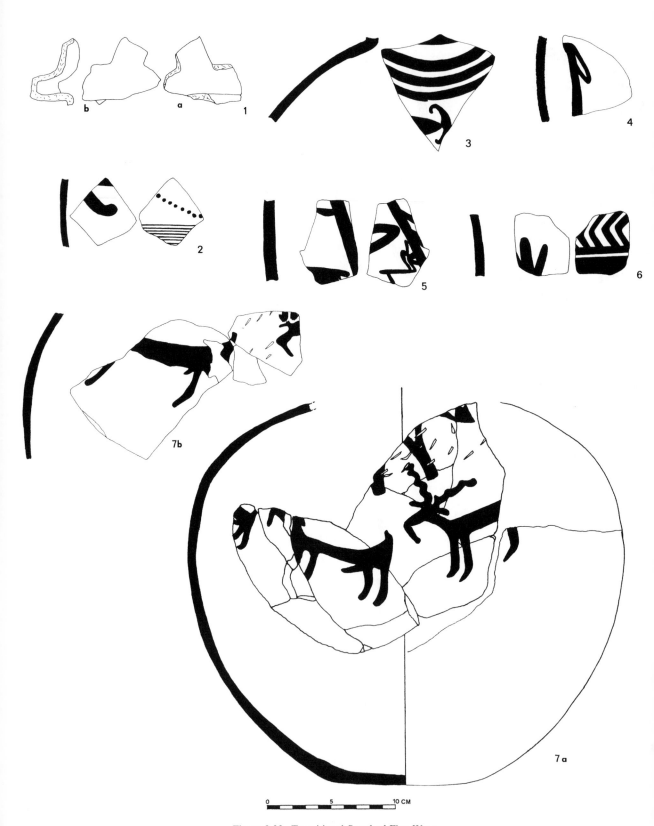

Figure 3.32. Transitional Standard Fine Ware.

Figure 3.33. Transitional Standard Fine Ware.

Figure 3.34. Transitional Orange Fine Ware.

Figure 3.35. Transitional Orange Fine Ware.

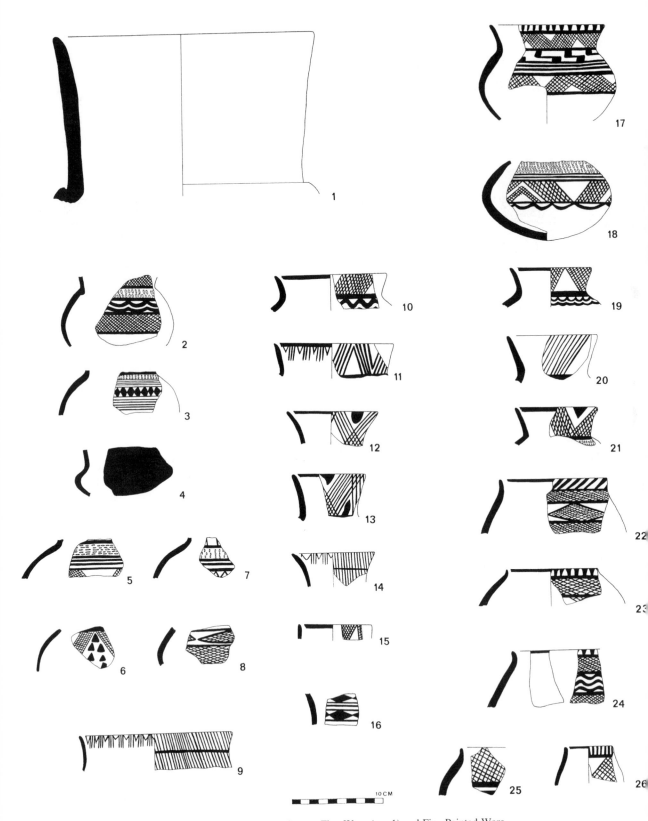

Figure 3.36. Transitional Orange Fine Ware (no. 1) and Fine Painted Ware.

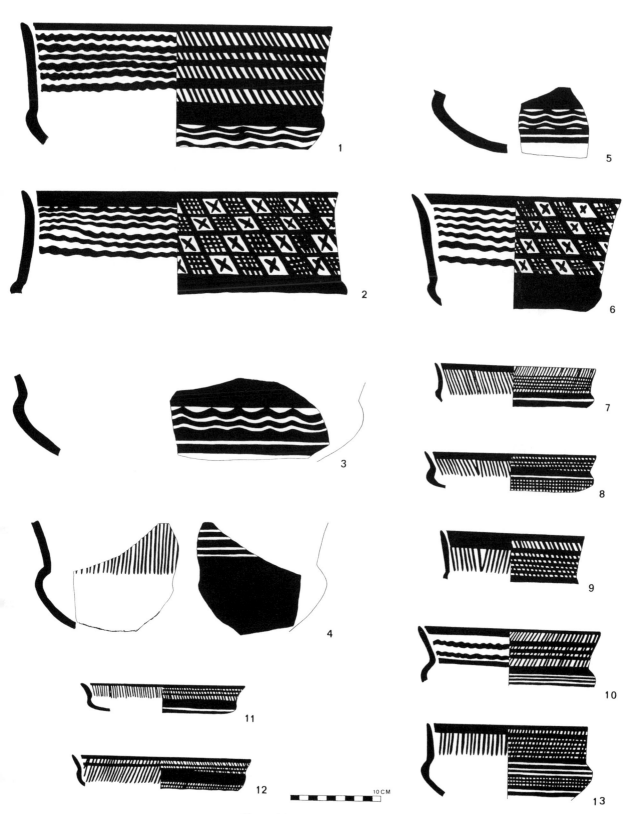

Figure 3.37. Halaf Fine Ware.

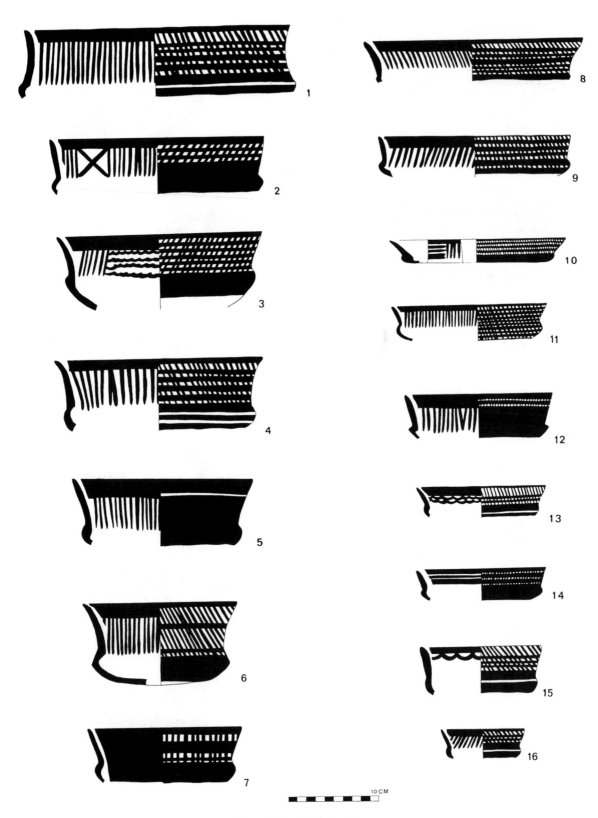

Figure 3.38. Halaf Fine Ware.

Figure 3.39. Halaf Fine Ware.

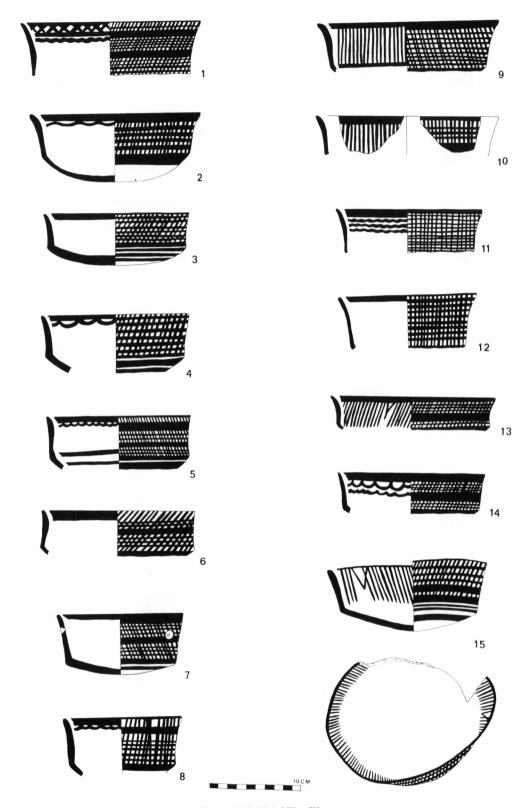

Figure 3.40. Halaf Fine Ware.

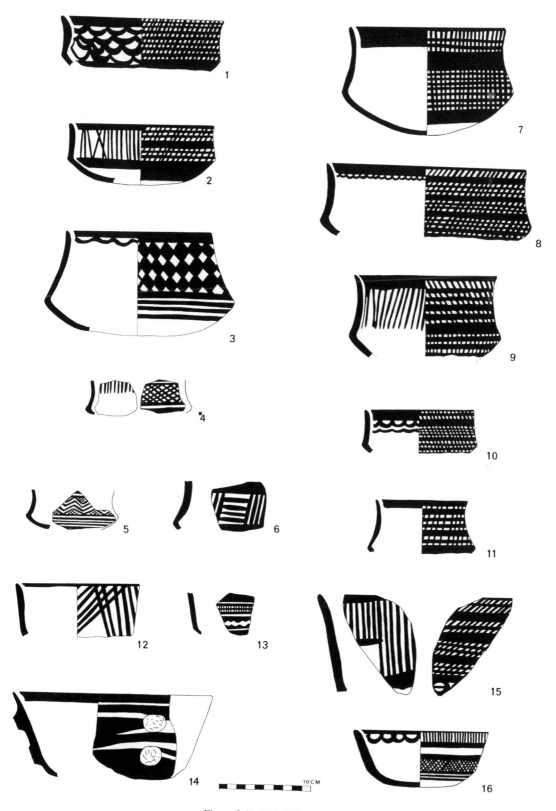

Figure 3.41. Halaf Fine Ware.

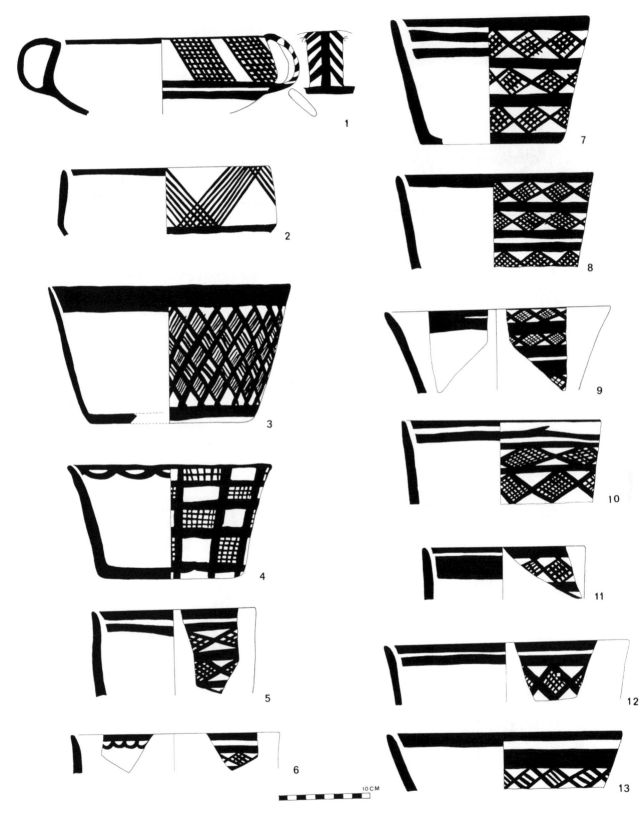

Figure 3.42. Halaf Fine Ware.

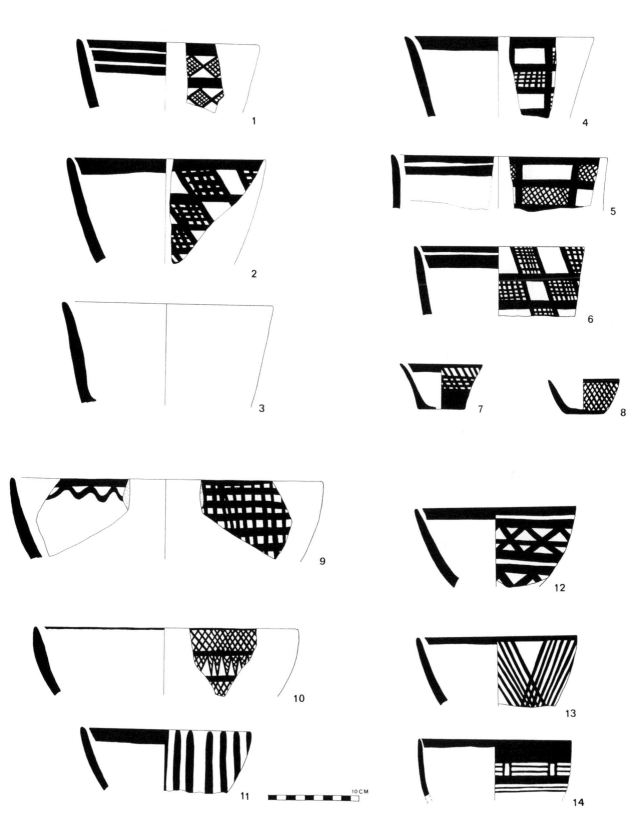

Figure 3.43. Halaf Fine Ware.

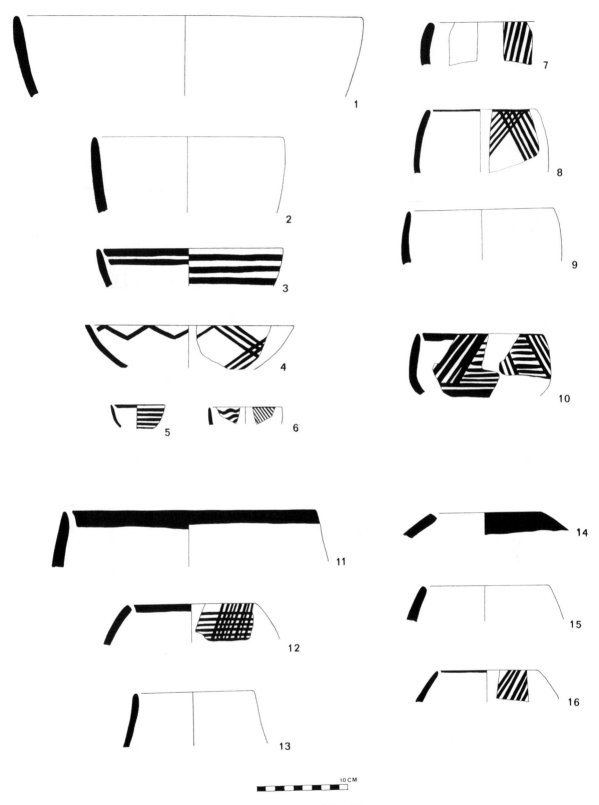

Figure 3.44. Halaf Fine Ware.

Figure 3.45. Halaf Fine Ware.

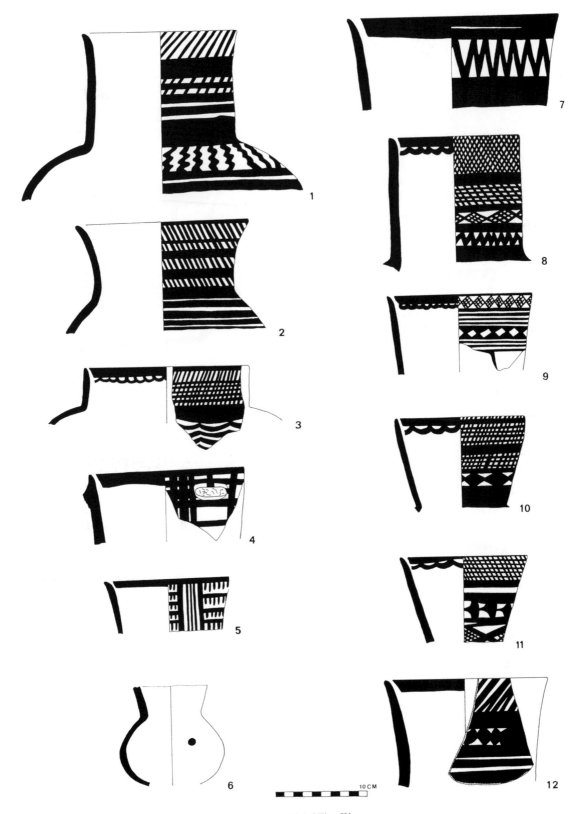

Figure 3.46. Halaf Fine Ware.

Figure 3.47. Halaf Fine Ware.

Figure 3.48. Halaf Fine Ware.

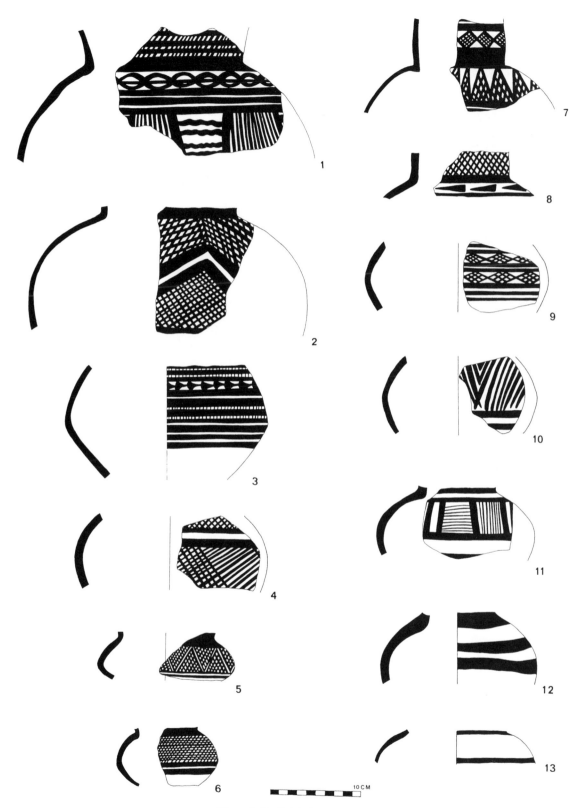

Figure 3.49. Halaf Fine Ware.

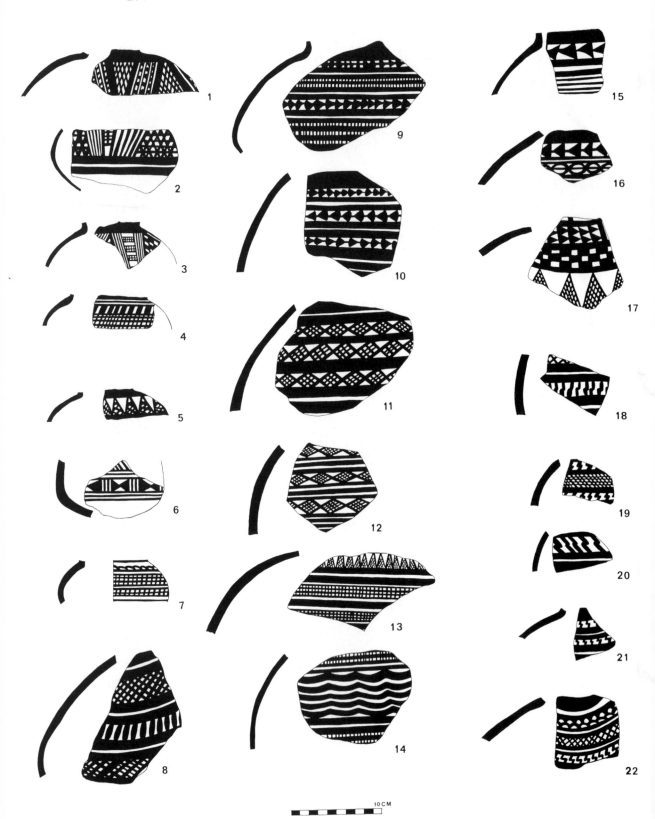

Figure 3.50. Halaf Fine Ware.

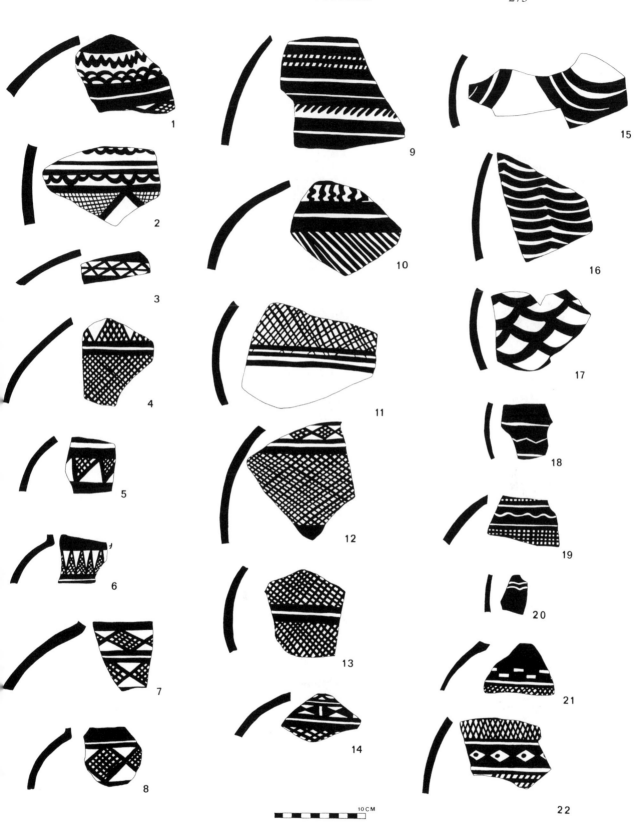

Figure 3.51. Halaf Fine Ware.

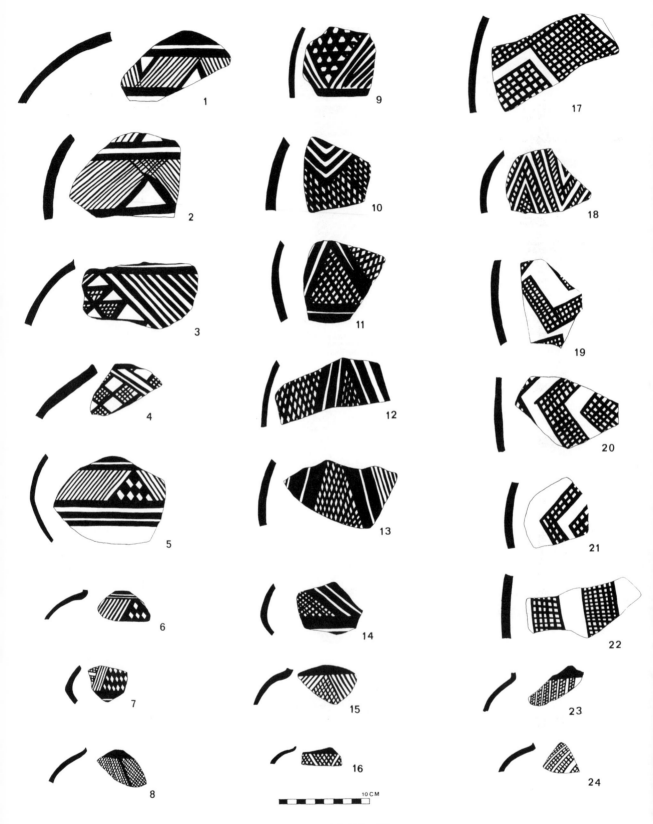

Figure 3.52. Halaf Fine Ware.

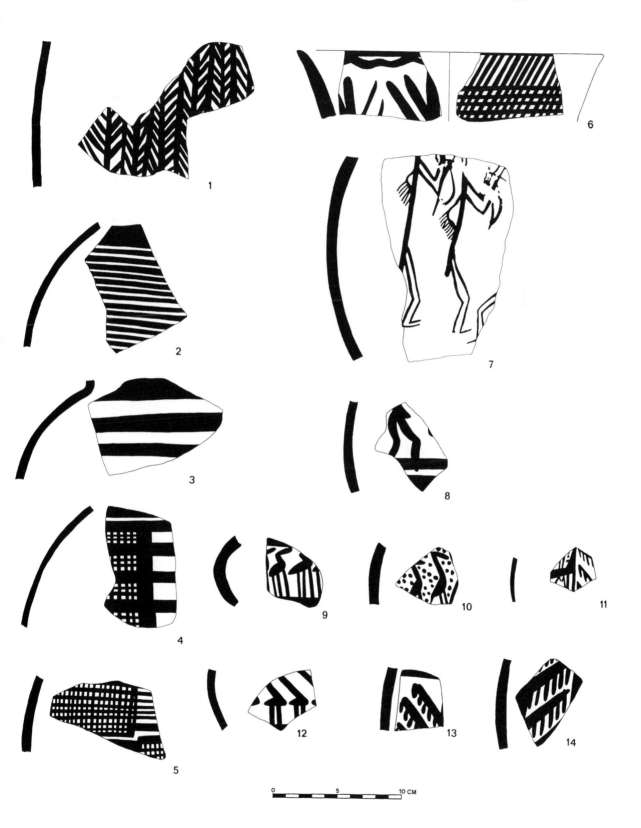

Figure 3.53. Halaf Fine Ware.

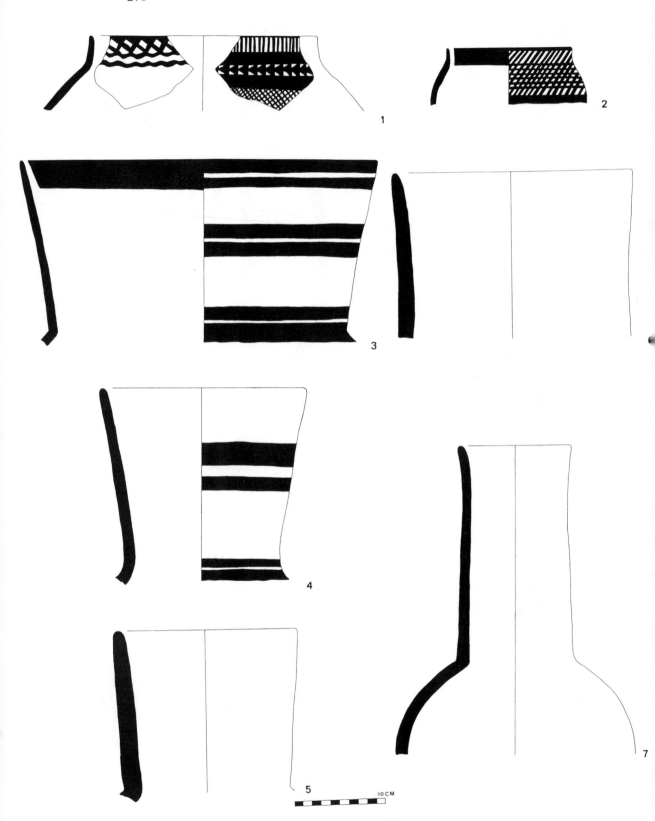

Figure 3.54. Halaf Fine Ware.

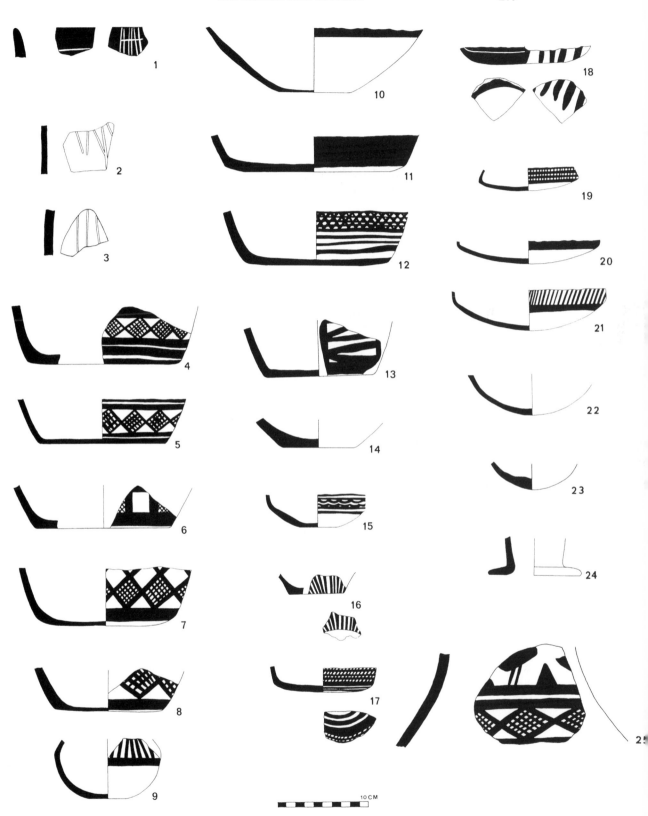

Figure 3.55. Halaf Fine Ware.

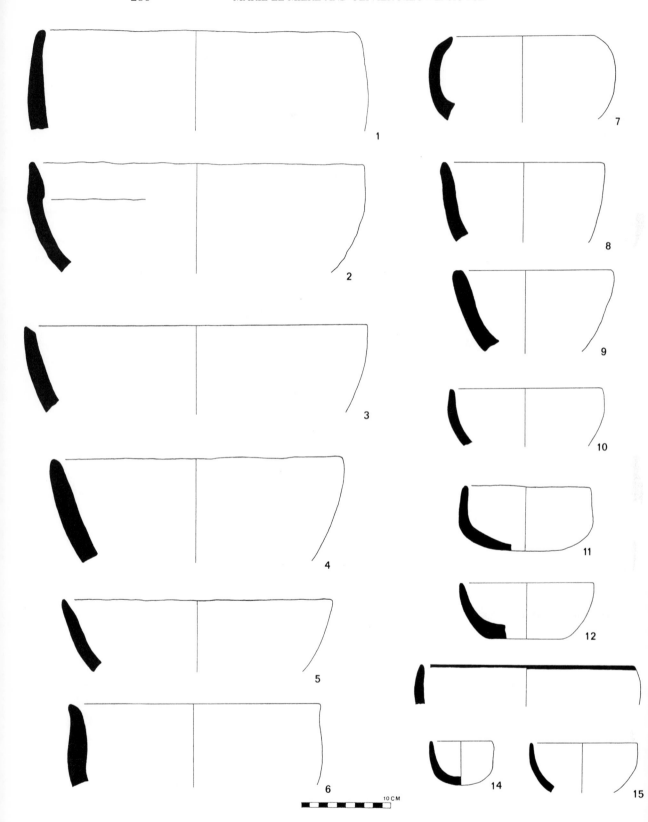

Figure 3.56. Halaf Vegetal Coarse Ware.

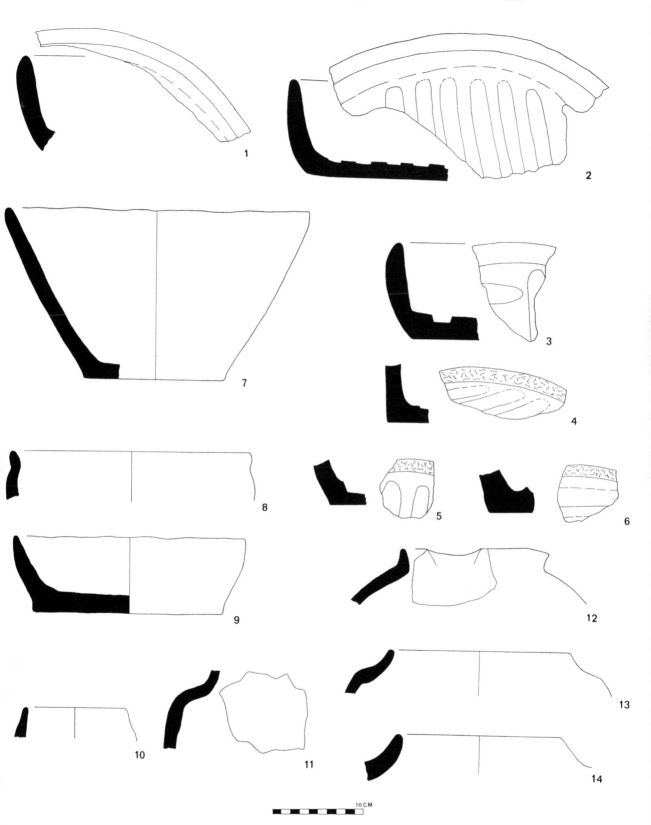

Figure 3.57. Halaf Vegetal Coarse Ware.

Figure 3.58. Halaf Vegetal Coarse Ware.

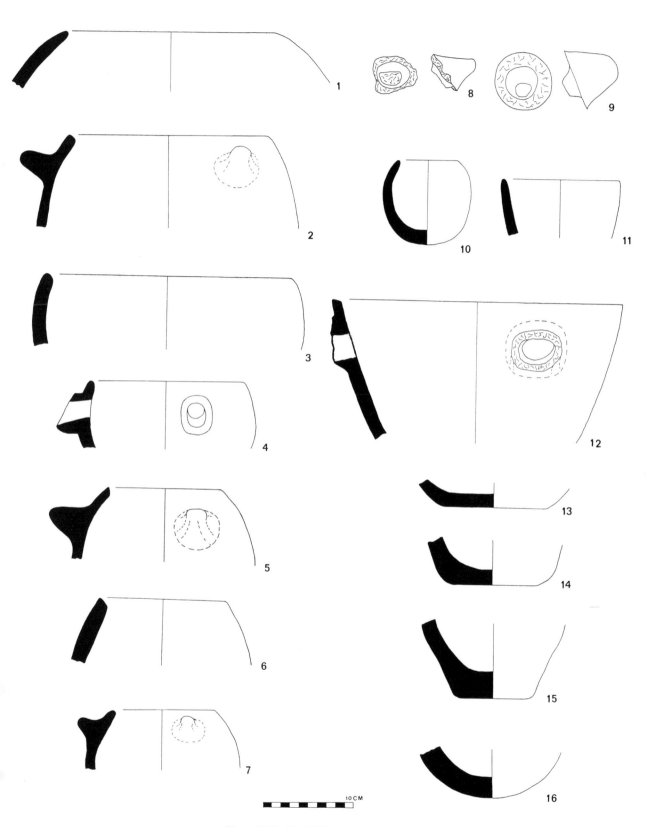

Figure 3.59. Halaf Mineral Coarse Ware.

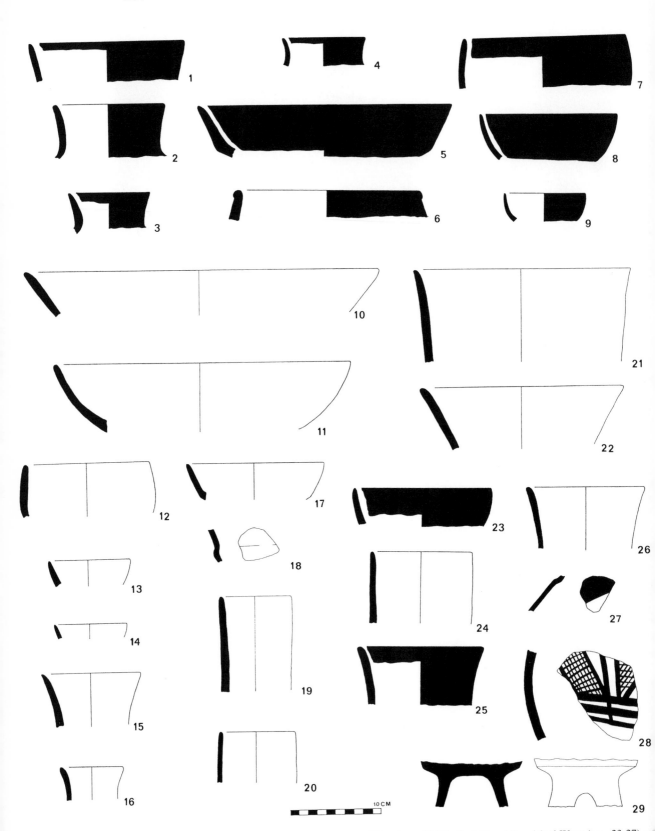

Figure 3.60. Halaf Red-Slipped and Burnished Ware (nos. 1-9), Grey-Black Ware (nos. 10-22), Dark-Faced Burnished Ware (nos. 23-27) and Orange Fine Ware (no. 29).

PRINTED ON PERMANENT PAPER • IMPRIME SUR PAPIER PERMANENT • GEDRUKT OP DUURZAAM PAPIER - ISO 9706

ORIENTALISTE, KLEIN DALENSTRAAT 42, B-3020 HERENT